The Way I Remember...

by

H.F.W. Proeve

1918 - 2014

Copyright © Elvira Boehler-Proeve, 2024

All rights reserved. This book is copyright. Apart from any fair dealing for the purposes of private study, research, criticism or review, as permitted under the Copyright Act, no part may be reproduced without written permission. Enquiries should be addressed to the editor.

Edited by Elvira Boehler-Proeve, PO Box 584, Tanunda, SA 5352

Cover photographs:

Front cover: Henry, at the conferral of his Doctor of Divinity award, 2005.

Photo on page 219: Henry, around 2004 followed by part of his manuscript, written on an envelope. He always used scrap paper.

National Library of Australia Cataloguing-in-Publication entry

A catalogue record for this book is available from the National Library of Australia

ISBN 978-1-7637149-0-8

Published by Immortalise in Hackham SA. September 2024.
Via Ingram Spark.

Cover design by Ben Morton

Contents

Foreword   4

Preface   6

Memoirs   7

Chapter 1 – The Queensland Decade, 1918 – 1928   8

Chapter 2 – The Victorian Decade, 1928 – 1938   41

Chapter 3 – The North Adelaide Decade, 1939 – 1949   78

Chapter 4 – The Nuriootpa Decade,
        1950 (January) – 1960 (March)   113

Chapter 5 – Point Pass Half-Decade,
        1960 (March) – 1965 (August)
  A: Point Pass Parish   130
  B: 'Part-Time' Church Secretary Double Decade, 1945 – 1965   141

Chapter 6 – Full-Time Church Secretary Double Decade,
        1965 (August) – 1984 (November)
  A: The Joint Union Committee (JUC) Years, 1965 – 1966   157
  B: The Secretary of the LCA   168

Chapter 7 – The Retired Couple Decade,
        1984 (December) – 1993 (December)   184

Chapter 8 – The German-Language Ministry in Adelaide   187

Chapter 9 – The Last Chapter   190

Foreword

"You did not choose me, but I chose you. And I appointed you to go and bear fruit…" (John 15:16). It was truly humbling for me to deliver the address drawn from this text at the funeral of 'HFW' (Henry Proeve). Henry's earthly remains were laid to rest in the Langmeil Cemetery in Tanunda, South Australia on 3rd October 2014.

Surrounded by vineyards in the Barossa Valley, another of God's chosen servants lies in the same graveyard as the pioneer Lutheran pastor, August Kavel. Both men grafted onto the "True Vine", our Saviour Jesus Christ himself. Ironically it was Kavel who had contributed to the split over doctrinal matters in 1846 which led to the formation of two separate synods, which Henry Proeve played a key role in reuniting.

Henry was brought up in a family where his father, sometimes poorly treated by the leaders of the Church, was also a pastor. This was not an encouraging start for Henry as, with his university degree, he could have chosen a different vocation in life. But a pastor he became. The loving Lord not only chose him as His child, but through the Church called him into the ministry and prepared him from his youth to perform the duties of Secretary of the Lutheran Church of Australia from its inception in 1966.

Formerly Secretary of the Joint Union Committee as two former synods looked to amalgamate, Henry had been well formed for the task. While this was not of his choosing, his hard work with many suggestions in the process, all behind the scenes, and not documented, became part of the official structure and direction for the Church, by which we are blessed today. "The Lord used the fellow-pastors and fellow-members of the Church to steer me into that avenue of service."

Henry was not a 'ladder climber' in a status-seeking era, even though his honours were many. He was a recipient of an Order of Australia Medal and recognised variously for his careful work on local church and community history. A keen archival researcher and contributor, it would have given him satisfaction that his own concept became a reality with a formation of the Friends of Lutheran Archives. (FoLA). How fitting that the first Honorary Doctorate bestowed by the Lutheran Church of Australia through its seminary would be conferred on Henry Proeve, even though he was already into his long and fruitful retirement.

We must remember that his work in drafting the Constitution of the Church in a disciplined and carefully detailed manner to fit that of an institution, which was required to meet the compliance of the state, was always done as a shepherd of the Church whose focus was on the salvation of souls. To this end he was meticulous and motivated.

Elected to a position of the Church, he lamented there was no call document as in a parish for this 'servant of the Lord', the calling clearly written on his ordination certificate. The Church had long overlooked such a practice for elected leaders. He had misgivings that perhaps he was seen as a legalist, especially as he drafted the matter of "Discipline, Adjudication and Appeals".

As much as he appreciated "good order", he did not want to be defined only as "the constitutional expert of the Church". He knew, however, that a confessional Church called to faithfulness also in this part of the world, under the Southern Cross, must abide under the cross of our Lord Jesus Christ. Our Church continues to be blessed through the work of Henry. He was a generous mentor when I was called into leadership myself. In vexed questions he gave clarity and wise, informed counsel.

"Hold that fast which thou hast, that no one take thy crown" (Revelation 3:11) was the confirmation text he used for his address to a lad at the same service at which he was installed as the North Adelaide pastor. These words were first used by the apostle John in an encouraging letter to the gathering of God's people in Philadelphia, to patiently endure their time of stress and trial. Henry knew times of sheer exhaustion, but was amazed at a gracious and merciful Lord who did for him what he could not do for himself. He also knew times of great joy.

It is no surprise that he was passionate about his role on the Hymn Book Committee of the Church and its liturgies. "I cannot imagine that any committee could be more dedicated in preparing the best possible hymnbook for its Church than this one."

These memoirs need to be told. Thank you to Elvira, his widow, and to former Archivist Lyall Kupke as her encourager and adviser. They have brought together Henry's own recollections of the events which led to the constitution of the newly amalgamated Lutheran Church of Australia. They have also included his personal Christmas letters.

The "crown" promised to believers is the crown of God's faithfulness to us. That is the glory of the "crown". It is our salvation. With that message Henry, the pastor, served at the bedsides of the dying and led worship, particularly for German-speaking congregations, which he shepherded well into retirement.

Across the former synodical divide, friendships were made. Through hymnody, Henry had a friend in Pastor Otto E. Thiele who penned the hymn to celebrate the union of the two synods (Lutheran Hymnal with Supplement 256 v3).

> *"Give us steadfastness, and keep us*
> *True to Thee, and to Thy Word:*
> *If in weakness we should waver,*
> *Strengthen us, Thine aid afford.*
> *Let us grow in grace and knowledge,*
> *Grow in faith and fervent love;*
> *Guide us, guard us, bless us, lead us,*
> *Till we share the home above."*

Rev'd Dr Mike Semmler (President/Bishop Emeritus, LCA)   2023

Preface

Henry Proeve (HFWP) wrote this story of his life and he was still working on it until two weeks before his death in September 2014. He had had the desire to record his story for many years. However, he wished to first write the Proeve Family History, which he had been researching for years. It was completed in 2007.

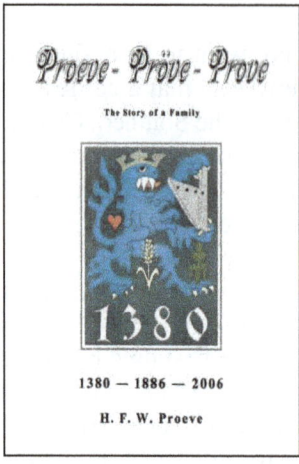

Already in 2003 Henry drew up an outline and then in 2005 he began to write his memoirs by hand on paper. In the following years he typed it while revising his earlier notes. However, he was unable to complete the story as he had planned in his original outline because of ill-health, which led to his death on Sept. 27, 2014.

As Henry's second wife, I, Elvira Boehler-Proeve, was involved in assisting him while he worked on it. After we had been married for one year he finally finished the Proeve Family History. He was then able to concentrate on his own memoirs. From 2011 his health deteriorated and so limited the time available or needed to complete and type his life story.

I know that Henry would have never published the memoirs as they were in September 2014, first for the simple reason that he had not completed them, but also because he was a very reserved man and would no doubt have revised or edited the story and have masked his own feelings far more in its final version.

After his death in 2014, I asked Lyall Kupke, former archivist at Lutheran Archives, to help me complete the memoirs. It was only possible to finalise these memoirs because Lyall gave much of his time and skills over a long time. I could not have completed Henry's life story in such detail without Lyall's digital skill and patience and his understanding of my need to complete the memoirs. Lyall and I had already been working at the Lutheran Archives for many years sorting Henry's book collection and papers. In the 19 years Lyall was Lutheran Archivist, he had gathered a good appreciation of and a large respect for Henry's role in the Lutheran Church.

How to complete his story took much soul-searching. We started to prepare the unfinished manuscript for publication. We added photos and used extracts from the Christmas letters which he started to write after Dorothy's death in 1993. Where we have used our own words, these are acknowledged in square brackets.

Most of the photos were chosen by me as I knew of most of the episodes and events in his life which were of great importance to him. He was very keen to use the diaries, pictures, maps and drawings especially from the American trip in 1927-1928, which he had carefully kept from his childhood. Lyall helped find suitable additional photos from the large collection at Lutheran Archives and wrote appropriate captions. Henry did intend to use photos to illustrate his story. He would not have used as many pictures as we have included, but we felt the pictures enhance the story and in a way honour him.

I hope that readers will look at the book with understanding of my wish to tell the uncensored story of a remarkable man, one that I loved very much.

Elvira Boehler-Proeve

MEMOIRS OF HEINRICH PROEVE

Halfway through my life I became aware of a hymn that has increasingly become meaningful for me. A 12-stanza hymn by Johann Heermann, *Geht hin, ihr gläubigen Gedanken*, caught my attention while I was engaged with Pastor Otto Thiele in a project assigned to us by the Hymnbook Committee that was preparing the Australian *Lutheran Hymnal*. The richness of thought in that hymn was inspired by the words of Ephesians 1,3-10, extolling the actions of God *'according to the riches of his grace which he lavished upon us'*. I immediately prepared a translation (1960), *Go forth, my thoughts, in faith and wonder,* which I have reviewed on several occasions since then, particularly to change the "Thee' forms to 'you' constructions. I place these Memoirs under the summarising content of two of the stanzas, 6 and 7, of this precious hymn, as expressed in the original German and in my translation:

Wer bin ich unter Millionen
der Kreaturen seiner Macht,
die in der Höh und Tiefe wohnen,
daß er mich bis hierher gebracht!
Ich bin ja nur ein dürres Blatt,
ein Staub, der keine Stätte hat.
	His creatures fill the earth and ocean,
	  fashioned in millions by His power;
	O what am I in this creation,
	  that He has helped me to this hour?
	Naught but a faded leaf am I;
	I am as dust that soon may fly.

Ja, freilich bin ich zu geringe
der herzlichen Barmherzigkeit,
womit, O Schöpfer aller Dinge,
mich deine Liebe stets erfreut;
ich bin, O Vater, selbst nicht mein,
dein bin ich, Herr, und bleibe dein.
	Maker of all, I bow before you,
	  whose love sets joy before my face,
	for I indeed am never worthy
	  of all your mercy, love, and grace.
	I am, O Father, not my own:
	yours am I ever, yours alone.

Members of the family at various times urged me to write down the things I remembered about the past. Mid-year in 2003 I essayed a beginning with thoughts absorbed into the above opening paragraph. I also wrote the prophetic words: 'Even now I fear it will be done in desultory stages'. I have had to make a five-year adjustment to the original words.

I begin today then (June 25, 2003) to put down what, for some unknown reason, as I rested in bed last night, finally formulated itself in my mind on the basis of some earlier thoughts. An overall picture sorted itself into eight periods, which can be classified as "decades", provided we do not define the term with absolutely precise chronological 'minute'ness.

The classification, slightly amended through the passing of time and recent developments to become nine, is as follows:

I.	The Queensland Decade: 1918 (November) – 1928 (October).	1
II.	The Victorian Decade: 1928 (October) – 1938 (December)	1
III.	The North Adelaide Decade: 1939 (February) – 1949 (December)	1
IV.	The Nuriootpa Decade: 1950 (January) – 1960 (March)	1
V.	The Point Pass Semi-Decade: 1960 (March) – 1965 (August)	½
VI.	The Full-time Church Secretary Double Decade: 1965 (August) – 1984 (November)	2
VII.	The Retired Couple Decade: 1984 (December) – 1993 (December)	1
VIII.	The Widower Decade-and-a-Quarter: 1993 (December) – 2007 (February)	1¼
IX.	The Closing Ninth Quarter-Decade: 2007 (February) – the present time	¼
		= 9 decades

Overlaid over these historical segments, like blankets across a number of them, there are several other 'decades' with their particular significance:
- the precious **Wedded Fivefold Decade, 1944 (August) – 1993 (December)**,
  covering the second half of III, and IV, V, VI, and VII;
- the **'Part-time' Church Secretary Double Decade, 1945 (August) – 1965 (August)**,
  covering the second half of III, and IV and V — the forerunner to the VI. Decade above
- the unexpected **'Macedonian Call' Double-and-a-half Decade, 1978 (April) – 2005 (March)**,
  covering the final half-decade of VI, and VII and VIII.
- the **'Tanunda Decade', 1987 (August) – the present time**,
  covering the latter part of VII, and VIII and IX.

Chapter 1

I. THE QUEENSLAND DECADE: 1918 — 1928
I. 1. The Family Background

The Memoirs must of necessity begin with pre-natal data, in order to avoid appearing on the scene like Melchizedek.

My father was **Hermann Waldemar Reinhold Proeve**, the eldest child in a family of ten children, who was born on December 5, 1888 on the cattle-run of the Auburn Station, north of Chinchilla, Queensland. His father, **Heinrich** Wilhelm **Pröve**, member of a family whose history in Klein-Eicklingen goes back to 1380, a wheelwright by trade, arrived in October 1886 from Klein-Eicklingen, a village 12 km from Celle in Hanover, Germany. Hermann's mother, **Emma** Anna Henriette nee **Beuschel,** arrived on the same ship from Soltau, West Prussia, Germany, close to the border of the Prussian Province of Posen, which had a strong Polish population. Their ship-board romance culminated in their marriage in November 1887 in Toowoomba, Queensland, ultimately followed by farming activities in the Toowoomba area.

My mother was **Clara Elisa Becker** (known in American circles as 'Lizzie', but enjoying the German diminutive 'Lies-chen' in Australia), the fifth of six living children of Friedrich **Wilhelm Becker** and **Katharina** Elisabeth nee **Preckwinkel**. The Beckers emigrated with four children from Ost-Kilver, near Rödinghausen, in Kreis Herford, Westphalia, Germany, to the U.S.A. in 1886. After farming in Nebraska and Saskatchewan, Canada, the family settled in St. Paul, Minnesota, U.S.A. Elisa was the first child born in America, born on April 1, 1888, at Hastings, Nebraska.

Photo: *Grandparents – Heinrich & Emma Proeve*

Father met Mother while studying for the Holy Ministry at Luther Seminary, Phalen Park, St. Paul, Minnesota, a seminary of the Lutheran Church Ohio Synod. Following their marriage in St. Paul on June 14, 1917, he immediately brought his young wife to distant Australia on a long sea-voyage from Vancouver, Canada, to Sydney on the ship *Makura*.

Hermann & Elisa

Wedding photo

The ship on which the newly-married couple travelled from America to Australia

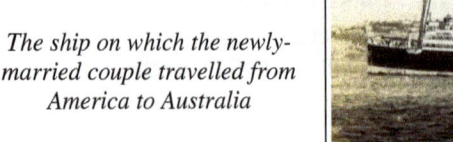

Chapter 1

I. 2. Infancy in Kulpi, 1918 – 1919

In the service of the United German–Scandinavian Evangelical Lutheran Synod of Queensland (UGSELSQ) Father and Mother took up residence in the manse at Kulpi, north-west of Toowoomba. They had secured a rubber-tyred sulky, which with a set of sulky harness had cost them £27 – the equivalent of salary for three or four months – and in it they set out for Kulpi on September 6. The parish had been vacant for well-nigh two years through the internment of the Australian-born pastor Theodor J. Fuhlbohm. In addition to the congregations of this parish, Father had to serve congregations 16 to 34 km distant from Kulpi: the three congregations of the next-door Goombungee Parish, vacant through the internment of another Australian-born pastor, Gustav Fischer, and some of the congregations in the next-adjacent Douglas Parish of the interned pastor Wilhelm G. Poland – a slightly-built, mild-mannered man with a false bone in his shoulder, who at the time of his 'capture' had been marched down the street, handcuffed like a felon. He had been serving in Australia (Queensland) for 26 years. On horseback or with his horse and sulky Father served this extensive prickly pear infested area. He recounted how some roads were reduced to 'single lane' by the pear, making it necessary at times to back the vehicle to a spot where two vehicles could negotiate their way past each other.

Father in sulky in front of Kulpi church and manse   *Father on horseback*

I was born on **Saturday, November 2, 1918,** in Wilsonton, near Toowoomba, in the private nursing home of the midwife Mrs. Claussen. She was the widow of the pastor A.C. Claussen, who had served the UGSELSQ at its Aboriginal Mission at Mari Yamba, near Proserpine, North Queensland, and as pastor at Highfields, near Toowoomba. I can claim to be a wartime baby by a margin of nine days. On November 17 I was baptised in the home church of the Proeves, Trinity Lutheran Church, Hume Street, Toowoomba, by the highly-regarded family pastor, Georg Heuer. Two siblings of Father, sister Emma and brother Emil, were my sponsors. My Father and I are rarities in the Proeve family in this sense, that we are the only ones with three Christian names. In my case they are a reminder of my grandfathers. Heinrich Proeve was **Heinrich Wilhelm,** Wilhelm Becker was **Friedrich Wilhelm;** thus I became **Heinrich Friedrich Wilhelm.** I used 'HFWP' as a type of 'logo' for much of my life; and when computers began to decree that considerations of space demanded that I had to omit one of the names, or themselves arbitrarily struck off the 'Wilhelm', I felt that part of my being had been amputated.

Grandmother holding me at my baptism   *Mother holding me*   *Mother and cry-baby*

Chapter 1

I don't intend in my memoirs to emulate a member of one of my congregations who claimed that he could recall something when he was only a few months old. My 'memories' of Kulpi are recollections of statements made by my parents. — I was a cry-baby. So much so, that neighbours said: *"Proeve's piano is on the go again!"* — The horse that provided the 'horsepower' for travel apparently had free rein on the property. One night the weatherboard house shook; but Father made the reassuring statement, *"It's only Toby, rubbing himself against the house"*. Next morning a neighbour enquired: *"Pastor, did you feel the earthquake last night?"*

I. 3. At Mackay, the most northerly parish of the UELCA, 1920 – 1924

At the end of 1919, fully a year after the Armistice had been signed, the interned pastors of the Lutheran Church were released from their enforced stay at Trial Bay in northern New South Wales, and could resume duties in their respective parish. Father was available for service elsewhere. The most northern congregation of the Church, at Mackay, 700 miles [1,100 km] from Brisbane, had been vacant for a lengthy period. The church authorities therefore decided that Father should serve there. The arrival of our family was delayed until March 17, 1920, because there was a lengthy shipping strike during the early months; and Mackay could only be reached by ship. I was an infant of a little over 1¼ years of age when I arrived there. It may have been on this voyage from Brisbane that a judge on board put his hand on my head that still lacked a good growth of hair, and said something to the effect of: "We'll make a lawyer of you yet".

Mackay did not have a harbour at that time. The ship anchored off Flattop Island and a tender transported the passengers to the wharf. Representatives of the congregation brought the pastor's family from the wharf direct to the church, and on the spot Father commenced a Sunday service with the congregation assembled there. He, in effect, had installed himself.

Photo: *Mackay church and manse*

In general the 'memories' of the years in Mackay come once again in the form of recollections of what the parents told me. Some faint personal recollections, however, linger in my mind, such as: riding in the sulky on some occasions when Father went out to Dow's Creek to conduct Sunday School; and water surrounding the manse to the height of several steps when the waters of the swollen Pioneer River could not flow into the sea on account of a king tide. — At that time Mackay could still be a centre for tropical ills. One of these was hookworm; and I have recollection of the small 'pill-box' type metal containers that had to be filled and forwarded when official checks against hookworm took place. Another ill was dengue fever; we all, my parents told me, suffered an attack. — As the centre of a large sugar industry Mackay had many sugar-mills. The homes near these were invaded by the swarms of flies that congregated where there were mills and it wasn't unusual for people, after finishing their plate of food, to turn the plate over, otherwise it was immediately covered with flies. Uncle George, when visiting the manse, sometimes made a point of searching it in an effort to find a fly. — Strangely enough, I don't have recollections of playing with my three cousins, the boys of Uncle Emil's family who figure with me on a snapshot.

Henry - in the middle of his cousins

Visiting Uncle Emil and family at Mackay

Chapter 1

I am not able to report from personal knowledge on my development, but I have found some reports by Father in letters written in December 1921 and January 1922 to his brother Ernst in Germany, who always longed for news from home. I quote from these in translation.

The letter at the end of December 1921 stated: 'Heinrich already this Christmas heartily sang Christmas songs, and even now sits sometimes with his toys and sings with all his might *"Alle Jahre wieder" ["As each happy Christmas"]* and *"O Tannen-baum" ["O Christmas Tree"]*.' Commenting on a photo just taken, he said that 'Heinrich wants to swallow the birdie that is said to fly out of the camera.' The letter written a month later added more: 'Heinrich is already learning to read; for he again and again fetches the newspaper or other papers and books, and then it starts off, "Daddy or Mama, what is that?"

'So he already has almost the whole alphabet in his head; and now he's starting with the numbers, saying "Daddy, one, two, three". We recently had a hymn with the tune *"Wie schön leuchtet der Morgenstern" ["How brightly shines the Morning Star"]*. Next day he sang the tune in such a way that everyone could hear what it was supposed to be; the words for it he composed himself. They were unknown sounds to us, but a few days ago he nevertheless wanted Lieschen to sing them with him. He can sing the following songs almost unaided: *"Herbei, o ihr Gläubigen" ["O come, all ye faithful"], O du fröhliche" ["O thou holiest"], "O Tannenbaum" ["O Christmas tree"], "Alle Jahre wieder" ["As each happy Christmas"], "Es ist ein Ros entsprungen" ["Lo, how a rose e'er blooming"], "Müde bin ich, geh zur Ruh" ["I am weary, go to rest"], "Breit aus die Flügel beide" ["Lord Jesus, who dost love me, O spread Thy wings above me"]*, and *"Du, du liegst mir im Herzen" ["You,, you lie in my heart"]*. He can already whistle quite loudly, and already tries to whistle tunes.' Father added that when the postman came with letters, 'he always wants to read them, and also likes to have the postage stamps'.

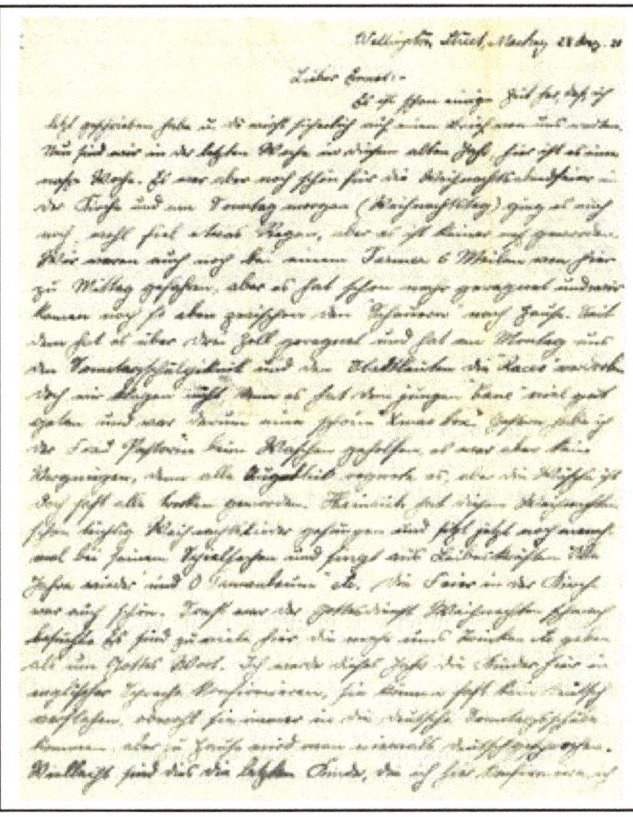

Father's letter to his brother Ernst in Germany

Henry's 4th birthday

When I further read in a letter written just after my 4th birthday, that 'Heinrich has already learnt many German and English hymns by heart, and he can hold many tunes on his own after he has heard them once', I realise (and appreciate) how strongly bilingual my upbringing was from the very beginning, and also how soon there began in my life the deep ongoing love of hymns, in reference both to words and tunes.

Photo on right: *Riding in the buggy with Father at Mackay*

Chapter 1

The isolation of Mackay was less burdensome when the rail link between Rockhampton and Mackay was completed. In April 1922, accompanied by three men and four women from the congregation, we boarded the train at 7.30 p.m., and arrived in Rockhampton at 9.00 a.m. next day.

After some hours the 'Rockhampton Mail' left for Brisbane, where it arrived shortly before 7.00 next morning. My parents told me there was a disconcerting feature about the carriages used at some stage of the journey; they were divided into completely self-contained compartments with two full-width seats across the carriage and a door on each side for exit on to a station platform. Any need for use of a toilet during the journey therefore could only be met if the train stopped long enough at its scheduled stopping places for the passengers to dash to the station facilities.

I think it must have been near the end of our residence in Mackay that the first indication of future intentions was given — at least that seems to fit in best with my memory of a verandah being the scene of action. 'Kirche halten' (i.e. to 'hold Church') was in my mind, and my parents had to serve as my congregation. They told me that singing hymns was a staple part of the 'service', and I did not forget to give a 'sermon', the contents of which were more mysterious than clear.

Mother, Father and Henry in Mackay, 1921

Henry, smiling for a photo for Uncle Ernst in Germany

The tropical climate in Mackay affected Mother's wellbeing, and ultimately made a transfer to another parish advisable. On Easter Monday, April 21, 1924, after a weekend of farewell services, the family moved south to the Darling Downs, to Goombungee, 27 miles [43 km] by road from Toowoomba.

I. 4. Goombungee, the address for four years, 1924 – 1928.

As I write this heading there comes a mixture of reactions that will become clear as the story of this segment of the Queensland chapter unfolds.

Neither the parish nor the pastor were strangers to each other when Father was inducted by the venerable Pastor G. Heuer in a service at Goombungee on April 28, 1924 — he had served its three congregations, Goombungee, Doctor's Creek, and Boah Peak for 2½ years from Kulpi. For me these years marked the commencement of my schooldays in the nearby State School. My clearest recollection of that is a brief time when the son of the headmaster (whether already qualified as a teacher, or not, I don't remember) asked us in a series of mornings what we had had for breakfast. Some adults were puzzled about the purpose of this interrogation; and I clearly remember the reaction of my Aunt Olga, of Toowoomba, when she heard about this: *"Tell him: a cupful of inquisitiveness"*. I don't recall any difficulties in coping with the beginning of my formal schooling. The event that stands out in my mind is the night when some fault in the carbide system of lighting that was used in the Goombungee Hotel, close by on the opposite side of Mocatta Street, turned the hotel into a burnt-out, twisted wreck.

Photo on right: *Goombungee church and manse*

Father bought a 'T-model' Ford for his parish work. It served him well, especially on the black soil roads in the area. I believe the story is true that there were instances of roads being signposted on the following lines: *'Impassable in wet weather to any vehicles except T-model Fords'*. These Fords had no gears; but in addition to a brake pedal they had a reverse pedal, which could be put to unusual use. An instance that Father recounted related to an occasion when a policeman suspected (apparently correctly) that the brakes on such a Ford were not in good order. Entering the vehicle, he asked the driver to drive, then insisted on more speed, and finally called out, "Now, stop!". The driver immediately pushed the reverse lever as well as the brake to the floor. The Ford stopped so suddenly that the policeman hit his head on the windscreen. — One of Father's members who accompanied him on a trip to Toowoomba apparently felt that such Fords had 'speed'. His account to a friend, as it came back to Father, was: *"Did Pastor make that car go! When we turned the corner from Russell Street into Ruthven Street on two wheels the car was singing 'Nearer, my God, to Thee'."* — One feature of the Ford provided me with concern: when the petrol in the tank, located directly in front of the windscreen, was low it did not flow into the motor on an uphill grade. This happened several times on the 'Charlton Pinch' on the outskirts of Toowoomba, where the road skirted a quarry. Father overcame the gravitational problem by backing the car up the 'Pinch', but I felt safer walking alongside.

Henry on his tricycle

Father in his T-model Ford

I ceased to be an only child when **Martin Waldemar** was born in Toowoomba 14 days after my 7th birthday, November 16, 1925. It is indicative of the high regard in which the parents held the family pastor, Georg Heuer, that he performed the baptism in Goombungee. The photograph taken on the occasion of his first birthday remains the visual remembrance of 'my little brother'.

One other, slightly odd, recollection relates to my health — but year unknown. I was childishly fearful when it was decided that my troublesome tonsils and adenoids should be removed. My nursing sister Aunt Frieda played a role in the ploy to divert my attention. She took me *'to see a man with a horse'* (probably associated with my interest in things), and he of course was waiting for me at St. Vincent's Hospital. As I lacked knowledge of the activity at this operational centre, I did not get a night-mare! — It was Aunt Frieda, too, who one day quietly reassured a worried grandmother that the very high bones on both my feet did not constitute a crippling abnormality.

Henry with Martin on his 1st birthday

Chapter 1

Festival at Hermann's induction at Goombungee. A typical open air mission festival of the early 20th century. Note that a motor car serves as pulpit and focal point of worship.

Proeve family gathering in January 1925 (Henry standing in middle row wearing braces). This was the first family photo since Ernst (back row, 3rd from right) came back from Hermannsburg after having been in Germany for 12 years.

I. 5. A Visit to the United States of America, 1927 – 1928

The memoirs now turn to ten months that naturally were of great significance to me in my juvenile years but, more importantly, triggered off an unexpected chain of events that completely altered the course and venue of our family life. I am therefore penning (hopefully in reasonable length) an account of our visit, which at the same time may provide a picture of what international travel was like in those days. The basic threads woven into this picture are provided by my own brief contemporary 'reports', material from our 'shipping archives' and American railway timetables, and brief extracts from a 100-page 'reconstruction', written with the help of my parents' recollections, that I introduced with the words: "Since even the best memory slowly fails, I have decided to set down the last reminiscences of that long tour ten years ago".

The reason for the visit was a solemn promise. When Father and Mother married in June 1917 they were well aware of the far-reaching significance of that step. The generations of our present times, living in a world in which distance is now measured by 'hours of flight', can scarcely grasp the reality of 'separation', often permanent, that such a step as international marriage brought about. The promise was given by the newly-wedded couple that they would return in ten years' time to visit the Becker parents. Despite low salaries, they saved in order to have the funds for the sea voyages.

[I.5.] 1. Preparations for the Journey.

In family papers I have found additional evidence how seriously my parents took this promise. Already in November 1925 Father made enquiries about fares for two adults and an 8-year-old son. The reply that a trip from Sydney to the U.S.A., then on to Europe and return "by the Suez Line" (an option that was strongly promoted by the New Zealand based shipping company) would cost £103 per adult and half fare for an 8-year-old (Third Class) immediately quashed any thoughts of including a visit to Germany in the plan — the total cost of £256/10/0 would have absorbed more than 2¼ years' salary! The alternative quote was the only one that could be entertained, viz. return journey, Sydney to San Francisco, or Sydney to Vancouver (Third Class), £50 each and half fare for an 8-year-old.

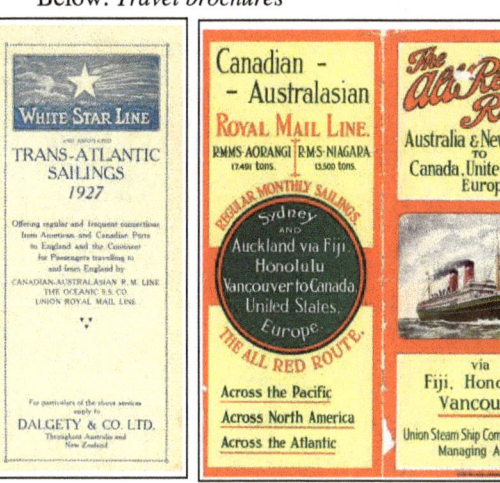

Below: *Travel brochures*

The negotiations in detail began a little more than one year later. In these times, when travellers wrestle with the annual 'ups and downs' of 'peak time', 'shoulder fares' and 'economy fares' offered by a large number of airlines, it can sound unbelievable that one year later, indeed two years later, the fares in 1927 were still the same as quoted in 1925. The additional 'infant' (Martin), however, added 10%, £5, to the original amount of £125. Additional financial figures that were written on the letter received from the shipping company in February 1927, completing negotiations, reveal the careful computations that Father made when he forwarded from their savings the required deposit, viz. "25% of the single passage money".

For he had to take into account additional costs: rail fares in Australia and the U.S.A.; some accommodation en route; the passport A58167 that cost 10 shillings; and two comparatively costly U.S. fees, viz. visa £2/1/8, and "Thirty-three Shillings and Fourpence ($8)" per adult as *"Alien Head Tax"*, paid via the shipping company by Father and Mother as persons who in American law were termed *"Straight Taxables"*, i.e. "aliens" who were not leaving the U.S.A. within 60 days. Our American-born mother was now an "alien".

In the meantime a shadow was cast over this careful planning of a visit to see once again the American parents – Grandfather Becker died on September 2, 1926.

Photo on right: *Part of the correspondence Father conducted over 2 years.*

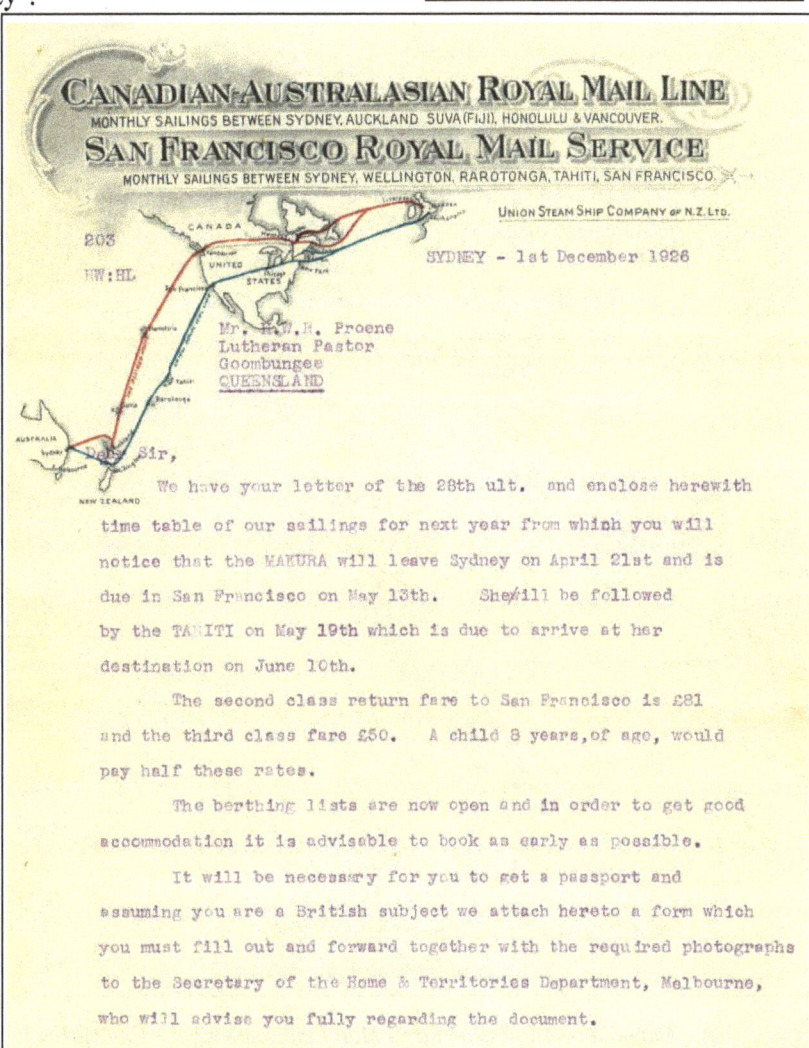

Chapter 1

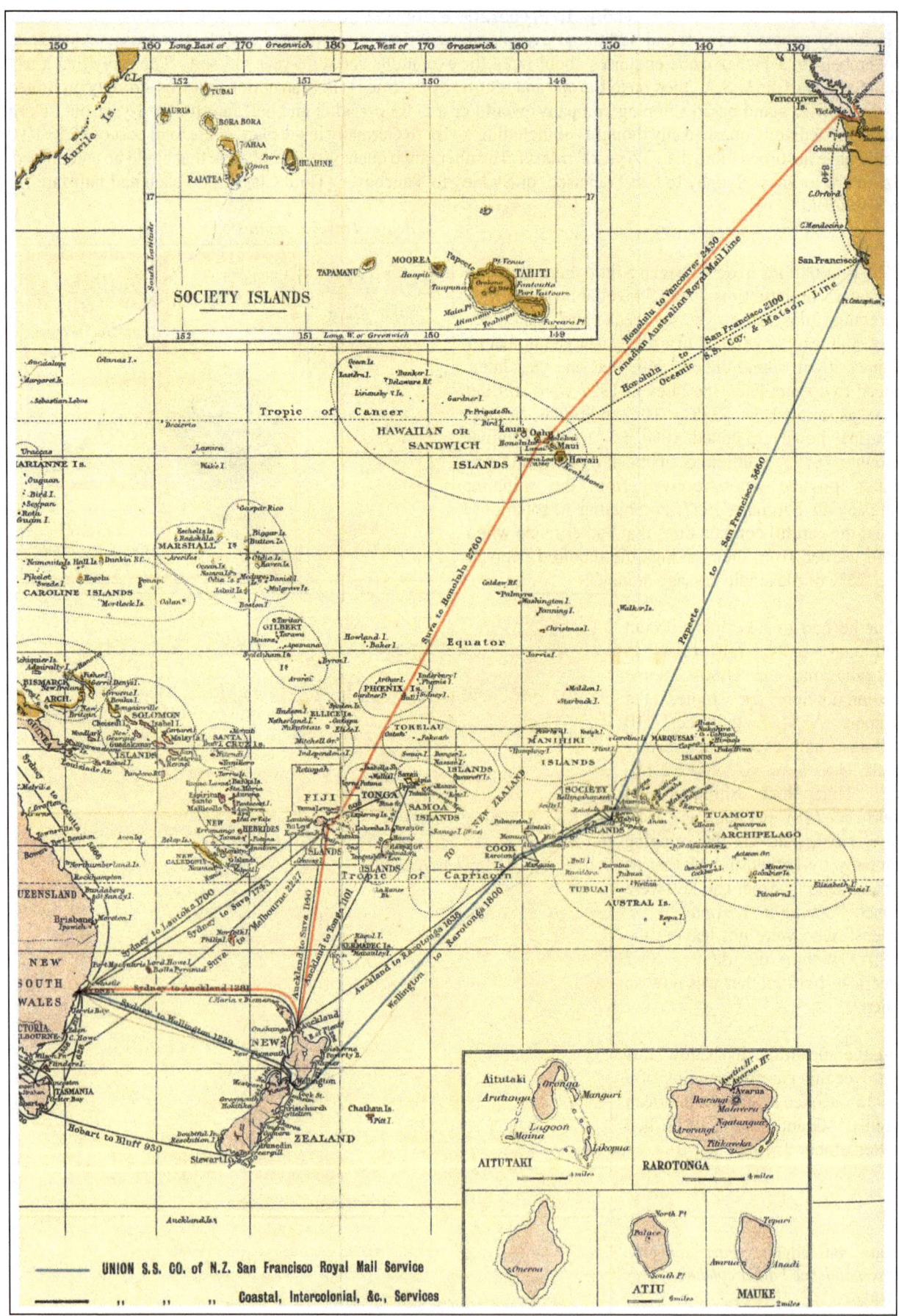

Canadian-Australasian Royal Mail Line, showing the route taken by the Proeve family in 1927.

Chapter 1

[I.5.] 2. The Journey Begins: Goombungee to Sydney

With six months' leave of absence granted to Father, and with a passage booked for Thursday, April 21, on the *R.M.S. Makura*, we set out from Goombungee on Easter Monday, April 18, 1927, for a last ride in the green 'T-model' Ford to Toowoomba. The Ford was to be sold there. We stayed for the night at "Seda", the home of Grandparents Proeve.

"Seda" the home of the grandparents Proeve in Toowoomba

Father starting the T-model Ford car

The next day we boarded the interstate Brisbane to Sydney train at 12.30 p.m., but had to change trains at the Queensland border station of Wallangarra because of the 'break of gauge' existing at the time. The journey, however, had to be broken next morning in Newcastle for two hours (7.39 to 9.50 a.m.), where we waited in the station while Father went to the American Consulate to secure the necessary visa.

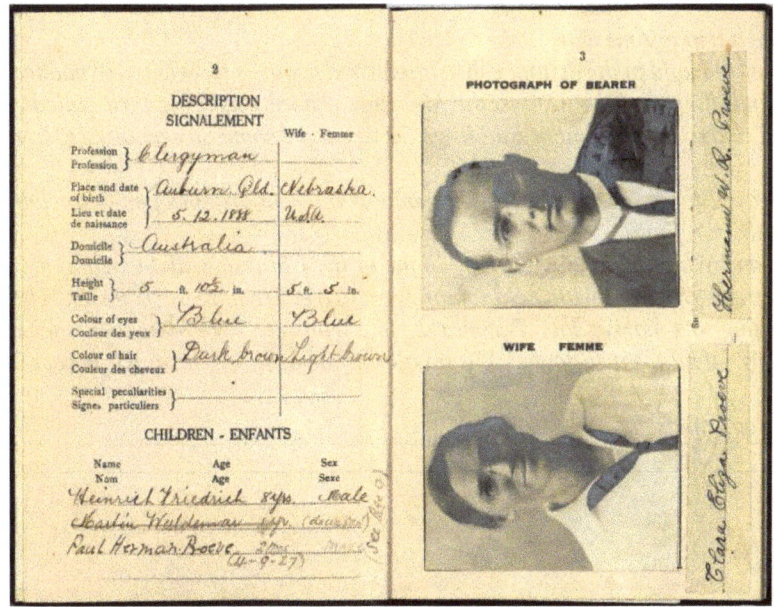

We arrived in Sydney at 1.10 p.m. on April 20. Accommodation was secured in a large boarding house, because the Peoples' Palace and all hotels were booked out with Royal Show visitors. Shortly before midday on the next day we visited a cousin in the Beuschel family, Aurelia Woods, living in the suburb of Carlton, and had dinner there. My sole impression is connected with the electric trains on which we travelled on that occasion: as it seemed to me, there was no driver, and the doors that opened and shut automatically were an impressive sight to a young lad.

The *Makura* was a twin screw steamer burning oil fuel, and at 8,075 tons it was the largest passenger liner of the Union Steam Ship Company of New Zealand Ltd. (As mentioned above, this was the ship that ten years earlier brought the young married couple to Australia.) It undoubtedly was nostalgia associated with memories of these two trips, ten years apart, that caused my parents, when the *Makura* came to Geelong about 10 years later on its last voyage, to go on board for one last look.

The departure took place one day later than the scheduled day (Thursday, April 21). On April 22, after having lunch (which in those days cost 3/0!), we boarded the ship for a departure at about 4.00 p.m. Aurelia Woods came to the wharf 'and saw us off with streamers'. The Third Class passengers were located in the front of the ship; the anchor was near our cabin, and created a rumble whenever it was lowered or raised. Mother and I, and Martin, were booked with four ladies in a 7-bunk cabin; the ladies, however, objected to my presence, so I had to go into Father's cabin. It was a men's cabin, a little distance away. There was only one passenger who was very sociable, my parents said; she was a Miss Fuller, who delighted to nurse Martin. Mother corresponded with her for a time, and she was shocked by the news of his death [*see page 27*]. During the voyage we used to sit in the bow of the ship, watching the waves. I believe there was much segregation of areas according to the 'Class' of the passengers.

Chapter 1

[I.5.] 3. From Sydney to St. Paul.

The two accounts that I wrote in 1927 serve as a summary of the journey from Sydney to St. Paul. The first (on page 1 of a "Big Chief Tablet' that I bought on June 6, 1927), was written that same day, 17 days after arrival. The second account followed a little later, written on sheet 7 of the same Tablet. The second account acts as a supplement to the first. Both accounts are given verbatim – incorrect spellings are therefore correct! – but are set out in paragraphs that mark stages.

In the sub-sections that follow I have added a selection of noteworthy features connected with our travel.

A Trip to America.   By Heinrich Proeve

We left Sydney Australia on the 22nd April 1927 to make a Trip across the Pacific Ocean to America. We arrived at San Francisco America on May 13th. We were a long time on the ship. When we were off the ship we got the inspector to have a look through our trunks and ports. We then went to the Continentiel Hotel with a Yellow Cab. We stayed there several days.

We went by the Free bus to the station. We crossed the Great Salt Lake and then arrived at Salt Lake City. We did not get out there but went on to Denver. When we reached Denver Pastor Kruger was there to meet us. He took us to his house. We stayed there two days.

We got to St. Paul Friday night. Auntie Lena and Uncle August were there to meet us.

We have been to Mounds Park, Phalen Park, and other places. Also in a lot of streets. Today June 6th I bought a globe, a tablet, and a purse. I have been to White Bear and Withrow and saw a lot of Lakes. The names are Heron, Mountain, Bald Eagle, White Bear, Crystle.

A Trip to America.

We left Sydney on the 22nd April and made a trip to America.

Wellington was our first port. When we saw the land in the distance the ship turned towards it. When we reached the land we got off and bought fruit etc., and afterward we went to the Museum. There was a big bird called a Moa, and fish, Kiwi's, birds, Pictures, Etc., and to the Parliment Buildings. There were some Street called Quay. One was Lambton Quay.

Raratonga was the next port. The ship stayed in the ocean. We bought some two dozen oranges penny for one orange. The Moers live there. They all walk barefoot.

Papeete was the next port. The Chinese and White people live there. Some of the Chinese walk barefoot, too. There are no footpaths by the sides of the street. We went with a chinaman for a drive. He took us six miles. The chinaman's car was a Ford. The next morning was market day. The market sold fruits etc. We bought, oranges, bananas, limes, paw paw, mangoes, etc. We then went to town. We bought a fan with Tahiti on it. It cost 2 shillings

We left Papeete May 2 at 12.30 p.m. for Sanfrancisco. .

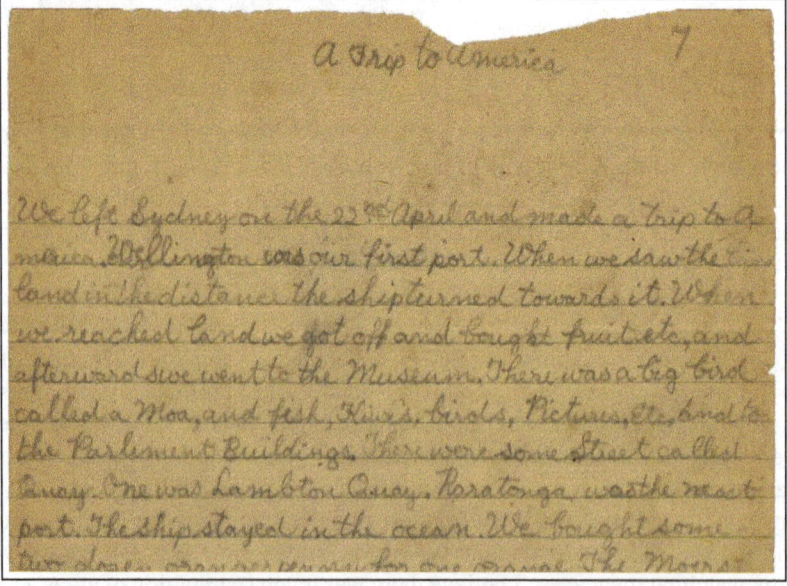

Chapter 1

[I.5.] 3.1. The Sea Voyage: Sydney to San Francisco.

The distance to Wellington was 1,239 nautical miles, and the voyage took 3½ days. I remember the crossing of the Tasman Sea as being extremely violent. The *Makura* pitched and tossed; this will have been particularly noticeable to those in the bow section of the ship. All had to hang on to rails in making their way along passages. After one had the under-foot feeling of 'down, down', the floor hit the feet as the ship suddenly made its way up again. Crockery and cutlery flew off the tables. — There was a medical inspection before we left Wellington.

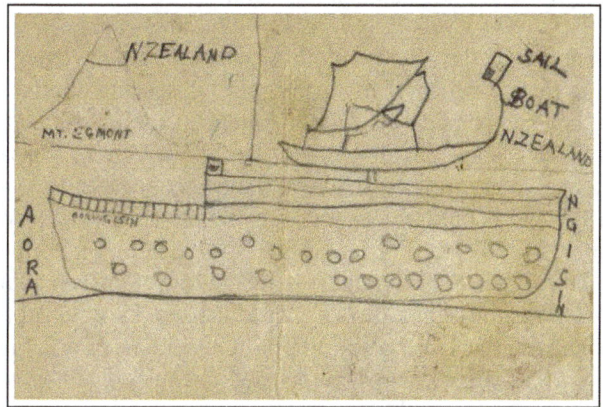 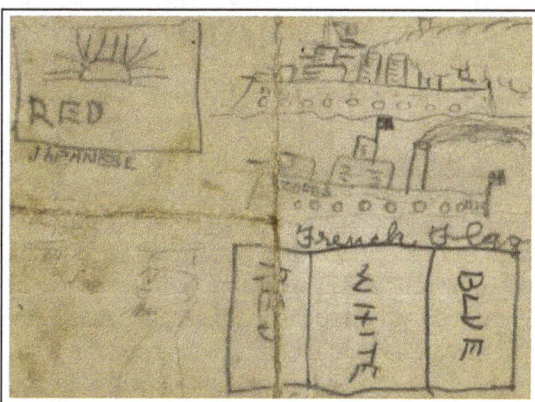

Henry's drawings on the back of the menus

Rarotonga (the correct spelling) in the Cook Islands lay 1,800 nautical miles from Wellington. When we crossed the International Date Line soon after leaving New Zealand, which created a repeat of one day, one man whose birthday fell on that day took full possible advantage of the spirits of the two days. — The comparatively unknown Cook Islands were unexpectedly brought back to my mind in December 1969, when I officiated in her home-church at the marriage of a country Lutheran girl who had fallen in love with a Cook Islander. For the first and only time in my ministry I officially had to identify what served as his signature by inserting the words '*I*.e' and '*E*.i' in the left and right quadrants, and '*His*' and '*Mark*' in the top and bottom quadrants.

The voyage of 650 nautical miles from Rarotonga to Papeete, the chief settlement on the island of Tahiti, was the shortest on the journey. The next was the longest stage, 3,660 nautical miles. It must have been about three days after leaving Tahiti that we crossed the Equator. It was usual practice to have a 'Crossing the Line' function on the deck, in which Father Neptune's henchmen dipped people who were crossing the Line for the first time into a pool. There are some mental visions of a 'bearded' Father Neptune, and of men whose faces, lathered in white, were 'shaved' with a big 'razor', and who then were thrown into the pool. This may well be a combined recollection, because the same was done on our return voyage to Australia.

A young lad's fascination with flags!

This voyage of 7,349 nautical miles ended on Friday, May 13. On board the *Makura* there was a deserter from the US Navy who, as we sailed across the San Francisco Bay, pointed out Alcatraz Island, where he said he would be spending his time of detention. The time taken to escort him off the ship and a medical inspection delayed our disembarkation.

Chapter 1

In San Francisco. We had a family room in the large Continental Hotel, very close to the heart of the city. After resting for the rest of the afternoon, we went to a café for tea, as the hotel did not supply meals. When the meal was over it was realised that we had no money to pay for the meal, because the Australian currency had not yet been changed into American. Fortunately the parents were trusted to pay next day, so all meals were taken at this café.

May 14 was a busy day. In the morning, by studying the seven or so folders that Father secured that day, the parents had to decide which of the many railroad systems should be used to travel to St. Paul. They had to set aside a hope they had shared with fellow-American friend Mrs. Alma Wiencke (the wife of fellow-pastor Edwin Wiencke in Queensland) that they could visit her parents in Kansas. They decided on a timetable that involved four systems, with a return via Canada, at a total cost of $159.85. — At a store a sailor's cap was bought for me for about $1.00, and I could be a sailor in my imagination. At 2 p.m., at the cost of $2.50 for each person, we went on the Thirty Mile Drive or Tour de Luxe of the Gray Line Motor Tours (as mentioned in my composition – *see page 18*). From Twin Peaks, roughly in the middle of the peninsula, and reached by a drive in the form of a figure 8, there were magnificent views of San Francisco, its Bay and the Golden Gate, and the Pacific coast. Near the coast we entered the 1,013 acre [405 ha] Golden Gate Park. The 'Portals of the Past' in it (specially mentioned by me) was a marble canopy. Supported at each corner by two Corinthian columns, mirrored in a small lake nearby – what it represented has not registered in family memories.

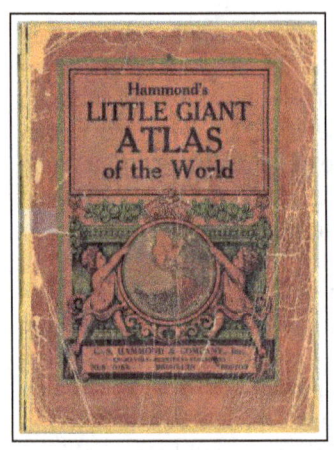

[I.5.] 3.2. The Train Journey: San Francisco to St. Paul

A frequent activity of mine during the months that followed in St. Paul was to retrace the route we took to reach St. Paul. The material for these 'journeys' was provided by the detailed timetables issued by the relevant railroad systems, and by an atlas that the parents bought for me, '*Hammond's Little Giant Atlas of the World*', which had maps measuring 125 cm x 175 cm, including an appendix of such full-page maps of each State of the U.S.A. The 1,150 mile-wide [1,850 km-wide] mountainous region from the Pacific Ocean to the Rocky Mountains in which the first part of our journey took place left an impression in my mind of travelling through many ranges. My 1927 descriptions are surprising in their brevity, as there were a number of very interesting sections. The "*free bus*" mentioned on the card (above) was provided by the Continental Hotel.

3.2.a. San Francisco to Denver

When the 'Scenic Limited' of the Western Pacific Railroad left the Union Ferry Station in San Francisco at 9.20 Pacific Time on Sunday, May 15, it went on to a ferry that carried it across San Francisco Bay to the Western Pacific Mole at Oakland. The train, running northwards, immediately began to make its way over ranges, commencing with the Coast Range. One of the longest canyons in the world through which a railroad passes, the magnificent 90-mile [145 km] long Feather River Canyon, pierced the Sierra Nevada Range at 4,995 feet [c.1,500 m]. As night fell the back of one seat was let down to fill the space between the two facing seats to form a bed. During the night we crossed northern Nevada and its series of ranges via a winding route, reaching a maximum altitude of 5,376 feet [c.1,620 m]. Just before midday on May 16, and a few miles inside Utah the railroad crossed the Great Salt Bed of Utah, which is about 8 miles [13 km] wide and 65 miles [105 km] in length. The train stopped to allow passengers to go for a stroll on the glistening white salt, a clean crystallised salt that is 98% pure as it comes from the Bed. Later the train ran so close to the Great Salt Lake and the mountains that held it back that there was a section where it ran on a causeway. We reached the capital of this Mormon State, Salt Lake City, at 3.15 p.m. Pacific Time.

The stay in Salt Lake City was short. At 4.30 p.m. Mountain Time (1 hour ahead of Pacific Time) the 'Scenic Limited', now part of the Denver & Rio Grande Western Railroad, continued its way south and then south-east, using river canyons to negotiate the mountainous areas into Colorado and the Rocky Mountains. During this second night the train took 8 hours till early daylight to negotiate a long climb of 202 miles [322 km], from 4,350 to 10,240 feet [1,326 to 3,120 m], to reach the summit in the Rocky Mountains – the Continental Divide in the U.S.A. – in a half-mile long tunnel at Tennessee Pass.

Chapter 1

Just over 100 miles [160 km] further on the eastbound descent, in the valley of the Arkansas River we entered the 10-mile long [16 km] Grand Canyon. Its most magnificent section is known as the 'Royal Gorge'. Like all daylight trains, our train stopped here for ten minutes at the Hanging Bridge. The river occupied the full space of 30 feet [9 m] between the sheer walls of the gorge, which towered up to 3,000 feet [c.910 m]; so the engineers anchored a bridge into these walls to hold the railway track. One man, standing alongside and gazing aloft at these rugged walls, said to Father: *"And then some people say: 'There is no God'!"* Amid the general impression of seeing huge mountains, this sight retained a little more detail in my young mind.

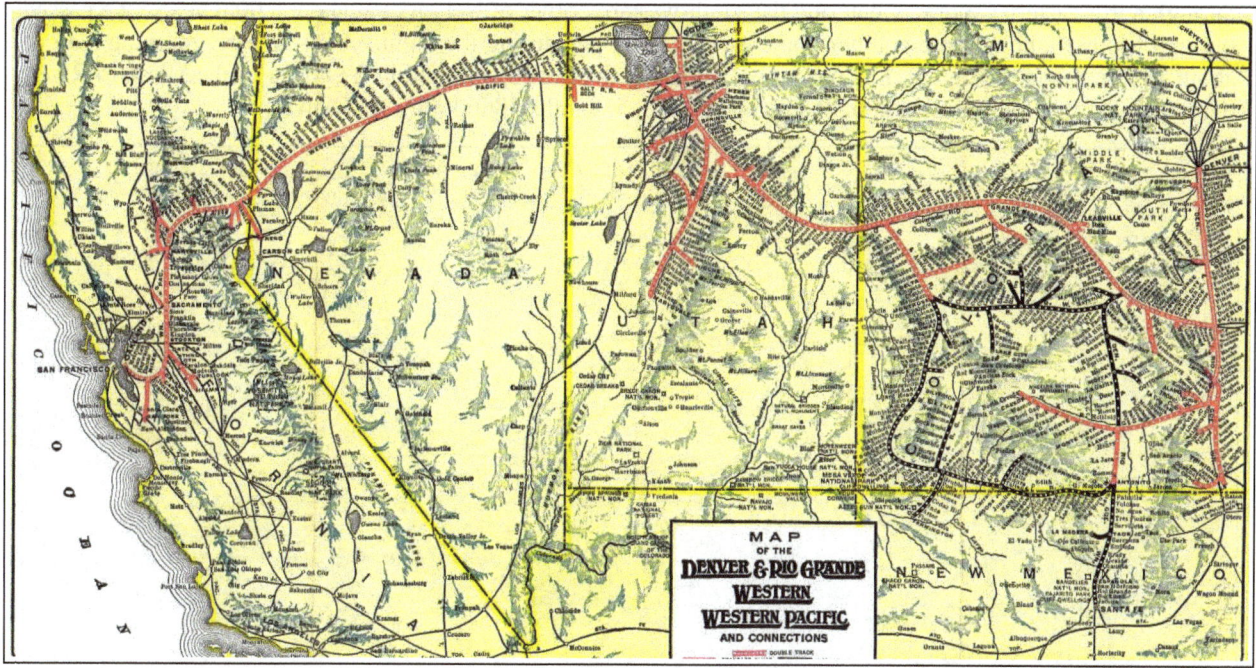

The first stage of the American journey (1,646 miles [2,649 km] from San Francisco) was completed when the train pulled into the new Union Station at Denver at 7.40 p.m. on Tuesday, May 17. — Very likely it was during this first stage that the conductor on the train, noting the non-American accent, asked Father where he came from. Father's reply called forth the exclamation: *'Australia! Australia! That must be a long way from here by train!'* — At this point I may add that ignorance about Australia was frequent in the U.S.A. Quite a number of Mother's one-time friends who had heard that she had married an Australian and gone there to live, made a point of visiting the Becker home after our arrival in St. Paul, and were amazed to see that it wasn't a black husband and black children that they were meeting.

In Denver. Pastor C.F. Hermann Krueger, who took us and our private luggage to his home, was a classmate of Father at the Seminary, and the best man at the parents' wedding. Naturally there was plenty of material for conversation during and after our first meal in an American home. Hermann planned to show us the sights of Denver next day; but one of his periodical attacks of rheumatism that developed and continued during our stay put an end to that plan. The leader of the Ohio Synod in that area, Pastor Martin Stricker, came to visit him, met Father, and stayed for the midday meal. Next day, Thursday, May 19, Pastor Stricker took us and our luggage to his home in late morning for the midday meal, prior to taking us to Union Station. During his conversations he offered Father a parish in Colorado if he cared to stay in America at the end of his holiday.

Eagle River Canyon, Colorado

Chapter 1

3.2.b. Denver to St. Paul.

The final stage of the journey to St. Paul, comprising 538 miles [866 km] to Omaha, Nebraska, and then a further 350 miles [562 km] to St. Paul, is covered in one six-word sentence in my 1927 composition [*see page 18*].

When we pulled out of the Union Station in Denver at 3.45 p.m. Mountain Time on Thursday, May 19, we were on the "Chicago Limited" of the Chicago, Burlington & Omaha line (the 'Burlington Route'). The mountainous section of our journey lay behind us. The final stage of our journey lay in the great plains of central U.S.A., through north-eastern Colorado, entering the south-western corner of Nebraska at about 8.00 p.m. So we passed through Mother's home state and her home town of Hastings during the night. After an early morning stop of about 15 minutes in the capital, Lincoln, we steamed into the Burlington Station at Omaha on the Missouri River, the eastern border of Nebraska, at 6.30 a.m. on May 20, 538 miles [866 km] from Denver.

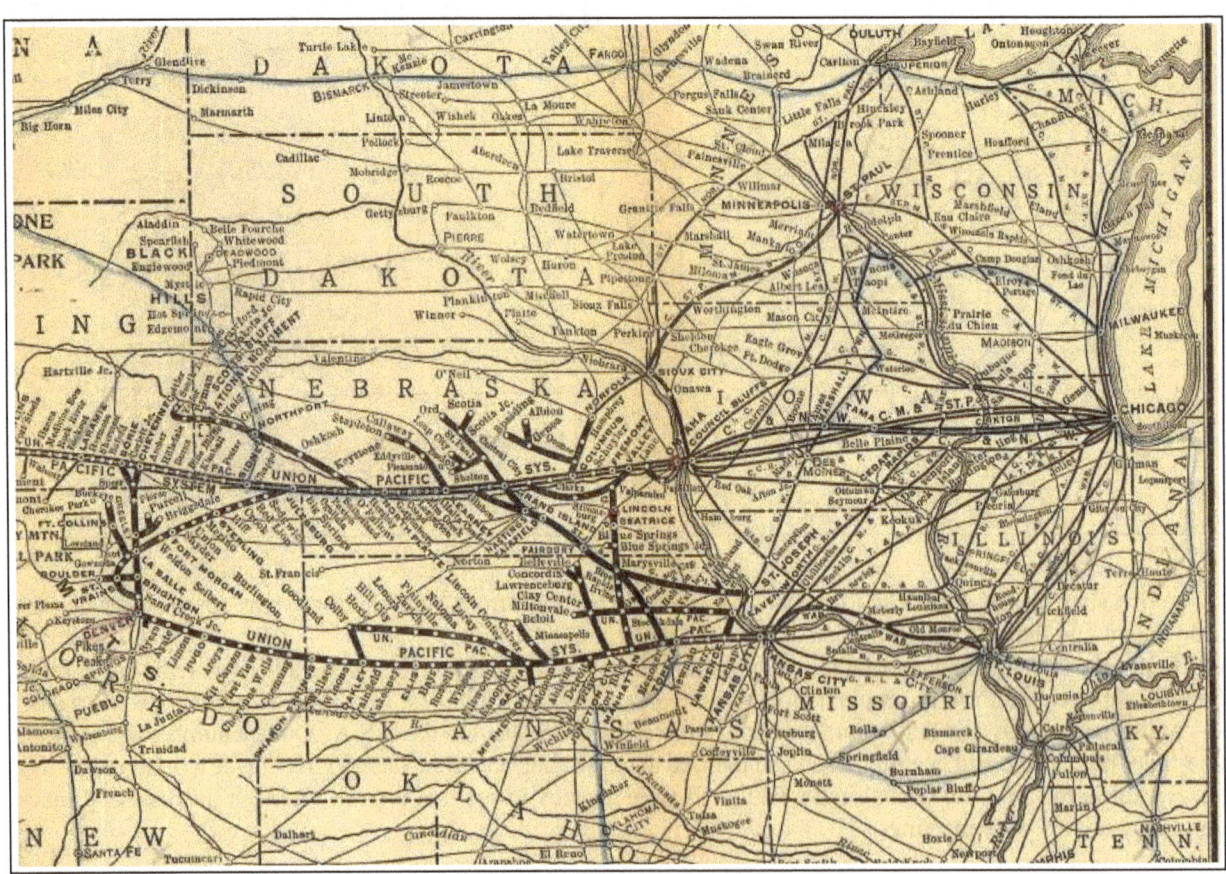

Denver to St. Paul, via Omaha

We had to get off the express that was bound for Chicago, and we walked to the nearby Union Station, where the train for St. Paul would leave. As there was a 1½ hour wait, we had breakfast at the Station before the last 11½ hour long stage began.

At 8.00 a.m. the Chicago Great Western train began its 350 mile [562 km] journey. It immediately crossed the Missouri to enter the State of Iowa at Council Bluffs. The route lay north-east across the level, rich farmlands of Iowa, maintaining an average speed of about 30 miles per hour as it bypassed most towns except Fort Dodge (plaster products) and Mason City (cement products), until the Minnesota border was crossed in mid-afternoon (c.3.45 p.m.). St. Paul lay only 100 miles [160 km] due north. At 7.45 p.m. the train journey of a little over 2,500 miles [4,020 km] was completed. Something of the parents' emotions is reflected in the words that I wrote ten years later in the 'reconstructed' description: *"Uncle August Becker and Aunt Lena were at the Union Station to greet us, and to take us to 941 Fremont Street in Uncle's car. Thither we went post-haste, where Grandmother Becker, crippled with rheumatism, but radiant with joy at our arrival, fondly greeted us. There was joy in the home that evening, but at the same time tempered with sorrow that Grandfather Becker was no longer there to greet us."*

Chapter 1

[I.5.] 4. More than Seven Months in St. Paul (May 20, 1927 – January 7, 1928)

[I.5.] 4.1. The First Two Months, May and June

The big house at 941 Fremont Street, in the eastern portion of St. Paul, stands in the centre of my memories of St. Paul. Standing on a north-eastern corner allotment, Forest and Fremont Streets, without a fence (the American style), it probably was imposing even to an adult; it certainly was to an 8-year-old. An Australian lad saw it as different from anything he had seen in Queensland, because (like all other houses around it) it stood elevated above the footpath – the 'sidewalk', a new word for his vocabulary. The allotment on which it stood sloped down to the sidewalk; but there were others that were filled against a stone wall along the street frontage and therefore required steps. The house was two storeys high, plus an attic and a cellar. All bedrooms were in the second storey; we slept in Grandmother's bedroom, which had an alcove; she slept in the next-door rear room, which had a heater that Aunt Lena used to light in the morning before Grandmother got up. The other two bedrooms were let as bedroom and kitchen to a German family named Weiss, parents and two daughters – a fact that remarkably has never been part of my personal memories. Aunt Lena slept on a davenport in the front room on the ground floor. The attic was rather out-of-bounds, being of a 'rumpus' room nature. Downstairs there were four large rooms: kitchen, dining room, and, connected by double doors, living room and front sitting room. In the living room there was a huge (at least in my eyes) 'Kalamazoo' heater, where Grandmother spent her painful days, gently rocking herself in her big rocking chair, and gazing through its large alcove into the street. There were two stairways leading to the top floor: the main one, wide and winding, in the main hall; the other, straight and narrow, from the kitchen, directly above the steps leading down into the cellar.

Henry in the snow in front of 941 Fremont St.

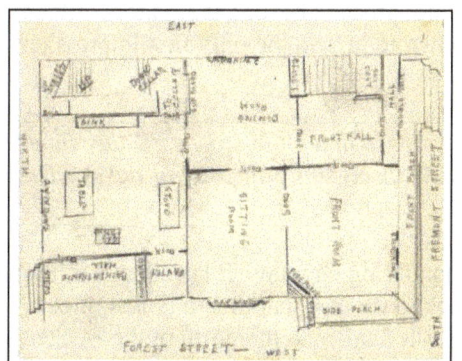 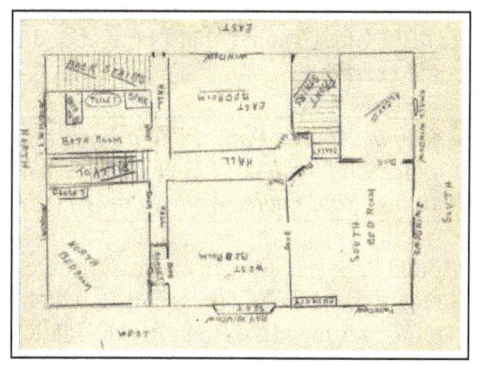

House plan at 941 Fremont St., drawn later from his memory

23

Chapter 1

There was much happy activity in these first months as summer approached, meeting family members and friends. Two days after our arrival was our first Sunday in St. Paul. Our usual place of worship was the church to which the Beckers belonged, in which the parents had been married, St. Paul's Lutheran Church, at the corner of Cypress and Cook Streets. Uncle August took us that day to visit Grandfather Becker's grave in Elmhurst Lutheran Cemetery, north of St. Paul proper. There were uncles, aunts, and cousins in the vicinity that I got to know in those first weeks.

• Uncle August, Aunt Elsie, and Loretta, at 1139 Beech Street were the nearest. Uncle worked as an engineer for the Minnesota Mining & Manufacturing Co., the only sandpaper factory in America (now famous as '3M'). Loretta, a little younger than I, the first cousin I met, was brought to Fremont Street on the second Sunday, as soon as she came out of a scarlet fever quarantine. I saw her most of all, because we were frequently in each other's homes. On these occasions we often used to read, like a play, the coloured comics that appeared as supplements to the St. Paul *'Sunday Despatch'*, which were full of the usual bravado and astounding escapades that are typical of the heroes and heroines in comics. Loretta would take all the girls' parts, and I all the boys'. I remember the hero in one of these being whisked off the ground when the tension that held down the branches of a huge tree to which he was bound was released. He got back to earth — as he hung aloft, eating for days bananas that grew all around him, he grew so fat and heavy (frame by frame) that the bough finally bowed to earth again!

Henry and Loretta holding Paul

The reference to Loretta brings to memory that at some later stage in my young life I declared to my parents that I would marry Loretta. This brought a rejoinder from them: *"You can't do that; she's related to you, and you're not allowed to marry someone you are related to"*. But I had a 'convincing' reply to that for my Father: *"Look what you did. You married your mother-in-law's daughter!"*

• Uncle Bill (Wilhelm), Aunt Marie, with Helen, William, and Richard, lived a little further along Beech Street. Uncle Bill also worked at M M & M Co., as a fireman. Our visits there were not as frequent as at Uncle August's.

• Uncle Henry and Aunt Anna, with four children (Eddie, Albert, Leonard and Lorraine) still at home, lived on a mixed farm (wheat, but mainly market gardening) at Withrow, north of St. Paul. To augment his income Uncle did some commercial travelling for the Rawleigh Company. The two youngest children, who were twins, were a year younger than I. Three daughters (Ada, Alma, and Mamie) lived in St. Paul with their married sister Lydia (Mrs. Otto Altmann). Otto took us for the first time to Withrow very early in June. Contact with them depended chiefly on the frequency of their visits to St. Paul.

At this point my 1927 writing comes to an abrupt end. It did not proceed beyond the bottom of the first page of the A4-size "Big Chief Tablet" that I bought and immediately wrote in. So the only first impressions on record are, as recorded earlier:

> *We have been to Mounds Park, Phalen Park, and other places. Also in a lot of streets. Today June 6th I bought a globe, a tablet, and a purse. I have been to White Bear and Withrow and saw a lot of Lakes. The names are Heron, Mountain, Bald Eagle, White Bear, Crystle.*

Indian Mound Park was an easily accessible and favoured spot during our stay. It lay about a mile south of 941 Fremont Street at the end of Cypress Street, which ran one block to the east, parallel to Forest Street. There were excellent views over the Mississippi River. Phalen Park lay about 2 miles to the north of the Becker home, with a large lake of the same name. Next to it lay the 15-acre campus of the Luther Seminary where Father had studied, and St. Paul's Church was nearby.

Chapter 1

I must also throw light on the globe that I bought. I did not contribute to the indoor lighting at Fremont Street! This globe was a small world that was mounted with the correct tilt on a stand, and it proved very useful in my studies in geography. And, for some reason or another, I listed *"a lot of streets"* in St. Paul and Minneapolis. That I *"saw a lot of lakes"* was inevitable in "The State of Ten Thousand Lakes".

It is surprising that I did not mention an event that has remained in my mind. On May 21, just after our arrival, Charles Lindbergh successfully flew cross-Atlantic to Paris in his "Spirit of St. Louis". His name was on everyone's lips. A local bakery printed some cardboard circlets with big wings, and *Spirit of St. Louis* proudly printed on it, which we children could put on our head; and Aunt Lena gave me a pencil sharpener shaped like an aeroplane. (I still have it!) Thus equipped, I was Lindbergh, flying around the world in the house at Fremont Street.

Mid-June was an interesting time, especially for the parents. Beginning on June 12, there were Commencement Exercises at the Phalen Seminary and its associated College; and the annual Synod of the Minnesota District, embracing Minnesota, North Dakota, South Dakota, and Iowa, followed.

This provided a good occasion for most of the 1917 classmates (also from other States) to gather in St. Paul for a week-long reunion. Three of them had pastorates in the District, one came from western Nebraska, and one even motored from Saskatchewan. Four were not present from remote areas: two from Texas – one of whom in his letter enquired whether Father would be inclined to accept a call in Texas –, one from Saskatchewan, and C.F.H. Krueger – with whom we had stayed in Denver, and who a little later paid a visit at Fremont Street. My particular recollection of this is the day that the classmates went for a drive and an al fresco picnic in the country north or northeast of St. Paul. I don't know whether it was already termed a 'barbeque' in those days; but I was impressed when somewhere in the area, around White Bear Lake, 'wieners' were cooked over an open fire and then put on sharpened stakes cut from the trees. This was followed by a visit to 'Wildwood', an amusement centre at White Bear Lake.

Picnic with Father's classmates and family. Henry seated at front, third from left.

I did not attend any school throughout the months in America. But I was 'in school' all the same; Father was the teacher. The 'Big Chief Tablet' still records some of my efforts. I wrote 'compositions'. There is quite an amount of history: a complete list of the monarchs of England and the years when they reigned; an 8-page essay ('192 lines', I recorded at its close) on Queen Victoria and her reign, including a section on the Federation in Australia. It contains geography, with a strong American content. Father supervised my arithmetic by means of oral mental arithmetic, and by setting and correcting 'sums': '407 shillings, bring them to pounds', '48,720 farthings to shillings', and additions – and there was a disturbing number of prominent X marks that did not denote an unknown quantity! The earlier-mentioned *'Hammond's Atlas'*, absolutely up-to-date as a 1927 production, with its excellent basic presentation of world countries and detailed presentation of cities and towns in the U.S.A., provided me with a knowledge of general geography that stood me in good stead in later stages of education, and at that time probably made me more knowledgeable of the U.S.A. than most American children.

Chapter 1

    I used those State maps for imaginary travels by rail, commencing at Washington D.C., and moving from State to State via each capital city. I could instantly name each capital. Even though Australia did not fare any better than being depicted with New Zealand on a one-page map, this atlas has been a lifelong 'treasure' — I bound it as a hard-cover book when its soft binding eventually gave way from constant use. — The Tablet also has drawings, both freehand and traced, coloured geometrical designs, maps, some American state songs; and a young lad's interests show up in lists: there are many lists, especially geographical, but also including 12 brands under the heading "Butter", and 78 different makes under "Cars".

School work in America – Geography, History and Mathematics

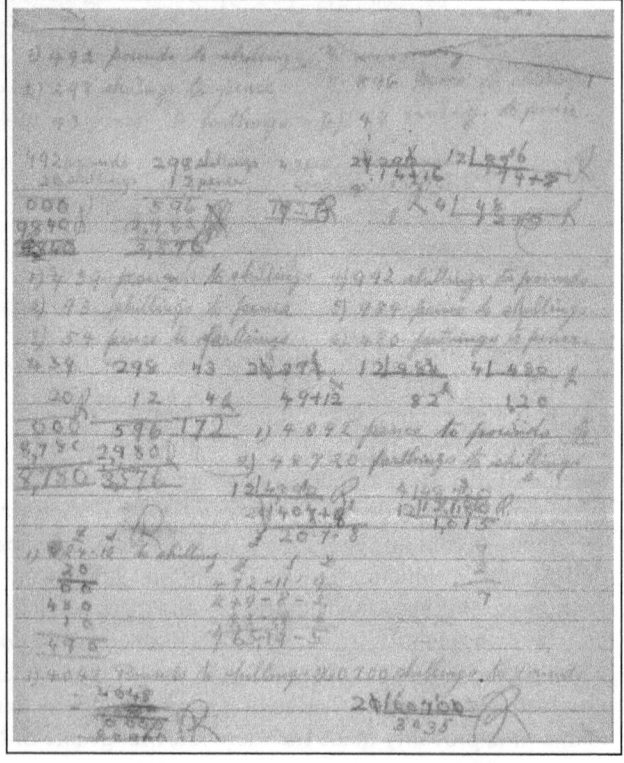

Grandfather Becker had bought a roller-wagon (also known as a roller-coaster), a rectangular wagon with a pole and closed grip in front, with which the wagon could be drawn along or, if thrown back over the wagon, with which it was steered. The two sidewalks around the house were a good spot for me to push it with the left foot while resting the right foot in its 'tray', or to steer it while being pushed around in it. I don't remember whether I took little Martin for a ride in it. Father attempted to prevent the problem of neighbourhood boys 'cutting the corner' so often with their roller-coasters that the grass ceased to grow. Some hours of amusement came from the cartons and cut-outs provided on packets. There was a brand of popcorn called "Cracker Jack", which gloried in the slogan *"The More You Eat   The More You Want"* – very good for sales! Occasionally allowed a carton, I got three small carts drawn by a horse, and a horseman on a horse, a kind of arch with an eagle and a clock, and a tramcar – all made of metal and painted. Somehow they helped to while away the hours. Armour's Cloverbloom Butter cartons had 15 Mother Goose Cut-Outs, all illustrating nursery rhymes. I got 6 series, which also served as amusement. In addition, part of the flap was a coupon. For two coupons and 10c the proprietors in Chicago sent their "beautiful Cloverbloom Mother Goose Painting Book", complete with paints, which were delicate tints on a palette, and a brush. I got one of these books, and thus was able to be an artist.

[I.5.] 4.2. Sorrow, Joy, Anxiety: July – October 1927

The summer months after our arrival were a delightful time. Then came the first shadow.

Martin's death. On Wednesday, June 29, Martin began to get feverish after breakfast. After our midday meal he suddenly got convulsions, and a Dr. Burfield was hurriedly called. Peeping through the double doors from the living room, I watched as he in the front room vainly tried to stop the twitching and writhing of my little brother with applications of hot and cold water. With his consent a children's specialist, Dr. Robert Rosenthal, was called. Suspecting meningitis, Dr. Rosenthal took Martin, still in convulsions, in his car to the nearby St. John's Lutheran Hospital. Martin's convulsions lasted for four hours. Next day double pneumonia developed. The services of a special night nurse were secured; we went to the hospital every day. Heavy-hearted, Father honoured an undertaking to give a lecture in German on Australia and the Lutheran Church at Springfield (137 miles, 220 km, distant) on the weekend of July 2/3. Next day, while briefly attending a Sunday School picnic in Phalen Park on America's Independence Day, Father and I were informed that Martin had taken a bad turn. It became evident that he was fighting a losing battle, and on July 7 he died. Brief life was here his portion: 1 year, 7 months, 21 days. In the Elmhurst Cemetery, where Grandfather Becker was buried, an adjacent plot of graves could be secured. On Sunday afternoon, July 10, Dr. R.A. Salzwedel, pastor of St. Paul's Church, conducted the funeral. Before we left America Father and Mother saw the simple stone that was erected to mark Martin's last resting-place.

Almost 80 years later it fell to me to deal with this one piece of American property that belonged to Hermann Proeve. A granddaughter of cousin Loretta desired to secure the rights over the remaining sites in that plot. As the executor of the estate of Hermann Proeve and then of Elisa Proeve I had to sign the documents, as prepared in accordance with American law and complete with the seal that Americans love to see on documents, transferring ownership as a gift.

The mixed pattern of sorrow and joy continued. Five days after Martin's funeral Mother's youngest brother, Gus, arrived by car with Aunt Jean and daughters Margaret, Jean, and Aletha, from Luseland in Saskatchewan, Canada (about 800 miles, 1,300 km, distant), for a stay of just under a fortnight. The nearest approach to a **family reunion** (33 family members, including 13 grandchildren) took place on the afternoon of Sunday, July 17, at Uncle Henry's home at Withrow – only Uncle Bill and family were absent. We were at Uncle Henry's farm about six times; on one such occasion we stayed for several days.

Chapter 1

The parents had the pleasure of visiting in the homes of professors serving in the Seminary in which Father had trained, also in the homes of some of the St. Paul Ohio Synod pastors. During the absence of one of these Father conducted services on three consecutive Sundays in his church.

With the family at Withrow. Henry seated at front, second from left

Paul's Birth. As one young life was taken out of the world; another young life was on the verge of entering it. The latter, I now know, had been an unexpected development after the arrangements to visit America had reached the point of being completed. Paul Hermann — the name stemmed from his birthplace — was born on September 4, 1927, at the home of August and Elsie at 1139 Beech Street. [As I write this I notice for the first time that two days previously the family had been mindful of the gap in the family circle created by the death one year earlier of Grandfather Becker.] It is perfectly understandable that cousin Loretta was brought to 941 Fremont Street to spend that day of birth with Heinrich. Later on, as a family snapshot of the two of us shows, she was able to nurse this infant cousin that had arrived in her home.

There is a poignant conclusion to this Heinrich / Paul / Loretta story that remains permanently etched in the mind. In 1991, as part of a worldwide journey, Paul and his wife Gwen visited the land of his birth and, unlike me, they met most of the American cousins. From that time on Paul repeatedly urged Loretta to visit us in Australia.

At last she did so; in 1999 she joined a group of 'Globus' travellers on an Australian tour, and was scheduled to stay with Paul and Gwen in Murray Bridge during the days that the others in her party toured Adelaide and surrounds. Early in the morning of September 15 Gwen and I met her at the Adelaide Railway Station upon her arrival from Alice Springs for a stay of two days and two nights. Loretta already knew, from a special message to her in Alice Springs, that Paul had died on September 13.

On the second day in Murray Bridge she was able by arrangement to see once again the cousin she once, as an 8-year-old, had nursed — now resting in a coffin in the funeral parlour. On the next morning I took her to Adelaide for a final farewell with the group that was on the point of continuing its Australian tour, and I returned to Murray Bridge for a final farewell in Christ Church Lutheran and the local cemetery.

Photo: *Baby Paul with the family (Sept 1928)*

A fortnight after his birth Paul was baptised in St.Paul's Church by Dr. R.A. Salzwedel; his sponsors were Aunt Lena and Uncle August. His health gave cause for grave concern, for he was a very sick baby, so that there was a danger of losing him, too. He had a weak stomach, and came under the care of Dr. Rosenthal. Great problems therefore arose relating to our return to Australia; at my young age I was at the time only slightly aware of these problems. The booking to leave Vancouver on October 19 on the *Niagara,* for arrival in November, when the six months' leave expired, had to be cancelled. The doctor's reports added one month to the next in opposing travel; the booking on the *Niagara* for December 14 had to be cancelled. Each time Father explained the worrying circumstances in letters to the Secretary of the parish. Thoughts about visiting some areas had already been abandoned. The finances for the visit, so carefully saved, became inadequate through the unforeseen developments. Father undertook to replace the wooden shingles on portion of the roof on a house owned by his classmate Hermann Krueger; I even climbed on the roof and nailed some of the shingles. Early in the autumn Father canvassed portion of eastern St. Paul, demonstrating the 'Hoover' vacuum cleaner and receiving a commission on his sales. It was not an easy task, because America was already entering into the period of financial recession that in time struck other countries as well.

Around September the Ford Company, which had important works in St. Paul, made a far-reaching announcement: it was replacing its renowned T-model car with a new model that was fully geared. Father took me along to the Ford Works to inspect the first Model A Ford car in its various types: tourer, coupe, etc. He was much impressed, and said: *"That is the kind of car I will get when we are in Australia again"*. And he did. The 1929 Model A Ford he bought in January of that year was precisely the same type as the 1927 model we saw at the Ford Works in St. Paul.

[I.5.] 4.3. Experiencing a Winter in America: November – December

It was unexpected to experience the start of winter. Father helped to put in place the special winter windows, stored in the attic, that were placed over the normal windows in a double-glazing effect. The winter was especially severe, even for Minnesota the worst for 40 years. One memory is frozen in my mind: One day I poked my nose out to read the thermometer hanging on the outside wall. It registered 20° below zero – and remember that on a Fahrenheit thermometer 'zero' is not freezing point; freezing point is 32°. [Uncle Gus in Canada reported the abnormal figure of 40° below zero.]

Aunt Lena and Henry

The first occasion of seeing snow fall was an exciting one for me, but disappointing, because I couldn't get that snow to stick together in a snowball. Yes, I was able to build a snowman before we left; and I also could render juvenile assistance to Father in shovelling snow off the 'sidewalks' at the Fremont Street property, a civic duty that fell on every householder. In Forest Street, a short distance past the Becker allotment, there were four vacant allotments. On the way to the tram with Mother and Aunt Lena, with sleet blowing into the face in blizzard-like conditions, I turned around and walked backwards. The butcher alongside the vacant allotments had cleared away the snow from his shop and piled it against the unshovelled snow at the neighbouring allotments. I plunged head over heels into this huge accumulation, and returned howling to 941 Fremont Street.

The extreme cold created a panic situation in December that I have not forgotten. Following a family visit to the doctor's rooms with Paul, Father and I walked off in the extreme cold to attend to other matters. A passer-by pointed out to Father that his nose was frozen. Father took off his glove to apply snow to his nose, but that hand froze as well. Finally the other hand froze too. Father turned back to rush to the doctor's chamber; and in an increasing panic I vainly tried to keep up with him. A stranger picked me up in his arms; it takes no imagination to feel the relief after panic as I was safely carried to those chambers, and could then watch the doctor thawing out the frozen areas — by applications of snow from his window sill.

Chapter 1

Unexpectedly I celebrated a birthday in the U.S.A., my 9th; but I don't recollect any details. We were not in the mood to celebrate the American Thanksgiving Day, Thursday, November 24, with the typical local feasting; but Dr. Salzwedel conducted a thanksgiving service.

The further delay to our return in December finally brought a Christmas in America, where Santa Claus (and even Mrs. Santa) was an important figure. The streets of St. Paul were decorated with green archways. Well before Christmas I drafted a letter that was not sent, but is a reminder of the modest (!) requests for me and the slightly startling ones for my 'little brother' that were in my mind. The requests are very heavily reduced from the original list of possibilities that are on record in my 'Big Chief Tablet'. American advertising skills obviously had infected me in this one and only approach to the venerable gentleman, here given verbatim:

> *Dear Santa Claus:—*
> *This is the first time I wrote to you. You will find me on the "Niagara' in Cabin No.   . The ship will sail for Australia. My name is Henry F.W. Proeve. I was nine years old the second of November. I want a Musical Top, Honeymoon Express, an American Flag, Touring a card game, Lotto, Modeling Clay, Saxaphone, and Sandy Andy. Well that's enough, I guess. I have a little brother, Paul, give him a Crowing Rooster in a coop, Teddy Bear, Grissly Bear, Tractor, Truck, Airplane, and a Musical Top. Well I'll close. From*
> *Henry Proeve*

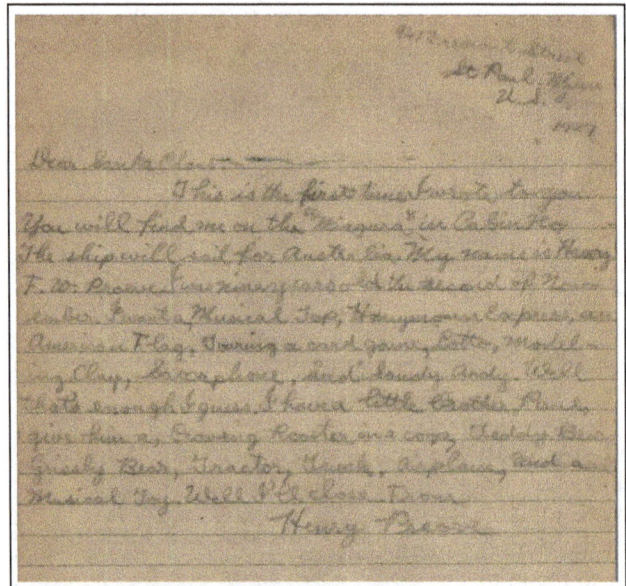 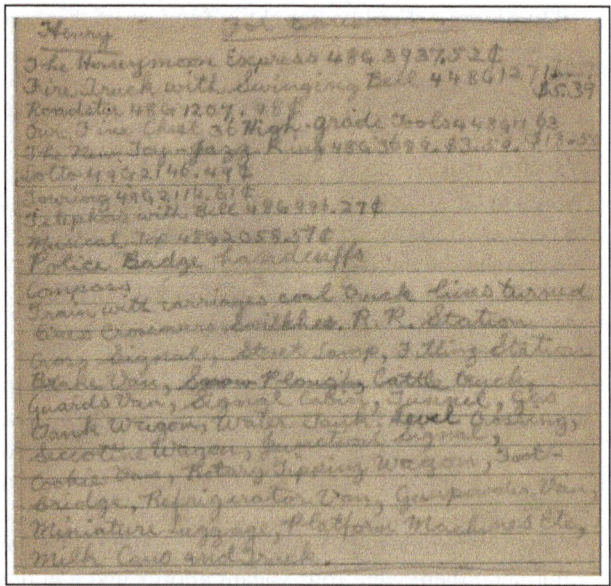

Letter to Santa   *Henry's first wish list to Santa Claus*

A snapshot of the Christmas tree in the Fremont Street home shows that I received my Lotto, and Tinkertoy and the Game of Horseshoes as well. St. Paul's Church did not forget me: I received a box of 'Golden Rule' chocolates and – still around in 2008 as a memento – the booklet "The Sweetest Story Ever Told".

Father continued to meet the problems created by our delay: Certificate of Death, and Certified Copy of Birth Record (which incorrectly recorded and thus ensured a 64-year-long use of the American form "*Herman*" by Paul, until a fresh application uncovered the mistake); a letter in November to the British Consulate General in Chicago with these documents to ensure necessary Amendments to Passport; a letter in December to the U.S. Department of Labor for Extension of Admission until 13 May, 1928, to ensure that the 'Welcome' mat was not withdrawn.

As a final American impression I refer to speech. Grandmother and Aunt Lena generally spoke Westphalian Low German to each other, and Mother soon remembered it again. That left Father and me rather in the dark, although Father after a while was able to get the gist of things, and even I picked up a slight smattering of it. My cousins thought my Australian English speech queer, and they, of course, sounded just as queer to my Australian ears. But by the time we left America I had acquired enough of the American twang that my schoolmates in Goombungee thought my speech was rather queer.

Chapter 1

[I.5.] 5. At last a return to Australia, January 1928.

Medical opinion finally allowed Paul to be taken on a long journey, but only on condition that he was immediately taken to a specialist in Sydney. The preparations for departure involved one feature that remained a lifelong recollection. The luggage included a couple of dozen tins of "Merrell-Soule Powdered Protein Milk. Physician's Sample. 2½ Oz." that Dr. Rosenthal provided as a special food that would suffice until arrival in Australia.

The return to Australia had always been planned for the alternative route, viz. via Canada, like the journey in 1917. It involved two railway systems: first the Minneapolis, St. Paul & Sault Ste. Marie Railway, known as the Soo Line, from St. Paul to Moose Jaw in Saskatchewan. From Moose Jaw the journey was to continue with the Canadian Pacific Railway to the Pacific Coast at Vancouver.

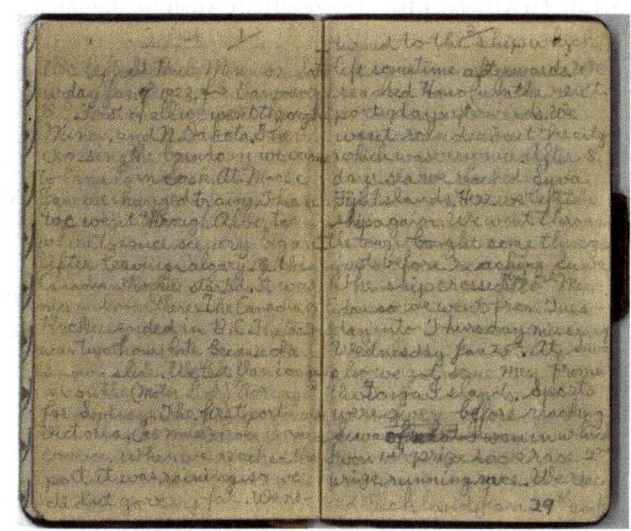
Henry's account of trip

Once again I let my contemporary account provide a summary of the trip. It was written early in 1928 as the opening entry of 5 pages (octavo) in a notebook that was given to me on the *Aorangi*. As with my 1927 accounts, I quote it verbatim, with its misspellings and concluding jumps of thought, but divided into paragraphs:

We left St Paul, Minn on Saturday Jan. 7th 1928, for Vancouver B.C. First of all we went through Minn, and N. Dakota. Then crossing the boundary we came to Canada in Sask. At Moose Jaw we changed trains. Then we went through Alberta where the nice scenery began. After leaving Calgary, Al. the Canadian Rockies started. It was nice and cool there. The Canadian Rockies ended in B.C. The train was two hours late because of a snow-slide.

We left Vancouver on the (Motor Liner) "Aorangi" for Sydney.

The first port was Victoria (85 miles) from Vancouver. When we reached the port it was raining so we didn't go very far. We returned to the ship which left sometime afterwards.

We reached Honolulu the next port 7 days afterwards. We went round about the city which was very nice.

After 8 days we reached Suva in Fiji Islands. Here we left the ship again. We went through the town bought some things. Just before reaching Suva The ship crossed the 180th meridan so we went from Tuesday into Thursday missing Wednesday Jan. 25th. At Suva we also got some men from the Tonga Islands. Sports were given before reaching Suva in which I won 1st prize sack race 2nd prize running race.

We reached Auckland Jan. 29th and left Jan. 31st. (Auckland's population is 189,000.) The first day we got off the ship and walked a little round about the town. Afterwards we went farther into the city. The next day in the evening we went to the town hall and saw the concert which was given by the Tongan boys or the Tongan Methodist Choir. The next day (the day we left) we went to Onehunga by the Onehunga tram and to the Zoolijical Park by the Glen Lynn Zoo tram. Coming taking the Herne Bay tram. The Tongan boys are in the care of Mr. Woods. They were adrift for some days. And suffered a lot. But luckily they drifted towards Suva, Fiji Islands where they came on board the "Aorangi" We left Auckland at 9.00 p.m. Tuesday Jan. 31st. Paul's prizes were a sailourgirl and a mill made out of feathers. I picked up some streamers when we left Auckland. At 8.45 p.m. a rat jumped all over the dining saloon making everybody squelling.

We saw land after we left Auckland 18 hours (from 9.00 p.m. 31st Jan. til 3.00 p.m. 1st Feb.) The same night of Feb. 1st a Mr. Trevaskis (whose address is at the back of the book) got word that his little girl who arrived with the "Makura" died. We got up at 6 a.m. for Medical Inspection. Then we got off the boat and had the luggage marked. We then took a taxi to the Strome House. The price for one day was 17 shillings.

We took the 1.55 p.m. train for Wallangarra.

We were at the Botanic Gardens, and saw monuments of Phillips, Flinders, Bourke, Sheakspeare, and Henderson.

We changed trains at Wallangarra the boundary of New South Wales and Queensland.

The hotel we stayed at Vancouver was the Hotel Dunsmuir.

We arrived at Toowoomba at 1.30 p.m.

Chapter 1

[I.5.] 5.1. St. Paul to Vancouver by Rail

It was a heart-rending farewell from the ailing Grandmother in her 76th year, and then a tearful one at the railway station from Aunt Lena, Uncle August, Aunt Elsie and Loretta, and Aunt Marie with Marie and Lydia Altmann on January 7.

5.1.a. To Moose Jaw. The return to Australia began at 11.00 a.m. Central Time on No. 107 of the Soo Line; and 45 minutes later the train left Minneapolis. There was snow everywhere on the journey. During the night the train proceeded diagonally across North Dakota until at 5.30 a.m. it arrived at Portal (562 miles [905 km] from St. Paul) on the North Dakotan border.

Canadian Customs officials boarded the train and checked the passengers' hand luggage. There was a 'double' change here: the locomotives of the Canadian Pacific Railway took over the jointly run train as No. 13 of the C.P.R. system; and as we were travelling west we entered the Mountain Time zone, which was one hour behind Central Time. Thus the departure time from Portal into Canada was 5.15 a.m. Mountain Time on Sunday, January 8. Soon after 11.00 a.m., after penetrating 130 miles, 208 km, into Saskatchewan, we were in Moose Jaw, on the important railroad route from eastern to western Canada. Here we changed to a train that came in from eastern Canada.

5.1.b. To Vancouver. The westward journey to Vancouver, 1,075 miles [1,720 km] away, began here at Moose Jaw at 12.10 p.m. Passing through the fairly level prairie land of Saskatchewan, it then climbed very gradually during the night (our second night of travel) through Alberta to the city of Calgary. In addition to its claim to be 'The World's Greatest Transportation System', the Canadian Pacific Railway fulfilled its boast that it ran through the Rockies in 'daylight hours'. After a 30-minute stop, we left Calgary at 5.15 a.m. on Monday, January 9, and ascended rapidly as we continued past the well-known holiday resorts of Banff and Lake Louise in a northwards sweep to cross the Rocky Mountains at the Alberta / British Columbia border.

Train route from Minneapolis to Vancouver

Here, at the Great Divide, there was a remarkable feature in the line that warrants mention – even if it has not figured in any recollections. In 1909 over 8 miles [12 km] of track and two Spiral Tunnels were constructed. Coming from the east the railway enters the first or westerly Spiral Tunnel, 3,200 feet [975 m] in length, under Cathedral Mountain 10,280 feet [3,133 m], and after turning a complete circle and passing under itself emerges into daylight, it then turns easterly and crossing the Kicking Horse River, enters the easterly Spiral Tunnel, 2,910 feet [887 m] in length, under Mount Ogden. Again turning a complete circle and passing under itself, it emerges once more into daylight, crosses the Kicking Horse River for the third time and continues westward into Field in British Columbia. A little further on another tunnel over 5 miles [8 km] in length shortened the rail distance by 4½ miles [7 km], and eliminated the need for snowsheds. Such sheds still stood on sections of the line built over the line at spots especially susceptible to snowslides. They spoilt the view, and sometimes obliterated it completely. There were none such in the Rockies in the U.S.A.

We spent a third night on the train, as it travelled south-west through British Columbia. Somewhere in the ranges in British Columbia the snowslide occurred that caused our delayed arrival in Vancouver at about 10.00 a.m. on Tuesday, January 10. The Hotel Dunsmuir, belatedly mentioned in my account, was used by the parents in 1917. On this present journey it provided the rest and accommodation for the remainder of the day and the night; all that was done was that Father attended to travel arrangements at the office of the Canadian-Australasian Royal Mail Line.

Photo: *Through the Canadian Pacific Rockies*

[I.5.] 5.2. Vancouver to Sydney by Sea.

The *R.M.M.S. Aorangi*, at Gross Registered Tonnage of 17,491 tons, was the largest ship of the Canadian Australian Line – "a new vessel, a high-speed motor-ship" (hence the extra 'M.' in its designation). Its length was 600 feet [182 m], breadth 72 feet [22 m], and depth 46 feet [14 m]. Its Commander was R. Crawford. Every four weeks it made a southward and then northward run between Vancouver and Sydney.

5.2.a. Vancouver to Honolulu. During the morning of Wednesday, January 11, we boarded the '*Aorangi*' to travel Third Class on what was advertised as 'The Smooth, Short and Enjoyable Route to the Antipodes'. On its way through Puget Sound to the open waters of the Pacific Ocean it called in briefly at **Victoria**, the capital of British Columbia, on Vancouver Island.

2,430 nautical miles from Vancouver, at **Honolulu**, the capital of the Hawaii Islands, the ship docked on January 18 for a stay of about 8 hours. What I did not mention in my account was that I drew a ship that lay in the port.

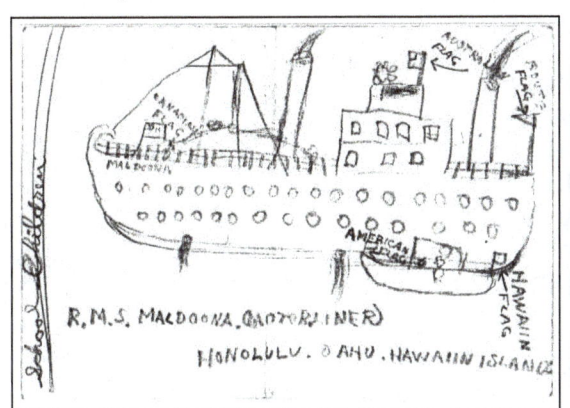

Henry at Honolulu

At a cost of 3d. per copy the '*Aorangi News*' could be bought during the voyage. Each copy consisted of 12 A4 sheets; 13 of these 24 pages were fully taken up by permanent advertisements. 'Latest Wireless News, General Notes, Topical News Afloat' were duplicated on the other pages, but most of these also had some advertising accompaniment. Two successive copies of this paper, issued after departure from Honolulu, have survived the passage of 80 years. The reason probably lies in a news item in Issue No. 7, dated 19th January, referring to a 12-member Sports Committee "*appointed by the 3rd Class passengers to represent them in the promotion of entertainment and games of various kinds, with special attention to the needs of the children, a special sub-committee having been formed for this purpose*". This news item included the following statement: "*At a whist drive in the 3rd Class saloon on the evening of January 16th, the ladies 1st prize was awarded to Mrs. H. Ravenscroft and the men's 1st prize to Mr. Proeve. Mr. Proeve generously returned his cash prize to the games fund*". I also took note of this by writing out on a menu card a report in a "Notice on Whist Drive" in the Third Class, which included the statement: "*The winner of the First Prize for Gentlemen has kindly denated* (my spelling, I fear!) *his cash prize of 6/- to the General Sports Fund to be used as prize money. The Committee extend their thanks to Mr. Proeve for his handsome donation.* — This issue also reported that at 8.00 p.m. the previous evening the vessel was 55 miles from Honolulu; the barometer was 30.06 and the thermometer 74 degrees.

Chapter 1

5.2.b. Honolulu to Suva. The stage to Fiji was the longest of the voyage (2,780 nautical miles) and took 8 days to cover. On the way we crossed the Equator, with usual 'Crossing the Line' ceremony, in addition to crossing the International Date Line.

The arrival in **Suva** took place among the world's early risers on Friday, January 27. Father hired a taxi for us to see a small portion of Viti Levu Island during the one-third day that we were there. — Several signatures in my notebook are a reminder of the presence of the fine young men from the Tonga Islands who became shipboard companions at Suva.

My parents made the comment that the passengers on the *'Aorangi'* were more sociable than those on the *'Makura'* in 1927. On this voyage a Mr. George Spreadbury, of Sydney, a member of the Sports Committee, was my frequent companion. The backs of 12 menu cards, undoubtedly for Third Class digestion, (9 of them from this voyage) became the manuscript for various activities, chiefly drawing, but on one menu recording as far as Auckland the daily latitude and longitude, and the daily nautical run! One of the final flourishes was a 'literary poetical effusion' that gloried in the Spreadbury title "Food Poetry. Grub Conversation", which I copied at the bottom as *"Food Peotry"*.

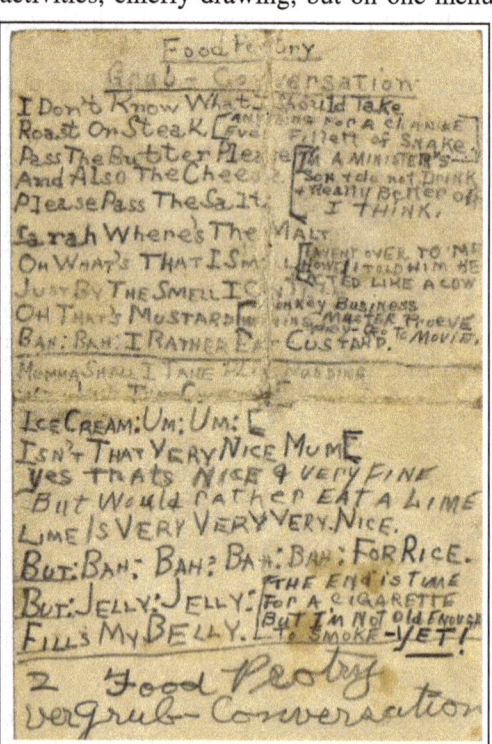

I think I have discovered the reason for that final fourfold outburst that now makes me feel sheepish, and I share it between me and you because it's found in the menus. From 9 daily menus available to me I quote what was available on the *Aorangi* for 'Dinner' [using '*&BR*' as a handy abbreviation]: "*Stewed Prunes & Boiled Rice*"; "*Stewed Apricots &BR*"; "*Rice Custard*" + for Tea "*Curried Lobster &BR*""; "*Stewed Fresh Pears &BR*" + for Breakfast "*Singapore Curry &BR*"; "*Stewed Prunes &BR*"; "*Iced Peaches &BR*" + for Breakfast "*Bombay Curry, BR*"; "*Stewed Pears &BR*"; "*Rice Custard*". What about the food that passed muster with me? "*Ice Cream*" showed up once, but "*Jelly, Jelly*" was not in our Class! – One of Spreadbury's contributions to this food for thought ran: "Monkey business, Master Proeve; when in Sydney go to movie", which indicates how he pronounced my unusual surname.

Photo on right: *Food Poetry*

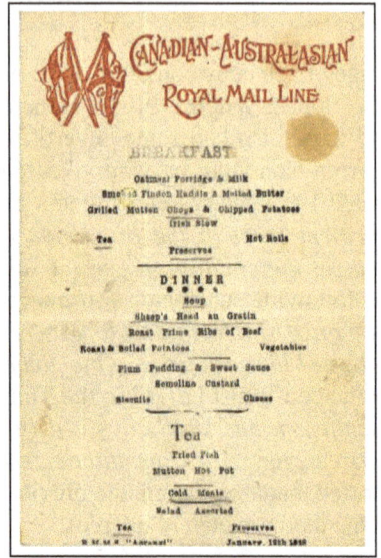
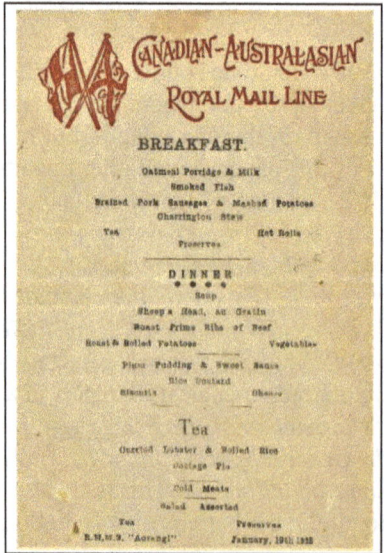
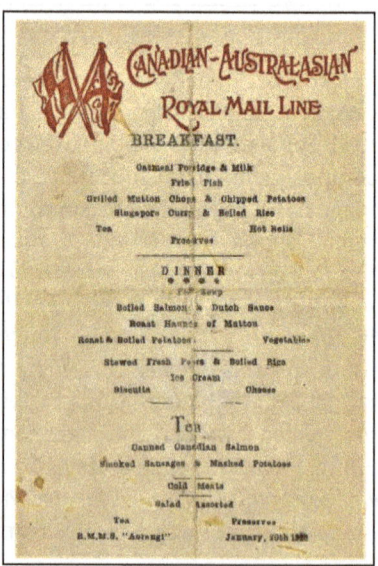

34

Chapter 1

5.2.c. Suva to Sydney. From Suva to **Auckland** was the shortest stage of the voyage, 1,140 nautical miles. The only addition I need to make to my full description of the stay in Auckland is to say that the trip to Onehunga was something of a visual geography lesson for me: we crossed the narrow piece of land that holds around 350 km of northern peninsula securely to the rest of the North Island, and looked over the western waters of New Zealand in the Tasman Sea.

The 1928 record of the final stage of 1,281 nautical miles from Auckland to **Sydney** reveals a boy who was conscious of time as he described the voyage along the northern peninsula before bearing west into the open waters of the Tasman Sea. — The Mr. A. Trevaskis mentioned in my account, whose Sydney address lay in Stanmore, was a fine man who had been active as the Chairman of the 3rd Class Sports Committee. His daughter, with mother, had just arrived in Sydney when she died. I wouldn't recognise him from a photograph; but I have a broad mental picture of my Father sitting often with him, extending pastoral care to him in his time of grief. Mr. Trevaskis decided that they could not remain in Sydney, and they left Australia.

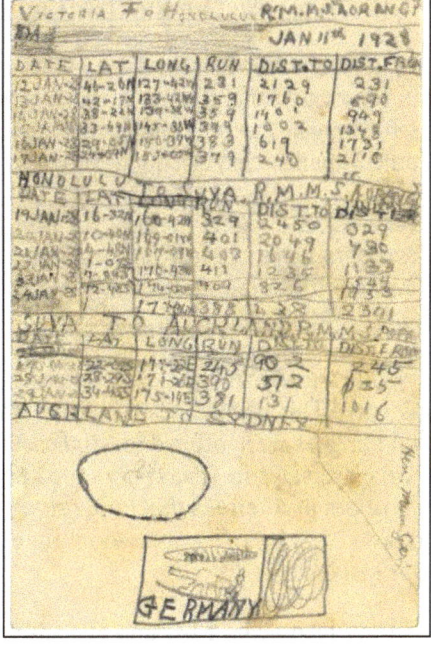

Photo on right: *Daily latitude & longitude*

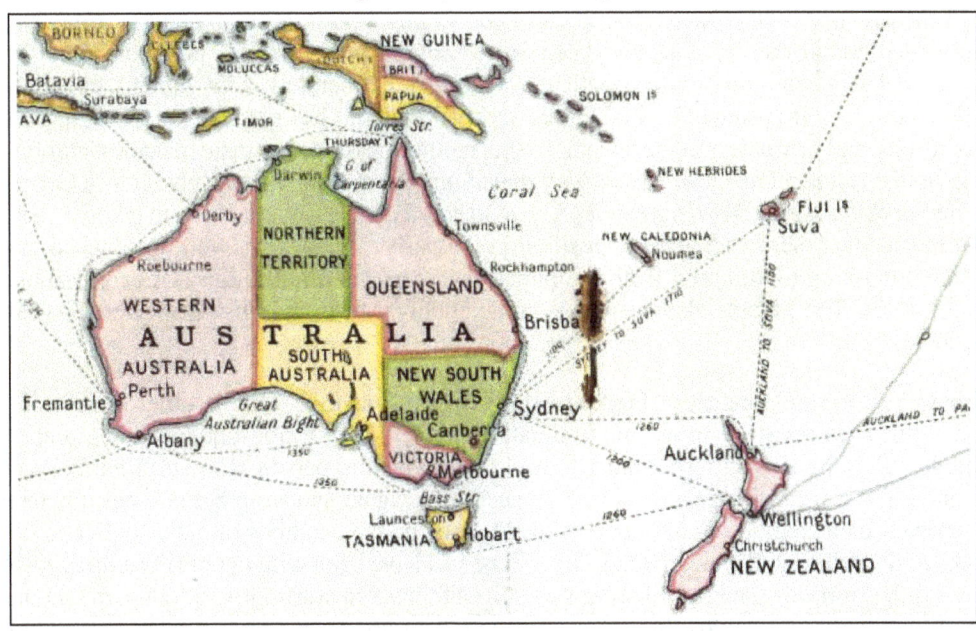

It was Saturday, February 4, when we arrived in Sydney. The voyage of 23 days over 7,631 miles [12,280 km] was over.

[I.5.] 5.3. Home at Last

My 1928 account is almost disorderly in its close, because the three matter-of-fact separate statements recorded there have sudden bursts of recollection about earlier parts of the journey interpolated between them. One more overnight train journey brought us home, leaving Sydney on February 5, and arriving in Toowoomba on the next day, Monday, February 6.

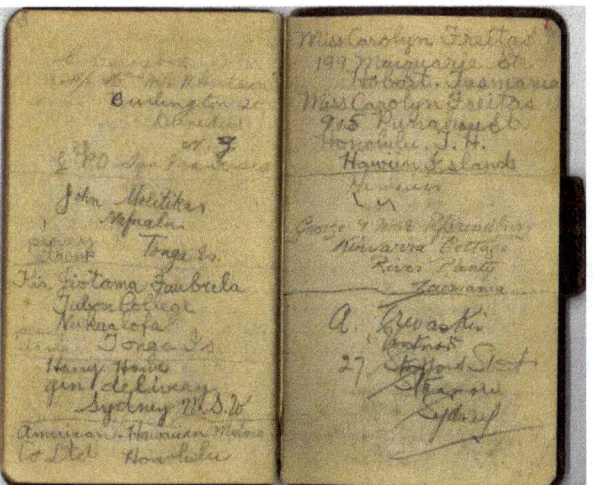

Photo: *Henry's collections of passenger signatures, including the Tonga boys*

Chapter 1

I. 6. The Unexpected End of the Queensland Decade, February to September 1928.

I don't know when or where Father received the letter that was to change the course of our life; but it awaited his return to Australia. It was not posted and it was undated; but it was addressed *'To The Rev. H. Proeve, Goombungee Parish'*, and it was very clear in its message. It was a dismissive missive that I have found in Father's papers and can quote verbatim:

> *'Dear Pastor. At a meeting of the above Parish held at Goombungee on January 31st 1928, when 33 Members were present, the following resolution was moved and Carried. It was moved that Pastor Proeve be given three Month notice from Feb. 1st 1928. this was second and Carried. Yours Faithfully [signature] Parish Secretary'*

While we were in the U.S.A. at least six approaches had been made to Father about entering into the local parish ministry. This began already when Father broke the journey in Denver. An offer came from North Dakota, and two parishes were offered in Minnesota, one of them being at Winthrop (only 75 miles [120 km] from St. Paul). Two classmates in Texas put out feelers for that State. Father's invariable reply had been: *'I have promised my members in Australia that I will return'*. The same heart-wrenching answer had been given to a pleading mother-in-law. I was, of course, too young to have a deep understanding of this thunderbolt that now struck in Queensland.

In my teen years I became aware of my parents' thinking about this. The shocked reactions of many parish members upon their return — *'We were told you were not coming back!'*, accompanied in some instances by an expressed desire to rescind the call that had been issued to another pastor — pointed strongly towards the explanation that Father's continued correspondence had been deliberately kept hidden from general parish knowledge. My later long involvement with Church archival material has not thrown any light on this; but the chatty letter of a contemporary pastor in Queensland to his mother (given to me many decades later for translation) made reference to the fact that Father *'had crumbled something into the soup'* in his parish — a German idiomatic phrase meaning *'made things awkward for himself'*, *'put his foot into it'* — by planning to go on a visit to America. The comment reveals that there was some opposition in the parish; and it may well be adduced that it was not difficult for this opposition to withhold from the parish members the information it received about the family problems in America. The parents also suspected some connivance in the District leadership, but not by the outgoing President.

It is possible to become melodramatic about an experience such as this. On the other hand, it is possible for those who have not been involved in a similar situation to view it in a non-understanding and therefore too detached attitude. Both parents suffered; but I think Mother was the person who suffered most. The pain of parting from an ailing mother whom she could not expect to see again and from her siblings, the pain of leaving behind in American soil a precious infant – pains not yet eased by the demands of daily routine in the Australian home to which, as she believed, they were returning – must still have been with her during a three-week shipboard 'inactivity'. And the worry of Paul's wellbeing was still with her. In warm, loving concern and understanding the members of the Proeve family took their 'Lieschen' into their arms and hearts in this stressful time.

Temporary Arrangements for the Future

The term "three months' notice" denoted that there was not an instantaneous eviction from the manse in Goombungee, but that we could remain there until the end of April. As far as I know that is what took place. The very troublesome question, of course, was: What happens after April? The Church authorities in Queensland – I think it will have been the Home Mission Committee in particular – made arrangements that Father, under the auspices of this Committee, should do some itinerant mission work in areas where Lutherans had settled, but were not under continued spiritual care.

Uncle George and Aunt Ruby came to our aid regarding accommodation. With their daughter Olga they had just returned to the Darling Downs from Mackay and bought a dairy farm at **Westbrook**. They lovingly opened their small home for us, and we moved in with them in early May.

Photo: *Westbrook*

36

Chapter 1

I was enrolled as a pupil at the Bunker's Hill State School, but (through lack of pupils at my level) in one grade lower than in my brief attendance at Goombungee. At that time, however, it became evident that no missionaries from New Guinea would be coming to stay in "Salem", the Lutheran Rest Home in Hume Street, Toowoomba, for such missionaries. It was arranged, therefore, that after three weeks at Westbrook we could take up residence in "Salem".

"Salem" remained our comfortable, but temporary, home until Queensland ceased to be our home State in September. It was the base to which Father returned after each of his rounds of visits as itinerant Home Missioner. In this capacity he visited Rosewood, where he conducted the first divine service that led to the establishment of a congregation, and (I believe) Beaudesert; to the north of Brisbane he visited Dayboro and Lacey's Creek, and the Nambour area, which was on the point of receiving its first resident pastor. My schooling took an upward turn, because in the Toowoomba South Boys' School I was again upgraded to my previous 'status'. Warm memories of my class-teacher, Mr. Biggin, a tall and to my memory already elderly man, have remained. He recalled the surname, because he had had George Proeve as a pupil.

Salem

It has quite recently come to my notice that the wheels that took us out of Queensland commenced to turn in May, when an official announcement appeared in the "Lutheran Herald", giving the information that *"The Home Mission Committee of the Victoria District intends to seriously take up the work in Ballarat next month"*. Inter-District negotiations must have arranged that when the temporary Home Mission arrangement in Queensland came to an end Father should serve as locum tenens in Victoria.

> **NOTICE.**
> The Home Mission Committee of the Victoria District intends to seriously take up the work in Ballarat next month. All Members of the U.E.L.C.A. who know of any members of our Church residing in or around Ballarat are hereby requested to send full names and addresses forthwith to Pastor G. Dohler, Natimuk, Victoria.
>   A. JERICHO, President Vic. Distr.
> Jeparit, Vic.

Photo on right: *Henry and Mother holding Paul, before leaving Qld*

The third item in my *'Aorangi'* notebook records the close of the 'Queensland Decade' of my life with very incomplete words. I reprint it in its total content:

> *Victorian Trip.*
> *Toowoomba Q to Sydney.*
> We left Toowoomba on Tuesday September 18th 1928 at 12.30 p.m. with the "Sydney Mail" train for Sydney. The first stop was Greenmount to let the "Sweeper" pass.

The 'Sweeper' passed. The Hermann Proeve family, however, stayed on the "Sydney Mail" and a little before nightfall on that day passed out of Queensland for good.

37

Chapter 1

> Trip to America. 1927-28.
>
> To write almost ten years after the event is always a difficult task, even with the most copious of notes. But when the only notes are some made for a short lecture, two short compositions by an 8-years' old lad, and railway & shipping folders, the task becomes infinitely more difficult. This is the position in which I find myself, but since even the best memory slowly fails I have decided to set down on paper the back reminiscences of that long tour ten years ago.
>
> First, may I briefly outline the reasons for this tour. When in June 1917 Father & Mother, very shortly after their marriage, left for Australia they promised Grandparents Becker that they would return in 10 years' time. To fulfil this promise was always their inmost desire, but unfortunately Grandfather Becker did not live to see their homecoming. In September 1926 he passed away.
>
> All the preliminary arrangements were made.

The start of the memoirs 10 years later

Father's letter to brother Ernst. 1922   *Ernst's reply from Hermannsburg, 1922*

Chapter 1

> St. Paul, Minn. Feb. 17, 1928.
>
> Dear Herman, Lizzie and Children:
>
> I hope you arrived home safely and are now again settled in your old home. How did it feel to be back again in your old surroundings? We missed you all after you were gone, especially little Paul and how is he now? It always seemed like we should be quiet when we got over to Mother's in order not to wake the baby. Well we miss you all and hope some day we can all live closer together and see each other more often.

Our American family enquiring about our trip home, 1928

```
TRAVELLING EXPENSES 1927                      Left Goombungee
                                               arr. Tmba by Ford
Photos 10/-, Passport 10/-    £1-0-0           Left  "   by train
Trip to Brisbane and meals                     arr. Newcastle
    etc.                      £1-10-0          Left  "
Railway fare, Tmba-Sydney     £7-13-9          arr. Sydney
Makura (Sydney-San Frisco)    £130             Left  "
Visum, Consul in Newcastle    £2-1-8           Rarotonga
Expenses in Tmba, and on way                   Papeete
    to Sydney, and in Sydney                   SanFrancisco 13 May
    first day                 24-0             St. Paul      20  "
Also meals noon and night     8-0              Left St. Paul 7. Jan. 1928
Train fares to Carlton and back  2-2           Left Vancouver 11 Jan  "
Lunch in Sydney before leaving   3-0
Wellington Expenses           10-3
Rarotonga, Fruits and beads   3-6
Papeete: Motor, fan, fruit    23-6             Sunday May 15.  34 tunnels
Tips to Stewards              9-0                      (117 miles)
Cards on boat and haircut,
    stamps                    4-0
Cigarettes on boat            2-0
San Francisco, 9.08 & 1.96    11.04
Continental Hotel             $ 5.00
Cap, films, milk etc., Frisco $ 2.09
Transfer charges              $ 1.75
Breakfast                       80 ¢
Expenses to Salt Lake         $ 4.40
Goggles and two meals, Utah   $ 2.05
Apples, oranges, cards (before
    Denver)                   $ 1.25
Figs, icecream, tea            .45 ¢
Expenses in Denver, Colo.      .79 ¢
Expenses from Denver to St. Paul 1.05
Expenses St. Paul, delivery   $ 1.50
_____
Return ticket, Railway        $ 159.85
Expenses to Vancouver         5.00
Vancouver Hotel room          3.50
Meals, bread etc.             1.50
Dextri Maltose etc., and tips 2.75
Cards, stamps: Vancouver and
    Victoria                   .40 ¢
Cards and stamps till Honolulu .45 ¢
At Honolulu, and deck chair   8.60
For sports on board           8 shill.
Suva and Auckland             10 shill.
```

Father's travelling expenses 1927

Chapter 1

Father's diary entry, Nov 1918, in his church almanac.

Chapter 2

II. THE VICTORIAN DECADE: 1928 – 1938

II. 1. At Natimuk: October 1928 – February 1929

The purpose of our travel to Victoria was reported as a news item in the *'Lutheran Herald'* of October 9, 1928: *"HELP FOR OUR VICTORIAN DISTRICT. Pastor Hermann Proeve from Queensland has been asked to come to the assistance of the home mission work in Victoria. He is at present relieving Pastor G. Dohler of Natimuk who is working at Ballarat"*. There were three congregations to be cared for: Natimuk, Horsham, and Green Lake. We shared accommodation in the manse with Mrs. Dohler and the two daughters of the family.

The three months spent in Natimuk hold a few memories for me. The difference in structure between the Queensland and Victorian education systems led, for the second time in the same year, to a 'demotion' of grade ranking. As a pupil in Grade V in the Victorian system I found that much that I was taught was a repetition of what I had learnt in Toowoomba. The importance of writing in the approved 'copy-book' style made it necessary to concentrate on discarding my Queensland style – which was rather stark in appearance – in favour of the florid Victorian style – which was full of loops. My school books of the time show that the changeover did not take place overnight. When adherence to "Copy Book" ceased at the close of my primary education I developed my own style of writing, which was a selection from both styles, chosen for speed, but also keeping beauty in mind.

Photo on left: *Proeve family at a church picnic at Natimuk, Nov 1928*

My 10th birthday does not raise any recollections. A brother of my desk-mate in the Natimuk School reminded me in later years that the desk-mate was Douglas Lockwood, a member of the talented Lutheran newspaper-publishing family, who achieved fame as a journalist with some radical ideas. One surviving memento of this time is a booklet of Shakespeare quotes given by the class teacher as a prize for spelling.

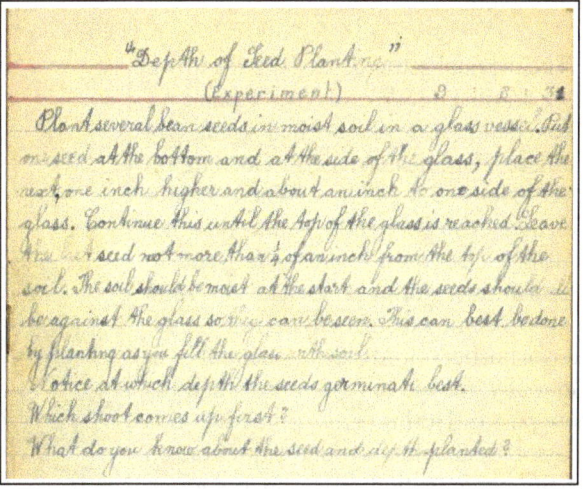

Copy-book writing

There is one matter, however, that I must record here, on account of its later significance. In the next-door parish of Dimboola the pastor was Wilhelm J.G. Schultz, whose wife was Clara. The Proeve and Schultz families had much in common. Wilhelm Schultz, an Australian from South Australia, had graduated from Phalen Park Seminary in the year when Father arrived in St. Paul. During a book-selling tour in one of his holidays Father had met and stayed with the Schultz family at their manse in Wisconsin. Clara Schultz also came from St. Paul – and in her mother found a soul-mate.

Wedding photo of Wilhelm and Clara, married in the USA

Chapter 2

The attempt to revive the cause of the UELCA in Ballarat was unsuccessful, and was therefore discontinued. Meanwhile the vacant Grovedale congregation issued a call to Father on January 7, 1929, and thus his activity as locum tenens drew to a close; but Victoria remained the District of the Church in which his activity continued.

Call document to Grovedale

II. 2. Grovedale: 1929 (February) – 1937

The Grovedale congregation had been without a resident pastor since May 1926. J.E. Auricht, studying for B.A.(Hons.) degree at the Melbourne University, served it mainly at weekends from Melbourne during that time. So there was rejoicing when the new pastor arrived. Once again the *'Lutheran Herald'* demonstrates how the church papers of that era, instead of concentrating on glossy sociological and psychological presentations as in later papers, let the Church know about life in its congregations as well as providing articles of theological guidance. Its issue of February 18, 1929, reported on the arrival of the new pastor in the most southerly congregation of the UELCA: *"The members of St. Paul's, Grovedale, are pleased to have a resident minister in their midst and showed their appreciation by giving the Rev. and Mrs. Proeve a surprise party in the Sunday School last Friday evening, Feb. 1, when everyone brought something to help fill the empty shelves in Mrs. Proeve's pantry"*. It also recorded that the welcome was made by Paul Paech (elder) and Frank Paech (chairman for the evening). Musical chairs, one of the popular items of entertainment of that era, was played, and supper was served.

The original settlement of Germantown (the original pre-World War I name of Grovedale) took place when eight Old Lutheran families arrived in Geelong on December 19, 1849. When Pastor Goethe, who was not aware that the 'pastor' [Jacobsen] whom he sent to Germantown during a vacancy in 1861 had been dismissed from the Hermannsburg Mission School in Germany, moved to replace him, and the new pastor (Herlitz) arrived in 1862, this 'pastor' was able to hold a major portion of the congregation. He and his group secured the manse and the original basalt church; in due course this group became a congregation of the ELCA.

St Paul's church, Grovedale

The smaller section of the 1862 division, which seems to have consisted largely of later arrivals from Germany, bought the two-storeyed Germantown Hotel as manse for Pastor H. Herlitz, and in 1872 built its quite commodious St. Paul's Church of brick. There was naturally a 'them-and-us' attitude in Lutheran circles. This is exemplified by the experience of new school-starter Walter Schulze, who strayed into Father's religious instruction in the Grovedale School, and was taken to task when he came home. *"Aber er hat nichts Unrichtiges gesagt"* *["But he did not say anything that is wrong"]* was his plaintive reply. Our relations with the ELCA Pastor Heinrich Hoffmann were very cordial. I was invited to daughter Aurelia's 21st birthday celebration, and was asked to propose the birthday toast; his son Martin and I mostly rode together by bicycle to Geelong High School, and the two fathers co-operated in fetching us and our bicycles home in instances of very inclement weather. They co-operated in answering family enquiries re baptisms etc. I received a good start from Pastor Hoffmann in a collection of New Zealand stamps – he had served as pastor there.

42

The church property had quite an imposing line of buildings along Torquay Road. The manse (on the site of the hotel), the church (with a prominent steeple), and Sunday School hall were quite widely spaced; and there was a remarkable depth of land along Heyer's Lane behind this façade – the remnant of a large original piece of hotel land. Thus there was room for a large garden around the manse, and enough land to have a commodious building close to Heyer's Lane that comprised a large garage, cowshed, and fowl-house, and an area in which a cow could be grazed. And I could hit a tennis ball against the back wall of the church. The manse was roomy, including a spare room in which we could accommodate visiting pastors or friends; but we had to wait a year or two before a telephone was installed, and initially we had to depend on lamps and candles for our lighting before electric light was installed.

Grovedale manse

[II.2] 1. St. Paul's Congregation: Life and Activity

Unfortunately there was disunity in the St.Paul's congregation, which ultimately affected Father's health. My assessment in mature years is that the larger group had been strongly influenced by a long period of ministry with Reformed Basle influence from the pastors G. Heyer (1868-1920) in particular, and R.T. Rohde (1921-1924). During World War I, for example, Pastor Heyer allowed his Presbyterian son-in-law Paton to occupy the pulpit in military uniform. Reformed Church influence, possibly through an architect, was visible in the total enclosure of the altar front with a rail, unlike the 'free access' of Lutheran church design. In the Sunday School Sankey's *"Sacred Songs and Solos"* set the style of 'hymns' with which the children grew up. Father introduced the use of the *"Lutheran Sunday School Hymnal"*. For some members there was *"too much Luther"* in Father's teaching and preaching.

On the other hand there was still some Old Lutheran element in the congregation, which demonstrated itself, for example, in a more consistent attitude towards worship attendance than some families had. In later years I discovered that the Paech family, for example, like South Australian families of the same name, came from Kay, an Old Lutheran stronghold. I used to lead old blind Mrs.Paulke on Sundays up quiet Heyer's Lane to her home; the name 'Paulke', I discovered many years later, was an Old Lutheran name in Hahndorf. My first German Bible was presented to me by Mrs. Paulke.

Services were still conducted in two languages according to a fixed pattern of English and German. The younger generation, however, was not quite so proficient in German as their elders. One year, for Good Friday and Easter and the preceding and following Sunday, the pattern meant that the younger generation was going to suffer through paucity of English worship. Father made one of these services bilingual. An elder, Mr. J–e, strongly objected and stated that Father had acted *"gegen die Religion"* (i.e. *"against the religion"*). I heard Father gently seeking to correct that by stating that Mr. J–e meant Father acted *"gegen die Regel"* (i.e. *"against the rule / regulation"*). But Mr. J–e repeated his previous wording, and remained so adamantly outraged that he left the congregation and joined the Church of England. The Church of England, of course, will have provided him with a German service every Sunday!! Local German speech had developed a broad Australian accent. I can still hear the choir singing the Gloria Patri (*"Ehre sei Gott in der Höhe"*) in the liturgy: *"Ar-*[as in *ar-row*]*-ray, Ar-ray, Ar-ray sei Gott* [as in *got*] *in dar* [as in *dad*] *Hay-yay-yay"*.

The choir functioned frequently; but sometimes it neglected practising as diligently as it might. One Easter Sunday it was less than adequate in its singing of an anthem marked by much repetition of *"Glory"*. This was immediately followed by Father's declaration according to the liturgy at that point, the beginning of the Epistle for the day: *"Your glorying is not good"*. Many of the anthems, which were of good quality, came from the appendix in the Presbyterian hymnal *"Church Praise"* – a hymn-book that I secured in later years and frequently consulted in connection with my activity in the Hymnbook Committee.

One liturgical quirk in its worship that Father was able to reverse (it needed to be <u>reversed!</u>) makes me smile, but shake my head, at the recollection of it. It was that the members knelt for the Confession of Sins – a praiseworthy practice of the Church. But in the process of kneeling they turned around and rested their elbows on the pews, and thus they presented rows of backsides to the pastor for absolution.

Chapter 2

There was a custom that at the Christmas Eve service with the Sunday School children the congregation provided a gift for each child; it was left to each child, however, to 'choose' the gift he/she wanted. Throughout the service the range of gifts chosen by the teachers was openly resting on a trestle top placed across two pews in front of the children. At times there were cries of disappointment when a child saw the gift he/she had been eyeing throughout the service chosen by a child whose turn to choose preceded his/hers. Father was not able to change the method, but at least was able to arrange that the gifts were covered with cloths.

The worship life of the congregation was quite strong. On Sundays services were held in the morning and in the evening. I don't recall how well attended the evening services were; mother and I attended most of the time. The festival days also were upheld.

Confirmation. Confirmation instruction was already given in English before Father came to the parish. My confirmation took place three days before my 14th birthday, on October 30, 1932. The memory verse that Father chose for me was: *"I am the resurrection, and the life: he that believeth in me, though he were dead, yet shall he live: and whosoever liveth and believeth in me shall never die"* (John 11,25-26). Unlike a settled family, the family of a pastor only rarely can develop a strong, perhaps lifelong, attachment to a particular church. The churches of my baptism (Trinity, Toowoomba, although totally rebuilt) and of my confirmation (Grovedale) probably come closest to having some degree of 'bond'. To these I would add Immanuel, North Adelaide, because my pastoral activity began there; later there were 22 years of membership and emergency activity in it, and even to old age I have had pastoral activity in it through service to its German-speaking section.

After their confirmation the young people in Grovedale became members of the Lutheran Young People's Society (LYPS), which met monthly. Father sought to deepen their spiritual knowledge with a study of the Augsburg Confession as the core of the Lutheran Confessions. I am not sure how successful this attempt was even at that time, when efforts were still being made to have the Lutheran Confessions serve as spiritual beacons. Occasionally the LYPS had a social, at which party games were played; and there was an annual popular picnic, usually on the beach at Torquay or Barwon Heads.

At the beginning of 1935 a fellow-confirmee, Frank Rossank, and I were called upon to exercise a type of steward's duty. We rang the bell for services, and controlled the ventilation via the windows. The bell-rope had to be held down for a few seconds at the right time to create a 'three-stroke' ring; this was quite a strain, so that the other ringer took over from the first ringer during the ringing process. In the nesting season the rope often brought down on our heads sparrow nests that rested on a ledge in the tower; so at times I made vertical trips up the ladder to bring the nests down. We two also were the pumpers who worked the wooden arm up and down that pumped air into the organ; I did it in the morning service, Frank in the evening.

Photo: *Confirmation, Oct 1932; Henry (back left)*

[II.2] 2. Some Snippets from Everyday Life in the 1930s

Some of the recollections about life in Grovedale will probably sound 'almost 'weird' to a 21st century generation; in addition to references at various points in these memoirs, some of them are gathered together under this heading.

Making ends meet. The pastor's stipend was not high in those days; when Father accepted the call his stipend was set down at £200 per annum. – in modern parlance, not quite $7.70 per week. When a depression set in at the end of the 1920s there came a time when this amount was not raised, and the shortfall created some monetary problems. Two things helped us out. On the area belonging to the church property we kept a cow, or more exactly, a series of cows (mainly Ayrshires), one of which was called 'Daisy'. From an early age I became one of the milkers. At the height of the milking period Mother could make an excess amount of butter, which was sold in Geelong. In the back shed we set hens to maintain a large flock of mixed variety, but mostly of a breed, e.g. Rhode Island Red and Plymouth Rock, that provided meat for the table when laying days were over. The surplus eggs likewise provided income.

Paul and Henry feeding the chooks

Behind the manse a roomy washhouse was erected for us. A new labour-saving device, a 'Hartwig' washing machine that worked on a suction principle to cleanse the clothes, was duly bought; pumping it for Mother with an up and down movement of the handle that operated this principle became one of the activities that strengthened my young muscles. The fork or spade for use in the garden that Father diligently tended to provide vegetables also strengthened my arms, especially when I was eradicating the mint that spread like wildfire under the brick path that led to the church. A less pleasant use was when I had to use the spade to bury the contents of the lavatory. This essential building stood in lonely glory in the back yard, a full cricket pitch length from the rear gate of the manse block. The 'cricket pitch length' of the dirt path served as the pitch on which I very frequently played cricket with Paul. To maintain his interest in being regularly beaten by his much older brother, he was permitted to bat in several consecutive innings, and I, after hitting his bowling around the paddock, would often bat left-handed. The washhouse also served another unusual purpose. Surplus milk from our cows was also made into cottage cheese by Mother; Father – and at that stage only he – loved this 'Quark' most of all when it was growing 'whiskers'. Its aroma caused it then to be banished to the washhouse. Lovely metwurst hung for months in the washhouse after there had been a pig-kill on some member's farm.

Hobbies or Pets. The interests of my young years went through a few passing phases. The nearest I came to having pets was that I once oversaw the hatching of two turkey eggs. The turkeys escaped the pot, but they didn't survive. Silkworms held my attention a little longer; I experimented with mulberry leaves from the tree in our backyard and with lettuce leaves, to see what colour silk thread I would get. And I had some canaries for a time. I collected birds' eggs, almost exclusively from the prolific sparrows and starlings. For many years I added to a large collection of rocks from the Geelong and Bendigo areas that I kept in the shed; but these had to be left behind when we shifted.

The most consistent interest as a hobby was philately. I retained what I collected, especially German stamps (in which Pastor K. Muetzelfeldt assisted me in Seminary days) and Australian stamps (which in the latest years has consisted in keeping the annual Collection of Commonwealth Stamps up-to-date). Interest in fishing did not develop in me. As a youth I fished with Laurie Hartwich in the Waurn Ponds Creek, which ran alongside their property; while munching raw quinces from their orchard, we caught a few minnows (which had no greater value than fishing bait, which we did not use). I accompanied Father to nearby Bream Creek; but he finally abandoned all efforts to be a successful fisherman there or anywhere else in the world.

What about dogs? I have a vivid recollection of standing in conversation with our next-door neighbour, Mrs. Cordingley, at her back door, when her Alsatian darted out of the back porch and flew at me at throat height. It seized my defensively raised right arm before she was able to gain control of the animal. As I was also, on an earlier occasion in my young life, bitten in the leg by a smaller dog that *"doesn't harm anyone"* (owner's assurance at the time), dogs have never been on my list of preferred pets. This was endorsed in my mind some years later, when a teacher at Geelong High School sent me to the house where he boarded to fetch something for him; my knocking and waiting at the front door was greeted by a collie that rushed around and, vying with me for height, placed its front paws on my shoulders, and kept them there until the lady of the house finally appeared.

Chapter 2

"Old King Cole's Court". The *"Geelong Advertiser"* ran a children's section, which it called "Old King Cole's Court". Children wrote letters to Old King Cole, sent in and/or answered riddles and puzzles, also took part in competitions, and received marks. The number of marks determined what standing they were given in the 'nobility' of Old King Cole's Court. I was a member of the Court for many years, and worked out such a system of gaining maximum marks, including creating crosswords and competitions, that there was no 'noble rank' left that could be granted me. An example of my productions that has survived the passage of time and many shifts, different from the many "Riddle-me-Rees", is my *"A New ABC"* that I prepared on July 31, 1934, and ran as follows:

Answers to Letters and Puzzles have A;   *B stands for Broadcasts, held almost each day;*
Courtiers and also Cub Notes start with C;   *The Drawings we send in start with letter D;*
E stands for Essays we write with much thought;   *F for the Features of Old King Cole's Court;*
Greetings King Cole sends to all if he can;   *H stands for Hobbies and How it Began;*
The Interesting Corner is of interest to all;   *Jokes delight Juniors ever so small;*
King Cole's Competitions we all try to win;   *L for the Letters and Limericks sent in;*
M stands for Music sent from 3GL;   *Numerical Enigmas with N you must spell;*
Old King Cole is our leader, you see;   *Pen Friend's Club and Puzzles have letter P*
The Question Box in our Page needs a Q;   *R stands for Rhymes, and for Riddles, too;*
The Serials by Seniors are enjoyed;   *Tricks at a party are to be employed;*
Unique is this Page, of that there's no doubt;   *Verses are plentiful when it comes out;*
A Welcome is given, whatever the age;   *When Xmas comes there's a special page;*
Young and old read Tuesday's paper when bought;   *Zealous are we to win marks in this Court.*

It seems to me that the popular "Riddle-me-Rees" of yesteryear have disappeared from the popular mind, and are now unknown. A "Riddle-me-Ree" that I provided in October 1936 for Old King Cole may serve as an example, but making it a little clearer by printing the important words in capital letters:

My first is in EBB, but not in NEAP,   *My sixth is in HERON, but not in QUAIL,*
  My second's in HARVEST, and also in REAP,   *My seventh is in ALTER, but not in CHANGE,*
My third's in ADO, but not in NOISE,   *My eighth is in MOUNTAIN, but not in RANGE,*
  My fourth is in MAIDENS, but not in BOYS,   *My ninth is in MORNING, but not in DAY,*
My fifth is in PIN, and also in NAIL,   *My whole is a sport that many folk play.*
        Answer: *BADMINTON.*

When I left the Court prior to going to Melbourne, Old King Cole emerged from his anonymity to correspond with me for a time as Charles McLellan (see below).

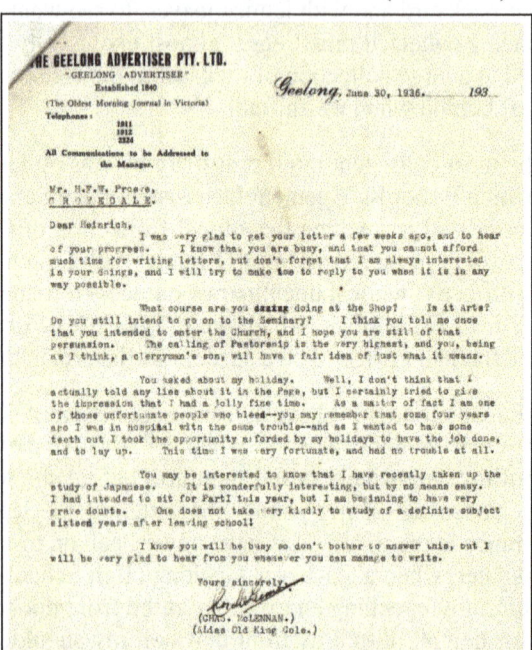

[II.2] 3. Three levels of Education

When I think back to my education and academic development over the years I realise that there were a number of factors besides the educational institutions that played a significant role. One was Father's interest in our education. He was very conscious of the fact that prior to his theological training his education had been no more than the basic primary level before he went out to work. He was therefore determined that his two sons should have the best possible education, and he encouraged us in our studying and searching. The second factor was that my own interest in learning caused me to do a lot of searching and collecting off my own bat. A surprising thing in the Grovedale manse was that there were still some books from Pastor Heyer's library in it. These included Meyer's *"Real-Enzyklopädie"* of about 15 volumes – a treasure-trove of information. I will later mention some specific use of it, but in addition I often read its articles at random. Unconsciously I thereby broadened my German vocabulary beyond that of usual household conversation. In my teens I began to take cuttings from newspapers etc.; these I initially pasted into my old exercise books –a saving device in financially tough years – creating several volumes of *"Knowledge in Scraps"* (as I entitled them).

I enjoyed writing essays. Sometimes this was a school curriculum requirement, sometimes it was invited competitively by some leading person in the community. The titles of books presented to me for my essays give some indication of the level of understanding among children that was taken for granted in those days. For example, the first presentation, for *"Empire Day, 1929*: *'Presented by The Hon. H. F. Robinson, M.L.C. for Essay on "The late Queen Victoria'"* – the book was *"John Halifax, Gentleman"*, by Mrs. Craik. And in the following year, as the prize from the Grovedale Mothers' Club for the "Dux 1930", I received *"The Complete Works of Shakespeare"*, edited by W.J. Craig. I think it was when a leading Geelong businessman, Mr. Belcher, following a world trip, offered one year's subscription to the city's Library as prize for the best essay on the ports he had visited (45 in all), which I won, that I, as a tender teenager and to the concern of the Librarian, concentrated on an English series that featured classical writers and read Charles Dickens, Thackeray, and the like. In a manuscript volume entitled *"Collected Essays"* 32 essays have survived (28 of which stem from the first three years of High School). The importance that May 24 (originally Queens's Birthday) retained as 'Empire Day' again shows up, this time in a general essay in May 1931: "Empire Day, and What it Stands for". Another public topic for an essay – a long one – in that same year was "Influence of Sea-Transport on Australia from Opening of Mail Communication by Steam to the Present Day".

Another activity to sharpen my wits began in 1931, when I started to write poems, entitled *"Poetical Essays"*. The first was an historical topic, in 34 lines, "The Monarchs of England", followed by a 29-stanza entitled "A Trip to America". The maturity of later years made me painfully aware of the weaknesses of these pre-teen efforts – I had carefully measured out the correct number of syllables in each line, but had forced them into unnatural emphases, as exemplified by the following 11-syllable couplet: "Then Ethelred followed after Ethelbert, And Alfred came to save Wessex from the dirt". (What a way to express being saved from destruction!)

[II.2] 3.1. Primary Education: Grovedale State School (1929-1931)

The longest period of education in the five State Schools that I attended was in the two-classroom Grovedale State School, No. 283, from 1929 till the close of my elementary schooling in November 1931, when I received Merit Certificate No. 207931, stating that I had *"completed satisfactorily the Course of Study prescribed for Elementary Schools"*. The school's number indicates its early origin as the congregational school of the pioneer Germans. It lay on a side road in the SW corner of Grovedale, about 1 mile from our house. On a piece of land behind the school stood the home of Robert Renzow, its venerable teacher, aged in the 90s, who was its first teacher. The wooden conductor's baton with which he conducted the church choir is a treasured memento of this man; with my father I often visited before his death, and the baton was presented to me by Dora, the daughter who so lovingly cared for him.

Grovedale State School – Henry front right

Chapter 2

Mr. Joseph Klippel was the teacher at the State School, of whom I have respectful memories, even though there was one occasion when I deeply felt that he had been unfair to me and others. One morning, through car trouble, he failed to arrive on time from Geelong, and quite a number of us, after waiting a considerable time – I think at least half-an-hour – returned home; he administered 'cuts' with the cane for not having waited longer! Every Monday morning we assembled at the flagpole, saluted the flag and pledged our loyalty to King and country, and sang the National Anthem. And then we marched into school. We had regular marching and drill, and we tended small garden plots as extra-scholastic activities.

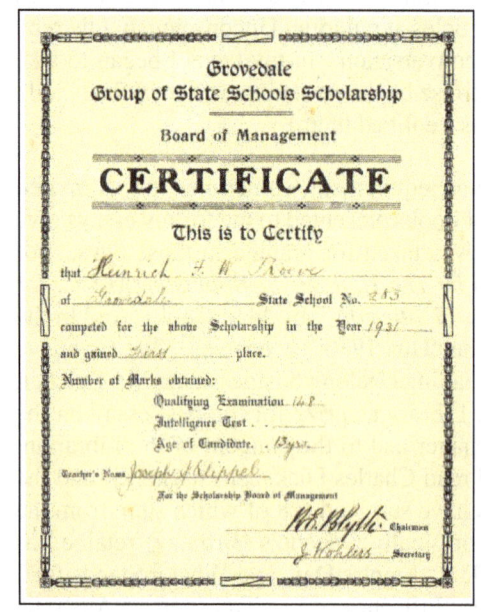

When Mr. Klippel had reason to teach in the second room, I was often made the monitor in the main room. I had been given school text books that had been used by uncles and aunts in Queensland, and from these (to give an example) I wrote words derived from Latin or Greek roots on the blackboard. Sometimes I had to take a junior class through the "Times Tables", as they were known: *"2 1s are 2; 2 2s are 4"* etc., which often finished with the triumphant shout by the class: *"12 12s are 144"*. That was the foundation for my lifelong use of mental arithmetic, even in the age when pocket calculators were being used to add 1 and 1 together.

I remember this closing stage of primary education with much appreciation. It provided a solid basis for further education, which I think is lacking today. I have mentioned the good mathematical foundation (for example, setting up simple balance sheets of "Receipts and Expenditure") – more advanced mathematics could be built up on it. We had a good grounding in English, through the drilling that we had in the parts of speech, and especially through the continual command to parse sentences. A Work Book of 1930 (Grade VI) has revived recollections of such forgotten terms as 'Principal Clause', 'Adjectival Clause', 'Adverbial Clause of Result / of Concession / of Condition'. All such things belonged to the now despised word 'grammar'. A grim joke of former years *("How's your grammar?"* — *"Oh, she's dead!")* is now reality. The phrase *"for you and I"* earned a red mark in the 1930s, now grown-up academics print it in their books; yesterday I heard a professor make a comparison *"like you and I"*. Correct spelling was insisted on. Spelling bees in school and in public were very much the rage in olden days.

The primary schools around Grovedale held annual sports days, the proceeds of which went into a local Scholarship Fund, from which the student with the best examination results from any of these schools was paid some scholarship money for secondary education. I won this scholarship in my final year, to the chagrin of some people who were put out by an 'outsider's' success. At the close of my secondary studies, when the scheme was closed down, the Secretary of the Scholarship Committee, J. Wohlers, in response to my letter of thanks for the scholarship, wrote that mine was the only expression of thanks that he had received in some 15 years of scholarship grants.

Chapter 2

[II.2] 3.2. Secondary Education: Geelong High School, 1932-1935

Attending the High School involved a 4-mile bicycle ride into Geelong, with two long climbs each way. In the morning there was often a land-breeze from the north; and around the time when the school lessons finished in the afternoon the wind shifted to be a sea-breeze from the south. So Martin Hoffmann and I, and other riders from the area, often pedalled into head winds. I developed strong legs from that. A Grovedale builder, Alf. Stein, used to drive his truck rather slowly. If he was on the road, I (or we) sometimes succeeded in grabbing its tray and being towed up the Grovedale hill or as a help against the head wind. I had this bicycle-riding exercise for four years. Photo below: *Paul and Henry with their bikes*

Mr. Robert Hagan was the 'Head Master' of the High School — 'Principals' only climbed onto the nomenclature ladder in a later status-seeking era. He was a much-respected man, ever ready to give sound advice. The holders of Merit Certificates were placed in Form E1, and I finished 1932 as the first in that Form. The subjects covered a wide range: English, Arithmetic, Algebra, Geometry, History, Geography, Science, and Drawing. A non-English language also had to be learnt; two of us desired to learn Latin: I because I had the Ministry in mind, Bert Siddle of Port Arlington because he wanted to be a lawyer. The only non-English language teacher in the school taught his home-tongue of French. Mr. E.J. Lewis agreed to brush up his Latin and be our teacher. Until this was arranged I heard three weeks of French, by which time the vivacious French teacher had taught me the French National Anthem about spilling the "impure blood". — I had to show a Geography term examination paper with 98% on it to the Head Master. The teacher, Mr. Jones, said that he had searched for some blemish to take away 2 marks; he found more in the next exam, because the mark was 92%. I loved geography, and happily drew maps when they were part of our week-end homework. Map-drawing became one of my delights until old age. But in Drawing as a subject (which included History of Art) I only secured 54% in one term exam result; later marks were better. My use of the paint-brush seems to have been my weakness.

On Tuesday of each week in the first year the boys in our Form went to the Sloyd Centre for practical training. I think Victoria must have been the only State to use the term 'Sloyd" (derived from the Swedish) to designate 'Woodwork'. Various kinds of wood were identified for us, and from these I sawed, chiselled, planed, put together a range of artifacts that has largely survived to the present day. As a result, I was interested enough in later years to purchase a workbench and suitable tools, and to make some household articles: a hot-water stand in the bathroom of our shack at Aldinga Beach; a huge set of bookshelves with adjustable shelves (14 feet high x 8 feet x 1 foot) for our temporary manse in North Adelaide; a smaller (124 mm wide) strong set of shelves, designed and built to hold a variety of items (including gramophone records), at Point Pass; a cupboard for the kitchen in Prospect; a set of pantry shelves in Tanunda.

From Intermediate Certificate to Leaving Certificate and Leaving Honours

As I reminisce about High School and read in my incomplete diary, I am struck how **broad the range of subjects** was that comprised my secondary education. That becomes evident in the following survey of the four years at High School, beginning with Form E1. [* self-taught]

1932 Form E1	*1933 Form Intermediate*	*1934 Form B Leaving*	*1935 Form A Leaving Honours*
English	English (mandatory subject)	English	English (1st class)
Latin	Latin (non-English language)	Latin	Latin (2nd class)
History	History		British History *[in 1934!]*
Arithmetic	Arithmetic	Mathematics I	
Algebra	Algebra	Mathematics II	* Greek and Roman History
Geometry	Geometry	Mathematics III	(2nd class)
Geography			
Science	Chemistry	Geology (science subject)	
	Physics	* German	* German (Exhibition)
Drawing	Drawing		

Chapter 2

Six subjects ran like a thread in the three years to Leaving Certificate level. Some came in as new subjects – the three 'Gs'. Geology became my compulsory science for the Leaving Certificate. I was keen to include German in my studies, and did so when I was able to programme time for what had to be my private study (as there was no teacher), Father serving as my 'corrector'. Greek and Roman History 'shot' into my mind at the end of Term I in 1935 while I was waiting for permission to leave the examination room after having completed an examination paper early.

After consulting the official syllabus I decided to try for Leaving Honours on my own, and in the next two terms I had books sent on loan from the Public Library in Melbourne, and read up many an article in my much-used German Meyer encyclopaedia! Some subjects were done in 'leapfrogging' style – that was the case in my privately studied subjects, as I bypassed Intermediate German and Leaving Greek and Roman History; but it was also the case in 1934 with Leaving Honours History: to our surprise Mr. Claringbold, my Intermediate History teacher who also taught at the Leaving level, suggested that I should bypass Leaving British History B and go direct to Honours. Mr. Hagan, whom we consulted, agreed.

My position as a student in Form A was unusual: I had already secured an Honours subject while in Form B, and in Form A I was studying two subjects under teachers and two subjects as a private student. At first I had to do my private studies in a room where a teacher was teaching, but the staff recognised that this was a disturbed way of studying and that I was disciplining myself in my private studies, and so I was allowed to study in whatever room was vacant. The School Certificate that I received at the end of 1935 shows the uniqueness of the situation: the line 'Subject' (where position in the Form was usually recorded) reads 'Special Award'.

School Magazine. In the third year (1934) the teachers decided that editing and production of the school magazine *"Flotsam"*, should be transferred from the teaching staff to the students. I was appointed by the teachers to be the Editor (together with Ron Pavia, a son of the Principal of the Gordon Institute of Technology), with an Editorial Committee of students, and the English teacher of Forms A and B, Miss Nellie Morrison, as the supervisor. We made many changes to the magazine, including a larger size. Miss Morrison insisted that I should include examples of my work in German, so my translation of Goethe's poem *"Erlkönig"* appeared in print. It must have been at a very early meeting of the Editorial Committee that I as Chairman asked: *"Is there anything that anyone would like to bring up?"* Pavia immediately picked up a nearby wastepaper basket and said: *"If so, do it in here!"* In all the decades that I conducted meetings after that I never again asked the above question to check if there was 'Any other business'.

Editorial Committee minutes

Geology was an enjoyable subject, and the Geelong district from the You Yangs to Anglesea was an area in which we had interesting geological excursions under a keen teacher, Mr. Alan (?) Coulthard. Mr. Coulthard put two of us – I don't recall the name of the other student – to commence a 3D map of the area. Using the large official maps with 10ft. contours and a pantograph to enlarge, we began the big task of drawing each contour on thick cardboard and cutting it out. We completed a portion with its hills and valleys, but the project could not be completed by us within that school-year. — The Leaving Certificate level in this subject must have been very good, because later, in Adelaide, a University student could make good use of my material for his studies.

A welcome supplement to the finances was the £15 paid to me as the Exhibition (i.e. award for the highest mark in Victoria) that I won in German in the Leaving Certificate examination.

My knowledge of German led to a highly unusual experience at the turn of the year 1935/1936. Two well-known aviators, the Pratt brothers George and Percy, lived in Geelong. Percy was deeply interested in gliding, which was still in relative infancy. Someone (I think the Pavias) passed on the information that there was a German student who might be able to translate a mass of German material on gliding that he had received. The excellent Muret-Sanders dictionary did not contain the multitude of technical terms that occurred in this material. Most of these words were German compound words; so I translated each part of these compounds, and that in very many cases served to give Pratt an understanding of the word. In return he promised me a ride in his aeroplane.

Henry in his High School uniform with Paul c. 1935

On March 4, 1936, a beautiful day, when I turned up at the Belmont Common along the Barwon River, he was more interested in his gliding. So I climbed into the seat of the glider behind the pilot; a car towing the glider raced across Belmont Common. In due course Pratt dropped the towrope, and as we slowly turned around to land again in the correct position I for a short time surveyed the view of Geelong and suburbs below me. "Oh, it was a glorious experience in the air!" was my recorded reaction. It got too late to go up in the "Wee Bee", his plane. — Percy's promise still had to be fulfilled. Next day I came again to the Common; his plane stood there, but he had great difficulty in starting its engine. As it spluttered Percy said: *"Hop in!"* I didn't hop; I tentatively climbed into the back seat of the two-seater plane, spreading my knees as far as possible to allow full play to the dual control ('joystick'). As Percy jiggled the joystick in his seat, the rear joystick played 'knock–knock' on my knees. *"I may need to make some big movements with the controls"*, said Percy, *"I need my brother's larger plane for you."* I climbed out, and there was less terror in my heart when my feet were again firmly planted on terra firma. — Before a further opportunity presented itself I had to leave Grovedale for the beginning of University studies in Melbourne. And so I had to wait until the 1950s for my first plane-flight.

I don't remember in which of the first two years at the High School it took place that on a day when I was not feeling well I (in accordance with school rules) stood as a non-player on the outskirts of the area where boys were playing cricket under the supervision of the Sports Master, Mr. Hobba. I looked away from the play; suddenly a strongly-hit cricket ball crashed into my face, just missing the right eye and breaking my nose with a vertical fracture of its bridge, and also fracturing the bones under my right eye. A doctor inserted a length of narrow lint into the nostrils (a huge length in the right one), and a short length of rubber tubing into both nostrils to aid breathing. For a long time I could not eat solid food; Mother made many an egg-nog, which I sipped through a straw. For the rest of my life I had a crooked nose, with a narrow left nasal slit, and a smashed right nasal area that often affected my breathing.

Chapter 2

[II.2] 3.3. Training in Music

The parents were very keen that we two sons should have a musical training. Early in our stay at Grovedale they arranged piano lessons for me with a Geelong teacher, Warwick Short. And they took out a loan in order to purchase a "Renardi" piano, on which to play. Mother especially held me to the necessity of practising; the only exception came on Good Friday and the following day. The piano is still in my possession. As Dorothy had very many pieces of piano music and songs, it was very often played by her, with the joy of singing associated with it.

Early in my musical development my interest shifted also to the organ as an instrument on which to play hymns. In this I was completely self-taught. Most of the time my playing took place on American organs; pipe organs were not so readily available in the churches and halls in which I played. In many places the instrument on which to accompany the hymn singing was a piano. It probably was in 1931 that I essayed to play in a service. Father had the idea that I could help him by playing in a service in Bendigo. I carefully and laboriously practised the tunes for the hymns that he had chosen. He also provided a list of the hymns and their tunes to an elderly man in Bendigo who was very fond of singing, had a good strong voice, but unfortunately also was very deaf. His pitch and his speed of singing, alas, did not coincide with mine. And at 'half time' the young player retired defeated in the tussle — 'half time' being the sermon. In later years I played quite frequently in Bendigo (17 times, according to a note that I have found among my diary papers); and on three occasions I played the Grovedale organ.

From early days I played a simple instrument of unknown name to me. It consisted of a tube about 1½ cm in diameter with a mouthpiece to blow into. On the opposite end there was a type of 'plunger', which one pushed in and out at various distances to create the pitch of the notes. I also played on the mouth-organ, but not in the florid style of the skilled player. The mouth-organ I used most was a little 'boomerang', about 8 cm long — so it really was a short one.

Photo on left: *Henry and Paul in their Sunday-best, 1934*

At the Seminary I took violin lessons from the College music teacher, John Meegan. With tips from him, I taught myself how to play the Immanuel College double bass in the orchestra that he conducted. For some musical interludes that we sometimes had at the seminary I learnt the Alto clef and played the College viola as part of a quartet. Playing the double bass and the viola ceased when I graduated from the Seminary, and playing the violin faded into nothingness in later years. My violin was passed on to my grandson Simon Wilksch. The musical interludes that we enjoyed in the home were duets that Dorothy and I played on the piano and harmonium respectively. My chief interest lay in classical music, orchestral and instruments associated with it, military band, piano, especially organ, and vocal. I gathered a reasonable set of records, and later of CDs.

Immanuel College orchestra, 1940. Henry standing at left with double bass

Organs and Hymns. There were two 'by-products' of my interest in music. One was that I developed an interest in the workings of organs. I took our own harmonium to pieces in Grovedale, noted and where necessary cleaned out the various sets of reeds that were operated by the various stops, and replaced pieces of felt where necessary. In later years, e.g. in the Kimba Home Mission Field, I sometimes, before a service, pulled out reeds and cleaned them up when they were 'misbehaving'. At Uncle Ernst's Immanuel Church, Point Pass, in my seminary days, I completely dismantled its Lemke organ, drew a plan of the positioning of its pipes, loosened their action where they were inclined to stick, and even tuned them gently. In response to the request whether the organ could be made a little louder to lead the singing, I experimented with bricks on the two sets of bellows, and put a half-brick on each bellow as sufficient to increase loudness a little without distorting the sound. What I did then was incorporated into the script for the ABC documentary on Lemke, *"The Pipes of Para"*.

The other early by-product was an interest in hymns and tunes. Knapp's *"Liederschatz"* in the Heyer books in the Grovedale manse provided me with information about German hymn-titles and writers of hymns that I started to note in my copy of the Australian Hymn-Book. I supplemented this, especially in reference to tunes, with information gleaned out of *"Church Praise'*, the Presbyterian hymnbook that was used in Grovedale for choir anthems. Father had a Layriz *"Choralbuch"*, from which I got to know chorales that we were not using. *'In dir ist Freude'*, for example, came to my delighted notice at that time. What this meant in my pastoral career is the subject of later memoirs.

"King of the Kids" at Point Pass with his cousins

[II.2.] 4. Sport in my Life

The reminiscences regarding my education at the third level, Tertiary Education, are no longer Grovedale based. They fall into the next period, centred on Melbourne. But this may be the place to reflect on that other aspect of life which nowadays prominently occupies the minds of the populace and occupies the pages of newspapers and the screens of TVs: viz. sport. Sport was less financially and still more recreationally orientated in those days; the more cricket, football, and tennis became a well-paid business, the more my interest in them waned. When I was at High School organised sport consisted of cricket, tennis, Australian Rules football, and swimming.

My juvenile interest in cricket (playing with Paul) continued at High School, where games were intra-school, with teams established at random. I followed with intense interest the fortunes of the Australian Test Team, when men played for the love of it, and radio stations went to great lengths to create the impression of "live" broadcasts of overseas contests in the only Test series that existed in those days, the Tests versus England.

I started to play **tennis** at the high school, and on one occasion was a member of the team chosen to represent Geelong High School versus Colac High School at Colac; but I don't remember the outcome. During the University years I played tennis occasionally with friends. And when I came to the Seminary I had in mind to continue to play some recreational tennis; but this did not eventuate for reasons enlarged on below. One final involvement in tennis came during my ministry at Point Pass: I played on Saturdays with the Point Pass Tennis Club team in a district competition.

Chapter 2

On the Immanuel College grounds the **cricket** pitch for practice lay just outside my study window in the Seminary. In response to frequent urgings to join in I went out one day to 'have a bowl'. My fast bowler's strong swing ensured that the ball was past the batsman before he got a bat anywhere near it — and playing in the College/Seminary team became my lot. *"The Echo"* assessed me as follows: "Has the build and makings of an excellent fast bowler, but should concentrate on direction and length. Useful batsman and slip-field". Erich Renner and I in 1941 set up a record score of 148 runs n.o. (not out) for the 7th wicket, to which Erich contributed 129 runs in a record-breaking innings of 164 runs n.o., and I contributed 19 n.o. runs, including a 6 off a 'block shot'! In that match I took 3 wickets for 9 runs; other figures included 3/37, 3/32, 3/25. As a fieldsman I mostly fielded at first slip. On one occasion, at Kimba, I managed to hold a catch wide to my left that the local press described as 'sensational'.

Photo on left: *Immanuel College cricket team, 1941. Henry standing third from left*

My interest in **football** was minimal. I had no personal prowess; my kicking was unsure, and I never was part of a team. At the Seminary, however, I functioned as a goal umpire in the inter-College competition in a manner that caused team members to say that seeing me between the goal posts gave them confidence. One occasion that fellow-Seminarists often reminisced about was at Christian Brothers' College, Rostrevor. With eyes fixed on the ball I moved backwards for a better view of the angle and fell head over heels over a bicycle that should not have been there. I rose to my feet with the fingers of two hands still raised to signal a goal.

It was my practice to establish and record the number and name of each player as he scored. At the close of one game at the Rostrevor college the supervising Christian Brother was approached by the umpire to identify "Number x", to whom he was going to award his vote for the "best and fairest player". (At the end of the season the winner of most votes received a much sought-after medal.) I was standing nearby, and when the Christian Brother had 'identified' the player I showed the umpire my notes, in which the numbered player had a completely different name. I had stymied a stratagem in which an attempt was being made to secure votes for their fancied recipient.

Swimming, or at least going to the Geelong Baths on Corio Bay, was organised by the High School as a school activity; but I did not learn to swim. In fact, when several boys one day pushed me off the Bath's boardwalk into the waters of the bay and then had to rescue me from drowning, my fear of being totally immersed in water was imprinted into my life. I loved to go to the sea, watching its moves, I felt comfortable in it paddling a little more than waist deep, but I floated with difficulty and without enthusiasm. Water in my ears has always been anathema to me.

Immanuel College A football team, 1940. Henry in centre, wearing a suit

Chapter 2

Games in the Home

    The above survey of sport in my life has set my mind thinking about recreation in the home in my childhood and since; and it has aroused a realisation that some games played in childhood appear to have disappeared. My parents were not stiff anti-pleasure persons. Often on a Sunday night, when the duties of the day were fulfilled, both parents or perhaps Mother would play with me. Dominoes figured frequently in this. There wasn't a pack of the normal cards (with diamonds, spades etc.) in the house, but an American card game called 'Rook' was popular with us. – There was a game with a cue that seems to have disappeared now, called 'Bobs', which required skills similar to those in billiards. A structure with a row of (I think) ten numbered openings, and with wings on each side to prevent balls falling off the table, stood at one end of the table. Shooting to pocket balls in the openings took place from the other end. – We played Nine-Men-Morris, and a similar game with dice that Mother knew from America, called 'Mühle' (i.e. 'Mill'). I also had a good Meccano set. In later years draughts and Scrabble were often played. Crosswords were a lifelong delight. Chess? Mr. Jentzsch soon taught me how to play it, but I forgot it through lack of ready players in later years.

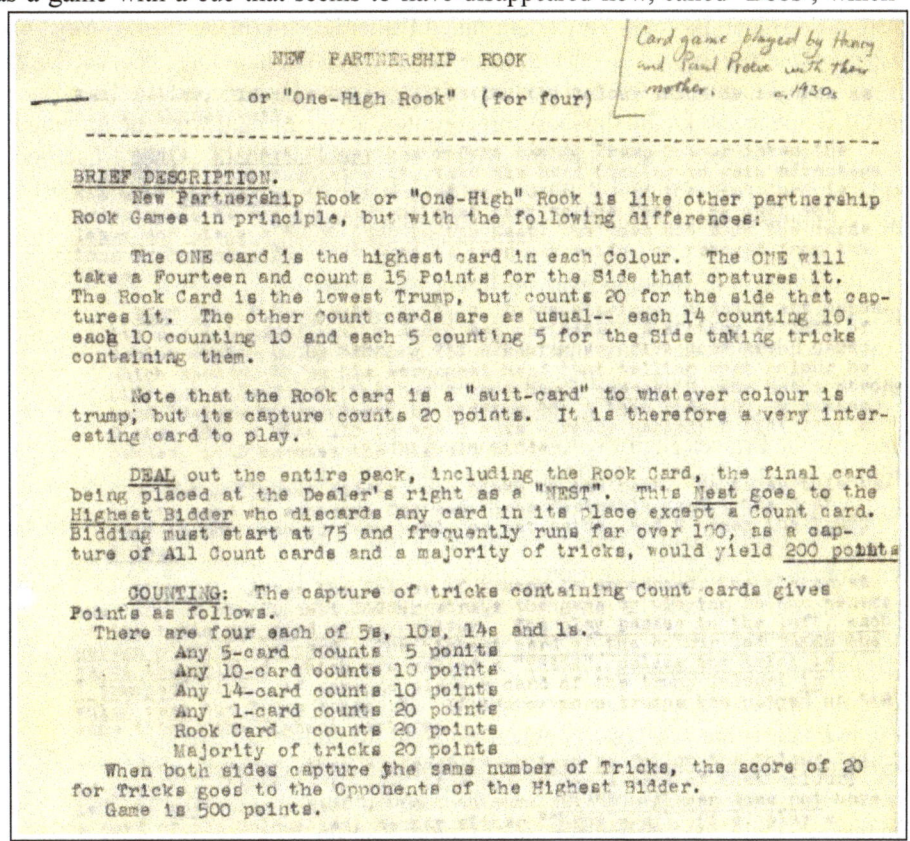

Rook, a favourite card game

[II.2.] 5. Geelong and Bendigo: Worship and Other Recollections

Services in Geelong. Neither Lutheran Church had a church in the city of Geelong before 1946, but both Grovedale congregations had members living in the city suburbs. For the benefit of his members Father established a preaching place in Geelong by conducting services generally every fortnight, beginning in the latter part of 1931 (4 services that year). The services were held in private homes, usually in the home of Adalbert Jentzsch; I sometimes at a later stage played the organ for these services. This small cause received strong impetus through a situation that developed in Grovedale. Fred Paech, on his way to ring the bell for a Sunday evening service in August 1935, was seriously injured when a car driven by young people of the congregation returning home from a beach outing at Torquay struck his motor cycle; and it seems they showed no remorse for what they caused their fellow-member; and one father staged a hostile defence of his son. The doctors battled for a little over 16 months in the hospital before they saved Fred's leg from amputation — but he had to wear irons on that leg for the rest of his life. This added to the differences in attitude etc. that Frank Paech had been having over a long period with the families of these young people, and he felt he could not continue to be associated with them in the same congregation. The strong spiritual life, liberality, and faithfulness of that family was a boon to the cause in Geelong, and led in later years to the building of the present Lutheran Church in North Geelong.

Henry (right) with the Jentzsch family

Chapter 2

Serving Bendigo. The once strong, then shrinking, congregation in Bendigo was transferred in 1930 to Father's care. It had been served for 61 years (in latter years from Melbourne!) by the aged Pastor F. Leypoldt (86 years old at retirement). It had lost its church through arson; and its state can be gauged from the statistics for 1931: 30 voting members, 30 baptised members, 30 confirmed members. It consisted almost entirely of widows and old maids, with a couple of old men; its services were still conducted in German. The later arrival of two related families hailing from Hamburg brought a little fresh blood into the congregation. When the District President, Pastor A. Jericho, installed Father he said (in German): *"Now, Brother Proeve, it is your duty to kiss off the old women!"* – that is what Pastor Leypoldt had done, because he baptised, confirmed etc. most (if not all) of them. On the first Sunday of each month Father conducted a service in the A.N.A. Hall, having travelled about 160 km by the most direct routes, about 240 km when he travelled via Melbourne. He usually went the day before, and visited the widely scattered members. Once I had become a reasonably confident organist – after my original baptism of fire in Bendigo – I often (finally almost invariably) went along, even from Melbourne; Mother and Paul frequently did the same.

In direct travel to Bendigo many different routes were used – hardly ever bitumenised. The most direct and most used by us was via Anakie–Ballan–Daylesford; another often used one via Bacchus Marsh–Gisborne–Calder Highway; rarely via Ballarat. The bitumenised road was the Princes Highway to Melbourne, and Calder Highway to Bendigo. — In those days, when 30 miles per hour (48 kph) was quite a fast speed, the journey took at least 3 hours. Many a time we avoided boredom by keeping an eye open for various kinds of birds, and recording our count. If the journey was at night we sang three-part rounds, like *O wie wohl ist's mir am Abend, mir am Abend, / wenn zur Ruh die Glocken klingen, Glocken klingen, / Bim—bom—, bim—om—* (in English, *O how lovely is the evening*). — When we went through Daylesford Father used to have a devotion (even Sacrament) with Mrs. Goodwin, nee Moll, and family. On the way there was a delightful walk to mineral springs at Sailor's Falls; many bottles at home were quite brown from the iron deposit that settled in them through our frequent filling of those bottles. On the other hand, if we used the top portion of the Calder Highway we came home many a time with a 4-gallon tin of excellent Woodend honey. One Sunday night Father arrived home with a large lump of snow still sitting on the running-board, deposited in a cold snap in the mountains around Woodend.

Mileage record, as always kept on trips

An orchard-owning family at Harcourt was also generally visited en route. The wife, Mrs. Gaasch, told an amusing story against herself: An Indian hawker called at their place, seeking to sell his wares. Mr. Gaasch, who had answered the door, seemed to be spending an inordinate amount of time with the hawker; so she finally called out very loudly to him, *"Ach, kauf doch etwas und laß den Esel laufen!"* (i.e. *"Oh, do buy something and let the ass run!"*). Some further time elapsed, so Mrs. Gaasch went to the door to check. The Indian hawker was just closing up his array of wares; he bowed deeply before Mrs. Gaasch and said: *"Der Esel wird nun gehen!"* (i.e. *The ass will now go!"*).

As some of the old ladies lived in areas surrounded by wild mining country with old shafts and heaps of rocks, I had an interesting geological time searching among and collecting rocks. I even found a rock with a tiny fleck of gold on it; but the large collection of rocks that I deposited in our Grovedale shed had to remain behind when our family shifted.

We stayed overnight with members. As time went on this was most suitably arranged with the two new families: Tonn at Golden Square, or Möller at Kangaroo Flat. Both men regularly drove trucks to Melbourne. One day, deeply engrossed in conversation, they walked along Swanston Street; coming to a cross street, they quickly glanced up and down, and set out to cross. A policeman's whistle pulled them up in their tracks, and he pointed to a set of red, amber, and green lights in front of them. This led to a conversation in general as follows: the Bendigo men, *"What are they for?" "Where do you come from?" "Kangaroo Flat"*. So the policeman patiently explained to the two men what each colour signified, and let them go with a caution not to do it again.

The Proeve family at the Möller home, 1934

In November 1936 the 80th anniversary of the congregation was celebrated. I wrote up the history for the occasion, using the Jubilee booklet of the Victorian Synod as its basis. — In January of the following year, during a holiday visit, when we camped in a borrowed tent in the White Hills Camping Ground, we saw a tent that very much impressed us. I measured and sketched it, and drew the plans for our tent to be made on its lines. We bought heavy waterproof duck for the roof, and thinner duck for the almost 6ft. high walls. The tent was 16 feet square; the centre pole was 9 feet high. When the various pieces, especially the four triangular pieces for the roof, had been cut out they had to be stitched together on Mother's Singer sewing machine. I did a large part of the sewing. It was a very very tightly wound together wad of duck that Father had to negotiate through the 'arm' of the sewing machine while I did this final sewing. It was a very comfortable and waterproof tent. The car was able to stand inside one half of it; camp stretchers, camp chairs, and cooking utensils were in the other 'living quarters' half. This tent served the whole family well on a Queensland trip, and later served my own family on camping holidays, in Archer Street North Adelaide as the 'garage' and storage space, and later as a marquee for family functions.

The tent Henry made

[II.2.] 6. Boarding in Melbourne, 1936-1937

At the age of 17 years adulthood took a new turn for me — the first stages of life in which the parental home would no longer be my unbroken dwelling-place began and, except for one year, became permanent. It was also the time when I had to buy a 'cut-throat' razor!

The University Student

The results of my Intermediate, Leaving, and Leaving Honours level studies were such that I was awarded No. 13 of the 30 Senior Scholarships awarded by the Government for study at the University of Melbourne. (No.1 scholarship was won by a brilliant student named Zelman Cowan!) Following advice from one of the High School teachers to do an Honours course, and after contact with Pastor J.E. Auricht of Immanuel College, an Old Scholar of the University, I enrolled for a combined History Course identical with his: History and German. These two subjects formed the three-year basis of my studies. Two other subjects at general level were required; I chose Latin I for the first year and English A for the second. The 'Honours' level in German included the study of Middle High German; in History it included the writing of essays on allotted particular historical episodes or characters, a detailed study of the French Revolution, and a 'special subject' in the final year.

Chapter 2

On February 9, 1936, Father took me to Melbourne. From that day onward Grovedale ceased to be the centre of personal connection for me: this was limited in the next two years to the educational vacations and an occasional weekend at home; and I ceased to be personally aware of daily events in Grovedale. Occasionally Father, perhaps also Mother, visited or passed through Melbourne. Otherwise the contact between us was by letter — as I write my memory says that there was never a telephone conversation between us!

I attended my first lectures on that February day; and that night was my first with the fine people who were to be my Melbourne 'parents' in the first year: our good friends Adalbert and Marie Jentzsch. In Geelong, finding no work, they had been living on the meagre 'dole' that was paid by the Government to the unemployed. For this Adalbert had to do work for a number of weeks on the Geelong to Ararat railway line near Maroona. They had now shifted to Melbourne, living above the pastrycook's shop at **301 Racecourse Road, Newmarket**. The room they made available to me was at the front, overlooking the busy street. The arrangement was that I paid £1/1/0 per week for board and lodging, but my washing would be done at home.

The Jentzschs moved back to Geelong (Belmont) at the end of 1936. For 1937 Pastor Steiniger found a home for me with Mrs. Varcoe at **262 Macpherson Street, North Carlton**. She was a fine matronly person, so highly regarded by my parents that in 1938 (when we were living in Melbourne) we continued as friends to have frequent contact at her new address. On the opposite side of Macpherson Street lay the northern boundary of the large Melbourne General Cemetery. I often walked to the University, and when I did so I traversed the paths within the Cemetery for almost one kilometre as a short-cut.

The three years that I spent in Melbourne had one focus: successfully to complete my chosen course of study in the Faculty of Arts in the University at Parkville. In fulfilling this I once referred to myself as having been "a learning machine".

Photo on right: *A letter for home which was occasionally written in the old German script which he was practising.*

58

Chapter 2

Had I not won a scholarship I would never have attended a university. The cheques for £10 that I received near the end of every quarter in the next three years as the Senior Scholarship made it possible, as they covered the University fees of £7/7/0 per quarter. The £15 that I gained in each year as the Exhibition in German naturally helped very much. And Pastor Ewald Steiniger, the German pastor in the Trinity Lutheran Church, East Melbourne, of blessed memory, persuaded an old businessman in his congregation, Mr. Grützner, to pass on to me (or for me) at frequent intervals 10 shillings per week. (Mr. Grützner probably will have recalled that Father conducted some services in East Melbourne when the congregation still belonged to the UELCA.) There were some teachers in the country who were doing subjects in private study; very soon after I came to Melbourne I began to send copies of my German notes, and less frequently of my History notes, to a few of them, and thus I earned some money. I once reckoned out that I earned 2 shillings per hour for my work.

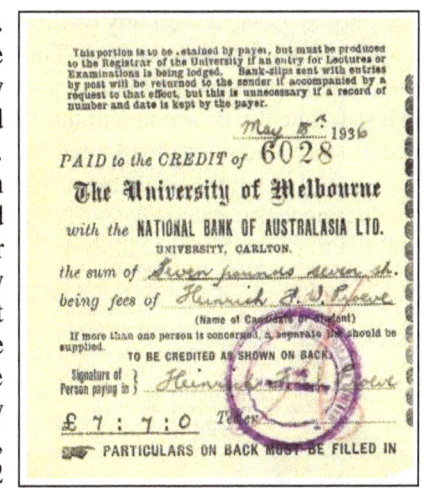

Receipt for payment of University term fees

The Steiniger manse was an open house to me at all times. Pastor Steiniger and his wife were very warm-hearted, and my comments in these Memoirs give some indication of how much he sought to help me. The family, especially the children, had wonderful help from a young lady from Walla Walla, Elsie Grosse. She liked writing and had a gift for it: poems and historical accounts relating to Walla Walla came from her pen. In later life she married Pastor Vic. Schultz. Pastor Steiniger was very much at home in English; he had served in England before coming to Melbourne, and he remained in Australia. He was no Nazi supporter, and did not deserve to be interned during World War II. — During the years when I was boarding in Melbourne I could also rely on other open invitations connected with Doncaster, from Pastor John Simpfendorfer (where I quite often stayed overnight), Mrs. Soderlund, and the W. Rieschieck family (with a son Ted), to stay for a meal, and longer. To travel through the orchard country or to wander through an orchard was a tonic.

Life at the University.

Compared with the previous necessarily regimented educational institutions, the University was a new and different world. The scheduled lectures, often only one or two for the day, were the only fixed features. My experience with privately studied subjects in 1935, however, had prepared me for the new system, in which I set up my own carefully thought out schedules of work, especially when essays had to be researched and written. I went to study in the University Library, a long narrow building, divided into bays by bookshelves and lined on both sides with mezzanine floors similarly divided into bays – one newspaper photo shows my friend Julian Wayden (marked with right X) and me (marked with left X) studying in it; or I went to the Public Library in Swanston Street.

Trinity Lutheran Church, East Melbourne

Chapter 2

I was not associated with any of the University Colleges and the social life that they included. My interest was almost completely academic. The only social activity that I engaged in was associated with my German studies (mentioned below), or associated with the two churches in which I worshipped, East Melbourne and (a little less frequently on account of the 12-mile bicycle ride involved) Doncaster. At East Melbourne I ultimately joined its small choir as a bass singer; in Doncaster I sometimes took part in Lutheran Youth activities. I watched the noisy fresher celebrations that marked the beginning of each year at the University, and that usually centred in conducting wars around the lake lying in those days in the University grounds. One year the forces of Gasolini fought the forces of Highly Salacious!

Doncaster Lutheran Church & manse *Pastor John Simpfendorfer*

The **History** section of my studies took me into a lecture theatre for lectures given by professors, into rooms for tutorials with tutors, and into the Libraries for research. I studied under two professors.

Prof. Ernest Scott — he couldn't pronounce his "r's" — sat firmly fixed at the lecture desk below us. Punctually on the minute, as soon as the clock on the Arts Building had ceased chiming, he rattled off the roll-call, not noticing or perhaps simply not reacting to the fact that many a name was answered, but not answered by the person named. Then he launched into the speedy reading, without pause or interpolation, of his presentation of his British History B material for the day.

This we wrote down in our own note form as fast as we could. Somewhere behind the writing desks in those tiers of seats there were also present Zelman Cowan, Chester Wilmot, Bruno Santamaria, and other later notables. Prof. Scott at that time had no academic degree. He was originally a journalist who wrote a number of notable volumes on Australian history; in recognition of this and his professorial work he was awarded a doctorate – I think it was at the time of his retirement, which took place at the end of my first year at the university, 1936. He stipulated the topics on which we had to write, and in due course had to read to him, the six essays that were part of the Honours section of our course. They were unusual subjects. On account of the first, "The Life of Richard Hakluyt", I have in my library 8 volumes of '*Hakluyt's Voyages*' in the Everyman's Library series, which glories in its original title: '*The PRINCIPAL NAVIGATIONS VOYAGES TRAFFIQUES & DISCOVERIES of the ENGLISH NATION Made by Sea or Overland to the Remote & Farthest Distant Quarters of the Earth at any time within the compass of these 1600 Yeares by RICHARD HAKLUYT*' — there are no misprints here; the original publication of these voyages etc. began in 1582!

The second topic on which I had to work at the same time was "John Milton's Smectymnuus Pamphlets". I had to go to the Public Library before I found out that the initials of five Presbyterian divines who wrote against episcopy created Smectymnuus; Milton attacked them. Other titles included "The Witchcraft Trials at Salem, Massachusetts", and the final one, "John Saris and William Adams in Japan". The witchcraft trials created a situation that caused me to write in my diary: *"My nerves are all a-tremble tonight. I hope I don't have to go through such a day again in a hurry."*

Professor Scott was very curt because I forgot to bring along my essay; then, at the end of his lecture, he called up three of us and practically accused us of stealing the Library copy of a book on witchcraft cases that we had consulted, and despite our explanations he declared that our names would be passed on to the Librarian; and then, after 'racing home' to Newmarket, I pushed my essay under his office door at the University. Eleven days later I noticed the 'missing' book was back in the shelves; but never a word of apology was given us.

One of his students related an experience that demonstrates Prof. Scott's excellent memory. This student found an old tome that dealt with the topic he had to write about. *"Scotty won't have read this since he was a pup"*, he said; and he wrote it out practically verbatim. After he had read his essay to the professor he received the assessment: *"There's one thing you forgot. You didn't put quotation marks at the beginning and the end."*

My second professor was **R. M. Crawford**, the successor of Scott. There is nothing about him that creates a picture of him in my mind; my diary note on the day of his first lecture, *"He is rather a thin man"*, has not helped me. In fact, for the whole of the first term he left it to tutor **Dr. Henry Hall** to be the lecturer in Australasian History, the subject for the second year of our course, as laid down by Prof. Scott. For the Honours section of our studies he introduced a new method, in which each student wrote a paper, which was then discussed. So there were no lectures; but there were no long essays either. At the time of his retirement many years later I, as one of his former students, received a letter requesting my assessment of his professorship. I ignored the request. I was in no mood to evaluate his qualities. When the results of the examinations at the end of my studies came out in early 1939, fellow-student in German Leonie Dunster wrote to me, congratulating me

ROSTER OF LECTURES 1936 (First year of studies at University of Melbourne)

	9 - 10	10 - 11	11 - 12	2 - 3	3 - 4	4.10 - 4.20
MONDAY	GERMAN I Lesebuch Room 23 Prof. Lodewyckx	—	LATIN I Translation Classics Theatre Mr. O'Brien	BRITISH HISTORY B (Pass)	GERMAN I Grammar Room 23 Mr. Egremont	—
TUESDAY	—	GERMAN I Reading Mr. Egremont's Room Mr. Egremont	—	—	—	—
WEDNESDAY	GERMAN I Phonetics Room 23 Prof. Lodewyckx	—	LATIN I Composition Classics Theatre Mr. Hunt	—	—	—
THURSDAY	—	—	—	BRITISH HISTORY B (Honours) History Class-Room Prof. Scott	BRITISH HISTORY B (Tutorial) Mr. Harper	—
FRIDAY	GERMAN I Room 23 Prof. Lodewyckx	—	LATIN I Translation Classics Theatre Mr. O'Brien	BRITISH HISTORY B (Pass) Prof. Scott	—	GERMAN I Tutorial Mr. Egremont's Room Mr. Egremont

on receiving Honours (Second Class), but expressing her displeasure that I was not given First Class Honours; Crawford had told a friend of hers in conversation: *"he never under any conditions gives First Classes in combined courses"*. My own reaction at that news was: *"I think his rule very unfair, especially since he alone upholds it"*. I have had difficulty in finding reason to have warm memories of him.

Dr. Hall impressed us as a fine lecturer, and later in the year (1937) four of us paid £1/2/6 each for private tutoring in 9 lectures. He suggested to me that I should use my knowledge of German to contribute an aspect of history involving German as my special thesis for the year. Prof. Crawford approved the research project as **"Dr. Ulrich Hübbe and the Torrens Land Act"**. The German newpapers in the vaults of the Newspaper Room at the Public Library became an important venue in my research. The librarian, Mr.Mossop, told me that he had been there for 15 years and couldn't recall that the German periodicals had been consulted. He finally gave me permission to go into the vaults and do my own searching. *"These vaults"*, I wrote in my diary, *"run under the Galleries of the Museum, are cool, long, stacked with papers, and dusty"*. I prepared a listing of every German publication I found there. Many years later, when the head of German at the University of Adelaide, Derek van Abbe, prepared a complete list of the German newspapers held in Adelaide, he enthusiastically added my list of Melbourne holdings to his.

Chapter 2

Five months after I began work on it my thesis was handed in to Prof. Crawford. My diary records the outcome. *"He gushed over it, like Prof. Scott with my last essay last year. He declares I have established my point moderately and convincingly, and says I should try to strengthen some of the weak points — e.g. one important quotation was not available, because the issue of the newspaper containing it was missing in the Melbourne collection — and then hand it in to an historical journal for publication".* That necessitated work in Adelaide; so it did not eventuate. I gave my paper a public airing when during the 1940s I was asked to speak on Hübbe at a meeting of the Goethe Society in Adelaide. Research by other persons in Adelaide had by then brought Hübbe's name to the forefront.

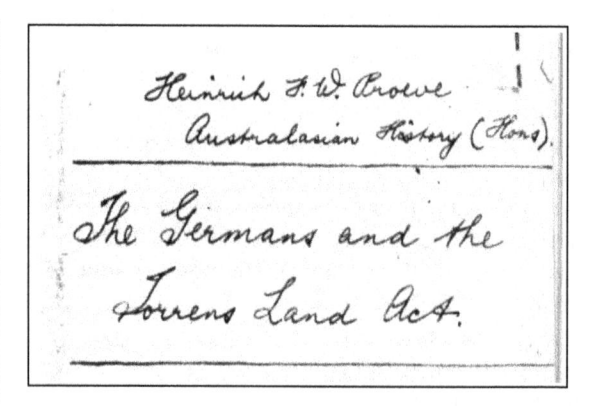

The two men who stand out in the **German section of my course** are the professor, Dr. Augustine Lodewyckx, and the tutor, Mr. Egremont. The professor was a most approachable man; his sterling work, *"Die Deutschen in Australien"* (1934), has for very many decades been a launching pad for much more detailed research. The Honours section of our studies included Middle High German, which remained helpful to my understanding of German; we had to learn portions of its poetry by heart. Prof. Lodewyckx's slightly guttural Flemish tongue occasionally was a little problem. At a Leaving dictation examination in my High School days that he conducted in Geelong he used a word that I had never heard before. Responding to my puzzled look he repeated it several times; and I wrote down what I heard but did not understand: the non-existent word *'Gatele'*. When I told Father about this problem, he recognised the word: *'Katheder'* (a lecture desk)! An important start to our studies was that we had to learn and do all our work in the old German written script; all my letters home, unless written in a tearing hurry, and Father's letters to me, were written in this form. The requirement to write out German phonetically according to the official rules of Vietor aroused a problem that I soon discussed with the professor: Should I continue to speak German in the Hanoverian style or according to this "Bühnendeutsch" (stage-German). He advised that I should adopt the official form. Instead of *'Tach'* I said *'Tak'*; *'Kriech'* became *'Kriek'*; *Sprechen'* became *"Schprechen'*. I wondered, in a letter home, whether my parents would understand me! Dr. Lodewyckx was away during part of 1937, studying the Icelandic language. Several tutors, especially his daughter Dymphna, filled in for him. — Much of our studies for two years centred on Goethe's *"Faust"*. Thereby I received a very detailed answer to the question that had troubled me as a lad, when I first heard this work mentioned: "What was so remarkable about Goethe's *"Fist"* that it received so much attention?"!

Mr. Egremont had been interned as a British citizen at Ruhleben in Germany during World War I. He knew the Australian Lutheran students from Neuendettelsau who were also there. The part that he played in my German course made his room and (for a particular reason) his hospitable home a much-used meeting-ground. It was through him that I was launched already one month after arrival into a temporary career in acting during these three years. This meant that, in addition to learning off by heart some Latin verses (in the first year), German poems, and Middle High German lines (80 of them in one instance), I was regularly learning lines for plays – in one instance for two of them on the same night. Play practice frequently took place in Egremonts's home in Armadale.

The **Deutscher Leseverein** (German Reading Circle), a gathering of the German students of a number of teachers of German (including a Mr. Ventur), usually met once a month, and listened to informative addresses on a wide range of topics. In addition there were German plays, in which we university students were an important component. I can recall six plays in which I and fellow-student Julian Wayden had a role. (I should introduce Julian here. His family was Jewish, coming from Poland; his father, who changed the name from "Weidenfeld", was a merchant. Julian and I worked together throughout the three-year course; but I had no contact with him after coming to South Australia. I was told that in World War II he was stationed in the Tatura internment camp as Major Wayden – and, I was led to believe, was not much liked. His German was excellent. When I asked Mr. Egremont why he was so often choosing me for plays, he replied that of <u>all</u> German students we two had the best German pronunciation.).

All plays produced in the DLV were repeated in the Deutsche Klub Tivoli. The first play was *"Fräulein Witwe" (Miss Widow),* in which I had to learn the art of 'stage kissing'; Mr. Egremont declared that I was wooden at it – but then, we weren't a kissing family, and I had no girls on which to practise. • This was followed by *"Brautschau" (Inspection of the Bride).* • In *"Goethe als Prüfungskandidat" (Goethe as an Examination Candidate)* I was the candidate into whom Goethe's spirit entered to give me the right answers; but Goethe's prompting muffed the answers! • Julian and I (I had the chief and long role as Flips) were the two tailors in the light-hearted *"Die Spitzbubenkomödie" (The Rascals' Comedy)* who made the emperor's clothes in the fashion of the well-known story – our emperor, however, kept his underwear on! • My role of Dr. Schön in the play *"Erdgeist" (Earth-spirit),* written by the playwright Frank Wedekind, introduced me to a vice. The heroine in the play had to make a complete change of costume while two of us were left on stage with scarcely any lines to say; and the answer to the problem of how to fill in time was that we should smoke. October 16, 1937 is the recorded date of my first smoke in preparation for the performance a week later — one Sunday afternoon in the 1970s, returning from preaching engagements in the Waikerie parish, I rolled the last bits of tobacco from a packet into a cigarette, smoked it, and did not buy a fresh packet next day, nor on the day following, nor ever after. • A *'Singspiel'* (play with song) had its origin in a request from the German Hilfsverein. Its title was *"Singvögelchen" (Little Singing Bird).* I played the role of an English lord (complete with top hat, white gloves, and spats) who was so annoyed by the happy singing of a lady with a lovely voice (Mrs. Reiter, soprano fellow-member of the Trinity Lutheran Choir) that I paid money (through my servant, Wayden) for her not to sing. My repeated cry of woe in my faltering German was *"aber sie hat <u>doch</u> gesingt"* (but she has sung all the same). This was so popular in the German circles that we had to play it five times. • Reference to the last play is held over because it became associated with particular circumstances in my life.

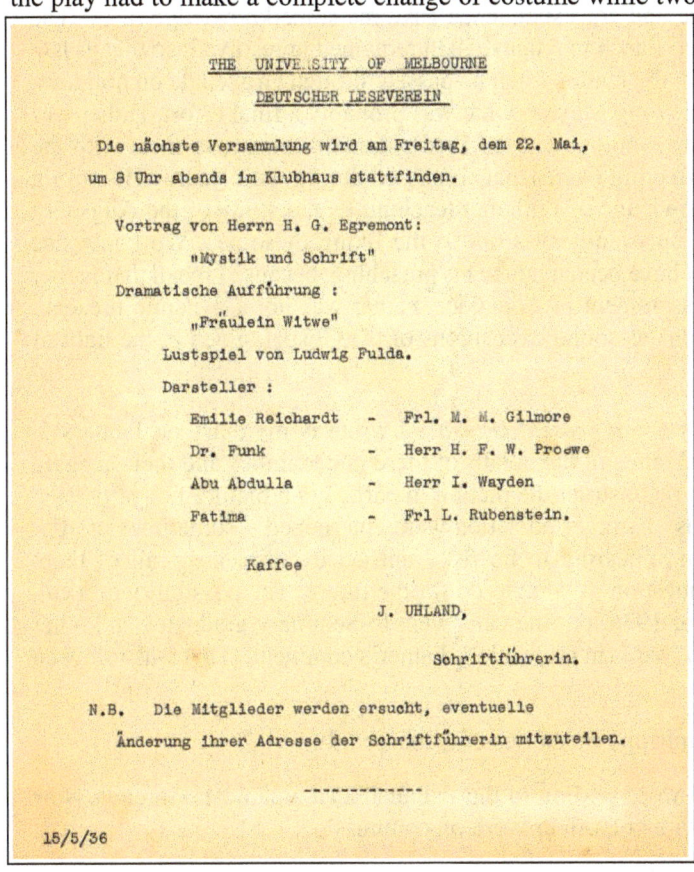

Program for the play "Fräulein Witwe"

Latin I was studied under a tutor, Mr. Hunt. Handing in exercises, in which we translated the set works from Cicero and Latin poets, constituted the bulk of our work. Mr. Hunt loved to roll off Vergil's verse. What I noticed was that his pronunciation of Latin words was much 'harder' than that used by Father according to his Hermannsburg training and 'harder' than what I had heard in any Roman Catholic chanting. His 'c' was a hard 'k' sound, not the 'tch' given (for example) to "excelsis"; his 'ae' was pronounced like 'eye', not like the German 'ä' of "Mädchen", as Father pronounced it.

Chapter 2

My one year in **English I** studies was spent metaphorically, but certainly not literally, at the feet of Prof. George Cowling. In his vigorous lecturing he used every inch of the podium in the lecture theatre, with the tattered ends of his robe flowing behind him. A much repeated mantra of his was that the word from the Anglo-Saxon was preferable to the alternative word from the Latin. In my own mind I could only agree in part: I preferred to say that I was bilingual, rather than to say that I was two-tongued! Cowling's publication *"The Use of English"* has had an honoured place in my library. We had to write many essays for the tutors. It was a relief for me that I fared better with the second lady tutor than I did with the first.

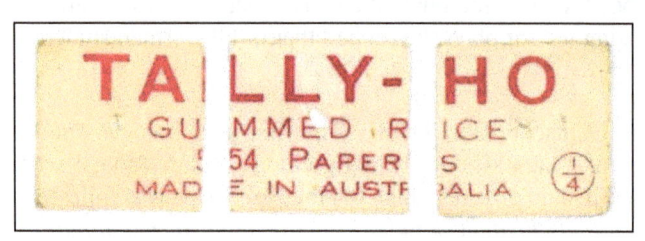

The Tally-Ho cigarette paper packets were not thrown away, but were used for protecting a file of papers when they were secured together. He continued this practice throughout his working life (see reference on the previous page to the end of smoking in the 1970s).

Years of uncertainty in Grovedale

I was in Melbourne, and so I did not have a day-by-day experience of the situation that my parents were facing in Grovedale in 1936 and 1937; but visits at home and correspondence gave me some knowledge of it. The tension that had been created by the accident to Fred Paech in August 1935 remained unresolved, so that as late as January 1937 Vice-President E. Sprengel took up the matter when he passed through Grovedale on holidays; but the irreconcilability remained. Even in the following May, in what was probably a final effort, Father was unable to persuade K., the father of the young man who had caused Fred's dreadful injury, to meet with the Paechs. But there must have been other matters affecting Father that simmered during these years. His strong Lutheran conviction and desire to give greater knowledge of Lutheran teaching (e.g. a study of the Augsburg Confession for young people after confirmation) apparently was not to the liking of some. We know one complaint was *"too much Luther"*. Reference must have been made to his preaching, because I recall that Father was asked to provide copies of his sermons for assessment in Adelaide. Father was not a dynamic preacher overflowing with oratory, but I regarded his sermons as sound expositions of the Gospel, given in the light of the Lutheran Confessions.

"The old year was one of uncertainty; the new year at present is also", I wrote in my diary on January 1, 1937. The passage of time has dimmed the remembrance of the details of these uncertainties and their nagging effect on the human spirit; but I have been able to reconstruct the picture in part. It's a picture full of twisted threads for more than two years, in which all kinds of suggested action were entertained – sometimes briefly, sometimes for an extended period, some of them appearing to be risky untried experiments – all of them supposed to be a possible answer to the pressing question of what to do for the future. The possibility of a call elsewhere was in mind already at **the beginning of 1936**, but the calls went to Seminary graduates and other pastors. *"So once again it's nothing in that respect"* was (in translation) Father's comment. That was followed by the suggested actions referred to above:

- Go to the North again (but there were unhappy memories of Queensland).

- Minister to Queensland members who were settling in the Pallamallawa area near Moree in New South Wales, supplementing the income with colporteur work on commission.

- Go to Light's Pass, sell books on commission, help at preaching, and run a farmlet (a plan proposed and strongly favoured by President Stolz). My own reaction to that was: "I don't think the former would pay, the second could scarcely be done if Father was gallivanting around, and the last would fall on Mum".

- A plan re Guluguba in Queensland, to minister to this isolated congregation.

- Father's thought: concentrate on Bendigo, but the Victorian pastors were not in favour of this because they saw no hope of building it up.

Chapter 2

The strain of waiting for correspondence from the President of the Church and/or the President of the District, or for any favourable development created a serious personal situation in October of that year. Father suffered some sort of heart attack – and he was not yet 48 years old. I believe the parents withheld from me the seriousness of this 'illness', probably so that I would not worry day by day in Melbourne. At that time I did not read this between the lines of a letter that Father wrote in the later stages, *'lying in bed'*, when he also penned one of his rare outbursts, writing about the inactivity of *"unser Volk" ("our people")*, compared with the helpfulness of neighbours to Mother. I really only became aware how serious it had been when he later told a light-hearted story.

Part of Henry's summary of his father's correspondence with the church officials, 1936-1937

He recounted the following: His doctor, who loved riding, rode out one day to Grovedale as part of his medical attention to Father. Father asked him whether he could shave himself again (and to my dismay I realised that he had been so sick that even shaving himself had been forbidden). The doctor looked meditatively at him and said: *"Yes, I think you can, otherwise you won't go to heaven!"* Then the doctor hurried to explain this strange statement: *"A young girl asked her mother, 'Mummy, do men go to heaven?' 'Why do you ask, dear?' she replied. 'I've seen many pictures of angels, and none of them have beards'. The mother thinks for a moment, and then replies: 'Yes, dear, men do go to heaven – but they only get there by a very close shave!'"*

The uncertainty dragged on into **1937** and soon became more intense. Steps that a pastor in the Wimmera who needed to shift should come to Grovedale must have already been well advanced. An after-service meeting was held at the end of February at which a member *"suffered for it"* that he opposed the proposal that Father should leave the meeting; in it reference was made to the future Frau Pastor as the *"best proposition Grovedale has had for some time"*. "We all feel it very keenly", I wrote in my diary. And there was as usual an evening service on that day, "by which time the atmosphere was not quite so electrical". On the first Sunday in February, when Father was in Bendigo, the members held an afternoon meeting; and next day the Secretary came, "who midst vigorous pants rubbing and umming and erring told us hesitantly that the Grovedale people were dissatisfied with present things". It is, I think, possible that he, mindful of the faithfulness with which my father ministered to his aged mother at Barwon Heads, was not in full agreement with this attitude. On the two days after Easter (March 29 and 30), while I was home for the weekend, Father and I packed his books, then my books and Paul's toys, into boxes, full of worries: "How long will we be staying on? When will we be able to shift to another parish? These are questions which torment us". One preliminary answer was the sale of income-earning 38 older fowls and 18 pullets in mid-April, leaving only a few egg-layers for home use. On May 9 the development was: "This morning P[astor] Jericho blew in and held a Coronation Day [George VI. on May 12] – Mother's Day sermon. This afternoon he held a meeting at which I was allowed to be present and listen in to them talking about the new parish, and the new minister etc. etc."

Chapter 2

The semester holidays began a fortnight later, and two weeks of packing household articles began in earnest, with Alma Paech and Mrs.Jentzsch as assistants, because May 30 was the last Sunday that Father preached in Grovedale and Geelong. The intensity of feeling at the time is demonstrated by two entries of mine during the packing: "Still more packing to do. But where are we going? and what shall we pack? and how shall we pack it? The Church will have much to answer for in its treatment of us." The other followed a visit by invitation to the home of Geelong members; they had a non-Lutheran boarder "who knows a lot of people in Murtoa. He knew a lot about the silly position in Vic. over the new parishes and P[astor] Proeve. What he said wasn't too complimentary to the heads of the Church and the members of it in Grovedale. I wished the big noises had heard him."

Photo: *Record showing the financial stress*

Pastor John Simpfendorfer advised Father to stay in the manse as long as possible. Various things were done to avoid being present next door when services were held in the church. On the first weekend we were in Bendigo, where Father conducted a service; on the next Sunday, when the incoming pastor came to Grovedale to conduct a service, we did a trip in the district. On another Sunday the parents came to Melbourne; and in July Father conducted two services in Bendigo, the second (at the end of the month) being his farewell service. President Jericho would not let him have the Bendigo field. The Light's Pass plan meanwhile was recommended by the Victorian Pastors' Conference; Pastor Simpfendorfer however, like Father, had his doubts about its feasibility. Reluctantly deciding that it apparently had to be Light's Pass, Father asked me to get carriers' quotes for removal to that spot in South Australia; in the meantime the household goods had to go into storage in Geelong, and the parents and Paul found a refuge in the Frank Paech home.

The temporary solution of getting away from the Grovedale area came in quite a different fashion. The triennial Synod of the UELCA was held in Queensland in 1937, and the Natimuk parish was happy to have the family during the absence of its pastor, W.W. Fritsch, as a delegate. Its 5 weeks there were marked by many emergency situations in the parish, and in other temporarily unmanned parishes, that took Father even to Mt. Gambier and up to Dimboola (where Pastor Schultz, the only other pastor left in Victoria, suffered a heart attack). It also brought a medical warning to Father to ease up, as worry had contributed to poor blood circulation. With a brief stay at Paech's between each stage, the parents and Paul made two interstate trips in October, the first via Dimboola to Uncle Ernst at Point Pass, as District President Heidenreich wanted to get to know Father as pastor and preacher. At the end of October the second trip began, in order to be present at the grandparents' golden wedding in Toowoomba.

Photo: *Parents and Paul at the Paech home*

For the last five months in 1937 I was bound to Melbourne. I could not join the parents in Natimuk during the 'swot vac.' on account of an infantile paralysis scare that isolated Melbourne; and I had to stay on in Melbourne when the parents left for Queensland, because November was the time for studies prior to examinations. With all my goods stowed at Steiniger's, I sat for my final Australasian History examination on November 18, and that evening caught the first express on a rail trip to Queensland. The joyful golden wedding service and celebration took place on November 21, the day after I arrived in Toowoomba. We visited relatives in the Darling Downs, commenced our journey to the South in mid-December, camping in our own tent on the way, which consisted of the New England Highway, Parramatta, and the Hume Highway. On Christmas Eve we arrived at the Frank Paech home, which then for a full month became our warm temporary home.

Grandparents' Golden Wedding at Toowoomba   *Henry joins the family at the Paech home*

II.3. Together for One Year in Melbourne, 1938

We made ourselves useful to our kind hosts. Paech's had a dairy farm. Milking machines were not yet the vogue, so the 5 Paech milkers were augmented by 3 Proeve milkers. During the years we had often done that on visits; on those occasions I had taken over the separating. So now, sometimes after milking one or two cows, I started up the separator and made it sing for a half-hour until about 36 gallons of separated milk stood in 9 tins. And the hay needed attention. A day standing on the haystack with Fred, pitching and turning sheaves on the stack and down from it onto a waggon made me a tired lad who still did the separating. In January ploughing began. I watched Fred do it; and then I tried my hand, first of all leading faithful old "Rose' as Fred, then Father, ploughed the garden, after which I scarified and harrowed it; but then branching out for 3 days (finally on my own) I ploughed in a next-door paddock with six horses. "Turning at the end of the paddock was most difficult; but I got the knack of ploughing to the right depth, adjusting the plough to the state of the ground, and I ploughed pretty straight too" – which was comforting in view of what Jesus said about "putting the hand to the plough" (Luke 9,62).

Photo on left: *Helping with the hay at the Paech farm*

In addition to the daily devotional exercises we were a home-congregation on Sundays with divine worship. In Geelong some of the families welcomed Father's visits. And I should add here that the Mr. J. who many years earlier had left the Church was warmly appreciative that Father again looked him up.

Chapter 2

President Stolz had said to Uncle Ernst on one occasion that he would be happy if Father were to make his own arrangements. That's exactly what was done at the beginning of 1938. Finances naturally played a big role in the deliberation. Turning all insurance policies into paid-up policies did not suffice; I calculated that I needed £120 for the year, which foreseeably would be covered by my Scholarship, the Exhibition in German, and Mr. Grützner's weekly gift. We made several day trips to Melbourne, visiting real estate agents who unsuccessfully showed us pieces of land that might meet our desire to run a cow and keep some fowls. The answer came on January 20/21. We saw a house at 247 Raleigh Street, Thornbury, very much a working-class suburb, available for £1/1/0 per week; it was in a moderate state of repair, the first in a row of houses in an unmade street with large open blocks round about. To have a cow was out of question, but we could have some fowls, and we could establish a garden (which I afterwards could help set up and tend). After another full day's visit to clean it out thoroughly with phenyl water, on January 26 we bade the family that indeed had been "friends in need" farewell, and arrived in Thornbury just before the van that brought our goods out of storage to our new home.

"The Lord provides"

What I wrote on the day it was decided to rent the house at Thornbury was indeed true: "We are naturally excited at the thought of going to Melbourne. Of course, things are still unsettled; we know not whither; but we do not wish to burden these good people here any longer." After a few weeks the Lord's answers to our prayers for guidance began. One Sunday near the end of February Father was asked to conduct the morning and evening services in Doncaster; and at the beginning of March the Natimuk parish (which was vacant through Pastor Fritsch's shift to Adelaide) gladly agreed to have Father's ministrations for three months, which continued for two more months; he returned home on several occasions for a brief stay with his family. — Just at this time Guluguba showed greater keenness to have Father come there, but it attached to its offer requirements that we regarded as "a bit harsh", namely to bind himself for 10 years, or lose the money he would have to invest in a house. In May another light appeared on the horizon in reference to future ministry: Uncle Ernst wrote that he would suggest Father for a call to the Northern Eyre Peninsula mission field, admittedly a large field, centred on Kimba, when the necessity to do so arrived later in the year; by September this became the reality for the future. Meanwhile, during August and September Father made several trips to the Wimmera to serve at Friedheim or at Natimuk. — In May further financial help came to hand in the form of more than £100 as Mother's share in the estate of Aunt Lena Becker in America.

Paul in front of the house at Thornbury

I for my part concentrated on my final University year: Modern History B (with quite an emphasis on the French Revolution) and German III (three students, Robert Cochrane, Leonie Dunster, and I), in which even before the academic year began I had been concentrating on Goethe's *"Faust II"*. My bicycle (now with light affixed) most of the time, otherwise the cable tram (which was the usual transport for Mother and Paul), occasionally the train, were the means by which I, or we, went away from home. In the absence of a car East Melbourne was the most usual centre of worship; but I went to Doncaster at times per bicycle, including evening rides to Youth Society meetings (returning just before midnight).

"In the valley of the shadow". I now record a few salient points from the "retrospective" diary, concerning the "five weeks crammed full with memories". On Tuesday, August 9, I went to the University Library to commence studying *"The Colonial Reformers"*, the important necessary "Special Subject" in the History section of my course that I had officially chosen the day before. Because it was late in the year, I recorded: "I will have to get going on that".

In the afternoon I got a sudden pain; I struggled on my bicycle to Pastor Steiniger's; he took me home in his car at 7.00 p.m. After a miserable night Father next morning contacted a specialist we knew, Dr. Theo Frank, who after examination arranged for immediate admission to the Royal Melbourne Hospital. Three doctors there had doubts about his diagnosis of appendicitis, but it was left to the discretion of the surgeon on duty. I was operated on in mid-afternoon; the official entry was "gangrene perforated appendix", and the doctor of the large Ward 8, Michael Woodruff, told me later: "Another eight hours, and I wouldn't have liked your case". I had a tube in a 'stab wound' in my right side to drain out pus, and had to lie up high to encourage drainage. I must have been at my lowest two days later: all I can remember is the look of concern on Dr. Woodruff's face. On that night I was supposed to have played the role of a wooden-legged apothecary in a play in the Deutsche Leseverein that had to be cancelled, *"Der Mörder" (The Murderer)*. And the next day was the day when the all-important 'swot vac.' began! I, however, was in no state to study.

Permission to sit out of bed for a few hours came to an abrupt end after two days, when my wound started to discharge and continued to do so for 11 days, accompanied most of the time by a high temperature. Then for two days I enjoyed being allowed out of bed again for some hours. On the second day I noticed a small swelling just to the left of the navel. When Dr. Woodruff examined it he said it was the first of its kind that he had seen, that some of the pus had come up along a fold in the stomach and had settled in the navel and would have to be drawn out. That confined me to bed again. On the last day of August I was shifted out to the balcony of the ward; and thus from the third storey of the hospital I had a view over the busy Swanston/Latrobe Street intersection. There were interesting fellow-patients out there, and an interesting view below. But after a few days pain increased and the navel began to turn inside out, forming what I called "Mount Disappointment". As a result, in the evening of September 8 I was given some capsules to swallow, and a dresser came around to remove the dressing over my navel. I knew what that signified – another operation. And lo! when the dressing was removed it was covered with pus – the swelling had opened of its own accord! After that there was good progress, so that on the afternoon of September 14 I walked out of the hospital, after having been five weeks in it, to continue convalescence at home. The worries about my physical wellbeing were over. Ahead of me were the worries of catching up on my academic work in time for the final examinations. (To complete the "worries" picture we had at that time let me add this: on October 12 Paul was operated on – for appendicitis! It was subsiding; but he had had several signs of it before. One can understand the reaction of the parents to this second case: "as we will be in Kimba next year, it is best to be on the safe side".)

In addition to the entire vacation study-time I also missed 1¼ weeks of lectures before I was strong enough to resume (on September 26) my attendance at the University for lectures and my visits to the Public Library for research purposes. The first of my final examinations was only 4 weeks away; so I drew up a Plan of Work, in which I discarded all but the essential according to my assessment of what would be regarded as essential, and so I hoped to finish the main body of studies before the examinations began. For a fortnight I concentrated on my Special Subject; at home I concentrated on an excellent book that I specially bought at a high cost (for those times) so that I did not need to go to a Library, and in the Public Library I studied a large number of Hansards on relevant parliamentary debates. In mid-October I switched to the requirements in the German course. On Reformation Day and the next few days the four final examinations in German took place: Middle High German; Deutsche Literaturgeschichte (History of German Literature); Unseen Translation; and Essay. This relieved examinee wrote: "I am quite confident and think I should do quite well". My most worrying problem, however, was the History section, because the final examination of the Course drew in the historical studies (at the Pass level as well as at the Honours level) of all three years. The first examination (in the third year subject, Modern History B at Pass level) followed three days after the German. The nagging concern continued: "When I think of all the British and Australasian History to be revised as well I sometimes tremble and fear I cannot get through for all my strict planning". Fortunately there was a breathing space until December. During this pressurised revision the usual pattern was that, if I did not go to the University Library, the studies at home began at 6.00 a.m. (sometimes 5.30 a.m.), but stopped at 10.00 p.m.

Chapter 2

There was another stream of events, not directly associated with my studies, that taxed my brain in those last months of 1938, viz. my roles in plays, to which I have made earlier reference. The performance of *"Der Mörder"*, long delayed by my illness, took place only 9 days after I was discharged from the hospital; the necessary support of a walking stick in my still weak state added to the genuineness of the "wooden-legged" presentation that I had to give. And 4 days after that another of the presentations of the popular *"Singvögelchen"* took place. During the following week I had to revive my memory of a long humourous recitation, *"The Bishop and the Caterpillar"*, for presentation as a desired item in the Doncaster Young Peoples Society's concert.

Before the year was out there were two more presentations: *"Der Mörder"* was played at the Deutscher Klub (November 19), and *"Singvögelchen"* at the request of the German teacher Mr. Ventur (December 3, which was two days before the first of my further History examinations). When thus presented en bloc in printed form these activities may well appear as a troublesome distraction, as they probably may have appeared to be at the time; but as I now reflect on these stressful months I find myself wondering whether they may rather have been a helpful safety-valve that prevented an academic "learning machine" from seizing up.

His bike was his means of transport

Start of the poem, "The Bishop and the Caterpillar", which people frequently asked Henry to recite at concerts

Chapter 2

Henry's dramatic involvement during his university days (1936-1938)

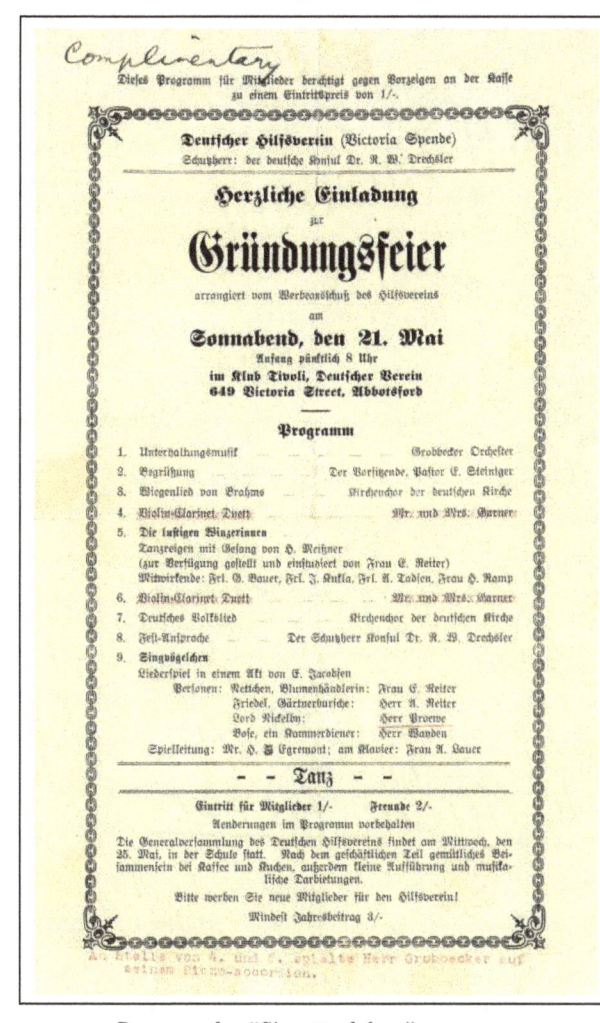

Program for "Singvögelchen"   *Henry as Lord Nickelby*

Program for "Der Mörder"   *Script for "Der Mörder"*

71

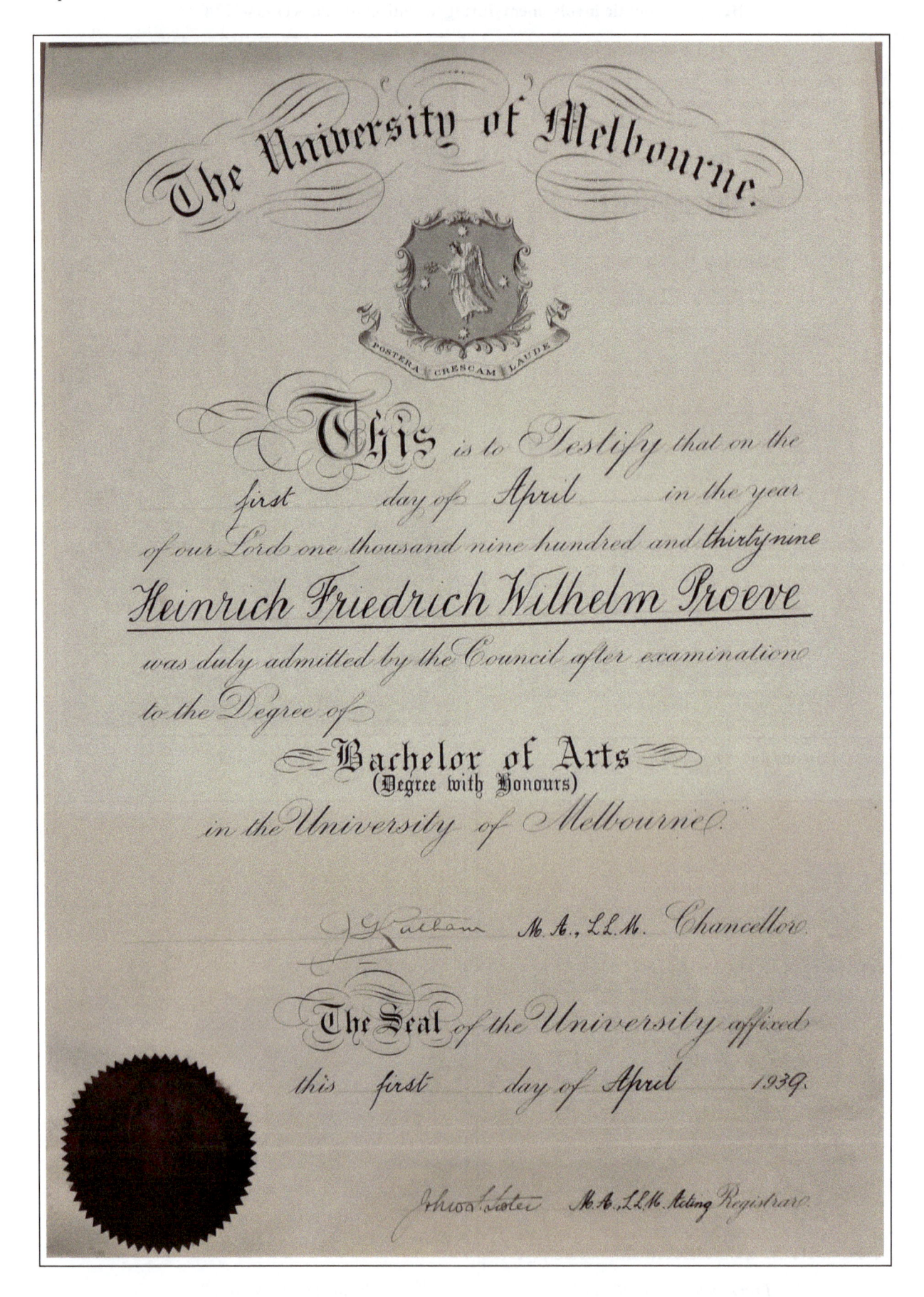

Chapter 2

The University of Melbourne

POSTERA CRESCAM LAUDE

This is to Testify that on the first day of April in the year of our Lord one thousand nine hundred and thirtynine **Heinrich Friedrich Wilhelm Proeve** was duly admitted by the Council after examination to the Degree of

Bachelor of Arts
(Degree with Honours)

in the University of Melbourne.

J. Latham M.A., LL.M. Chancellor.

The Seal of the University affixed this first day of April 1939.

Johns Sister M.A., LL.M. Acting Registrar.

Chapter 2

Farewell, Victoria! The last month of life in Victoria naturally consisted of winding-up. Packing our home libraries was a break from learning. Ascertaining the best way to have our household goods removed to Kimba involved making various enquiries. A table and some other items were placed on auction as being surplus to our needs; and one day, after the parents had left Melbourne, I walked to Northcote and collected the proceeds. They amounted to 1/6! There were farewells to bid or to receive. The Doncaster Young Peoples Society invited the congregation to participate in a farewell social for us. On the next day, our last Sunday (December 11), my record reads: "This morning we went to the Reichskirche and paid our farewells to all the kind friends there, and tonight we went to Doncaster." – this had been our worshipping practice for quite some time. – "This afternoon we called around at the Hospitals and as proof of our gratitude left 5 guineas at the Royal Melbourne and 1 guinea at the Children's. With the prospect of a steady position before us we felt we could afford to show our thanks."

Packed and ready to leave for Kimba, 13 Dec 1938

Next day the parents and Paul left in a heavily loaded car to go to Paech's at Waurn Ponds, from where they then continued to Dimboola on the way to Point Pass via Bordertown.

In the early part of this month I sat for two History examinations – British History B, and Australasian History. When the parents left for South Australia I stayed with the Steiniger family because I still had three examinations in the next five days: Modern History B (in which I correctly concentrated on studying the French Revolution), and two in my Special Subject.

In the morning of December 16 I sat for the last of these examinations. When I left Wilson Hall my feeling of concern had disappeared; what I had written "made me feel elated over the ultimate result". I went back to Steiniger's to pack my belongings. That wonderful friend took me to the Spencer Street Railway Station — it was, to the best of my recollection, the last time that I saw him — and at 7.00 p.m. on that same day, with a ticket for Port Augusta that had cost me no more than £1/15/6 in my pocket, I was being carried on The Overland towards the State in which all further decades of my life have been spent. The tight margin in Adelaide to board the Commonwealth train for Port Augusta, 10 minutes according to schedule, was made easier by a delay in departure. As planned, we met in Port Augusta. I arrived there at 2.02 p.m. (14 minutes late); the parents, having driven from Point Pass, arrived at 3.03 p.m. "Together we covered the last 100 miles to Kimba, arriving at 8 o'clock".

On **December 17, 1938** we were in a new fixed home after years of uncertainty.

Study notes for the French Revolution

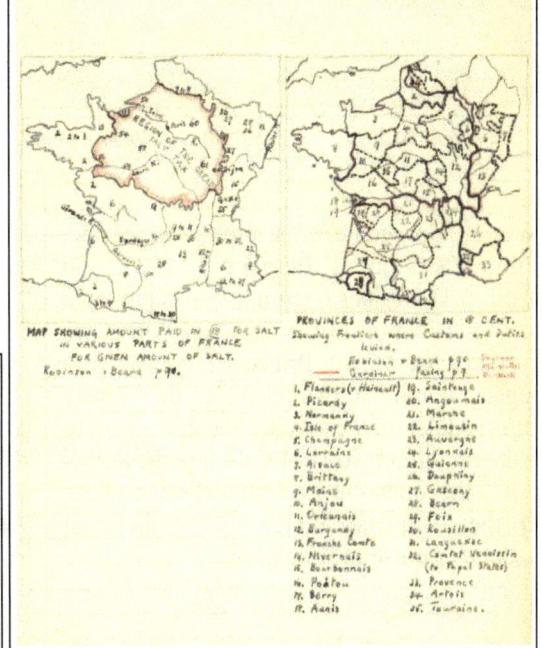

73

Chapter 2

II.4. Happy Travellers in and out of Victoria

Travelling, especially in Australia, has always been 'in the blood' in our family. Paul and I inherited that from our parents; and both of us were inclined to make written descriptions of our trips. I make reference to this because travelling, sometimes for family reasons, sometimes to 'see places where we have not been', began in Victoria. As a preliminary example I give the following: the hacking of the Great Ocean Road (in what has sometimes been termed a 'shelf road') out of the coastal cliffs between Anglesea and Lorne as an undertaking to provide work for returned soldiers was one of the highlights of the early 1930s. Father undertook this difficult journey, well knowing its problems. The need to remove cliffs without the mechanical help of our modern age caused the road to be one-lane, with spots for passing the traffic coming in the opposite direction hacked out of the cliffs at frequent intervals. That meant that in travelling it was necessary to keep a sharp lookout to decide whether one had to wait at a passing bay for oncoming traffic. As I recall it, there was much tooting of horns as warning signals. There were no guard rails to prevent cars from falling into the ocean below. Many years later, when I travelled there with a caravan, I had a sense of relief that I was travelling from Lorne to Geelong, and therefore was close to the cliffs.

We visited **Queensland three times** while we were in Victoria. The first of these is written up in some detail, because what I record here is in many respects typical of travelling in those days.

The **first trip** was in many respects a 'trail-blazer' for us, and quite a remarkable feat at that time. I wrote it up in such detail that when cousins Karl and Erich Mutze showed their copy of it to their teacher he got them to read it out in serial form in the school (apparently as a kind of Australian geography lesson). Road maps were rare, but someone made a Pearson's map available to us, which served us well for a large part of the journey.

[Some years later Father bought an invaluable help for 2/6, that served us well on later travels. It was *"The Herald Road Guide, 1933 – Detailing the Main Roads of Victoria—the Interstate Routes to Sydney, Brisbane, Canberra and Adelaide—and the Adelaide–Alice Springs Route—in Speedo-Maps"*. The importance of 'Hotels' as the sole source of accommodation is evident by indicating this against the towns that had them. Advertisements in *"The Herald Road Guide"* indicate that a usual rate was around 13/6 per night and £4/4/- per week, but the price could be as low as 10/6 per night and £2/2/- per week — the alternative to hotels was to use a "Camping Ground", which we did as much as possible.] I was the navigator and recorder in the back seat on this trip.

Written description of trips, always done in pencil

We left Grovedale, after a morning service, in mid-afternoon of **January 1, 1931**, and stayed in Doncaster overnight. — Our route was quite circuitous: from Melbourne we travelled east on the Prince's Highway into Gippsland, and had two punctures on the way to Bairnsdale; on the way we secured a pass to see the important works at Yallourn: the Power House, the open-cut coalmine (brown coal), and the Briquette Works that made coal briquettes for use in fireplaces.

Photo on right: *A much-treasured road guide*

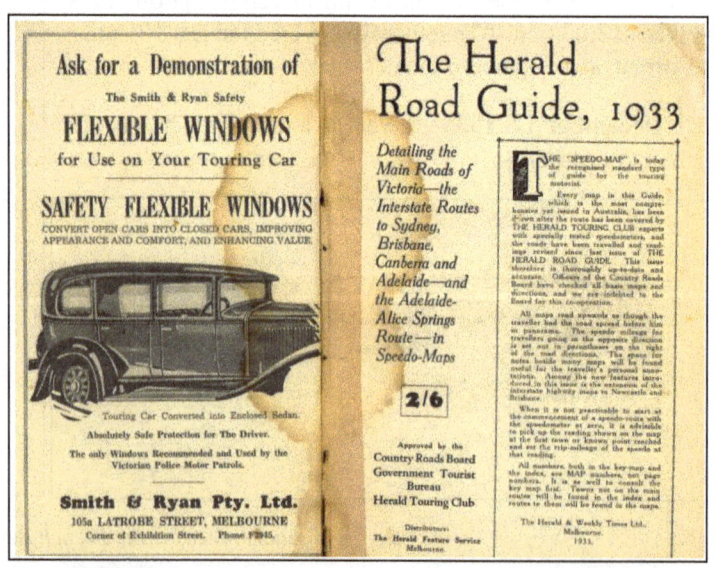

In Bairnsdale we stayed by invitation with a Pearce family whose tuberculous daughter Father had been ministering to spiritually on Bendigo visits. Next morning, at their gate, we had a blow-out, and put on the spare wheel. A short distance further, at the main road, that wheel blew out; just in front of us was a garage where a new tyre could be bought. Tyre trouble like that was frequent on our early travels; but we were spared that on the rest of this journey to Toowoomba. We camped at Eden in SE New South Wales on the next night (196 miles for the day). — As it was necessary to secure permits for any interstate travel at the first police station we caught up with this lack next day at the police station in Bega. Travelling up the coast towards Wollongong we camped at Kiama (245 miles). We had to cross two rivers by punt, which is the most used term on *"The Herald Road Guide"* maps; but it has now fallen out of use. — We left the Prince's Highway north of Wollongong, in order to bypass Sydney by travelling up the beautiful Bulli Pass to Campbelltown, Liverpool to Parramatta. Beyond Sydney, according to the maps we had had access to, we had to cross the Hawkesbury River by ferry at Wiseman's Ferry (at a fee of 1/-) in order to travel north.

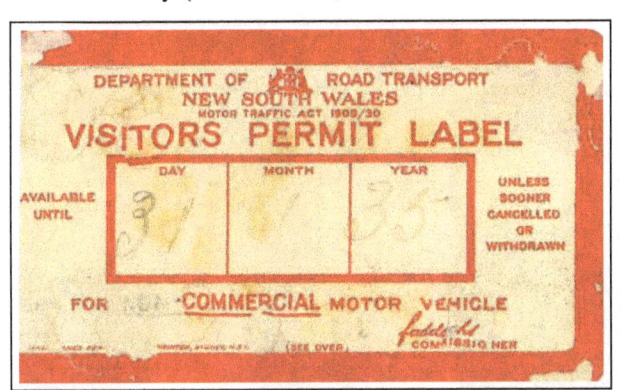

Some of the travelling permits that were needed

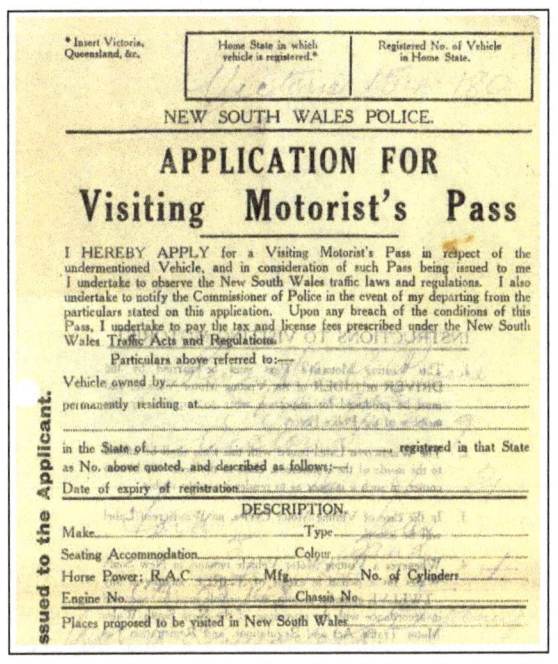

Climbing a long steep hillside only about 10 yards from the ferry we left the road to Gosford and Newcastle and continued straight ahead, soon crossing the Macdonald River by Book's Ferry ("worked by turning a handle by hand"!). The generally 'fair road' up this river valley deteriorated when we passed through two gates and entered the Wollombi Ranges, "something we have never forgotten. The road became much worse, being dissected by many gutters, and the hills became steeper, and the country more rugged. Speed, so as to get up the hills a reasonable distance in top gear, was impossible because of the state of the road, with the result that we had to get into second gear at the bottom of the hills. At Mount Manning we had to make a 'Devil's Elbow' turn, augmented by a few deep gutters, and then a very steep mountain to climb. Of course we immediately got into second, but were soon in low gear, and we reached the top of the mountain very, very slowly." From Wollombi we branched off to Singleton on the Great Northern, now New England, Highway, and camped beyond Scone at Wingen railway station. It had been a rather gruelling 14-hour day with 270 miles of travel. Close by lay Mt. Wingen, a burning mountain with smoke issuing from fissures in the ground, coming from the subterranean combustion (it is said, for 2,000 years) of a thick seam of coal.

A good road helped us next day, when we were prepared for a long run for the day. Breakfast in Tamworth (90 miles), then the Moonbi Range and the lovely scenery of the New England Range through Armidale and Glen Innes to Tenterfield – by this time we had covered 259 miles. We had been told not to travel through Wallagarra, so we continued on the Highway on its original route, following the mountain border towards the north-east as far as a tiny settlement called Legume, a few miles from the Queensland border. We were soon waiting for a gate in a fence to be opened – the border. The road through the Macpherson Ranges consisted of tracks through paddocks and up hills. So we blundered our way to Killarney in the dark, and then to Warwick and Toowoomba, arriving there at about 1.00 a.m. We had covered 400 miles in that long 19½-hour day; and 1,350 miles (2,170 km) on the 6-day trip. Our normal daily mileage lay between 196 and 269 miles.

Already in northern New South Wales we saw people staring at our car, and could see that they were saying, *"A Victorian car!"* In Toowoomba Uncle Fred Mutze's garageman said to him: *"I hear there's a Victorian car in Toowoomba – I don't believe it!"* We spent 12 days with the grandparents and Aunt Olga in Toowoomba, and with the Mutzes (Wilsonton) and Uncle George (Westbrook).

Chapter 2

Commencing on **January 19**, the return journey mostly followed the coastal highway (Pacific Highway) from Brisbane to the outskirts of Newcastle. The large rivers that fed into the ocean necessitated crossings by punt: Logan (Beenleigh); Tweed (Tweed Heads); Brunswick (Brunswick Heads); after avoiding several Clarence 'ferries' by travelling through Lismore and Lawrence, Clarence River (Grafton); Bellingen (Raleigh); Nambucca (Macksville); Hastings (Blackman's Point); Manning (Tinonee near Taree); Hunter (Hexham Ferry). We were told of a new road to Sydney (largely made of cement), and of a new ferry, Peat's Ferry (fee 1/10), over the broad Hawkesbury. It didn't run like the usual punts, which were hauled in a direct line across the water; this was a ship with uniformed officers and carried cars in a double curve across the river. From Sydney our route led along the Hume Highway, via Albury, to Melbourne. Our daily journeys ranged from 193 to 265 miles (310 – 426 km). On the way, as usual, we bought hot water for tea or coffee (generally at a hotel), and camped five nights at spots beside the road. We arrived in Grovedale on **January 24**, and had travelled 1353 miles on the return trip, and 3,167 miles for the entire journey.

Visiting Uncle George (Henry middle back)    *Visiting Zeckomskis, 1937 (Henry in back row, 3rd from right)*

The second trip began on **Dec. 31, 1934**, and five days later we were in Toowoomba, having travelled via Albury to Sydney and via the New England Highway (and a clearer route into Queensland through Wilson's Downfall and Stanthorpe) to Toowoomba. My records show that we travelled a little over 1,100 miles (about 1,800 km), most of the time over a 12-hour per day period (but with a 3.00 a.m. start on the last day), initially at a speed of 30 to 32 miles per hour (48 – 51 kph), but generally at an average of 25-26 mph. (40 kph). We visited relatives at Westbrook (Uncle George), Kulpi (Blanck family), and Kumbia (Uncle Carl Dunemann), until we left on **January 15, 1935,** via the coastal highway to Sydney. This time we travelled through the Blue Mountains and visited Jenolan Caves. A hair-raising largely narrow road, which clung with its loose stones to the side of mountains, was part of our travel to Goulburn. Canberra (still a young capital city) was a focal point of our return trip. The final section lay through Cooma, Bombala and Gippsland, concluding on **January 24**. The trip totalled 3,252 miles.

The third trip, **October 29** (for the parents and Paul) – **December 24, 1937,** was associated with the golden wedding of the grandparents, as mentioned at the end of II.2 in these Memoirs. This time I did some of the driving on the homeward journey. Leaving Toowoomba on December 16 we stayed three nights at Uncle George's at Mt. Kent; then, camping at night in our new tent, we again bypassed Sydney by going through Parramatta. The new feature this time was a visit to the Hume Weir. The journey ran smoothly, except for two car problems: tyre trouble (which we had on every trip on account of the condition of roads) and a leaking radiator hose.

Visiting Dunemanns, 1934 (Henry at back, 3rd from right)

76

In **1933** we travelled to **South Australia**. Leaving Grovedale on **January 6** we spent three nights in Mt. Gambier, where Father conducted services. Via the Coorong to Meningie (9th), and via Adelaide and Tanunda to Point Pass (10th). During the fortnight's stay at Uncle Ernst's we visited Pastor P. Breier at Stonefield. Leaving Point Pass on January 25 we visited Mildura, and then travelled south to Dimboola and home via Ballarat, where we arrived on **January 27**.

In **Victoria** we went sightseeing in **January 1934** (3rd to 9th), going through an area largely unknown to us: Daylesford, Maryborough, St. Arnaud (an oasis on a hot day), Charlton, Inglewood, and Bendigo (where a service was conducted).

Another limited journey in Victoria took place in **January 1936** (9th to 24th). Almost a fortnight was spent in the manse at Mt. Gambier, where Father conducted services during Pastor E. Sprengel's holidays. I think it was on this occasion that at Millicent everyone stuck to the pews, due to the heat, and left a clear imprint when, with at least two tries, they struggled to their feet after the sermon. The pews had been freshly varnished! When we left Mt. Gambier on the 21st we travelled via Edenhope to Dimboola. The final day's travel to Grovedale was made via Ballarat.

I have been reminded of a practice that we, like other drivers, used in those days to conserve petrol, but we did it with caution, especially if we were in areas where we didn't know the road. The practice was legal at that time, and was called 'coasting'. The engine was put out of gear into neutral at the top of hills, so that the car 'coasted' downhill. *"The Herald Road Guide"* printed the following: *"CARE IN COASTING. A general rule for safety is never to coast in neutral down a steep hill unless swift changes into gear can be made when desired. Missed changes during such coasts can mean burnt out brakes or a fatal crash."*

II.5. A Muted Epilogue.

Over the years I have seen many photos of proud graduates, wearing academic robe and bachelor hood, pictured in newspapers perhaps with admiring relatives or friends, or given pride of place in the family home. The sight of these has sometimes awakened a mild sense of disappointment. Had we still been in Melbourne on Saturday, **April 1, 1939**, my Mother would have had as a birthday gift being present in the Wilson Hall at the University, and seeing her son wearing the academic robe and hood of a **B.A.(Hons.)**. On that day she was in Kimba. And her son was in Adelaide, going into the city in the morning, and in the afternoon playing cricket as top scorer with 27 runs in the team's total of 97, and taking 1 wicket for 2 runs as bowler. No gown and hood, no photo provides a reminder of the occasion – just a certificate that arrived later and has never been framed. I don't recall receiving any local congratulations. — It was some kind of embarrassed feeling and desire not to be regarded as "cocky" that caused me for very many years to leave off the "(Hons.)" portion in official listings of my degree. It began with the two editions of "The Echo" that I edited in my Seminary days, and continued in the listings in the Almanac of the Church and on the official letterheads when I was an official of the Church. I ultimately realised that I was falsely listing what had been officially conferred on me. Since then I have received some other certificates, but I lay the greatest store on the certificates that I received upon graduation from Immanuel Seminary and ordination as a "called and ordained servant of the Lord".

Entry from the 1938 diaries

Chapter 3
III. THE NORTH ADELAIDE DECADE: 1939 – 1949

The heading for this chapter of my Memoirs is not a slip of the mind. My life in South Australia commenced in mid-December 1938 in Kimba, but this was a 'home' address, where for four years I resided for a few months in each year during vacations, feeling very much 'at home'. North Adelaide was at first largely, and then permanently, my place of residence.

Photo on right: *Kimba manse*

III. I. Experiences at Kimba

Our removal from Melbourne to Kimba was so arranged that the outgoing pastor, Hugo Stiller, could introduce Father to this far-flung home mission field – the **Northern Eyre Peninsula Mission Field** – during the remaining weeks of 1938. Father's ministry commenced on January 1, 1939, and was scheduled for an initial period of six months, in order to establish whether his health would stand the rigours of much travel between its many centres. Kimba had only a short time earlier been made the centre of the field, but it lay on its eastern extremity. Most of the centres in the field were preaching places, where services were conducted in halls or homes. When Father began his ministry they were: Kimba (which had the manse, but no church); Kelly and Buckleboo (near Kimba); Ballumbah, Pallinga, Cootra East, Cootra West, Koongawa (to the south-west and west); (along the central Eyre Peninsula railway) Warramboo (congregation with the only church in the field), Wudinna (in a home at Mt. Wudinna), and Yaninee; Cungena, in the Streaky Bay area (congregation in the far north-west; church dedicated in November 1944). These 12 centres, most of them very small in number, were soon reduced by members shifting or undertaking to worship at another centre. Cootra West, Cootra East, Yaninee, and Ballumbah closed in 1939/1940; Wudinna in mid-1944. Caralue replaced Pallinga as the centre of worship for the group in that area.

After the service in the Koongawa hall, 1939

The field, however, expanded towards the east. Already in 1939 Father began visits with home devotions in the developing industrial town of Whyalla (120 km by the direct sandy road) and in its iron ore mining centre Iron Knob (totalling 140 km from Kimba to Whyalla). Services commenced in 1940 (for a short time with some help from other pastors), and Whyalla was added to the field. From coast to coast, i.e. Whyalla to Streaky Bay (where hospital visits were at times necessary) was a total of 370 km – a greater distance than Adelaide to Port Augusta; normal pastoral travelling thus involved an average of 1,600 km (1,000 miles) per month on unsealed, sometimes sandy, roads. Kimba welcomed us with a **heatwave** that included many Fahrenheit 'centuries' – up to 107 degrees (42 degrees Centigrade) – in January. I went along with Father on his visits; we often sat on concrete floors as the coolest spot in the house, and we ate what the people could offer in that time of drought, viz. mutton from their flocks and cucumbers from their garden. I had a problem with cucumbers; but worked out that if I discarded the seeds they did not repeat so badly on me.

Along the Whyalla-Kimba road, next to the pipeline, 1940

My memories of the 'West Coast' are on the whole pleasant. We did have some early experience of disadvantages associated with its remoteness from the 'Mainland' (as the area east of Spencer's Gulf was sometimes called). The price of vegetables and fruit was high, on account of cartage costs. But Father's keenness to do gardening in due time provided vegetables, and in season the fairly prolific quandongs provided a little fruit (and their hard, round, pitted centres provided Chinese Checker markers).

A serious disadvantage showed up when our furniture arrived at long last on February 3 – 48 days after our own arrival. For almost 7 weeks Mother had been sleeping on the two car seats, the rest of us on camp stretchers; boxes provided our seating. We were pleased to see the West Coast carrier arrive with our furniture; but he was a carrier, and not a furniture removalist. Not one piece of packing had protected the furniture on its 300-mile journey from Adelaide; the table had rubbed, the sofa was especially badly affected, the washing machine had several holes punched into it. The carrier of course declared that the furniture was in this condition when he had picked it up from the Melbourne removalist's depot in Adelaide.

The people were very friendly, ready to share what little they had, ready to help when necessary. They greeted one another (even if unknown to each other) when travelling. We did the same; and we got into an initial habit of greeting the passing motorist when we were travelling on the 'mainland' towards Adelaide, i.e. south of Port Augusta, until the puzzled looks reminded us that we were in a different world. I was able to provide some help for Father. Whenever I was home in Kimba during the next years it was the natural thing that I, now equipped with a South Australian licence, relieved Father of the necessity of doing the driving. Many a time this already took place en route from Adelaide to Kimba at the end of a term. I soon gained experience in picking the best part of the road (when there was no traffic), and in negotiating sandy ridges and sometimes boggy flats. Early in 1940 I drove the car on my own for the first time, in order to have it serviced at Waddikee by the Kobelts. On the return journey at night I had to deal with a petrol choke; with no torch along, I pressed the backing sheet of a duplicating stencil under a headlight to reflect light into the engine while I worked three times to clear the choke.

A more strenuous occasion of helping followed six days later, a Sunday, when the car used an inordinate amount of petrol and stopped red-hot 9 miles (about 15 km) from Kimba. I set out at 11.00 p.m. for a 2-hour plus walk in the moonless night, lifting my feet with every step, so that I did not scuff the corrugations in the road. With a container full of petrol on my parcel carrier I set out on my bicycle, and was back at the car a little after 3.00 a.m. A broken carburettor jet, followed by the carburettor breaking apart, forced the two of us to camp in the car until the first passing car took the carburettor into Kimba, and mechanical help got us home at dinnertime.

In January 1940 Father established a parish paper, **"The Lutheran Messenger of the Northern Parish, Eyre Peninsula"**. It appeared quarterly, a folded quarto sheet printed on both sides, which I typed twice on my portable typewriter (the first time as a rough copy; the second time with enough extra spaces to 'justify' each line) and duplicated in 100 copies on a simple flat-bed duplicator with a roller that had to be inked up with every application. To my present amazement, as I checked my bound copy of the paper, I have discovered that I did this for Father until the end of 1945; he then had it printed at Auricht's Printing Office, Tanunda.

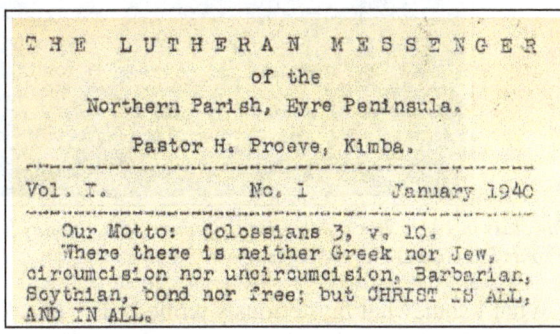

My Future Career — What shall it be? As long as I was still a university student the matter of my future was not yet pressing. But there were questions that had been raising themselves. In the light of my Father's experiences did I still want to serve in the Ministry of the UELCA? There were times when some negative feelings went through my mind. Might I become a **secondary school teacher**, with History and German as my particular qualifications? But that would not be within the Church, as J.E. Auricht taught those subjects in the only secondary school in the UELCA.

Photo: *Henry's portable typewriter*

Chapter 3

Another line of thought began when Prof. Lodewyckx during a December 1938 gathering in his house suggested that I should apply for a **Humboldt Scholarship**, as he believed I had good prospects of being granted one. Study at a university in Germany? I had never contemplated that. Pastor Steiniger thought that the fact that I wished to enter the Holy Ministry would cause the Nazis to look askance at an application from me. The German Consul provided a reference. "But I don't feel too keen about entering", I recorded. In answer to an enquiry from us, Pastor J.P. Löhe of Immanuel Seminary advised: "No!" – I later became aware of his opinion of University education. The Lord's hand was in all this. Had I applied for and been awarded such a scholarship I would have been in Germany when World War II broke out. The desire held from boyhood to serve in the Ministry of the UELCA held out against all doubts and temptations. Life in North Adelaide, first of all with years of study, lay before me.

III. 2. The Seminary Student in North Adelaide, 1939-1942

On February 24, 1939, after a stay in Point Pass and attendance with Father at the District Synod at Light's Pass, I was at Immanuel College, Jeffcott Street, North Adelaide. Siegfried Held took me to the room he had as an auxiliary teacher; he placed before me an idea he had already discussed with the Seminary lecturers, viz. that the two of us should be absolved from Proseminary studies on account of our university studies – Sieg was still a student. We quickly made written application (in German). That evening we were informed of the outcome: "The arrangements for our studies are that Held and I and three others, [Philipp] Scherer, [Herman] Pech and [John] Biar, will be in the Proseminary only one year and then go into the Seminary. The teachers could not see their way clear to dispense with the Proseminary altogether. The other three were added by P[astor] Muetzelfeldt because they had been under him for the previous year doing the course of the Lehrerklasse [Teachers' Class]."

The class in 1941. Back: John Biar, Herman Pech, Stanley Schilg, Henry Proeve, Sieg Held, Erich Renner, Philipp Scherer. Front: Les Grope, Victor Wenke, Colin Scheer.

What I somewhat mysteriously termed "The Break-in for the Seminary" (diary), involving the three Seminary students, Norman Keller, Laurence Leske, and Len Loffler, and us newcomers, took place on February 27 in the presence of the three teachers. We were **ten new students** in all – one of the largest intakes that Immanuel Seminary had –, the additional five being Leslie Grope, Erich Renner, Victor Wenke, Colin Scheer, and Stanley Schilg. Of these ten, four of us were the sons of pastors; the fathers of almost all others were strongly involved in their local congregations, some also in District church affairs. Those who know German can hear what we heard on that day of initiation into theological study, as recorded by me: "Director in his address had a dig at us two University students. He admonished the class *'sich vor den Irrwegen der Welt und einer weltlichen Bildung zu hüten, und sich vor Abwegen zu hüten, die selbst von inmitten der Klasse kommen können'* (i.e. *'to be on guard against the wrong ways –or paths– of the world and of a worldly education, and to be on guard against misleading ways, which can even come from within the class'*). He quickly glanced in our direction several times." So – welcome to the Seminary, potentially subversive students!! Pastor Muetzelfeldt, in charge of the Proseminary, then met us on our own. "He declared our class was uneven: *Wie Kühe und Pferde in einem Pflug'* (i.e. *'like cows and horses in one plough'*)." — In the afternoon "we started lectures". I didn't use this term again; instead, I wrote "Lessons (I won't call them lectures) today". I certainly had not expected to be instructed by dictation.

German and English Lessons. There were more lessons in German than in English. I have heard much criticism of this, partly (I think) because after World War II we have become supersensitive to the use of German. It can be difficult to make an objective assessment of it. The decades that have elapsed since then have demonstrated that the fears of church leaders in those days that the loss of German (at least among the pastors) could result in a loss of firm Lutheran consciousness were not without ground. Total reliance on theological writings in English has been leading to a greater absorption (perhaps unconsciously) of Reformed theological teaching, e.g. there is a strong tendency to link consecration with justification as the ground or basis for our salvation instead of being the result or fruit of our salvation. *"Trust and obey* (which is synonymous with "have faith and do good works"); *for there's no other way to be happy in Jesus* (which is senseless if it is not a synonym for "eternal life") *than to trust and obey"* – this did not get into the Lutheran Hymnal when the Hymnbook Committee was at work; now it is chosen and sung with gusto. What has happened to the Lutheran conviction that "we are saved by faith alone, by grace"? Instruction in German and the use of German books made us at home with a source of true Lutheran theology that is only partly available in translated form. There could have been a greater use of English for some subjects, e.g. church history; and we had a successful changeover from German to English in Dogmatics, when the lecture notes of a committed Lutheran teacher with a German background, Dr. M. Reu, became available. We had his books on Homiletics and Catechetics in English from the outset.

There were two of our number for whom we felt sorry: Wenke and Schilg, as both of them only became familiar with German in lessons at the College, which of course did not reach the level of the academic German in theological writings. We admired the diligence with which Wenke especially sought to overcome his handicap. As he sat in the front desk, directly in front of Director Löhe, he (more than all of us) was called upon: *"Na, Victor, referiere mal"*. *"Referieren"* involved repeating what one had been told in a previous lesson, or what one had read up as an assignment. Victor diligently went through the allotted subject, and made what we all did (but were not supposed to do), so-called "gardening notes" which were summaries of the allotted subject. On one occasion in Church History, mischievous senior student L.L. mixed up Victor's "gardening notes". The inevitable *"Victor, der vierte Kreuzzug"* (i.e. the Fourth Crusade) was followed by Victor furiously searching in his notes and repeating at regular intervals, *"der vierte Kreuzzug"*, until Director intervened with *"Was ist es mit dem vierten Kreuzzug"* ("What about the Fourth Crusade?"), and, I think, turned to someone else. The use of German verbs can be a trap for the unsure; Victor once managed to end a sentence with *"gehabt zu haben hätte"* (i.e. 'had to have would have had').

The Campus and Seminary Life

In view of the changes made on the campus it may be helpful, in order to understand references to **Seminary life** in these recollections, to provide a pen-picture of **Immanuel College / Seminary campus.** Three buildings stood on this large allotment. Facing Jeffcott Street as No. 104 stood the **former Angas College**. The entire central portion was the residence for the Löhe family (J.P., wife, and unmarried daughter Ingeborg); in it (even in the clock tower) was a vast library, for Director Löhe was a keen purchaser of books, and rarely came home from his (usually daily) walks into the city without one or more. In the northern wing at ground level the large dining-room and kitchen (with underground pantry); above these, boys' study rooms, bathroom and toilet facilities. In the southern wing large class-room, and study rooms; above these, large boys' dormitory, and study rooms. Sieg Held and I occupied the north-east room as bedroom for two years because there wasn't room in the Seminary; Sieg's bed was so hinged that it was up against the wall during daylight hours – our study was in the Seminary. At the eastern end of the allotment with a separate pedestrian gate, as 196 Ward Street stood single-storeyed Immanuel Seminary, the **former Whinham College.** The Riedel family lived in the eastern portion. The larger classroom and a larger study room lay on opposite sides of the main entrance. Along the western portion, facing an open campus towards the College, the large dormitory, study rooms, and bath and toilet facilities. Their doors opened up to a long open area, at the northern end of which (back of the building) lay a smaller classroom.

Immanuel College (formerly Angas College)

Chapter 3

The third building was the **Gymnasium** ('the Gym'), which was used for sport purposes and for concerts. Behind it an old stabling building, used by highly respected 'Vater' G.B. Linke for his work as handyman. Two splendid Moreton Bay fig trees stood near the northern wing of the College; and a tennis court fronted the Gymnasium. The girls were housed in the Girls' Hostel, a two-storeyed building two doors north of the College.

Immanuel Seminary (formerly Whinham College)   *College gymnasium*

Between lessons (and in other free time) we often congregated outside the back door, at a gate which could be opened to Ward Court, where we awaited the arrival of Director Löhe (with the cry *"Es kimmt!"*) or of Pastor Muetzelfeldt. And if the cry was *"On the drum"* we raced across to the Moreton Bay figs because that cry (inherited from a previous class) signified that grapes from some congregation's Harvest Thanksgiving had arrived and were waiting there to be enjoyed. We had our meals in the college dining room at a long table next door to the Löhe family; visitors to the College (e.g. College Board members) were accommodated at our table. The weekly menu was rather firmly fixed. Bread with Marmite or Crosse & Blackwell's fish paste were an ever-present filler. (We thus had "C.B." – our nickname for "*Collegium Biblicum*", an explanation of the biblical text by August Vilmar that was dictated to us by the Director – as spiritual food in the Seminary, and "C.B." (Crosse & Blackwell's) – *"Pass the 'C.B.' please"* – as bodily food in the College.) We had to eat fast, to be finished when the Director and family appeared to be finished. (I write "appeared to be", because on one occasion I had reason to go to Director's door immediately after the midday meal, and he was still munching.)

After the midday meals the Director read from a book. For a very long period it was the record of Sven Hedin's travels; this led me to write for our topical song at the Break-up Concert at the end of that year (to the tune of "Little Brown Jug", with apologies for possible misspelling of the river and the person that figured for weeks in the readings): *"With Sven Hedin we've travelled far, and now in wild Tibet we are. The Boksangsangbok us has vexed; we'll meet the Tushilumpo next"*. On Sundays the above was replaced by singing for an half-hour spiritual songs from *"Die Kleine Missionsharfe"* (i.e. *"The Small Mission Harp"* – or in our more colloquial term *"The Mission Ukelele"*) to Director's accompaniment. Morning and evening devotions followed the respective meals; Seminary students, usually Herman Pech, played the organ, speeded up by Inge Löhe, if deemed necessary, to Director's desired tempo. And so the Seminarists once rallied to the defence of their organ-playing fellow-member by speeding up a *'Missionsharfe'* song so much that Director's playing fell apart.

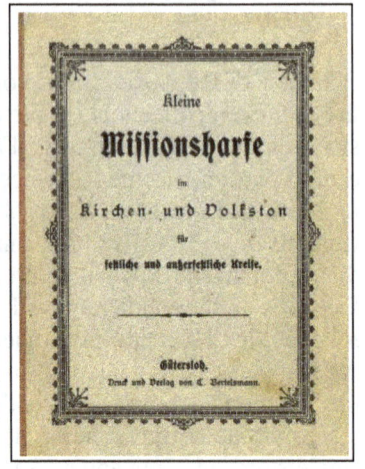

As I seek to describe our **Seminary life** I preface this with a reference to the document that controlled it, our ***Hausordnung***, i.e. 'House-rules'. The last one had particular importance: *"Unterhaltung eines Liebesverhältnisses oder Verlobung während der Studienzeit ist streng untersagt"* (i.e. *"Maintaining a love relationship or engagement during the time of studies is strictly prohibited"*). But Laurie Leske was regularly and openly visiting Hilda Riedel next door. On one occasion his pyjamas were hidden in the boot of his parents' car, who also were next door, to be taken home to Freeling. On another occasion Laurie came late to the dormitory to find his bed hanging from the open rafters. When his engagement was announced immediately after his examination I pinned the page announcing it on our notice board in the open area, and opposite the announcement I lined up the rule in our *"Hausordnung"* with red arrows pointing to the two items boxed in red. While Pastor Muetzelfeldt was chuckling over this he motioned Pastor Riedel, who happened to pass through this open area, to view it, with the lighthearted comment: *"Gut, nicht wahr!"* (i.e. "Good, isn't it!"). *"Huh, huh!"* was the forced response.

82

Chapter 3

Sieg Held was already courting day-school teacher Dulcie Gehling when we entered the Seminary. Later on, when Ruth Rechner was the Girls' Representative on *"The Echo"* Committee, I as Editor was quite happy to let committee member Les Grope discuss with her any *"Echo"* matters that related to the girls. After further keeping of it in the breach thereof the rule was abolished. — Every evening we took it in turns, alternating English and German, to conduct devotions (Scripture reading and prayer). We formed ourselves into a **Seminary Society**, often with visiting speakers to address our monthly meetings. At Sieg Held's prompting those who were interested – I think it was all of us – formed a **Musical Appreciation Society**. Individual members researched the life and activity of a composer and, if possible, illustrated his music with records from Sieg's good collection. The singers in our midst formed a **Male Choir** – most of the time a double quartette –, which sang at times in the North Adelaide church, and provided items for the College break-up concerts. We were the backbone of the College football, cricket, and tennis teams, and of the College orchestra. All actors in plays were Seminarists, even for female roles!, except one year when Agnes Dobson, a talented actress directing the trial scene in the *"Merchant of Venice"*, managed to persuade Director to allow a female Portia to be 'imported'. I was given the role of Shylock. Miss Dobson chose Sieg Held and me for roles in Shakespeare's *Richard II* that she planned for her acting group – my role was to be that of Bolingbroke – but fortunately nothing came of it.

The Musical Appreciation Society

Some Notable Events during the Early Seminary Years

Illness and Death of Pastor Edwin Wiencke. I refer to this because it had its impact a little over 3 years later on my personal career. Pastor E. Wiencke had come from Queensland to take over the North Adelaide Mission Field from its founder, Pastor J.J. Stolz. About the middle of 1939 he took ill, and this proved to be terminal (December 20th). During the latter part of the year, as one of three seminarists who had licences, I fairly frequently took pastors or seminarists in his Willys 77 car to conduct services or to pay home visits. Our family was saddened by his early death, because there had already been a connection with Pastor Wiencke in Queensland, and Mrs. Wiencke and Mother felt bonded as fellow-Americans. The care of the North Adelaide field was again taken over by Pastor Stolz, helped by other local pastors. This lasted for almost 3½ years, broken only by a 2½ month locum tenens service by the newly arrived, then unjustly interned, refugee Alfred Zinnbauer in 1940.

Chapter 3

War with Germany. The impact of the war that broke out at the beginning of September 1939 came gradually. The first sign that the Lutheran Church would be targeted came within a fortnight with an attack on Lutheran schools, which were defended by two letters in "The Advertiser" on September 15, one of them being written by a returned soldier. – The Government Archives, when released many years later for perusal, revealed that one person wrote to the Military Intelligence, stating that he had heard the Immanuel College girls singing, as they went along the street, a German national song that he recognised; it was the *"Lorelei"*! – One day a man stuck his head in the Ward Street gate and called out to us as we were standing at the back of the Seminary, *"Go back to Germany, you bloody Huns!"* – One Sunday evening a large round stone was forcefully rolled down the sloping floor of the Wellington Square church while Pastor Stolz was preaching; Stan Schilg and a soldier went on the chase and caught one of the culprits – his name was Helbig. When we embarked on a concert tour in 1940 Sieg Held and I translated the German songs we were singing into English in order to avoid giving offence in sensitive districts.

In December 1939 John Biar and I received a call-up to military service, as we were in the age bracket that was chosen in the first conscription of the war. We both were passed as A1 fit for service, but we received an exemption as theological students.

In Kimba the local policeman, Senior Constable Fox, visited Father one day. After some general conversation he indicated that he was on official business: he had received orders to search Father's house. *"Can you give me something to take along, so that I can show that I have been here?"* said he. – At a later stage of the war Father was one of a team of spotters that sat in a special small building with direct telephone communication with Adelaide, ready to give warning of the approach of Japanese planes. On one occasion when Father was away I took his place for a 4.00 a.m. to 8.00 a.m. stint.

The most serious evidence of official suspicion of us came on the day (November 14, 1940) when we seminarists watched in amazement as two buses pulled into the College grounds and soldiers poured out of both with bayonets fixed and rushed to the College building and the gates. College and Seminary students were herded into the College dining room. There we seminarists were bodily searched. I had a pocket diary, which the soldier quickly paged through and then put down. Another soldier said to the seminarist he searched, *"I don't suppose you have any firearms on you"*. The central part of the College, especially the tower section, was searched. Apparently there had been reports of night signals coming from the tower; the source, we believe, must have been the torch light in the tower, switched on by the Director on nocturnal visits to the toilet. In the Seminary, classrooms and some studies were targeted and left in a mess, but Sieg's and mine remained untouched.

Immanuel College Concert Tour 1940. *"The Echo"* of 1940, in an unsigned article on pages 12-14 entitled *"The Concert Tour – May 1940"*, contains my description of this highlight of 1940. To this I would merely add that the photograph shows how the Seminary students were the backbone for such major undertakings on behalf of Immanuel College; there were three students from the College in the group. My own contribution on this tour was playing a role in both plays, *"The Crimson Coconut"* (a rollicking comedy) and *"Deep in the Earth"* (a poignant play set in a mine that even brought some members of the audiences to tears), and as a member of the orchestra and the male choir. The "bomb" in the first play consisted of <u>two</u> coconuts, well hidden in a bucket – one in its natural colour; the other, allegedly on the point of "going off", painted red.

Tour party at Point Pass, May 16th   *Back home again, May 23rd*

Concert Tour. May 1940.
The Party
Packing-Up (May 10th)
Interested Spectators
Ready to go

Editing "The Echo". For the second time in my life I was called upon to edit the magazine of a school. This was already set into preliminary motion in my first year in the Seminary (1939). An additional position (Assistant Secretary and Humour) was created in the Editorial Staff to accommodate me, with the openly stated purpose of having me as Editor in the next year. For the 1939 issue, using the mistakes of the writers of essays for the magazine, I contributed an article that I entitled *"The Inglish Langwidge"*, and I selected one page and six half-pages of contributed jokes. The reason for the half-pages was that we wanted people to read the 1½ pages of advertisements on each double-page spread! — I duly edited *The Echo"* in 1940 and 1941. My Editorial in 1940 reflected on the problems that had increased as World War II progressed. The Northern Printery Limited at 77 O'Connell Street (now part of the North Adelaide Village site), owned and operated by Bruno Andersen, deserves special mention in my Memoirs in recognition of its help, which went beyond technical skills, in producing the magazine. Two former scholars who have figured in the literary world contributed. Paul Pfeiffer contributed three poems to the 1940 edition: *At the Window* (p.38), *Poem* and *Nondum* (p.40). I identify poems contributed anonymously at that time as having been written by Colin Thiele: in 1940, *Midnight* (p.24) – with a small doubt, as I have not written in the name in my copy, *The Gum* (p.32), *Sonnet: To the Poets* (p.37); and in 1941, *Evening* (p.24), *Harvest* (p.30).

"The Echo" Editorial Staff, 1941: HFW Proeve, LB Grope, Rev JE Auricht, SA Schilg, RH Rechner, R Pech

Chapter 3

The "Petition", 1941. At the beginning of August 1941 there was a development that was never forgotten in our class. In reading my diary I have become aware that it was already there in embryonic form in my November birthday celebrations in 1939, when we "discussed problems that confront us as Seminarists, especially how we can make our time of studies more fruitful". In 1941 it began as a very lengthy discussion in a meeting of the Seminary Society (of which I was the Secretary) regarding the work at the Seminary, especially its course of study. Informal discussions took place for a couple of days, in particular by Held and Pech, Grope and Renner however also taking part. More and more grievances were ventilated, and statements were formulated in German; but I was not present at these discussions, as I was in bed after having some teeth extracted. Three days after the Seminary Society meeting, following further daily discussions and amendments, a 3½ foolscap-page document (cut on stencils by me) was handed to the College and Seminary Council for consideration; copies were handed to each teacher. It stated our attitude to the presentation of the subjects we were studying: dictation of material, reading of extra material, style of questions. Pastor J.J. Stolz said that its tone was good, much better than the one adopted in a similar development by the class that graduated in 1939; one Council member said it was "a serious matter"; Pastor Stolz said "it was of concern to the whole Church"; we heard that Pastor Riedel was approachable, but Director became '*fuchswild*' (i.e. furious), threw the document on the table and walked out.

In the lessons on the following day Director launched a three-quarter hour, on the second day an even more bitter-sounding hour-long offensive against us. This included a bitter remark about those *"who have not properly gone through the University, and there have got to know something, and where they have tasted something"*. He was greatly relieved when we assured him that we were not against the content of Dr. August Vilmar"s '*Collegium Biblicum*".

When the final semester of 1941 began there were some changes. The dictation of *"C.B."* ended when John Biar and I had cut the stencils of the sometimes edited version that had been dictated to a previous class. One other change was that the dictation of *Philosophische Grundbegriffe* (i.e. '*Philosophical Basic Concepts*', dubbed '*Philosophical Groundgrips*' by us) was replaced by lessons on philosophy by Pastor Muetzelfeldt.

Three photos on the page:
Extracts from the Petition of 1941, which they handed to the College and Seminary Council and their teachers.

Preparing to be preachers and teachers. The final semester of 1941 brought with it the feeling that we were moving towards our final goal. In succession we prepared a catechetical demonstration, with the North Adelaide children as the recipients. I prepared my catechesis on Psalm 121 – a happy choice, because at a later time I could use basic thoughts in a sermon that had overwhelming significance for me. An even more significant sign of progress was the preparation of the first sermon. The classroom sermons were given alternately in English and German, under the supervision of J.P. Löhe (English) and W. Riedel (German). Sieg Held, the senior in age, elected to preach in English, so my sermon, based on Luke 9,51-56, had to be in German. After a study of the text, a 'disposition' (outline of sermon development) had to be approved by the supervising teacher. And the sermon had to be learnt – no copy or even notes allowed in the pulpit! The preacher chose a fellow-seminarist to be his critic in addition to the supervisor. When I preached my first sermon on October 30 I got stuck in a section where I had never got stuck during the learning process, and that sparked seven more memory failures in the first section, but then I settled down. "That is not to be criticised" was Pastor Riedel's comment, adding that when one preaches for the first time it was better to get stuck in the beginning, rather than to be too ready with words. Two days later Mrs. Irene Klante, of Warramboo, brought the well-made pastoral gown she had completed. The realisation was really brought home to me: I can now be called upon to preach publicly. At the end of November I knew that I would be serving in Queensland during the next holidays; Pastor Stolz had been bearing that in mind for quite some time, because my aged grandparents were in Queensland.

'Vicarage' in Queensland, December 1941 - February 1942

Unlike my four fellow-students, who served in other Districts of the Church, in Queensland I preached at or conducted many services (38), and for a time was on my own in ministering to a parish. When I arrived in Toowoomba on December 15 I knew nothing about planned services, except that I was to commence in Toowoomba. Mr. W.C. Schneider was in Queensland on a tour of promotion of Immanuel College; I found out that if I served in places that he did not visit, it was expected of me that I would promote the College in a brief address.

In Toowoomba. During the rest of December I stayed with the grandparents and Aunt Olga, and under the supervision of Pastor H. Rogge preached at eight services in his Hume Street (Trinity) parish. The first of these began on Friday (19th) in his country congregations, with a Christmas service in Narko. I recorded this momentous occasion in the following words: "Then I had to mount the pulpit for the first time. Some moments previous to this my heart beat heavily, but I felt quite composed as I faced the congregation for the first time. I felt strengthened by God at that important moment. Impressions rushed in a torrent through my mind, impressions that can barely be disentangled. At no time did I feel uncomfortable or unsafe".

Narko was followed by Christmas services in the other two outlying congregations, Maclagan and Kulpi. This was the area where Father had commenced his ministry and where I spent my first two years. The warm reaction of some people was embarrassing, yet comical.

Trinity, Toowoomba

In Kulpi, in keeping with the practice that announcements followed the sermon, Pastor Rogge reached the point of thanking me for my sermon. Old Mr. B-n immediately rose to his feet: *"When the parents left they were given a send-off, and the congregation sang 'God be with you till we meet again'; and, behold, today now we meet again. This young man was only a baby at the time, and here now we have him in our midst again. And I think that for a young man he preached a very good sermon. I know what I'm talking about, as I was chairman at the time. And as a mark of respect to his parents and to this young man I call upon the congregation to rise in honour of them".* And the packed church thundered to its feet. — In another congregation an old Mr. S-r, who had been a neighbour of the Proeves at Westbrook, approached me, and the following conversation ensued: *"Is that old Mr. Proeve in Toowoomba your grandfather?"* *"Yes".* *"Well, who is your father?"* *"Hermann Proeve".* *"Hermann Proeve your father! No, no, I can't believe that, I can't believe that!"* (He shakes his head and turns half away.) *"No, no, I can't believe that – Hermann Proeve your father!"* *"But still, that's the case."* (I reply smiling.) *"No, I can't believe that!"* (and off he goes to Mrs. Sch-g.) *"This young man means to tell me Hermann Proeve is his father. Is that so?"* *"Yes."* (So he comes back, shaking his head and cutting similar capers to the amusement of many nearby.) *"Well, I suppose I'll have to believe it; but Hermann Proeve your father?!"* And still shaking his head he retreated to the back seat of his car.

Chapter 3

I was very much aware, as I preached three times in Trinity Church over the Christmas period, that **my grandparents** and Aunt Olga were **hearing me for the first time**. They said that I preached at a good speed, neither too fast nor too slow. And when grandfather added on the last Sunday in December (28th): *"Das war eine gute Predigt, die du gehalten hast" ("That was a good sermon that you gave")*, those few quiet words were worth more to me than any other words of praise.

On the day before that last sermon in Toowoomba a telegram was delivered from **Aunt Emma Boettger** (Father's sister, married to a missionary in New Guinea), stating that she was **in Cairns**; and in the evening of the last day of 1941 she was in the arms of parents who wept with joy. The war against Japan had taken a serious turn for the worst at the end of 1941, when British warships were sunk off the Malaysian coast, and the Japanese army was marching forward to Singapore. It was expected that Papua-New Guinea would ultimately be in their sights. All mission women and children had therefore been evacuated in a freight plane (with boards on cases as seats) from Lae to Port Moresby, then by passenger plane to Cairns, and by special train to Brisbane. Some were remaining in Queensland, but the majority (70 or more) were continuing south. Towards the end of my stay in Queensland some doubts began to arise whether I would be able to leave; there was talk about closing the state borders, and of facing the Japanese advance at "the Brisbane Line".

Darling Downs commitments. Only in the beginning of January did I know what my further programme would be in Queensland. In that month I was with pastors in the Darling Downs, sometimes for about a week, preaching in 12 congregations: with Pastors G. Venz (Highfields), H.W.L. Prenzler, like Father a student at Hermannsburg (Goombungee), A. Simpfendörfer (Haden / Douglas), E.V.H. Gutekunst (St. Paul's, Toowoomba), N.G. Sander (Chinchilla). On January 1st there was an innovation that took getting used to: at 1.00 a.m. the clocks were moved forward to 2.00 a.m. – the beginning of a new phenomenon called '**Australian Summer Time**' (but dubbed 'Daylight Saving Time'), which was supposed to 'save lighting and fuel'. For the first time I was involved in 3 services on a Sunday (which soon was the normal pattern of services), and on some occasions the service began at 9.00 p.m.! In the Goombungee parish in particular the focus was on me as the boy who had left a good 13 years previously. – Conversation with the pastors in most cases turned to the **"Petition"** in which we had been involved. I fully expected this, as Norman Keller had written to us in November: "The 'Seminary Riot' is viewed with regret and disgust by most of the Queensland brethren, and for this reason I would feel terribly sorry for that one of your class who would come to Queensland during the forthcoming holidays". The first with whom I discussed this was the venerable family pastor whom I respected, G. Heuer. He was interested in how Pastor Muetzelfeldt was faring, as he hoped great things from him. (He had nursed Pastor Muetzelfeldt as a baby in the Hermannsburg Missionsanstalt.) In his own student days they had to appear before Director Harms because they had protested against one of their teachers as being liberal and chiliastic. Nodding several times as he read the petition, he finally said: *"Wenn ich da unten gewesen wäre, hätte ich es auch so gemacht". "Es freut mich, daß wir solche Studenten im Seminar haben, die solchen Ernst zeigen."* *("If I had been down there I would also have acted like that." "I am pleased that we have such students in the Seminary who demonstrate such earnestness.")* I found that among the pastors with whom I spoke there was much understanding of our position.

Locum in South Brisbane. Travelling on an early train from Toowoomba to Brisbane on January 31 I felt a little dejected, wondering whether I would ever see my grandparents and aunts again. And I wondered, too, what Brisbane had in store for me – this much I knew: there would be plenty of work. For three weeks meeting the spiritual needs of the South Brisbane parish was in my hands. It began with conducting divine services on the next day: South Brisbane in the morning and again in the evening, and Eight Mile Plains in the afternoon. That was the service programme for three Sundays, and it required six sermons. My much used sermon on Psalm 121 opened the series. I had to search the Löhe library for some helps to prepare some extra sermons. Ash Wednesday fell into the time I was there, and I found out that I needed two sermons for a morning and evening service in South Brisbane. I was totally unprepared for this. Various emergencies made it impossible for me to prepare the second sermon before that day. After the morning service "I immediately fled into the study like a hunted human being" (as I recorded in my diary); using the disposition of a sermon by a Ludwig Sabel that I had found, and thoughts from Matthew Henry's exposition of the Bible, I preached on Matt. 26,6-16, feeling that "in spite of its hurried preparation it was not futile".

Photo: *Nazareth Lutheran Church at South Brisbane*

And next day I felt "as free as a bird, knowing that there was no necessity for me to prepare any more sermons". (On my last Sunday in Queensland I was with Pastor G. Dohler, conducting three services in the Ipswich parish.)

Photo on left: *An example of the records that Henry kept for every service he conducted*

Before breakfast on the Wednesday in my first week I was called out to visit an 85-year-old Mr. Schneider, who (the family thought) was dying. I read 2.Timothy 2,3-13 from my German New Testament, prayed the verse *"Wenn ich einmal soll scheiden"* *("Lord, when I am departing")* and the Lord's Prayer, followed by the blessing. In the ensuing conversation I took the opportunity of quoting and expounding Psalm 121. His thankful family told me at my next visit that he had said, *"Der Pastor hat mir einen herrlichen Psalm vorgelesen"* *("The pastor read to me a magnificent psalm")*. I visited him several more times as he became weaker and died 6 days later. Pastor Otto Adler conducted the funeral next day. There were five or six other persons, including one who was terminally ill, in sick beds at home or in a hospital that I ministered to during these weeks. Each occasion led me a little further in the way of being a "Seelsorger" with the Word of God and prayer. — One day a Müller couple came with their child, who was not expected to live, asking for baptism. I accompanied them to the home of Dr. F.O. Theile, Director of New Guinea Mission, who was basically in home detention after having been interned for four months at Graythorne. When he asked who the sponsors were, they mentioned two names and added, *"and of course Mr. Proeve"*. In this stunning fashion I became a sponsor for the first time in my life! It did not become an ongoing responsibility – the little boy died a few months after my return to South Australia. — At the meeting of the Youth Society I on one occasion gave the talk I had gradually evolved as a substitute for Mr. Schneider, giving it the title "Immanuel College and Seminary and Its Surroundings". In this context, as an afterthought, I would add that on my round of country congregations with Pastor Rogge a Mr. Mayer spoke to me about this matter in connection with his two sons – and they came to Immanuel College at the beginning of the new academic year, Reinhard and Rolf.

Extract from Henry's diaries kept while he was doing vicarage

Chapter 3

When Pastor Max Lohe returned from his attendance at General Church Council meetings in Adelaide I braced myself for his reaction to our Petition. During the first couple of days his brother Wilhelm (Bill), with whom I had spent congenial hours, and he discussed their father in my presence in the study: how he was excellent as a translator into English, how he was sound in his pronunciation of English, how he was marvellous in music, how they had never heard him play a wrong note. I took it in, and said nothing. Reaction came just once, on the day after his return. *"I must say that I was very disappointed in your attitude in your petition. I didn't like the tone at all."* He kept on repeating those words *"I must say"* like a refrain during our conversation. He said that if he had been down South at the time he would not have taken it lying down, as the College Council had; and he had told the Council so. He admitted that there were many things that needed improvement, but his attitude was that we, since we were students, had no right to suggest any. My attempts to explain various matters that he raised did not make any difference; but he was not personally antagonistic. He presented me with a copy of the history of the South Brisbane congregation and a much appreciated copy of F.O. Theile's history of the Lutheran Church in Queensland.

The financial remuneration for services at that time was 10 shillings per service, with travelling expenses payable out of that. At the 20 services in the Darling Downs congregations I was generously given offerings that amounted to about £18. I had been prepared to have just my travelling expenses covered, but I was a little disappointed that the generosity of the Darling Downs was taken into account as making it unnecessary to pay anything further for my 11 services in the South Brisbane parish and 3 in the Ipswich parish. When we compared our experiences during the end-of-year break, I found that I had had very much more preaching etc., but most of the other seminarists had also been able to do seasonal work to help their financial situation.

Further away from the 'War Zone' – or was I? It had been arranged that Esther, the youngest daughter of widowed Uncle Carl Dunemann should go South with me to be fostered by Mother and Father. After a worrying week of co-ordinating arrangements for her travel from Kumbia and mine from Brisbane for the commencement of Seminary lessons – and with a constant fear that travelling over the border was going to be stopped – we left Brisbane on February 25th, and arrived in Adelaide in the morning of February 28th. That evening I wondered whether I had come closer to the 'war zone'. Paul and I accompanied Mother and Esther to the newspaper office, where at midnight they got on Mrs. Birdseye's bus for Kimba. Then Paul and I had to walk through the blacked-out streets to Immanuel College. The blacking out of Adelaide got on my nerves, because this had not been the case in Brisbane. The cars drove with just a narrow slit permitting light to come from their headlights. Our study window was covered with brown paper and had blackout paint smeared over the paper. In the vestibule of the Seminary a blue light burned. No light was allowed to shine outside; no street lights burned. In Brisbane I had been to a few homes where some sort of air raid shelter had been set up, and precautions were being taken in general against flying glass, but life was not as affected as in Adelaide.

Esther with the Proeves at Kimba, Feb 1942

1942: The Final Seminary Year and Year of Upheaval in North Adelaide

The Seminary studies began two days after my return from Queensland in a heatwave that topped 109.6° Fahrenheit (43.1° Celsius); but we were very soon involved for about a week in Air Raid Precautions (ARP). Shelters for all students in the event of air raids were created; Pastor W. Riedel's motor shed was the one to which I was allotted as deputy leader (under Mr. G.A. Keller) and as first-aid man. (All seminarists had done a course in First Aid with The St. John Ambulance Association, and held a certificate. My Certificate No. 28130, dated 4.11.40, certified 'that Heinrich F.W. Proeve has attended a Course of Instruction, and has qualified to render "First Aid to the Injured".) In the eyes of the Immanuel College authorities it also qualified me to be asked to instruct Immanuel College students in first aid when the College was relocated to Walkerville.

Chapter 3

With Erich Renner as my assistant we met the problems of the motor shed as best we could: viz. the big doors of the shed with no lock inside to keep them shut; a loft with books overhead; a motor car with petrol fumes. In the Seminary itself its internal Box Room became the shelter, with the large bagatelle table and a grand piano (that nobody played because its notes did not hold their pitch) as our chief protectors, and big tomes out of the Seminary library for added overhead protection! Most seminarists were deputy leaders and first-aiders or fire-fighters. Sandbags for bagging doors and for fire-fighting were prepared. One morning there were frequent 'alarms' in order to get us used to the dispersal of all students: I had to call the roll of our group, and had to have the key to the motor shed with me wherever I went. In addition we all were kept busy blacking out all rooms in the Ward Street building.

Ten Days to Vacate the Immanuel College Property

After all this work, only 23 days after the Seminary had begun its new year, Director Löhe had a telegram from Melbourne in his hand, informing him that the Air Force was taking over Immanuel College and Seminary. A message from the Air Force representative at Keswick indicated that this would probably take place at end of term. Two days later (March 26), however, the blow was more severe: we had to be out in 10 days (April 5), for a takeover on Easter Monday.

In *The Echo 1942,* pages 22-24, there is a description of the transfer of the College and Seminary, entitled *'From North Adelaide to Walkerville'*, which I wrote in careful wording. It provided an anonymous nucleus for the description in D.E. and I.V. Hansen's book *'with Wings'*. In these Memoirs, as one of the few living participants, I wish to fill in more about those 10 days of desperate high pressure, especially adding how the Seminary was affected. I am convinced that our joint labours at that time and the constricted life we had in the relocated Seminary, were a cement that bound us tightly together throughout the following years.

There was a flurry of thinking during the first two days (March 25th and 26th). One mooted plan for the future was to divide the institution into North Adelaide sections: Tynte Street church and hall as central for the school; the boys to go to Verco House in Molesworth Street (to be bought); the girls to stay in the Book Depot in Ward Street; the seminarists to go to 39 Hill Street. Another line of thinking, which many in the Seminary favoured, was that the Seminary should go into the country — enquiries were made at Point Pass, and Tanunda or Nuriootpa were mooted. On those days I, as deputy librarian of the Seminary library, stamped about 1,500 library books in preparation for shifting.

Tynte Street church

On the third day (27th) a clearer picture of possible developments began to emerge. Mr. Schneider's suggestion to buy two adjoining properties in North Walkerville became the focal point of hopeful negotiations. It was decided that the Seminary would shift into the Girls' Hostel, and that made it possible to commence, as stage one of the removals, the shifting of the Seminary and the Löhe family. Held and Biar immediately prepared a scale of the two floors of the Hostel, while Scheer and I sorted out the Seminary library into categories of 'primary' and 'secondary' importance and 'not needed'. We all started packing up our own libraries.

A major task opened up on March 28th, when Director Löhe led me into the sanctum sanctorum that no one had seen, his study. A great troop of seminarists was soon staring at a massive array of shelves in almost all rooms and in the tower, and facing a task of shifting each book – a task that was to take us three days to carry out, including Palm Sunday (March 29th), when Director agreed to our request to continue working on the last day that all College lads were with us. — The Löhe family first of all had to be convinced that its idea of occupying the entire ground floor and a large room on the upper floor as sewing room made it impossible for us 10 seminarists to live, study, and have lessons upstairs. Slightly modified, Biar's plan of distribution was adopted. During those three days frantic work was carried out at two locations.

Preparing sandbags

91

Chapter 3

Our activities in those initial days were divided between four removal projects that were simultaneously in progress (each with its own working group), and with the large fifth one still looming. These were: **1.** The Löhe family, with furniture and library from the College to the Girls' Hostel; **2.** The Seminary, with furniture and our own possessions, from the Seminary to the Girls' Hostel; **3.** Riedels from the Seminary building to the Tynte Street church porch and hall (furniture) and to 39 Hill Street (residence), plus the Church Archives with its very heavy fire-proof safe to Tynte Street hall; **4.** The College girls from the Girls' Hostel to the upper floor of the Lutheran Book Depot at the corner of Ward and O'Connell Streets; and finally **5.** The entire College to Walkerville. To shift Pastor Muetzelfeldt's few items back to his house was a bagatelle in all that turmoil – I did it in a cricket cart!

During those first three days the centre of frantic work was at two locations: in the Löhe study books were carefully taken down from the bookshelves and the bookshelves were dismantled – (each section and its shelves was given an alphabetical numerical identification); at the Hostel these were set up by Scherer (who bore the brunt of altering and setting up the bookshelves throughout this undertaking). The two rooms in the Hostel facing the street were separated from rooms behind them by a curtained partition (left room), and by a sliding door (right room). Both these openings were closed with long bookshelves: to the left on March 28th by Scherer and Biar; to the right on March 29th by the five of us who first had to pull it down in the study. The Löhe family thus had rooms facing the street, as they desired: bedroom on the left, study on the right.

The books were moved in this fashion: A 'chain-gang' of College boys was formed, on the first day, from the study to the front lawn of the College. Renner, initially with Held and Biar, was in charge inside the study, taking down the sections in undisturbed order, and sending them out to me (who was in charge on the lawn) to place them on the grass in identified order. When the shelf was in position in the Hostel, I packed the books on boards, and sent them section by section to Biar, who placed the books in position again. With the constant switching around of jobs to be undertaken, on the next two days I sent the books per College students direct from the study to Renner in the Hostel, as we had to be careful outside with occasional showers. The horse stable at the back of the Hostel became a repository for a bookshelf of excess books, also for Seminary library books (packed in a piano case).

The Kelly Gang   *The Otto trucks*

It was an act of total dismay when carefully sorted books in the shelves in Director's study were pushed out of sight by one of the packers into the cavity between bookshelves and sliding doors to make way for more arrivals – to be discovered in the following year when the sliding doors were accidentally opened! At 4.30 p.m. on March 30th Renner and I solemnly shook hands. Our probably conservative estimate of the number of books handled was 20,000. The Head stood and gasped to see his study cleaned out; he couldn't grasp it, and he couldn't grasp either how we shifted all those books across in such a comparatively short time, and that he could find books where he had had them in the College – except those, of course, that 'disappeared' into the above-mentioned cavity. The time, however, had been long enough for Renner and me not to get nightmares about it.

To give an idea of the variety of tasks we seminarists faced I add that on the Sunday Grope organised a 'chain-gang' of College students that shifted 5 tons of valuable mallee roots across the backyard of the neighbouring old maids' (Labatts') property to the Hostel backyard, where Biar stacked them up.

Chapter 3

Our problem was the lack of transport. In my wartime write-up in *The Echo* I obviously could not make reference to it; but I have no hesitation to record in my Memoirs to the permanent disgrace of the Air Force that it <u>refused</u> to provide any assistance in removal. (When the Army at that time took over Concordia College with 7 days' notice for a short-term use as military hospital, it provided transport.) On March 30th Pastor John Doehler and wife Frieda arrived with a trailer that he had bought. From March 31st Evans of Evan's Fruit Shop in O'Connell Street, willingly made his horse and delivery cart available. Two gangs worked for three days with this equipment: the 'trailer gang' helping John Doehler; and the 'Kelly Gang', with Pech as the driver, using the horse and cart. Hampered a little by showers, between them they carried out the first four removals. This involved a large amount of co-ordination, especially at the Girls' Hostel, where furniture was being moved in, and furniture was being moved out. Negotiating narrow staircases and sharp corners with large pieces of furniture was difficult, and often required that such furniture was lifted over balconies and lowered from upper storeys to the ground by ropes, or vice versa lifted up in the same manner. After March 31st the seminarists had only 13 senior College boys to give them invaluable assistance. They were George Mutze, Gerhard Proeve, Victor and Ivan Roennfeldt, David Lubke, Ken Leske, Paul Renner, Vincent Jarick, Rufus Pech, Les Schliebs, Konrad Hartmann, and (during the day) Conrad Otto.

Photo on right: *While the billy boils*

Attention to the final major removal began on April 1st. Two long wings of a boarding school had to be shifted. Everything had to be brought to ground level in and around the courtyard: the beds, bedding, and wardrobes of a large boys' dormitory; the furnishings of private bedrooms / studies; the desks, chairs, and teaching aids of several classrooms; the tables, chairs, and bookshelves of boys' studies; the long tables, chairs, and other items in a large dining room; the crockery and kitchen equipment, the contents of a commodious cellar and of kitchen staff quarters. Two lorries (one with a trailer) provided by Mr. G.B. Otto arrived, and after the long-awaited news came through that the contract for the purchase of the Hawker property had been signed at 5.00 p.m. we rang the school bell in sheer delight, and loading up of the lorries commenced. The teachers now took the lead: A. Doecke controlled the activity at North Adelaide; G.A. Keller was to be responsible at Walkerville, but he asked me to take charge of the gang that would work there, and at the end of the next day he gave me the key. The fully furnished house of course was not yet available, but the large garage stood at our disposal. It measured 39 x 24 ft. [11.88 x 7.32 m], with two small rooms alongside, 8 x 8 ft. and 8 x 5 ft. [2.44 x 2.44 m. and 2.44 x 1.52 m.]. It had a pit, into which we stacked chairs.

With my chosen 'Walkerville Gang' (Schilg, Scheer, Mutze, Lubke, and a couple of others) I went out on Maundy Thursday morning (April 2nd) to await the arrival of the fully laden lorries. We handled five loads that day. We put long tables and forms across the strong rafters to serve as a sort of floor for the stacking of furniture up to the roof. Pictures and similar things that needed careful handling were mainly stored in the larger of the two small rooms (the 'library'). The smaller room served as the 'kitchen', the receptacle for all kitchen utensils, jams, and kerosene tins filled to the brim with pickled eggs. Spilling a little of the vile-smelling brine over ourselves turned us into 'stinkers'. We were relieved that we could see vacant space in the garage; and the farewell words of the Doehlers before they left for a Maundy Thursday service in their parish (*"You seminarists have done a magnificent job in working and organising"*) cheered us with the knowledge that Director Löhe and his whole family appreciated our efforts.

Good Friday (April 3rd) meditation was well-nigh swamped out by the worries of the terrific problem that still lay before us. Two Otto trucks, again one with a trailer, stood in our yard. They could not go out on the road, but they could be loaded with more College furniture, this time with Grope organising, in preparation for a big 'putsch' on Saturday. I took my gang out to Walkerville that morning to finish the incomplete stacking of what was there, and then played the organ for the afternoon North Adelaide service.

Chapter 3

In pious German Lutheran circles the day after Good Friday is "der stille Sonnabend" ('the quiet Saturday'), but April 4th was far from 'still'. It was a drizzly day with heavy work to be done. Three loads of furniture had to be packed away in the morning; in the afternoon there was another load. The big arrival, however, was the 10 tons of mallee roots that Biar had loaded in the morning. With shrinking numbers we worked as a 'chain-gang', passing the roots up to the stackers, especially Schilg, who ensured that the wall of roots (the width and height of the sliding door) did not interfere with the working of the door – a marvellous job! — On Easter morn (April 5th) I took my reduced gang out once more: the last load of furniture was sent out; when stacked away there was a space of about 8 x 4 ft. left near the big door. In the afternoon I played the organ for the Easter Communion service in North Adelaide. And Immanuel College and Seminary stood empty on the stipulated date

Hawker House at Walkerville – our new home

Immanuel College stood ready to receive Air Force men. We were there early on Easter Monday to shift the 5 tons of sand dumped before the kitchen door for air raid precautionary measures. We expected any minute to see Air Force men stream into the yard. But nothing happened. Building up the sides with sandbags, we unloaded the sand into that last remaining space at Walkerville. We then had an annoying anticlimax to all the shifting!

Mr. Keller had arranged another trip in order to take away a wash-trough in the washhouse and the old grand piano in the Seminary (which we had deliberately neglected in the hope that its existence would somehow be ended in the war situation). We six men plus driver struggled to shift the unwanted piano from the lobby to the truck, and onto the truck, and off the truck into the Tynte Street church hall; then Scherer and I continued to Walkerville to unload the wash-trough. At about 11.00 a.m. I shut the main door, scrambled over the stumps and furniture in the dark, and turned the key in the side door for the last time. — And in the afternoon a very annoyed Director Löhe made his way to Air Force headquarters to inform them that after they had hurried us out of the place, we could not be responsible for keeping urchins off the grounds. (The urchins were there on Sunday, digging up vegetables etc.; with two others I went out late that night in an effort to catch some of them.) The Head's action led to an occupation at the end of that so officially stipulated Easter Monday – there were <u>six</u> Air Force men in the building.

Next day, a little epilogue. Held and I, as the only two seminarists still on hand, helped Director Löhe shift a few things at the new Seminary, but for most of the morning we cleaned up, and dug in the garden plot that was to come into use. Pastor Auricht, Headmaster of the College, however, received permission to collect some of the firewood that was still left on the College heap. After we had loaded up his brother-in-law's utility in the afternoon, I took it to his home in Prospect; one trip became two trips for his benefit, because we discovered a 'nest' of mallee roots under bits of twigs and rubbish.

Seminarists – resting at last!

Chapter 3

The big shift was over. All of us had finally drifted off into a holiday. The Doehlers most warmly invited me to come to Murray Bridge. On Wednesday morning, April 8th, with two cases strapped down on my parcel carrier, and cycle bag with tool kit on my back, I set out per bicycle. I rode without the benefit of any road signs – these had been removed to bamboozle the enemy. I enjoyed a 3½ hour stay in the hospitable Petering manse in Hahndorf, continued up hill and down dale, and reached Murray Bridge a little before 6.00 p.m., having covered the 52 miles [83 km] in a little under 5 hours of pedalling time. During the 5 days that I enjoyed with them I got to know John Doehler in his geniality and quiet humour very well. His visitors' book contained amusing verses by the Pastors J.P. Löhe and L.E. Kuss, punning on *"Loh" ['ardour']* and *"Kuss" ['kiss']*. *"When later I approached the old boy about giving a 'Kuss' to a 'Löhe' he was not very pleased"* was John Doehler's wry comment on his courting of Frieda Löhe. I gladly assented to preach at the three services in his parish. On April 14th I returned to Adelaide in the comfort of their car, with the bicycle on board, and later caught a train to Point Pass for the second portion of my holidays. That was the occasion when I dismantled the Lemke organ [*see page 53 of memoirs*]. I preached at three services in Pastor Materne's parish, which was in Uncle's care. Uncle had a triple baptism at one of these. His comment that two of the mothers did not go much to church was exemplified when one of them, standing a metre away, balancing on one leg with her baby in one arm, tried with open hand to throw a 'thanksgiving' coin into the collection plate on the left end of the altar, and only managed to pitch the coin on to the floor, where it did a long roll.

Walkerville Revisited. The 'gentlemen of the Seminary and the upper school', according to a circular from Dr. S.P. Hebart that I received in the evening of April 20th, were expected to resume work next day. Through arriving in the afternoon of the 21st, I missed the commencement. The seminarists and College officials attended at Walkerville at 11.00 a.m. to receive the key. But it didn't arrive. They boiled a billy tea out there with the utensils at their disposal from the garage. Around 1.00 p.m. the key arrived. President-General Stolz very much desired a solemn official opening to mark this beginning of a new era for the College. He read Psalm 121 in the presence of Board members Hebart and Lehmann, the College teachers, and the seminarists. The youngest girl present carried the key. The procession solemnly proceeded to the main front door; but the key wouldn't fit. The procession went around to the door at the other end of the entrance hall; but the key wouldn't fit. The procession finally entered the building via the kitchen door at the back, but with much less decorum.

Photo on left: *Hebart, Stolz and Lehmann enter the building*

The next days, with senior College boys also on hand, and under the direction of the teachers, the contents of the garage were transferred into the building – except the mallee roots, which went outside the garage through a window, and the sand. The teachers' task of working out where to place the contents of a 30-room College into a 15-room building was unenviable. — For two days Sieg Held and I stained floors in this fine building. Then I offered to do jobs of quite a different nature. The Matron had reluctantly acquiesced to Mr. Keller's choice as her room. I offered to kalsomine its walls – a task done entirely on my own, with her furniture already in place. So I had to move furniture as well as the ladder, and had to be careful not to splash kalsomine. On two other days I worked on the small room in the tower (I called it the "Tower Room"). Mr. Keller accepted my offer to do it up because visitors would pass through it on their way to the lookout and its magnificent views. There was scarcely a square foot free of cracks, because the Hawkers originally had a large flagpole that extended down into this room for added strength and footing. Two big holes where the plaster had fallen away on account of vibration had to be filled up, and then, in order to cover the cracks, I did the kalsomining in a colour similar to that in other parts of the building.

The new College was ready for a Service of Dedication on April 30th. At the close of the service the teachers were profusely thanked by church officials for their work. Then plain-speaking Pastor Lehmann closed his speech by saying that those who should be specially thanked were the seminarists and older boys and Mr. Keller. John Doehler endorsed this with a hearty "Hear, hear!"

Chapter 3

Life at 132 Jeffcott Street, North Adelaide

After a long break due to the transfer of College and Seminary we resumed lessons on May 4th in our new classroom.

The new "Seminary' was not a commodious place. The ground level rooms were largely devoted to the three-member Löhe family, with one for Miss Kuhl (our matron), and the kitchen and dining room for all residents. We ten seminarists had our studies, classroom, and sleeping section upstairs. University student boarder Colin Thiele was also there until July. The Senior Study was just as dark at 11.00 a.m. as at 11.00 p.m., due to blacking out. As there was insufficient sleeping room I was one of the five who had our beds on the balcony, which faced west, the direction from which the weather generally approached. Large blinds between the balcony posts were our sole protection against the elements. So we were not 'wind-proof', and on at least two occasions very violent storms with driving rain drove us indoors, with our mattresses on the classroom floor or on desks. Pastor Riedel had to conduct one lesson with the classroom in this turmoil. We balcony-sleepers placed newspaper sheets under our mattresses to preserve a trifle more warmth underneath. Our clothes were stored in the small bedroom.

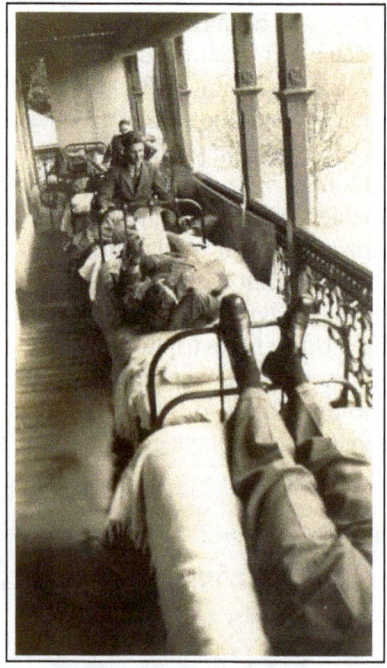

Sleeping on the balcony

Calls to serve as preachers increased in number during these closing months for the five of us who were licensed to preach. I, for example, could help Uncle Ernst as he served two parishes. On one occasion Pastor Albrecht Fehlberg, of Yorketown, who had forgotten to arrange for guest speakers at his parish Mission Festival, appealed to his good friend Director Löhe for help. He turned to Sieg Held and me, and we both managed at short notice to transform a classroom sermon into a foreign mission and home mission sermon respectively.

Photo on left: *Loading furniture at North Adelaide*

Silver Wedding and Silver Ordination Celebration. One occasion naturally is particularly memorable for me. The parents' silver wedding anniversary fell due on Sunday, June 14th, and Father's silver anniversary of ordination on June 24th. It seemed to be impractical for us two sons to come home, as was their desire. A last-minute urge caused me to travel home unannounced on June 13th; Paul could not come because the College was in quarantine. Late that day I walked into the Kimba kitchen, to the complete surprise of the parents, and for the first time in nine months. And next day I conducted the thanksgiving service with the combined congregation of members from Kimba, Kelly, Buckleboo, and Ballumbah. It was the first time my parents heard me preach. My text was Psalm 121. "I felt rather shaken for a moment or two on this occasion, but steadied during the service", is my record of this auspicious occasion. On the next day I returned to Adelaide.

A Varied Day. October 7th began with normal lessons with Pastor W. Riedel. In the afternoon I had to get the double bass violin somehow from the Seminary to the College. So I put my two luggage straps around it, slung them around my neck, and mounted my bicycle with the big bass at my side. A few people goggled and smiled as I cautiously made my way, with a slight breeze blowing, to Walkerville; I greeted them with a wave, and passed on. After tea at the College there was orchestra practice, then a return to the Seminary. The news there was a bombshell: Pastor Riedel had been whisked away during the afternoon by the military authorities! — As a result of Pastor Riedel's internment, my third and final class-room sermon was preached before J.P. Löhe. He advised me to complete my preparation in German, based on the disposition approved by Pastor Riedel. I believe that this was the last sermon in German preached in the Seminary.

The Church authorities selected me to be the student who provided a reference for Pastor Riedel. At the hearing of his case – he told me later – frequent reference was made to the fact that he had written a brochure against Freemasonry and all secret societies – presumably so that the Freemason 'judge' would take that into account as an attitude that agreed with Hitler.

DECLARATION

IN THE MATTER of the detention of
WOLFGANG RIEDEL

I, **HEINRICH FRIEDRICH WILHELM PROEVE** of North Adelaide Theological Student solemnly and sincerely declare as follows:-

1. That I am a Bachelor of Arts of the University of Melbourne.
2. That I am 24 years of age.
3. That I have been a Theological Student of the Immanuel Seminary at North Adelaide since February 1939.
4. That Mr. Riedel (now interned at Loveday) was my constant tutor during the whole of the time that I have been at the Seminary.
5. That the said Mr. Riedel has from time to time told his pupils that they should increase their knowledge of the English language with a view of assisting the further development of making the Lutheran Church an Australian Lutheran Church and thereby destroy the idea that the Lutheran is exclusively a German Church.
6. During the years that I have attended his lectures I say without hesitation that Mr. Riedel on no occasion has uttered a word derogatory to the British Empire.
7. That the said Mr. Riedel also lectured to me and other pupils on the subject of Ethics which embraces loyal sentiments to the Empire and such sentiments are expressed in prayers for the King, the Governors of the Commonwealth and all those in authority. This forms part of the general prayers used in the Lutheran service every Sunday.
8. That I believe that other pupils in the said Theological class would support the statements made in this my declaration.

And I make this solemn declaration conscientiously believing the same to be true by virtue of the provisions of the Oaths Act 1936.

DECLARED by the said HEINRICH FRIEDRICH WILHELM PROEVE at Adelaide this fifth day of November 1942.

H. F. W. Proeve

M. Fleming JP

Chapter 3

Further Steps Towards Ongoing Activities in My Life

A review of the years of study at Immanuel Seminary makes me realise that in some things in which I had been interested as a 'young apprentice' I was being led like a 'journeyman' from private activity into public service.

The prosaic task of **proofreading** was one activity. My apprenticeship with the Geelong High School magazine was followed by proofreading the two *"Echos"* that I edited. The further development began in 1940, when W. Riedel asked me to proofread the two brochures that he wrote as Secretary of the UELCA Intersynodical Committee, entitled *"Was hindert die Einigung?"* and *"What hinders the Union?"*. Then in May 1941 he suggested me to the hymnbook authorities as a proofreader of the new printing. That opened up a new world in my other interest, the hymnological field.

As for further proofreading? Perhaps I will take time one day to calculate how many thousands of pages I have proofread in printing General Synod Reports (17 Conventions) and other reports and editing *"Lutheran Heralds"* for the Church, not to mention parish papers in North Adelaide, Nuriootpa, and Point Pass, a goodly number of histories of congregations (at least 7), and Schulz and Proeve family histories.

The **hymnbook**, however is the striking example of being led into public, continued activity. I have referred earlier to my private interest from the days of youth in hymns and tunes. In my Seminary days I continued making notations in my hymn-book and recording other material, using the Seminary library as one source. Julian's invaluable *"Dictionary of Hymnology"* was a prime source; the second-hand hymnbooks of other Churches that I bought provided cross-references. Pastor Muetzelfeldt made available to me a book by W. Nelle, providing information on hymns in the Westphalian *"Gesangbuch"*. My appointment, together with Sieg Held, as proofreaders (for the UELCA) of the new edition of the *"Australian Lutheran Hymn Book"* opened a new world of opportunity, as it drew attention to what I had been researching. The edition that was being set up in the printery of *"The Advertiser"* was important in local hymnody: for the first time the UELCA was given co-publishing rights with the ELCA, and J.J. Stolz had thus become a prominent member of the committee overseeing its publication. There was a separate printing for each Church; thus the Common Order of Service no longer appeared as an "Alternative Order of Service", but as the Order of Service in the UELCA edition. The writers and translators, who previously had been listed in the Index of Hymns or of Translated Hymns, were to be named under each hymn.

A few examples of some of the developments during this time of proofreading may be of interest:

- The notation in the original hymn-book for Hymn 343, *"I do not come because my soul"*, was the slightly mispunctuated *"F.B., St. John"*. In the proof-sheets the writer was identified as *"St. John of Damascus"*, who flourished around 800 A.D. When I told Pastor Stolz that the ascription was 1,000 years out, and should read *"Frank B. St. John, 1878"*, he noted my research work with surprised interest and instructed me to make any comments at any time on hymns.

- Sieg Held and I found that the proof-sheets for the new edition contained many mistakes, especially in punctuation and in the use of ":" as a sign of antiphonal singing / recitation. Using the previous edition as copy was the cause. These mistakes were too many to alter without incurring extra cost, but we had to provide four copies of our alterations for the ELCA and UELCA representatives for future reference.

- The only hymns listed in the "Index of Translated Hymns" in the original hymn-book were the German hymns. At Pastor Stolz's request I began typing an Index of Translated Hymns which included missing German titles; but I also pointed out to him that there also were translations from the Greek, Latin, and other languages. He discussed this with Dr. O. Nichterlein (ELCA head of publication). Because the various indices had not yet been set up, it was arranged that my Index of Translated Hymns should be set up, and also that I should draw up the index of all hymns in the hymn-book, and include the names of writers / translators. My 12-quarto-page Index of Hymns (603) was in Pastor Stolz's hands the next day. When I commented that there were 6 Norwegian, 15 Danish, and 1 Swedish hymns that I did not know, he in his strong sense of 'getting things done' immediately mailed letters to Pastor Sternquist (Swedish pastor in Melbourne) and C. Bjelke-Petersen (retired Danish pastor in Kingaroy), seeking answers.

- My "Index of Translated Hymns" was completed when Pastor Bjelke-Petersen, through his daughter Agneta, forwarded his carefully researched answer. There was one gap in my list. I had overlooked including in my list Hymn No. 375, *"God His watch is keeping"*, allegedly *"Danish, alt[ered]"*. Pastor Stolz had an answer to the problem: viz. we could provide the title from other hymn titles that we had: *"God"* was *"Gud"*; *'watch'* was *"vag"*; hence *"Gud Sin vag"*. I felt uneasy about this: first lines in other languages were not necessarily similar to those in the English translations; and *"watch"* in the missing hymn was a noun, not a verb like the Danish *"vag"* in *"Watch, my soul, and pray"*. I consulted a Scandinavian dictionary in the Public Library, and found that *"vag"* was indeed a noun. Had we printed *"Gud Sin vag"*, every person who understood Danish would have been bemused and amused to find that the hymn *"God His watch is keeping"* was based on a Danish hymn that began *"God His hole in the ice"*!

There is an interesting aftermath. In reply to a letter that I wrote, Pastor Bjelke-Petersen found in research that the "Danish" hymn was a translation (more accurately, a paraphrase) by H.A. Brorson of a German hymn in a totally different metre. After a good deal of searching I established that the German original was a slightly rare hymn, *"Gott der wirds wohl machen"* *["God will do it well"]*, by Ernst Stockmann. When the new "Lutheran Hymnal" was prepared, a totally new translation by O.E. Thiele and me, based only on the German, was accepted.

> Immanuel Seminary,
> 196 Ward Street,
> NORTH ADELAIDE,
> South Australia.
>
> March 24th, 1942.
>
> Pastor Bjelke-Petersen,
> KINGAROY.
>
> Dear Pastor,
>
> Although a complete stranger to you I am bold enough to approach you for assistance in a matter which greatly interests me. The information I would like to have is in connection with the Scandinavian hymns in our Australian Lutheran Hymn-Book. I was able to help in the preparation of the new edition of our hymn-book last year as a proof-reader. In addition I drew up the list of translated hymns. To help me in this our President-General, Pastor J. J. Stolz, got information from you regarding the Scandinavian hymns and handed it on to me. Now, however, I would like to continue my private work on the hymn-book, and would like to know more about these Scandinavian hymns.
>
> In the enclosed sheets I have noted down all the Scandinavian hymns in our hymn-book. I have given all the information I have concerning them so that you can check up on the correctness of it. In addition I have asked for more details; and I hope you will be able to answer the questions I have asked in those sheets.

Hymn-book Assessment with J.P. Löhe. In May 1942, to my surprise, I was appointed by the Publications Board UELCA to serve as the amanuensis who would record J.P. Löhe's much sought-after reactions to the hymns and tunes in the Australian Lutheran Hymn-Book. Part of my fulfilment of this task began when I, at G. Dohler's request, transcribed all of JPL's tunes into a manuscript book. I also noted down all that I could find in JPL's private hymnbook. Personal working together only began at the beginning of November; but his interest soon warmed, so that almost every Saturday morning one to two hours were spent together in the classroom, where we had an organ. There wasn't the stiffness of a teacher / pupil situation in a lesson; the human side of JP came to the fore as he frankly spoke to me of his reactions to the hymns and tunes, during which his opinion of what should be expected of hymnody in the life of the Church was impressed in my mind. I wrote down his reactions, often in the original German in which they were spoken. We were one-third through the hymnbook when the meetings had to cease for 1942. They resumed next year at the end of May, after I had settled into my parish.

Chapter 3

Final months in the parental home

After a few examinations, which the teachers really did not want, we graduating students went home to prepare for the final examinations. This was the closing five months of my life in the parental home. The first half was marked by preparing examination papers: in Apologetics – a 16 foolscap-page treatise on Roman Catholic apologetics (in German), for which I had collected material for quite a time; in Catechetics, the sermon – for which I chose John 5,19-29 as text. This was followed by swotting for the oral examination day.

Christmas turned out to be an unforgettable event. Leaving Cungena, where I gave the children's address on Christmas Eve, we reached Wudinna by pushing the car the last half-mile into town – the car had a broken cog-wheel on the camshaft. Father managed to borrow a buckboard, with which he took Mother and Esther Dunemann to Wedding's at Mt. Wudinna, where he conducted the afternoon service. Paul declared he would accompany me to Warramboo. Setting out on foot in the hot sun at 3.23 p.m. in a recorded temperature of over 100 degrees (hotter on the open road), carrying a kitbag with gown, liturgy, and Bible and a supply of hymn-books, we walked non-stop to Wannamana siding in an hour (4 miles). After two brief stops we reached Kyancutta, where we had a cool, refreshing drink from a tank – our water bottle had warmed up. We began to do 15-minute one mile stretches. After 15 miles of walking, 2 miles from Warramboo the first car came into view. Our welcome pick-up was Wally Gerschwitz of Cungena! "Although a little weary in the legs, I felt like taking the service and preaching" in a well-filled church.

The two **final examinations** in writing (Dogmatics and Church History) took place in North Adelaide on February 22 and 24. We were completely unsupervised – no handshake was required of us! After our final oral examination, and comments on our written papers, on **February 26** we were told, after a break that we had passed. We each received a certificate signed by J.J. Stolz and J.P. Löhe, declaring us *"Worthy and Well Qualified for the Ministry of the New Testament"*. Then Pastor Stolz intoned: *"The vacant fields are ..."*. He said, as we knew, that Pech was going to fill a position at Immanuel College while doing additional studies; *"Ersatz [substitute] for North Adelaide"* (which we were all awaiting with trepidation), *"Proeve"* – I heard that with mixed feelings. The remaining three then knew that they were destined for Queensland. There was no valedictory service at this time; that was replaced by a farewell service in North Adelaide on April 11. Meanwhile we all returned home to be ordained.

Sunday, March 28, 1943. "A day, the depth of which one cannot really put into words. I can only say it was a great and wonderful day for me: of which one can experience but a few in his life", is my record at the time. Uncle Ernst arrived in Whyalla two days earlier. St. Paul's Church, Warramboo, was the only church in the parish, and centrally located for the parish service and annual meeting. The problems that a wide-flung parish with small numbers faced showed up in the attendance, which I could record in detail in my diary: from Warramboo, 7 families (15 adults, 5 children); from Cungena, members from 3 families (6 adults); from Pallinga, 1 family (3 adults) – a total of 24 adults and 5 children. They were 5 family groups: Wagner, Havelberg, Klante, Gerschwitz, Kobelt. How many ordination services have had such a small attendance? I for my part have always treasured it in my remembrance. Uncle Ernst preached the main sermon, based on Malachi 2,7; Father followed briefly, based on 2.Timothy 2,1-15, especially the first and last verses: *"Thou therefore, my son –* no doubt a word with special meaning to him, *be strong in the grace that is in Christ Jesus. Study to shew thyself approved unto God, a workman that needeth not to be ashamed, rightly dividing the word of truth."* It was a moving moment for all when a father ordained his son, assisted by an uncle (whose ordination greeting was 1.Chronicles 28,20: *"Be strong and of good courage, and do it: fear not, nor be dismayed: for the Lord God will be with thee; he will not fail thee, nor forsake thee, until thou hast finished all the work for the service of the house of God".*

The whole gathering at the Ordination service

Chapter 3

The words of old Mr. F.W. Wagner when he warmly shook my hand after the service were particularly fine. In his typically solemn and pleasant way he said: *"Nur eins! fest trauen auf Ihn!"* *['Just one thing! Firmly trust in Him!']*. The certificate that declares: *"after having been duly examined and proven himself a thoroughly capable and worthy Candidate for the Ministry of the Gospel ... has been duly ordained ... May the Exalted Head and Lord of the His Church endue our Brother with the Gift of His Holy Spirit for the Salvation and Edification of many and to the Glory of His Name! May the Lord bless him and make him a blessing!"* This, and the Graduation Certificate issued on February 26, are my treasured recommendations.

The weeks before duty began: A life-changing discovery. As I think over events for these memoirs I have for the first time realised that Saturday, April 10, when I left Kimba to be present at the farewell service for our class, marked the close of the 24 years that my parents' home was my home, and that the first steps towards establishing my own home were looming. And this soon included an important discovery for my life.

I accepted a renewed invitation from our good friend Pastor W.J.G. Schultz to stay a while in Dimboola. As I was denied the necessary permit to travel interstate by train, I decided to get there by bicycle. I boarded the South-East Express – the train to Mt. Gambier – in the morning of April 15 for Bordertown. Laurie Leske was waiting for me with the message that WJGS would meet me in Kaniva at 4.30 p.m. Losing sense of time at Leske's created the events that followed. They took me and my bicycle by car 5 miles inside the border, and (as we later worked out) we missed the Schultz car by about 5 minutes. I rode 10 miles into Kaniva in 37 minutes, arriving about 15 minutes after WJGS, who, believing he must have missed me, left for Dimboola. I telephoned Dimboola (before he had arrived back). While he set out at 7.00 p.m. with Dorothy I rode 6 miles in the moonlight without a light. At milepost 262 [miles from Melbourne] we met. – Dorothy and I reflected on this each time we passed that spot in later years.

On Palm Sunday (19th) I preached at a service in Ni Ni and gave a talk on "Archaeology and the Fall of Jericho" at the LYPS evening meeting in Dimboola. After a game of Chinese Checkers Dorothy and I continued to talk. Suffice it to say that neither of us had known how much we wanted each other. She did not know how I felt until I spoke; and I did not know that she did care for me. The entry, 'I trembled like an aspen leaf at this new and strange feeling that surged through me', expressed at the time how I felt when it became evident that my fear that she had another interest turned out to be unfounded.

I helped out in services while I spent further days in Dimboola in new-found happiness. On Good Friday in Arkona (Jeparit parish), and preaching in Dimboola. On Easter Sunday I preached at Katyil and Ni Ni and conducted the full service in Dimboola, with WJGS and wife, Verna and Grace, in the congregation, and Dorothy at the organ.

A memory of the last night before I left Dimboola: I had knelt down before the hearth to turn over the log, so that it would go out. Dorothy knelt down too. In the dying light of the fire I asked her: *"Are you watching the fire go out, too?"* She replied, *"No, I was praying"*.

III.3. The Pastor in North Adelaide

My first problem in taking over the North Adelaide Parish was to find board. Several days of fruitless enquiries ended when Miss Selma Maass of 118 Margaret Street, North Adelaide, offered board at £1 per week, £1/2/6 with washing. Her aged mother, the widow of a mariner, had died shortly before. She was legally still married to a Rechner (a distant cousin of J.J. Stolz), who unfortunately was in a mental institution. She was a fine, motherly soul belonging to the Bethlehem congregation in Adelaide (ELCA), of whom I have fond memories. There was no telephone in her home, but it was arranged that until I could have one installed – which only took place five months later, in October – messages could be relayed at given times, mindful of their hours of sleep, through Perryman's bakery nearby.

Sunday, May 2, was the date of my introduction, when I preached my 'introductory' sermon, based on John 20,19-23, to a congregation in which I could see nine pastors. The next day I received a great surprise when I was told about the call meeting that followed the brief service. There were 59 voting members, who voted as follows: as No. 1 choice, G. Dohler 30; as No. 2, M.R. Stolz 32; as No. 3, myself 46 votes! — I inherited the use of Dr. K.J. Basedow's Dodge car; but was assured by the Chairman and Treasurer of the Home Mission Committee, to which I was responsible, that I could also claim tram and bicycle expenses as travelling expenses. During the next fortnight J.J. Stolz on several occasions took me to outlying suburbs to introduce me as his successor.

Chapter 3

Wide Experience in City Mission Work

The North Adelaide Parish (Home Mission Field) consisted of **North Adelaide** (the only organised congregation, worshipping in the one-time Primitive Methodist Church, Wellington Square), and as preaching places, **Hope Valley** (F.B. Dallwitz's dairy home, Modbury), **Magill** (lodge room, Magill Institute), **Semaphore** (in a hall), and outlying **Morphett Vale** (Sauer's bakery home). The "working agreement" from the Home Mission Committee stipulated that in addition to the above my sphere of work included the Lutheran City Mission. This comprised visiting the hospitals and rest homes in Adelaide, the three mental institutions (Parkside, Northfield, Enfield Receiving Centre) and the Adelaide Gaol. I received no request to attend at the last-named. But I was very quickly thrown into the other areas already in the first week! On May 6, arrangements for the wedding of a non-Adelaide couple on June 5. On May 7, news that I had to conduct the funeral of G.A.Tschirpig, of Pyap, next day. The hospital visiting began three weeks after my introduction. My experience in Queensland stood me in good stead; but I am especially thankful for the one gift that I received at my ordination – 10 shillings from Mrs. Gus. Klante of Warramboo, with which I purchased J. Sheatsley's *"The Lord Thy Healer"*.

The patients, mostly from the country, were generally unknown to me, and their illness was also unknown, so that I did not know how life-threatening the illness was. Their spiritual knowledge and state was also unknown to me. My attempt to awaken a spiritual memory in a German lady by referring to loved hymns, especially the well-known *"Christi Blut und Gerechtigkeit"* *['Jesus, Thy blood and righteousness']* aroused no memories in her; but a spiritual link was established when I quoted the spiritual song *"Gott ist die Liebe"* *['God is love',* translated as *"I know God loves me"]*. In the Royal Adelaide Hospital I became aware that certain cases were in certain Wards, e.g. heart cases in Flinders, gynaecological in Da Costa, eye in Ophthalmic. Most of my visiting was centred on RAH (where on one occasion I had 10 to visit), Memorial, Calvary, and Ru Rua Hospitals; and most of the patients were in hospital for a short time only. A young lady from Light Pass, Beatrice Hermann, lay with both eyes bandaged for many weeks in the RAH; when I visited her after the bandages were removed she expressed her joy that at long last she could 'see' the 'voice' that had meant so much to her, and I naturally rejoiced with her in thankful prayer.

At mental institutions. Visiting the three mental institutions as a young inexperienced man, beginning in mid-July, with J.J. Stolz accompanying me on two initial visits, threw me into the unknown field of ministering to persons who were not normal. The work in general took place in sections or wards. 'Lutheran' groups were brought together by the staff; Enfield Receiving Centre was the early-stage institution where I was more likely to have only a few people to minister to. At Northfield there was a common room with a piano in which the inmates could gather, and sing. A former ELCA pastor who had had a nervous breakdown could play the piano brilliantly for the hymns, provided he was in the necessary mood. At Parkside (later generally called Glenside) there were some 'formidable' wards, like Z Ward for the most dangerous cases, where up to two entrances were unlocked and immediately locked behind me upon my entry. If we were gathered in a small room, I normally saw to it that the people were in the room and I was near the door; but on one occasion I noticed (a little worriedly) that I stood opposite the door. I geared my devotional meditations at Sunday School level, according to how I assessed the understanding of the people. The devotions were generally well-received; but it could happen that the gesticulating of some persons in front of me put a strain on concentration. I had to cope with the unexpected. For example, on one occasion I announced a hymn, and before I could begin singing one inmate started off, singing his own tune in a loud voice and with a curious stress on words; no two stanzas were alike, so all one could do was listen to his musical treatment of the words. At the close of devotions small packets of sweets were handed out, which (as I correctly surmised) attracted a 75 per cent non-Lutheran attendance in some places.

At **Parkside** one day I had quite a lively time as I went from Ward to Ward to speak to two ladies (generally) at a time. At the first Ward one lady talked volubly, commencing in English, but in spite of my best efforts to follow I did not notice when she switched to German; the other lady was motionless and silent. At the next Ward there was such screaming that the nurses inside did not hear my ringing; a nurse from outside had to let me in. As I sat with my little group on the edge of the verandah at the next Ward a young woman with one hand strapped into a leather 'muff' cried out, *"See that woman, she's a sorceress"*; and when a nurse came to get her she let out a blood-curdling yell, *"Minister, minister, help me! The devils have got me!"* The surrounding mood became disturbed, and after a while some solid object went hurtling through the air behind me along the verandah. At the last Ward, which I was visiting for the first time in one of several buildings "enclosed by a fence, like at the Zoo", one woman started talking very loudly: *"Meinen Jesum haben sie genommen und verbannt. Sie haben mir die Brust halb abgerissen, um ihn zu kriegen"* *['My Jesus they have taken and burnt. They have half torn off my breast, in order to get him']*. It seems that she had had a picture of Jesus which was somehow burned or destroyed. On days like that I returned home exhausted.

It was essential to remember important points in reference to particular people. In Z Ward it was vital not to mention the blood of Christ to a man who had unsuccessfully tried to end his life by slitting his throat. Approaching him one day when he was working in the garden of the Ward, I could hear threatening muttering in German and see a raised spade; still facing him, I changed into reverse, and quietly exchanged greetings and farewell with *"Bruder Martin"*.

One lady at **Northfield**, from whom I hoped to secure some personal information (baptism, confirmation, etc.) for the congregational record of members, provided this one day in quite normal German conversation until she made reference to *"die Kinder" ['the children']*. I continue the conversation in English translation: *"Whose children?" "Ours". "Did you have many?"* A gentle, whimsical smile played on her lips: *"I am not quite sure; but about 68,000."* I had to bite my lips to retain composure. Later in my visit, on the Northfield farm, I tried to find out more about a man I deemed to be Scandinavian. But he merely repeated the last words of whatever I said. Once, when I didn't know what he had said, I as a matter of form said, *"Ugh, hugh!"* He of course immediately said *"Ugh, hugh"*, then spoke a few more words, said *"Ugh, hugh"* again, said a few more words, followed by *"Ugh, hugh"*, added a few more words, and again *"Ugh, hugh"*. A few more German words, with gesticulations, came out, and finally he took the lapel of my black coat and said, *"Nachtzeug!" ['Night-wear']*. It was then, as I rode back home, that I could break out in saddened laughter.

Z Block at Parkside mental hospital

Around Christmas time special get-togethers were arranged, when those present received honey biscuits in addition to sweets. The biscuits were provided by Ladies' Guilds in the District congregations. Treasured possessions of mine are simple framed pictures that ladies of Parkside bought in the city to express their thanks. I believe that many of those who were in these institutions suffered from dementia or Alzheimer's disease, and today would be treated quite differently.

Many of those whom I visited spoke about their problems, e.g. one lady was not sure that she had a soul; so I was faced with many spiritual matters for which I had no ready-made answer from Seminary days. This two-year ministry of mine caused me ever after to have an inwardly angry reaction whenever I heard someone speak disparagingly about 'asylums' and those in them.

A City Mission funeral that I conducted in August 1943 at the Centennial Park Cemetery attracted quite a measure of attention; it was the funeral with full Air Force honours of a 28 year-old Lutheran member of the Women's Australian Auxiliary Air Force (WAAAF) who had been stationed at 4STT, Immanuel College. J.J. Stolz and I had visited her in hospital. JJS made it the subject of a news item in the *'Lutheran Herald'* (28 August), with a summary of my address to the Air Force personnel. I believe he was anxious as much as possible to draw public attention to Lutheran military personnel in order to counter as much as possible negative reaction to the Lutheran Church.

My City Mission work ceased in May 1945, when Pastor Alfred Zinnbauer was appointed and installed to carry out the duties that had been mine. A Lutheran City Mission Committee was established to oversee his work, with W. Riedel as Chairman and me as Secretary. The Committee has had much criticism levelled at it by biographers of Zinnbauer, and I believe it is justified to say that there is a large measure of unfairness in what has been written. The UELCA did not have unlimited financial resources; because it was not operating a prosperous goldmine it had to allocate carefully what amounts of the giving of Church members were available to each of its wide range of activities. Zinnbauer found it difficult to serve as the member of a team; he was much more at home launching out into sensitive, time-consuming social welfare work for the refugees who began to stream into the State, than being a pastor who was a spiritual 'Seelsorger'. A pastor who accompanied him on a round of visits at the Royal Adelaide Hospital recounted that his most frequent message to the patients was *"Have an apple – Have an orange"*. No record of his many baptisms, confirmations, marriages, burials, has survived; as a result there are people who do not know for sure that they were baptised. When W. Riedel resigned from the Committee in frustration, I became its Chairman until I transferred to Nuriootpa. I sought, for example, to co-operate with Zinnbauer in arranging bi-lingual services (including the singing of hymns bi-lingually) when Swedish ships were in port.

Chapter 3

This and That about the Parish

Called and Installed. It took six months before the matter of my call was finalised. After a fairly lengthy deliberation G. Dohler declined the call. And M.R. Stolz who had been chosen as second candidate received his call-up as military chaplain just at that time, and therefore did not came into consideration. On October 15 I received a letter from J.J. Stolz, stating: *"You are free to accept the call"*. I asked him about the significance of that unusual statement. He explained that in the course of their lengthy correspondence the Council of Presidents felt that although this was an appointment of a graduate according to Church rules, under which the graduate did not have a voice of decision, I had already had a good deal of experience in the parish, and if I had *"sehr starke Bedenken"* ("very strong doubts") about staying there, I could advise them of this, and receive consideration; hence the *"free to accept"*. He asked me how I felt. I replied,*"Bange" ("Afraid")*. He said he could understand that; and added that it was better that way than too cocksure. He said that I naturally did not attract by vivacity etc., and thereby draw large crowds, but he also added that he wondered whether such attraction would really be lasting.

First part of Call document to North Adelaide, Semaphore, Morphett Vale, Magill, Hope Valley and the City Mission

It was December 12 before District President John Doehler was free to install me. A remarkable convergence of religious activity caused it to be a service of amazing ecclesiastical richness, which J.J. Stolz commented on in the *"Lutheran Herald"*. During the year I had been engaged in activity that was more City Mission than parish in nature. A soldier from Milang, Keith Schwartz, had not been confirmed, and an uncle of his arranged with me that he would come to me once a week for instruction before call-up. He was ready for confirmation. My former classmates Les Grope, Erich Renner, Colin Scheer, Stan Schilg, Vic Wenke had completed their studies, had sat for their examinations without having time for revision of their studies (their addition to the Ministry was so eagerly awaited), and were now to be farewelled. At the same time they were to see their former classmate, who had co-operated with them, e.g. making his class available to them for confirmation instruction, installed. And Holy Communion was to be celebrated on account of the confirmation.

Imagine the procession that moved into the church. I headed it with my confirmand during the singing of *'Jesus, lead Thou on'*; the graduates followed two by two, then the District President John Doehler and the pastors assisting in the installation: J.J. Stolz, K. Muetzelfeldt, H.W.R. Proeve, J.E. Auricht, S.P. Hebart. The first rite was the confirmation. Pastor Stolz pointed out that my address for the confirmation, based on Revelation 3,11: *'Hold that fast which thou hast, that no one take thy crown'*, gave the graduates occasion to examine themselves as to their willingness to keep their confirmation promise, also by complete surrender to the Lord in the Holy Ministry right to the end. The second rite was my installation, followed by the farewell to the graduates. After the graduates had received a blessing with laying on of hands the worshippers, in Pastor Stolz's words, "ascended to the Tabor heights of the Holy Sacrament, both the means of bringing the Lord quite close and a pointer to the goal towards which every minister, indeed every Christian, is pressing on, the Real Presence of the Lord in eternity".

In addition to Keith Schwartz I gave weekly confirmation instruction to another candidate from a country parish, a girl student from the Hahndorf parish, Jean Meissner of Meadows. It was quite a tie to go every Tuesday during the school terms over a period of eleven months to the home in Kensington where she boarded. Pastor W.E. Petering confirmed her with his Hahndorf class.

The list of addresses of members and contacts that I received from Pastor Stolz and Mrs. Zinnbauer covered the entire metropolitan area because I had four preaching places. My log-book of visits in 1943 has 209 addresses; in 1944 it rose to 243. I said at the time in Home Mission addresses that if I could instantaneously turn addresses into membership I would have a congregation / parish of 400 members. My bicycle was my usual means of travel in the important rounds of visiting. Later I bought Gerhard Graue's autocycle, with which I could travel about 140 miles per gallon of petrol; my ration was 4 gallons per month. The monthly ration for the car was 8 gallons; one visit to Morphett Vale used up 2 gallons of that ration.

Photo on right: *JJ Stolz's report in the* Lutheran Herald

> PASTOR H. F. W. PROEVE INDUCTED AT TYNTE STREET LUTHERAN CHURCH, NORTH ADELAIDE.
> The fine attendance, necessitating the use of the extra seating accommodation on the gallery, bore testimony to the joy of the members again to have a permanent pastor, and to the fact that the pastor to be inducted has endeared himself during the months of his locum tenency. The lessons of the day, third Sunday in Advent (12th December), on faithfulness being the requirement in a minister of God (1. Cor. 4: 1ff.) and on John the Baptist, not a reed but a prophet and more than a prophet. (Matt. 11: 2ff.), made the day eminently fitting for an induction. The first part of the service was conducted by the locum tenens for the previous three years, Pastor J. J. Stolz; the induction by the South Australian president, Pastor J. Doehler (text the Sunday epistle), the concluding part by the newly inducted. It was a sight that impressed: the president before the altar, flanked by five pastors (E. Auricht, S. Hebart, K. Muetzelfeldt, J. J. Stolz—all members of the congregation!—and Pastor H. Proeve sen., father of the new pastor), before the altar step the pastor-elect, behind him on the first step leading to the altar platform, six lay-members of the parish, elders, officials, representatives of preaching places. But hymns and lessons and the address had the main share in making the service a memorable one. God bless the new pastor of the North Adelaide parish!

My main problem was to **stimulate attendance in the preaching places**, especially in Magill. The place of worship was dreadfully primitive – a lodge hall at the rear of the property, in which 'the All-Seeing Eye' dominated, and the children disappeared under the stage for Sunday School. Very few members owned a car; I picked up members for all preaching places, travelling some quite circuitous routes. The faithful attendance of Mrs. H.S. Fienemann and her three children, who rode their bicycles 4 miles each way to attend, encouraged me to continue services at **Magill** when only 2 persons formed the congregation. I felt convinced that the time would come when the suburb would develop; but I unsuccessfully put the idea to the Home Mission Committee to purchase an allotment and erect a simple hall on it as a centre of worship.

In **Morphett Vale** the strong anti-German feeling, which had closed the Presbyterian church against use by the Lutherans, ultimately made it advisable to close the preaching place, because the 'patriots' were targeting Sauer's bakery business with boycott.

In **Semaphore** the hall was almost invariably in a mess if elections had been conducted on the previous day. The attendance however was encouraging, and caused me to consider organising a small congregation. I was shocked when my successor closed down the preaching place.

Photo on left: *Petrol ration tickets*

When the Dallwitz home and dairy at Modbury was sold, a new centre of worship was found for **Hope Valley** in the Gilles Plains Hall. Its modern continuation, via Hillcrest, is the present congregation at Dernancourt.

I was asked by the Home Mission Committee to investigate the possibilities of commencing services in **Salisbury**. Armed with a list of names culled from the electoral rolls, J.J. Stolz accompanied me on the initial trip; the initial prospects were not promising. On my second visit I rode my bicycle the 12 miles to the area. On a rough track along the Little Para River up-stream from the Old Spot Hotel I found a Jaensch family which was preparing to shift to Burnside; it promised to join North Adelaide, because its members felt a spiritual need. The son and daughter received confirmation instruction at a slightly higher age than usual. And at the daughter's request I officiated at her marriage in Adelaide soon after I had shifted to Nuriootpa.

Chapter 3

On my 25th birthday I was overwhelmed in the **Muetzelfeldt home** by a sense of inadequacy; for it was a house of death. It had been my privilege to minister to Mrs. Muetzelfeldt during her terminal illness, and now the Lord had mercifully released her from her suffering. I was very much the junior in the home as I sat there with my respected and richly experienced teacher and J.J. Stolz. The family wanted me to conduct the entire funeral service, but had no objection to J.J. Stolz delivering the funeral sermon. The realisation that the sense of loss would strike my teacher very deeply made me feel completely inadequate to remind my experienced senior of his source of strength in the future. – Exactly thirty years later my birthday received a similar indelible stamp – the death of my father.

Before the year ended my preaching ministry received an extension. I had close contact with many nurses, and had been asked by the District authorities to cultivate this contact. Nurse Scherer – Lena, if I remember correctly – nursing at the **Royal Adelaide Hospital** as one of the 18 UELCA and 9 ELCA nurses there, was able to arrange that I conducted an 8.00 p.m. service in the well-appointed Hospital Chapel on December 31. It became fixed practice that I conducted such a service on the last Sunday in the months when there was a fifth Sunday.

The Home Mission Committee asked me to strive for an improvement in the giving of the parish. The parish agreed to the introduction of the **Duplex envelope system** that was coming into use more and more in the UELCA. These envelopes were divided into two sections: one for the support of congregational needs, e.g. pastor's salary; the other for Church undertakings, Australia-wide and District, as fixed by synodical resolutions. A change to this system was not made obligatory, but its adoption did create an improvement in the giving. A brother and sister in one of the preaching places, whose father did not adopt the new system, when they were confirmed asked for envelopes into which they proposed to place offerings from their pocket money. I quietly took notice of their 'setting aside' for the Lord: sometimes it was 3 pence, sometimes it was 6 pence.

When Pastor W.W. Fritsch took over the St. Stephen's congregation in Wakefield Street he established a simple parish paper, the *Adelaide Lutheran Messenger*, a double-sided sheet folded to form 4 pages. The fourth page was made available to the North Adelaide parish. The time came that it was advantageous for St. Stephen's to have use of the fourth page. In an amicable parting of the ways I therefore established the *Immanuel Lutheran* as our monthly church news sheet; and we exchanged copies of our papers for the benefit of those members who were keen to be kept informed on developments in the sister-parish.

One activity of mine was not mentioned in the Letter of Call; **the control of pigeons in the church.** The Wellington Square Primitive Methodist Church (also known as 'Tynte Street – pronounced 'Tint') was a square building with lofty 40 foot (12 metre) parapet walls. (In a flight of fancy it was possible to picture the church as being a giant square inkwell. H.F.W. Roehrs one day in a clever pun asked me the question: *"Predigst du noch immer im Tintenfaß?"* ("Are you still preaching in the Inkwell?") The roof of the main building sloped into a square box gutter against a parapet wall. There was a full-length porch on the Wellington Square frontage; its roof sloped away from the parapet wall to the box gutter that ran around the building. The plaster-board ceiling sheets, which were nailed from the underside, had pulled through the nail heads on account of the weight of pigeon droppings resting on them. The pigeons had ready access into the church. One Pentecost Sunday during J.J. Stolz's ministry one pigeon masqueraded as a dove for the whole of the service.

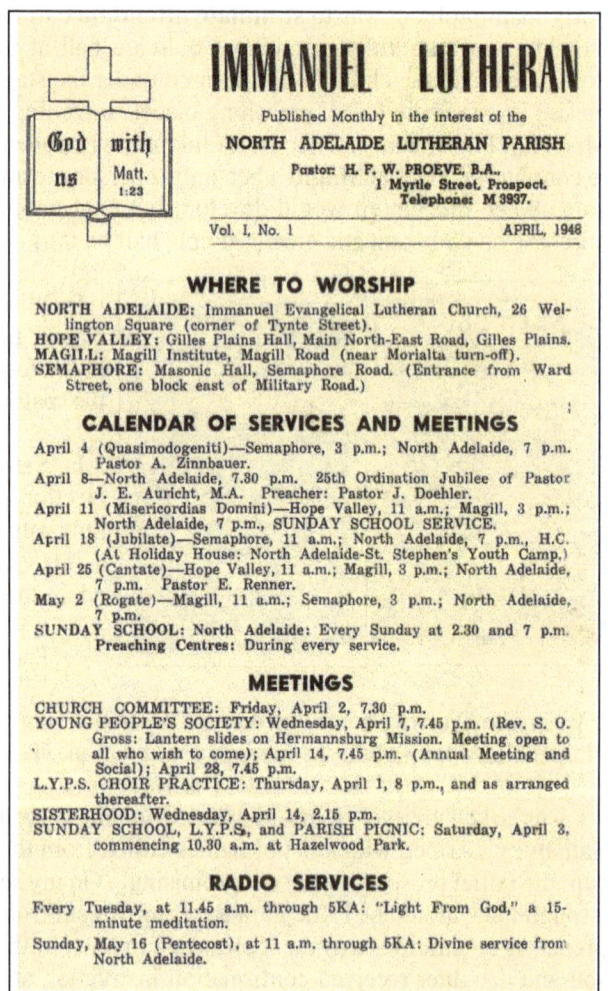

IMMANUEL LUTHERAN

Published Monthly in the interest of the
NORTH ADELAIDE LUTHERAN PARISH
Pastor: H. F. W. PROEVE, B.A.,
1 Myrtle Street, Prospect.
Telephone: M 3937.

Vol. I, No. 1   APRIL, 1948

WHERE TO WORSHIP

NORTH ADELAIDE: Immanuel Evangelical Lutheran Church, 26 Wellington Square (corner of Tynte Street).
HOPE VALLEY: Gilles Plains Hall, Main North-East Road, Gilles Plains.
MAGILL: Magill Institute, Magill Road (near Morialta turn-off).
SEMAPHORE: Masonic Hall, Semaphore Road. (Entrance from Ward Street, one block east of Military Road.)

CALENDAR OF SERVICES AND MEETINGS

April 4 (Quasimodogeniti)—Semaphore, 3 p.m.; North Adelaide, 7 p.m. Pastor A. Zinnbauer.
April 8—North Adelaide, 7.30 p.m. 25th Ordination Jubilee of Pastor J. E. Auricht, M.A. Preacher: Pastor J. Doehler.
April 11 (Misericordias Domini)—Hope Valley, 11 a.m.; Magill, 3 p.m.; North Adelaide, 7 p.m., SUNDAY SCHOOL SERVICE.
April 18 (Jubilate)—Semaphore, 11 a.m.; North Adelaide, 7 p.m., H.C. (At Holiday House: North Adelaide-St. Stephen's Youth Camp.)
April 25 (Cantate)—Hope Valley, 11 a.m.; Magill, 3 p.m.; North Adelaide, 7 p.m. Pastor E. Renner.
May 2 (Rogate)—Magill, 11 a.m.; Semaphore, 3 p.m.; North Adelaide, 7 p.m.
SUNDAY SCHOOL: North Adelaide: Every Sunday at 2.30 and 7 p.m. Preaching Centres: During every service.

MEETINGS

CHURCH COMMITTEE: Friday, April 2, 7.30 p.m.
YOUNG PEOPLE'S SOCIETY: Wednesday, April 7, 7.45 p.m. (Rev. S. O. Gross: Lantern slides on Hermannsburg Mission. Meeting open to all who wish to come); April 14, 7.45 p.m. (Annual Meeting and Social); April 28, 7.45 p.m.
L.Y.P.S. CHOIR PRACTICE: Thursday, April 1, 8 p.m., and as arranged thereafter.
SISTERHOOD: Wednesday, April 14, 2.15 p.m.
SUNDAY SCHOOL, L.Y.P.S., and PARISH PICNIC: Saturday, April 3, commencing 10.30 a.m. at Hazelwood Park.

RADIO SERVICES

Every Tuesday, at 11.45 a.m. through 5KA: "Light From God," a 15-minute meditation.
Sunday, May 16 (Pentecost), at 11 a.m. through 5KA: Divine service from North Adelaide.

Access to the church ceiling was gained via the gallery, which stretched back over the porch, where there was a manhole giving access to the box gutter and a manhole over the main building. Both wooden covers were broken, and the problem was only solved when I nailed them together and wired them down. I shudder now when I recall how I crawled around on the ceiling rafters, trying to pull up sheets with wires. One day I chased out 15 pigeons, collected 25 eggs and 9 young pigeons. Pigeon droppings blocked the box gutters, causing overflows down church walls; I lowered 24 4-gallon kerosene tinfuls of droppings over the wall into the street. Painting the wall required the hazardous task of holding tightly to and climbing up the longest ladder that the building firm of Webber & Williams could offer, placed on a sturdily built school desk.

Which Church is the 'Evangelical Lutheran Church'? One experience illustrates the relationship between the two Lutheran Churches at that time. After his marriage Monte Rieger wanted to join the North Adelaide congregation. So I wrote to the pastor of the Bethlehem Church, Flinders Street, asking for a peaceful dismissal. The Bethlehem pastor (later a good friend of mine) asked a retired pastor in his congregation to speak to Monte. Monte was deeply troubled when he was told by that pastor that he would be breaking his confirmation vow if he joined the United Evangelical Lutheran Church in Australia in North Adelaide: '*You promised to be faithful to the "Evangelical Lutheran Church"*' – *and that is us!*' I showed Monte my '*Liturgy and Agenda*' that the UELCA had given me – it was the '*Liturgy and Agenda*' of the Lutheran Church – Missouri Synod – and I pointed out that my confirmees also promised allegiance to the '*Evangelical Lutheran Church*'. This attempt to hold a member by making false capital out of the technicality of a name did not succeed. But my trust in the ELCA received a shaking by this.

Interior of the Tynte St church

Non-parish Activities

Being stationed in Adelaide led to a number of **extra duties** that W.W. Fritsch and I had to carry out. One has been mentioned earlier: membership in the **City Mission Committee**. – In the latter part of 1943, at the request of the S.A. District authorities, I approached the commercial radio stations with enquiries whether they would accept a religious radio programme. The stations 5AD and 5DN were not interested, but 5KA, which broadcast from Maughan Church, was willing. *"Fifteen Minutes with the Lutheran Church"* went to air in January 1945. Fritsch and I were members of the **Committee for Broadcasting**, I as its Secretary. I prepared scripts, which had to be submitted beforehand for censoring, a requirement that applied only to the Lutheran Church. I also read the devotions prepared by pastors not in the Adelaide area, and stepped in at short notice if pastors forgot. I continued this activity, which was quite a bind, until my shift to Nuriootpa. – Fritsch and I also served as the S.A. District representatives on the **South Australian Council of Social Service**. – As the **Church Archives** had been shifted to the Tynte Street Church Hall when Immanuel College was taken over, I became the Custodian of the Archives. I guarded them with an aura of liberally applied anti-vermin naphthalene flakes around the piled up cartons.

The laymen Frank Rothe and Jack Starick and I (as Secretary) were appointed to serve as a **Commission on the Pensions Fund.** We investigated several schemes, including two that had an insurance superannuation backing, but found that the most financially viable was to supplement the Government pension payment with the maximum allowable supplement that the Church could provide. Relief to the pastors was given by taking over their private Ministers Widow Relief Fund as a Fund run by the Church. (For many years I typed and duplicated the minutes and financial statements of this Fund. It was always a puzzle to me where to put the apostrophes: *Ministers'* was clear, because there was more than one Minister who had a widow; but what about *Widows'*? – how many widows was a Minister allowed to have? Should this be *Widow's*? – but the Ministers did not all have the same widow! What did I do? I omitted all apostrophes.)

Chapter 3

I continued the activity in which I had previously been engaged. On Tuesday evenings for about 2 to 2½ hours I was together **with J.P.Löhe**, resuming the study of the hymn-book. Then during 1944 the Publications Board, which had been relocated in Queensland because the pastors up there were critical of the Board members in South Australia and were convinced they would do a better publishing job, asked JPL to review the manuscript it had prepared for a prayer book, *'Lord, Teach Us to Pray'*. He was very critical of some of the prayers, and surprised me by suggesting that I should write a prayer for 'A woman with child'. It was accepted for the book. – A few years later I was appointed to the **South Australian Liturgical Committee** – the beginning of a long association with liturgy, worship, and prayers. The association with men who had studied liturgics – R. Held, T. Hebart, W.F. Roehrs, T.G. Obst – was an enriching experience, with the setting up of Orders of Service and prayers for particular occasions, such as burial of an unbaptized child (sparked by an experience I had in Nuriootpa), burial of a suicide, and burial in case of doubt.

To an increasing extent I was **drawn in by J.J. Stolz** into his literary activity, which was very prolific. Every fortnight an issue of the *"Lutheran Herald"* appeared, with editorials, articles, reports from his pen. The manuscripts were placed before me prior to going to the printer, because JJS wanted his wording to be checked. I appreciated the thoughtfulness of his writing, and I certainly did not alter the sense of what he wrote. He was inclined in somewhat typical German style to write what is dubbed *Bandwurmsätze'* ('tapeworm-sentences') in German. There were occasions when I recast such sentences into three sentences. JJS fully agreed with my recast forms. – The manuscript of his *'Almanac'* articles were handled in the same way. He had the gift of summarising the year's events in articles on world affairs and in surveys of development in the Church. A good friend of G.A. Keller, the parliamentarian Archie Cameron, bought the *'Christian Book Almanac'* each year, because he was so impressed by those surveys of world events.

The Married Man

Marriage and Homes. Dorothy came across to Adelaide in November 1943, and stayed with a friend whom she knew from Peterborough days. What many friends had been suspecting was thereby proved to be true – I had a lady friend. When I then went across to Dimboola in 1944 my autocycle provided the transport. I put it with the petrol tank empty on the Overland as far as Bordertown; there I poured two wine-bottles of petrol (carried in my kitbag) into its tank, and then eked out its economical 140 miles per gallon by also peddling the machine as a help to be warm in the night-air. That is how I made my 'engagement' trip. – But I had to make a second trip some months later. The health of Dorothy's mother deteriorated, and she died on the Friday after Easter, April 14. I naturally conducted the Sunday services two days later. At mother's specific request we continued our planning for our marriage day, August 29.

Getting married during wartime years had its difficulties. Dorothy had to use precious clothing coupons to have a simple wedding dress made. More difficult was the matter of travel connected with the wedding. The bridegroom obviously would receive a permit to travel interstate by train. I made enquiries regarding travel by my parents. I found out, to my surprise, that it was not self-evident to issue them with an interstate travel permit. I had politely manipulated my wait for the interview until the moment when I saw that the senior officer in charge of permits, a Mr. Stolz, was free. From him I received the assurance that when the parents arrived in Adelaide from Kimba on their way to the wedding they would be granted permits. It was obvious that others we had in mind, Paul as best man, Dorothy's brother Bill, Margaret Proeve as our organist, had no hope of receiving permits, and it was arranged that Father Schultz would collect them at Bordertown. My parents duly arrived from Kimba, but Mr. Stolz was not on duty when we attended for the permits. *'Not available"*, we were informed, and it was only when in surprise I stated, *"But Mr. Stolz stated ..."*, that these appeared on the table. – The number of wedding guests was small, but the church was filled with members from the parish and other friends of Dorothy.

Photo: *Henry & Dorothy, Lorna Boehm, Grace Schultz, Paul Proeve*

Quite a number, especially among the ladies, felt a good deal of concern for the bride when the organist began wedding march strains and there was no one near the altar. The wedding party was following the European custom of entering together in procession behind our two fathers. It was a day of muted joy: there was one person missing – a dearly loved mother who had been lovingly cared for, a dearly loved friend [to Henry's mother] from the same far-away homeland. – We had no honeymoon, just packing days. Five days after the wedding we were at 118 Margaret Street, North Adelaide, and I was carrying out normal duties in the North Adelaide pulpit.

The matter of where to reside found a preliminary solution through Dorothy also being a boarder with Miss Maass. Because provision had not been made in the District budget for a married man's salary, my remuneration until the end of 1944 remained at the level of a single man. Dorothy's natural desire to be the housewife came to fulfilment in the next year, when we were able to rent half of the home of aged congregation members H. August and Mrs. Koch at 1 Myrtle Street, Prospect, where family members had moved out. The 'flat' consisted of two rooms on the right side of the central passage, the former dining room, now kitchen, through which the Kochs had access to their kitchen, and a bathroom and toilet adjacent to our kitchen.

Mrs. Koch was a quiet gentle lady, who had to exert a quieting influence on her husband on the occasions when he looked too long into a glass. One day (April 14, 1945) we heard a thud; Dorothy answered the anguished cry of Mr. Koch that *"Mrs. Koch needs you!"* I could find no pulse in the body that lay on the bedroom floor beside the bed. It eventually [in 1948] became evident that someone in the family had to move into our section of the house, and so we had to make other arrangements. But the story of how we came into our third home has its own peculiar features, and is best left to a later part of our North Adelaide experience.

Hermann Heinrich: Friend extraordinaire of North Adelaide. It is a joy during the course of a long ministry to recall how the indifference of some congregational members was counterbalanced by the dedication and enthusiasm of others. In North Adelaide it was the willingness of a friend who was not a member of the congregation that did this. Hermann Heinrich's association with North Adelaide predated my ministry. Heinrich was a well-to-do member of the South Kilkerran congregation in Yorke Peninsula with a great love for his Church. During J.J. Stolz's ministry he loaned North Adelaide the money for the two-manual Estey organ which improved the accompaniment of hymns in broadcast services. The fact that his daughter Hildegard had married a Rechner cousin of Stolz possibly was a tie in this helpful relationship. Heinrich was particularly anxious to see North Adelaide own its own church. He heard a rumour that the Anglican Church was contemplating selling the historic Christ Church in Jeffcott Street – the Bishop's church – and asked me to investigate and report back to him. The answer rather obviously was negative, but it was followed by his request to continue to investigate the possibility of securing a building or an allotment, and to contact him immediately if I found anything.

Early in 1948 nothing came of the proposal, approved by Heinrich, to purchase the former manse of the Wellington Square church alongside the church, or the large vacant block of land hidden behind the manse and the church. The Standing Committee on properties of the Methodist Church was opposed to any sale. At that very time I heard that the Church of Christ proposed to sell for £1,000 a large allotment (56 feet x 210 feet) at 139 Archer Street, on which a stone building stood as the first stage of a church complex. We were granted a first option lasting four days to decide. Mr. Heinrich immediately agreed to give the £1,000. On the fourth day Ben Dallwitz and I filled in the necessary forms, and while Ben was paying out the deposit money a phone call came through – the Returned Soldiers' League was making an offer to buy the allotment! God's amazing blessing rested on the generosity of a friend!

A home at Archer Street. When it became obvious in 1948 that we could not remain in Myrtle Street any longer, Dorothy and I surprised the parish authorities by proposing that we move into the building in Archer Street. I am unfortunately now unsure of some of the details. The building, to the best of my recollection, was 16 feet x 32 feet with 14 foot high walls, and had been used as a food-processing factory with an uneven concrete floor poured over the wooden floor. It was difficult to secure the necessary building to turn the building into a residence.

Photo on right: *Henry at work on the new 'home'*

Chapter 3

A full-height masonite wall created a main room about 16 feet deep. The other half was divided into a kitchen and a bedroom by an 8-foot wall. A window was inserted into a thinner section of the northern wall. On the opposite side a window was turned into a doorway from the kitchen, with steps leading down to a besser-block attachment that was added to house the laundry and bathroom. The existing toilet stood at the far end of the allotment. I was the 'architect' who drew up the plans, including the elevations, for submission to the Adelaide City Council; Edwin Wilksch (foreman in the building firm of Webber & Williams) was the builder, ably assisted by other members who were handy with their hands. Monte Rieger did the electrical work. (Some years later in his willingness to put his gifts into the service of the Church he installed electric light at the Hermannsburg Mission Station.) In the back yard we set up the large tent I had made. That was the garage for our car and the shelter for our spare furniture.

We became 'parents' so suddenly that it created a turmoil of emotions at the time, and was a great surprise to our Proeve and Schultz families. The normal time of adjustment to the realisation that a new life was going to be entrusted to us was completely missing. The circumstances were indeed amazing, commencing with the unexpected pregnancy of a close nursing friend (Margaret M.) of Eileen Dahlenburg (Dorothy's brother Clarrie's fiancé), who also had become a good friend of ours. Like other nurses, she occasionally spent her day off with us. We three stood by her when she had a daughter as a single mother and were the sponsors when I baptised Carol. We occasionally had mother and daughter overnight in our home, and often cared for Carol during the day while her mother carried out her duties (often up to 80 hours per week) as cook, housemaid, and general domestic in a home where its quick-tempered members became increasingly nasty. And it was a pleasure to have Carol. The day that brought a new dimension to our life was January 27, 1948. When mother and daughter arrived in early afternoon the mother poured out her heart to Dorothy, stating that she had for a long time been thinking what was best for Carol, and that she was convinced that the best was to entrust Carol to us for adoption, not for fostering. I was staggered when they told me this, particularly when her answer to the question *"When?"* was *"Now!"* She left on her own, and we had a dearly loved 'daughter' with us! She immediately won the hearts of a surprised family and a surprised congregation.

Lutheran Women's Association. Dorothy was very much interested in the involvement of women in Church activities – not in the modern feministic push to play prominent authoritative roles, but in service. In her first year at North Adelaide, when interested women came together to pack honey biscuits and sweets, supplied by ladies' guilds in the S.A. District for Christmas distribution in the hospitals and mental institutions in Adelaide, she successfully broached the matter of forming a Sisterhood (our preferred term). – A more important development, however, took place, affecting the UELCA. J.J. Stolz quite correctly said that Dorothy was the 'spark' that set the women's movement alight. The North Adelaide Sisterhood agreed with her suggestion to invite the women in the S.A. District, who came in large numbers to Adelaide with their husbands to attend the Royal Show, to have a pleasant afternoon in North Adelaide as guests of the Sisterhood. Dorothy invited the wife of retired Pastor C.J. Siegle of Murtoa to attend. Mrs. Siegle had on one occasion arranged a get-together of women in Victoria, and she was the guest speaker about the avenues of service in which the women could combine. The gathering, chaired by Dorothy, reacted with enthusiasm, and the Lutheran Women's Association was established next year at a meeting at St. Stephen's Church, Adelaide. The chairperson of the day, Mrs. W.W. Fritsch, was elected as President, Dorothy as Secretary. That is the official beginning of the LWA, but the North Adelaide initiative conceived it. Ultimately it became a fruitful Australia-wide movement.

My involvement in constitutions – 'constitutional expert of the Church' became an albatross around my neck – began in part with this organisation, as John Doehler and I drafted its constitution. The other involvement was the incorporation of the North Adelaide congregation (which adopted the name "Immanuel" at this time), when it became the possessor of real estate.

Joy and Sorrow in the Family. Father Schultz started to stay with us at fairly frequent intervals during 1947, and he puzzled us with cryptic references in our visitor's book to *"(all-) important business"*. This became clear when on October 8, 1947, he married Hildegard Rechner, nee Heinrich, of South Kilkerran, whom he had known as a member of his South Kilkerran congregation during his pastorate in Peterborough, 1921-1926. We rejoiced with them. But only five weeks after the wedding he sustained severe injuries in a side-swipe collision with a truck near Dimboola. Eileen, Clarrie's fiancé, agreed to serve as a special nurse, so I waited until she arrived in Adelaide from her nursing position on Yorke Peninsula, and drove through the night to Dimboola and Horsham in a nightmare trip. Faulty attention to the timing gear caused oil to be sprayed inside the bonnet of the car, and I used up a tin of oil on the journey. The patient, who lost his right arm through the accident, lingered for not quite four weeks until his death on December 11. Hilda was fortunate to retain an eye that hung right out of its socket; the skill of the local Dimboola doctor rescued it from the removal that the other doctors advocated.

A Pointer to the Future

What a 1945 election led to. I was on the point of closing my North Adelaide chapter when I became aware that I had not referred to an event that ultimately completely changed the nature of my service in the Church – full-time in the administrative side of the Church. As the years of my ministry went by I became more and more aware that completely unforeseen circumstances set my career on a course that no one could ever have envisaged in 1945. That was an important year in the functioning of the UELCA. For the first time since 1937 (on account of the war) the General Synod of the Church was held. Two officials were not standing for re-election: J.H.S. Heidenreich as General Vice-President, and J. Doehler as General Secretary. The regulations regarding elections played an important role in the proceedings, with particular emphasis on exhaustive ballots as the method of voting. The General Pastors' Conference had the sole right to nominate one candidate, or at most two candidates, to the General Synod. Not all pastors were members of the General Pastors' Conference and Synod delegates; the pastors of each District elected a number of pastors in proportion to the number of confirmed members in that District. These pastors could choose their nominee from any of the pastors except those who indicated that they were not standing. If a candidate had a two-thirds majority he was submitted as the only nominee to the General Synod. If no candidate had a two-thirds majority, successive ballots were held, with the lowest candidate eliminated in each fresh ballot. – All this would have meant nothing to me, because I was not due to go to General Synod. But the Lord of life and death intervened; he called Pastor Franz J. Lehmann out of this life on May 4. So I had to go to the General Synod as the first emergency pastor of South Australia. Uncle Ernst Proeve, S.A. District Secretary for about 12 years, was a few votes short of the two-thirds majority, but did not pick up enough votes in successive votes, so that at the end of the balloting I was also a nominee. I was convinced that General Synod would vote for Uncle Ernst – but to my amazement (and the amazement of the assembly) I was elected by about 10 votes. There were some members of the Church who felt some concern that a 28-year-old pastor was elected to a senior position.

I have naturally wondered what contributed to such a vote. In South Australia I have become fairly well known through almost twelve months of broadcasting, but that did not influence the Victorian, New South Wales, or Queensland delegates. There was a contingent of younger pastors from Queensland, who quite possibly may have voted for me. J. Doehler chose Edward Helbig and me as minute secretaries at the prior Pastors' Conference, and we were commended for our minutes, which we wrote up at night and read at the beginning of the next day; that may have also drawn attention to me as a secretarial candidate. – After 1945 I was re-elected unopposed in 1947, 1950, 1953, 1956, 1959, 1962, and 1965. And 1966 ushered in the threshold of a new secretaryship, which is the subject of a later chapter.

Pastors at UELCA General Synod at Walla Walla, NSW, 1945

It seems to me that the 6¾ years of my activities as the pastor of North Adelaide may figure more prominently in these memoirs than longer periods of later activity – that the latter will be delineated in broader sweeps of the 'paint-brush'. I surmise that this is due to the deep impression that it had on me.

Chapter 3

Photos from trip to Bethesda Mission, April 1949

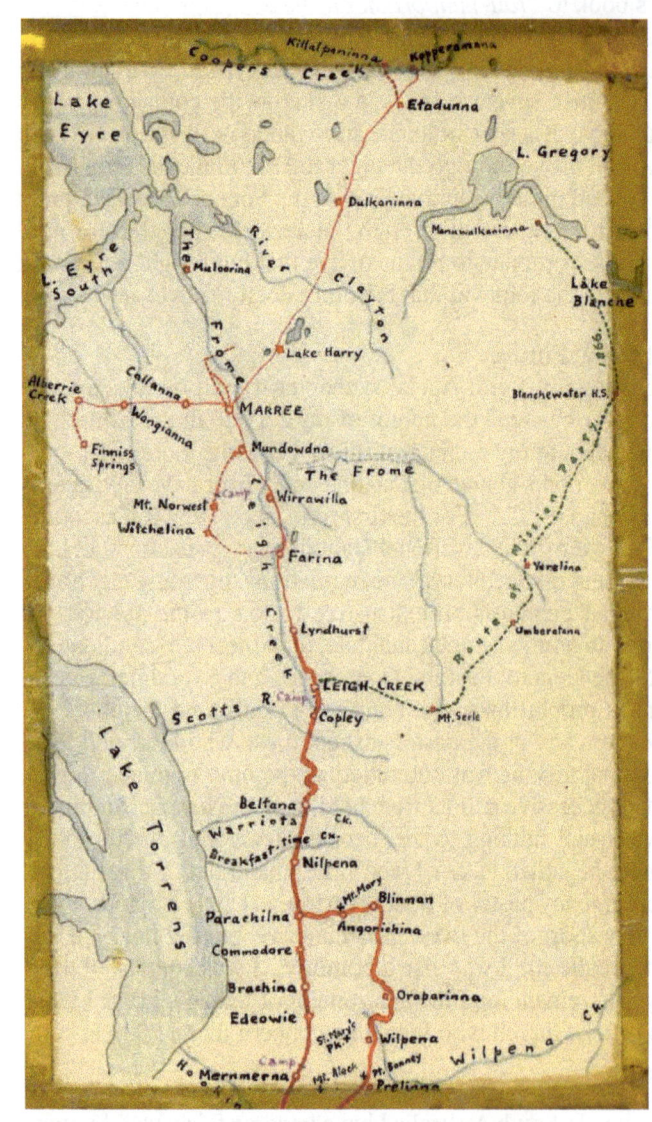

Bruno Doecke, Theodor Vogelsang, Henry Proeve, & Ernst Proeve leaving Point Pass

Ruined building at Kopperamanna

Visiting at Finniss Springs

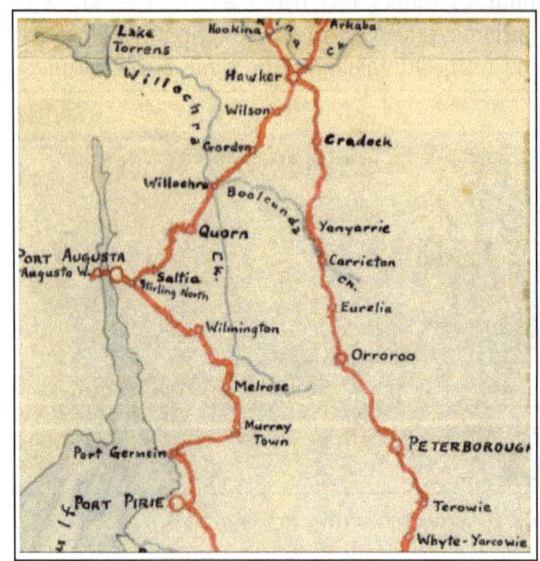

Henry's handwritten maps of the trip

Visiting at Marree

Chapter 4

IV. THE NURIOOTPA DECADE: 1950 (January) – 1960 (March)

When Pastor Richard Held retired the S.A. District authorities put into effect a plan to make Nuriootpa the centre of a **new parish**. Neukirch, after 6 years still the unattached remnant of Pastor F.J. Lehmann's Eden Valley parish, was added to it. For the town of Nuriootpa this was a notable development – for the first time it had a resident minister of any denomination. It was a large parish, and therefore a completely new experience for me. Nuriootpa had 488 baptised and 426 confirmed members, Neukirch had 128 baptised and 84 confirmed members, a total of 616 baptised and 510 confirmed members. – My predecessors had served their congregations for very many years. The 47½-years of R. Held's ministry meant that many middle-aged members in Nuriootpa had not known any other pastor, and for a time made comparisons between the old and the new. In Neukirch the 33½-year ministry of F.J. Lehmann had been cushioned by the 4½-year locum tenancies of W. Flierl and A.G. Simpfendorfer. – This was the parish into which I was inducted on January 29, 1950, by Pastor R. Held.

Photo on left: *Original St Petri church, Nuriootpa*

My initial problem in Nuriootpa was to establish who were the members for whom I was responsible. There was no written list, except for the list used by the Treasurer as he collected the *Pastorgehalt* (stipend) payments – and this list was far from complete. I had to do a lot of questioning, and I gradually discovered that members of about 12 Lutheran congregations lived in the Nuriootpa area. At the end of my first year a couple presented themselves as 'members of Nuriootpa' with a baby to be baptised; I had been told that they belonged to Strait Gate, Light Pass. When I ceased my ministry in the parish it had grown to: Nuriootpa, 750 baptised members (increase 262) and 536 confirmed members (increase 110); Neukirch, 118 baptised (decrease 10) and 86 confirmed (increase 2) members.

This may be the point where I add that my ministry in this growing parish was also marked by frequent assistance as preacher or even as locum tenens in neighbouring congregations, particularly in times of vacancy or of illness of the incumbent pastor. On checking my services record books I was surprised to find how often this happened. I helped by conducting services in 16 congregations of 8 neighbouring parishes; in 12 of them I provided occasional assistance (one service, up to 4 services). But I was closely involved in 4 congregations, namely Stockwell, Ebenezer, Daveyston, and Angaston.

Photo on right: *Neukirch church*

This was in the first half of my Nuriootpa ministry, often in an extended locum tenens situation. H.F.W. Roehrs called on me to help in his Stockwell congregation in three periods: 4 months (end of 1950-Mar. 1951), occasional services (1952, 1954), 6 months (1955). Serving Ebenezer was a natural development through the bonds between Neukirch and Ebenezer: 7 months (1953 during August Simpfendorfer's absence as refugee chaplain), 4 months (1954 during the vacancy when he left Light Pass). The three terms in the Daveyston congregation, serving it with its usual one service per month, has caused me to be listed as one of its pastors in the references to it in the history of Greenock: 5 months (1953), at the same time as I was serving Ebenezer; 5 months (1955), 2 months (1958). My serving Angaston 7 times was spread over 5 years (usually when its pastor was engaged in other Church service).

Chapter 4

My ongoing yet temporary service made it possible for me to initiate a change in Daveyston before an incoming pastor arrived. The congregation still used Sankey's *Sacred Songs and Solos* as its English hymnal. When I conducted a baptism (a rarity in this ageing congregation) I could not find a baptismal hymn. I suggested to the members that they should adopt the *Australian Lutheran Hymn-book*, as used in the neighbouring congregations where they worshipped at times; and they agreed. The floor of their substantial St. John's Church was interesting; its tiles were laid in an effective diamond pattern. When the Education Department bought the property to enlarge its school grounds, the church was demolished.

The Manse

The first major combined undertaking of the newly-established parish was to build a manse in Nuriootpa for the first resident minister in the town. The strong Building Committee of the parish had the heads of three building firms as its nucleus: Carl Juncken (C.O. Juncken Pty Ltd.), Laurence Mader (Burley & Mader), Arthur Liebich (Liebich Bros.), who had agreed to work co-operatively; also Oswald Krieg (Krieg Brickworks). The three firms were able to supply a large number of tradesmen who were members of the congregation and who were highly skilled in the various sections of the building trade. Very many of these, plus some congregational members who were not in that trade, were willing to supplement the contracted work with voluntary assistance; this was of great financial assistance to the parish. The Nuriootpa parish made the western portion of its Church Hall allotment available for the erection.

The UELCA had just at that time drawn up guidelines for the erection (or renovation) of manses, in which the emphasis lay in providing as much inbuilt furniture as possible (linen presses, built-in wardrobes, kitchen and pantry shelves, bookshelves in the study), and including a visitors' bedroom. It was hoped thereby ultimately to spare pastors the costs of some personal furniture and lessen the costs of transfers in the future. Carl Juncken, who visited us in Adelaide to find out what we 'wanted' in the manse, heartily endorsed the UELCA guidelines that I placed before him, and with the full assent of the Building Committee incorporated them into his plan. His early death in 1950 prevented him from seeing the project completed; Laurie Mader took over his guiding role.

Nuriootpa manse

It was still a time of strict post-war building restrictions because of scarcity of building materials; so a building permit had to be applied for as the first step. The permit that was granted required one less room to be erected. For practical reasons this meant that the study, which was planned as a south-east attachment with a separate entrance, could not be erected; the permitted building then formed a perfect rectangle. The building was still in early stages when our son David was born in June 1950; and behold! the regulations allowed an extra room to be built, because we now had a boy as well as a girl in the family. So the foundations of the study were immediately added with an accidentally enlarged width according to the original plan.

I pause in these manse memoirs to record a couple of unusual features connected with David's birth. It was in the wee hours of a wild winter's night, marked by broken branches on the road, when I took Dorothy to the Angaston Hospital. Fathers at that time were taboo at births, so I did my normal morning round of religious instruction lessons. When I got home there was still no news from the hospital. After lunch, as I arrived at the hospital, I met Dr. F.W. Hoopmann, who was leaving. *'Have you heard what happened?'* the doctor called out. *'No –o –o'*, I replied, with some sense of foreboding at these words. *'You have a son!'* Ah, what a relief! — Almost immediately after the birth notice appeared in the newspaper a very confident seller of insurance appeared at the manse door. Three year-old Carol accompanied Ruth Stoll (who was caring for us at the manse) to the door. *'Ah, you're a sturdy little girl'*, said the salesman to Carol as opening gambit; *'What do they feed you on? on Glaxo?'*. *'No'*, was the instant reply of the three-year old, *'on PLATES!'*

While the manse was being built we lived for about 22 months in Fourth Street that Mrs. Altus made available for rental by the parish. The current problems associated with securing necessary materials slowed down the completion of the project.

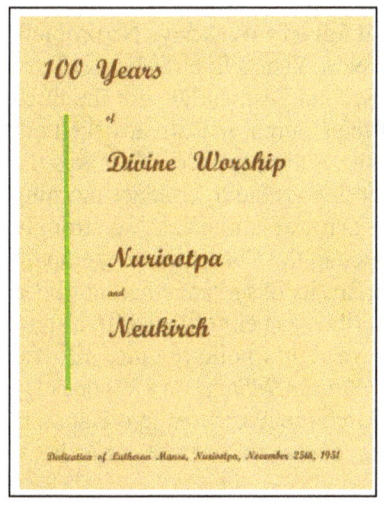

The erection of the manse was regarded as a memorial of 100 years of worship in Nuriootpa and Neukirch. I researched and had printed, with the above as its title, a history of the two congregations. It was available on the day, November 25, 1951, when the manse was dedicated by Pastor F.W. Albrecht. The provision of so much inbuilt furniture provided some personal problems regarding redundant furniture for us; for example, my tall set of bookshelves, built for our Adelaide residences, found use in father's studies in Stonefield and Tanunda for many years.

In 1958 the careful initial planning of the manse was demonstrated and bore fruit when it was resolved to add an additional north-western room as the "visitors' room". The plaster on the existing wall could be carefully chipped away at the spot shown on the original plan, to reveal the doorway that had been bricked in for this future addition.

Matters of Worship

There was a good tradition of worship in the two congregations. Even when it was part of a three-congregation parish Nuriootpa had held two services every Sunday, whether preaching or lay-reading: one in the morning, one in the evening. Of course, as in all large congregations, there was a substantial percentage of 'sleeping' members. The percentage of these was small in Neukirch; the level of spiritual life there brought joy to the pastor's heart. The initial basic structure of the service plan for the parish therefore was shaped like this:

Sunday 1: 10.00 a.m. Nuriootpa (preaching);
   10.00 a.m. Neukirch (reader) or 2.30 p.m. (preaching);
   7.30 p.m. Nuriootpa (preaching, especially if a.m.
               service German, or reader).
Sunday 2: 10.00 a.m. Neukirch (preaching);
   10.00 a.m. Nuriootpa (reader);
   7.30 p.m. Nuriootpa (preaching).
There was alternate sharing of time on high festival days.

One change in times of worship helped to spark a gradual rethink throughout the UELCA regarding worship before the usual 10.00 or 10.30 a.m. service. In 1952 Sieg Held experimented in his Tanunda, St. John, parish with conducting some 8.30 a.m. services during the warmer season. As Christmas drew near in that year Neukirch (mindful of what had happened in Tanunda) suggested that instead of a 2.30 p.m. service on Christmas Day (according to basic structure) an 8.30 a.m. service should be tried. Christmas Day morning was delightful, the afternoon was very hot. What members said among themselves after that experience was resolved in a meeting in February 1953, viz. In place of 2.30 p.m. services, 8.30 a.m. services should be conducted till mid-year. During the summer there could be two morning services: Neukirch, followed by Nuriootpa. Such a time of worshipping was so foreign to previous thinking that the early worshippers faced questions like: *'Are you turning Roman Catholic?'* Nuriootpa followed suit more hesitantly and less frequently; on Easter Sunday 1953 it gathered at 8.30 a.m. for the morning service, and on Christmas Day at 9.00 a.m. Neukirch's flexibility regarding time made it possible for me, using 1953 as an example, to conduct regular services in Daveyston and in Ebenezer, in the absence of respective parish pastors, and even to assist in the Angaston parish.

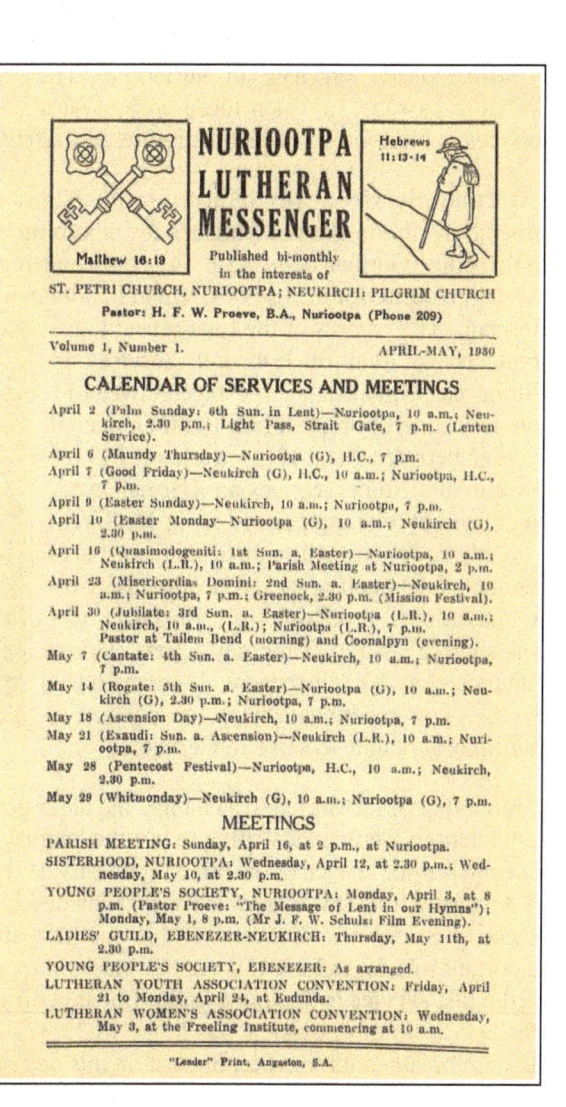

Chapter 4

There was a problem of varied nature regarding services for religious days that fell on a **weekday.** No problem with Christmas Eve and Christmas Day, Maundy Thursday and Good Friday, New Year's Eve (Sylvester Eve) and New Year's Day; and no problem regarding the German services on the Second Festival Days at the three high festivals. The Festival of Ascension, one of the earliest high festivals of the Church, had already died out in some areas of the Church, e.g. in N.S.W., but survived in S.A., usually as an evening service. That was the case in Nuriootpa; in Neukirch however, as a strongly rural congregation, it was possible to conduct morning services. – January 6, however, as Epiphany Day and the end of the 'Twelve Days of Christmas', so strongly upheld in the Orthodox Church, apparently has not survived as a weekday service in the Church. My attempt to reintroduce a service on a weekday fell away after my departure from the parish; its observance had not been consistent enough to take root against an attitude that can probably be best described as being filled with a spirit that thought: 'We've had enough "church" at Christmas and the end of the year; it's holiday time, also for pastors'. – Neukirch still adhered to celebrating the Fourth Day of Repentance (*Vierter Bußtag*) on a Wednesday in November. The delightful story was told me that many years earlier a Neukirch member went into Kapunda after the morning service, still dressed in his Sunday finery. A Kapunda resident expressed surprise at his dress. *'Don't you know,'* replied the Neukircher, *'Today is our BOOZE day!'*

There were excellent teams of lay-readers in both congregations; but the absence of a pastor at the service unfortunately did have some effect on attendance in Nuriootpa in the evenings. As the years passed by I began a substitution of some evening lay-reading services in Nuriootpa. The first type were **'Hymns Services'**, at which, in addition to normal Scripture readings, the words of the hymns constituted the message. I chose a variety of hymns, usually 7 in number: Lutheran and non-Lutheran, well-loved hymns and hymns with tunes that were less well-known; I introduced new tunes that the Hymn Book Committee was introducing into the coming new hymnbook. I gave information about the hymns, especially their origin, and about the hymn writers and tune composers. I conducted 22 of these in Nuriootpa and 4 in Neukirch. – From 1957 I also conducted 11 **'Bible Study Services'** in Nuriootpa. The sermon was replaced with a Bible study style treatment of a Scripture passage, in which those present were encouraged to take active part. – I also experimented with 3 services in Nuriootpa at which **religious film-strips** provided the message within a liturgical framework.

German Services. My ministry in the Nuriootpa parish took place at a time when there were still some generations in the Barossa parishes for whom the German language struck chords in the heart, or who at least could follow German quite well. My comments regarding Communion services have already revealed that there was still a desire for the use of German in both congregations – e.g. the Neukirch Male Choir very often sang in German. The records of the time reveal that I conducted a total of 114 such services in Nuriootpa (with an annual average between 11 and 13), and 105 in Neukirch (with an annual average between 9 and 11) – a total of 219 for the parish. Some services in German were conducted by visiting pastors or, in Neukirch, by readers. In those 10 years of ministry I also conducted 13 such services in other Barossa congregations: Stockwell (5), Ebenezer (4), Gnadenberg, Nain, Langmeil, Rest Home Tanunda (1 each). There were also many other Barossa congregations where the pastors at that time were able to serve in German.

St John's, Tanunda, interior

A number of factors led to a change: the older generations dying, the lessening in number of pastors who were competent in German or willing to use the language, 'patriotic' objection to its use. So the situation developed that one service at each of the three high festivals was conducted for the entire Barossa by Pastor Norman Sander of Angaston, then by Wladimir ('Ken') Jaworski in St. John's Tanunda, and finally by me by courtesy of the pastor of St. John's. Concerning this one-time stronghold of the Lutheran Church where German played an important role for at least 150 years, I place on record in these Memoirs that I conducted what has turned out to be the **last service in German in the Barossa on Good Friday, April 10, 2009, in St. John's, Tanunda.** The *Predigttext* on this occasion was Mark 15,33-37. The language of the founders of the Lutheran Church in the Barossa breathed its worshipping last on this occasion – unheralded as such, unnoticed, unrecorded, and largely unwanted.

The Sacraments. In Nuriootpa my ministry was marked by many **baptisms** (207 in number). In August 1951, according to what I was told locally, I conducted the first quadruple baptism in the church. I conducted 5 such baptisms. In addition I had 5 triple baptisms and 21 double baptisms. On such occasions I had to play the part of a 'sergeant-major' to ensure that orderliness reigned. But best-laid plans can go astray. At one of the quadruple baptisms, as the first child was held over the font, I proclaimed: '*A.B., I baptise thee in the name etc.*'. The sponsor holding the child began to quiver strongly, and quavered: *'Pastor, you gave the wrong name!'* I straightened up, surveyed the 19 persons around the font, and saw that the group that I had said should stand in third place had placed itself at the head. So I announced to the congregation: *'The child that we have just baptised is named C.D.'* I had been prepared for such an occurrence! The day before, in confirmation instruction that was dealing with baptism, I had put the question to the children for discussion: *'If a pastor happens to give a wrong name at baptism, should he baptise again?'* Under my guidance the children gave their opinions, and the outcome was that they realised that, as important as the naming of a child might be, the essential feature in baptism was the baptising with water.

During the years I made two changes in connection with **Holy Communion**.

I increased the opportunity to commune from the once per quarter that was usual at that time; my services records indicate for 1953 the following: in Nuriootpa 11 English and 7 German communion services, in Neukirch 5 English and 5 German; for 1954, in Nuriootpa 8 English and 6 German, in Neukirch 6 English and 6 German communion services. At that time a long-held practice was still upheld in the modified form that those who desired to commune announced themselves (generally in groups) before the service in the vestry to the pastor or to the allocated elder to be recorded and to participate in a pre-Communion prayer.

I increased the number of communion services to 12 per annum in Nuriootpa, so that the opportunity to commune was offered more than 4 times per annum. I have not been a sacramentalist in the sense that I advocated that every service, or every second service, should be a communion service. It seems to me that the preaching in the church becomes poorer, and that is an element of opus operato (thinking – good work) in the attendance. I also introduced an Epiphany service in the parish, and I was disappointed when my successor dropped them.

The second change was connected with the distribution of the Sacrament. In Nuriootpa it was still the practice to have strictly separated tables, first of men, then of women. A couple, Otto Kruger and wife, who joined Nuriootpa after shifting from Yadnarie (on Eyre Peninsula), had been used to communing together. In response to their query, I placed the matter of communing together, with explanations, before a meeting of the congregation. It agreed that this should be permitted, leaving its introduction to me. This took place at the next English communion service – the strongly attended Good Friday service. In accordance with my instructions there were three segments in the distribution: first the time-honoured practice, viz. tables of men, followed by tables of women, finally those who desired to commune together. The result was amazing! There were a few tables of men and of women (possibly about 2 of each), and the majority of communicants came as the third group. One couple who had celebrated their golden wedding quite recently were deeply moved as they declared this was the first time they had communed together. I followed this same procedure about twice, and then it was no longer necessary.

Religious Instruction of the Young.

My ministry in the Nuriootpa parish was my one ministry in which a **Lutheran School** figured. This Neukirch School was a combined venture of interested members of the Neukirch and Ebenezer congregations without being supported by the two congregations. The one-time manse used by Pastor E.D. Appelt on the Neukirch property served as its building. The school was opened in the year before I came, and on December 17, 1959, Pastor George Venz conducted the closing rite, so that its existence coincided almost exactly with my ministry. The Ebenezer pastor and I were its spiritual leaders. At the very first service that I conducted in Neukirch (February 5, 1950) I inducted its second teacher. The turnover of teachers was by no means a reflection on their dedicated service; they enjoyed the full confidence of the parents who supported the school, and successive State School Inspectors praised their work. They were: Gladys Leschke 1949, Rhoda Wiencke 1950-1951, Vera Dittrich 1952, Betty Ahrens 1953, Ruth Wegner 1954-1957, Helen Wiencke 1958-1959.

Former Neukirch manse, used as Lutheran school

Chapter 4

56 children received Christian instruction during these 11 years. The closure of the school was accelerated by the removal of the large Ben Kleinig family to Cookes Plains, and the successful examinations of a large Grade VII class, leaving only about 9 children in the school. The parents had kept the school going by foregoing attractive things of life. For example, the B. Kleinig family did not buy the new marvel of communication, a television set, because to them the school was more essential.

The alternative form of instruction for children was the **Sunday School**. Both congregations had one and were blessed with interested and capable teachers. With the full co-operation of its Sunday School Committee I immediately inaugurated regular meetings of the Nuriootpa Sunday School teachers, at which teaching methods etc. and problems connected with the Sunday School were discussed. Neukirch teachers sought opportunity to participate on occasions. An example of the results of such discussion was that interested confirmees were encouraged to attach themselves as assistant to a teacher and thus learn the art of *teaching* through observation. – A problem that increased as the years went by was the housing of eight classes in the increasing large school of over 100. These met in the commodious Church Hall. As a first step metal screens with a canvas insert solved the problem of the distraction of sight of other classes, and lessened the distraction of sound. Ultimately, at the end of 1958 the bold plan of building **Sunday School Rooms** was decided upon by the congregation because it was envisaged that in four years' time the Sunday School would have more than 200 pupils. Laurie Mader planned the building, with input from the teachers; it was commodious, and included several rooms that could be screened off into two rooms. The building was erected partly on land north of the church hall / manse block that had been bought by the congregation. The members of the congregation reacted wholeheartedly to an appeal for voluntary labour, so that the main expense was the cost of materials. The project began on February 7, 1959, with clearing of the site. On May 24 the foundation stone was laid by the highly-esteemed member who had served as teacher for decades, O.J. Krieg. The demands on time created by hosting the General Synod of the UELCA, delayed the completion of the project before I left Nuriootpa, but I was invited back to officiate at the dedication of the building.

Nuriootpa church hall

I have a vivid recollection of the meeting at which the above-mentioned purchase of property was decided upon, because of the strong action I took at it – an action never before and never again contemplated. Very many members had been openly speaking in favour of the purchase before the meeting took place. When the meeting began the former chairman of the congregation asked whether there was a quorum present – we knew he was against the proposal. I was well versed in the minutes of the congregation and had noticed at the time of reading that under this man's chairmanship there had been many meetings without a quorum. I replied that there was not a quorum present, but that I had noticed that many previous meetings had been conducted without a quorum, and therefore considered that this meeting could proceed. The proposal to buy was wholeheartedly adopted, and endorsed (as required by congregational rules) at a second meeting. But the ex-chairman, whose word had once been equivalent to law, and who suffered from what he called 'arthuritis', suffered so serious an irritation (*-itis*) of 'Arthur' that he attended no more meetings.

The third area of religious instruction of the young was **religious instruction in the State Schools**. Here, and in the presentation of work with organisations in the parish I will (to avoid unnecessary repetitions) include comments relating to the Point Pass parish as well.

In North Adelaide I had limited involvement at the North Adelaide Primary School. In Nuriootpa it became a full morning's undertaking: Nuriootpa Primary School (where I was for a time a member of the School Committee); Nuriootpa High School, together with other Lutheran pastors, where I had the senior forms; the full school at Ebenezer and at Stockwell Primary School (at the request of H.F.W. Roehrs); and for a time, at Father's request, at St. Kitts Primary School. I took this opportunity very seriously.

As a help to remembering my instruction I traced and duplicated small Bible History illustrations with a brief summary, which the children pasted into a special religious instruction exercise book. This was a time-consuming activity; but I believe it was worthwhile. Later, on several occasions former pupils expressed their thanks for my instruction and its visual presentation. Two Uniting Church girls at Ebenezer received prizes from the Uniting Church Sunday School in Nuriootpa for excellent biblical knowledge. Their mother told me, she commended them for this. *'But don't forget we had Pastor Proeve at school'* was their reply. – Some senior boys in the Nuriootpa High School group were somewhat of a problem with their lack of attention and antics. I stopped short in my presentation one day, and said nothing for a time until their actions stopped. *'I'm worried by the actions of some of you'*, I said. *'It's not the first time I have seen such actions, but they did not worry me on that occasion; but this time it worries me. The other occasion was at the Parkside Mental Hospital!'*

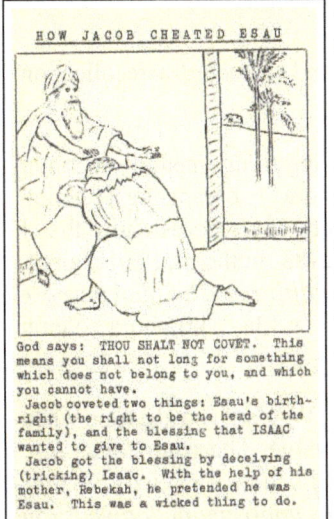

In the **Point Pass parish** I had a similar day in schools, with instruction on the same lines as in Nuriootpa; but it involved more time and a wider area. It began in the morning in the Eudunda Higher Primary School, where we three Lutheran pastors (M.T. Renner, E.W. Wiebusch ELCA, and I) taught. Audrey Schutz of Point Pass accompanied me to teach the youngest class, for which she, after my example, prepared illustrations. When Adolph ('Ardie') E. Schirmer replaced Wiebusch he took out the ELCA children from the combined groups. At that stage the traditional ELCA attitude must have been lingering in his system; after the amalgamation he was a highly valued worker in the LCA. – Before lunch there was instruction in the Robertstown Primary School, where Nellie (Thusnelda) Pfitzner taught the junior children. After lunch, eaten somewhere between Robertstown and Black Springs, I had the entire school at Black Springs Primary, about 37 km distant from Point Pass.

Bible History illustration

Confirmation instruction was the next stage in the instruction of the young. To me this was a vital time of instruction, which warranted preparation and clear, thoughtful presentation. Standing at the threshold of adulthood, it was the opportunity to establish them in their faith by means of one of the Symbolical Books of the Lutheran Church – Luther's Small Catechism. In some sections, especially the Ten Commandments, I encouraged them to think through the meaning of these sections. I expected them to know the Catechism text, and according to ability to learn the most pertinent Scripture passages set out in the exposition of our UELCA catechism, and selected hymns. I was pleased if they answered questions in their own words, not in the words of the exposition. – An answer in a confirmation examination before the congregation in Point Pass continues to raise an approving smile on my face whenever I recall it. One of the boys was not gifted to learn by heart. Following my usual practice of letting the answer to a question sometimes determine my next question, when the word 'hypocrite' was used on this occasion in an answer, I asked the question: 'What is a hypocrite?' The boy's hand shot up, so I naturally let him answer. *'Please, Pastor, someone who goes to church on Sunday and swears on Monday'*. As an impressed elder put it: *'I didn't think it was in him! It shows that he understands'*.

In Nuriootpa I had some large classes of more than a dozen children, and the total number that I confirmed was 90 in Nuriootpa, 31 in Neukirch, and 4 in Ebenezer. R.B. Reuther had managed to get permission from the Nuriootpa High School to teach his children in released time on Tuesdays. I inherited this permission too, and taught my children for a time on Tuesdays as well as on Saturdays. The confirmation in Ebenezer (due to a vacancy in the parish before Pastor G. Venz came) is a reminder that my class was greatly increased in size by teaching Strait Gate Light Pass children (Pastor Reuther's absence), and on two separate occasions Bethany parish children (Pastor Roehrs being ill, and on the second occasion away in Europe, but back in time to confirm) – in the vicinity of 40 children!

Confirmation class, 1951 – one of many classes

Chapter 4

Treasured memories of my confirmation teaching is that three of the boys trained to be Lutheran pastors: Marcus Schultz (Nuriootpa), Dr. John Kleinig (Neukirch), Vernon Schutz (Point Pass); and 5 of the girls served as wives of pastors: North Adelaide – Ruth Linsenmeier (Clem Schmidt) and Laurel Sander (Dr. Ivan Wittwer); Nuriootpa – Carol Proeve (John Wilksch) and (Neukirch) – Edna Heintze (Peter Welke); Point Pass (Julia) – Jennifer Henschke (Geoff Hartwig).

In Nuriootpa, from 1951 onwards, by decision of the mothers, girls wore small veils at their confirmation. This was a practice not unknown in the Lutheran Church, but it did not survive after my departure from Nuriootpa.

I am reopening this section in August 2013 as a result of receiving a letter, and to record a recollection connected with confirmation that has been aroused in my mind.

28 years after I had left Nuriootpa several 'confirmation girls', including according to my memory Marilyn Elix (nee Gladigau), contacted me that they had been seeking present whereabouts and were organising a reunion of all those that I had confirmed in Nuriootpa. A very good percentage attended. My records show that I conducted this unusual and moving Confirmees' Reunion Service on August 28, 1988, in the St. Petri church, and preached on Matthew 5,13-16. My sermon notes record the theme: *Continue to fulfil your Christian purpose in life: for you are salt and light.* This, I pointed out, was a glorious opportunity (v.13a, 14a) and a solemn responsibility (v.13b, 14b-16).

The above-mentioned letter from a Mrs Margaret Symonds, nee Zerner, in Harvey, WA, arrived at a time when ongoing health problems had considerably lowered my spirit and view of life's value. The letter said: *"I'm writing from the past as I am one of your old confirmees from St. Petri, Nuriootpa. I believe 1958 was the year and at the time you were our resident minister. I felt like writing to you to express my appreciation for what you did for us all, those many years ago. The firm and invaluable Christian foundation you instilled in us to prepare for life is only appreciated through maturity. When I see young people who have no proper guidance these days I feel very thankful for your teaching and help. ... The Barossa has certainly changed since we lived there, but I have lovely memories of living in Nuriootpa, having experienced warm friendships that have continued to this day and being brought up in a loving Christian God-fearing family.* ... That has been one heart-warming answer to the question that many a pastor has admitted passes through his mind at the time of confirmation: *'What will become of these young people?'*

The final stage of work with the youth was the **Lutheran Young People's Society** (in the ELCA known as the 'Luther League'). The usual span of membership was after confirmation until marriage. I have the impression that rural youth were slightly more likely to be consistent members than town youth were – I believe this applies to Neukirch (25 and 23 at beginning and end of ministry) and Nuriootpa (46 and 63) respectively, and to the basically rural congregations that constituted the Point Pass parish. There was good leadership available in all Societies.

25th Youth banquet

The amount of talent available in the Nuriootpa Society made possible very creditable annual concerts, including choral items and plays; the entrance fees were adults 3/6, children 1/6! The combined Ebenezer-Neukirch Society, in which we two pastors alternated in supervision, also held annual concerts. Bible studies were a regular in all societies, and talks with a religious background were frequently given. Both societies conducted socials at times. Various games (e.g. musical chairs) were the chief feature; dancing was taboo at that time, except for some forms of square dancing (first introduced in the Luther League). A devotion and (in Nuriootpa) the singing of the two last stanzas of *'Now rest beneath night's shadow'*: *Lord Jesus, who dost love me* and *My loved ones, rest securely*, closed the social. I was aware that some less spiritual youth from other quarters who shopped around for such entertainment could pass the comment, *'Now comes the commercial!'*

Work among and with the youth was enjoyable, but it also involved a good deal of time and effort. For quite a number of years I provided a duplicated small 'flyer' to announce the next Nuriootpa Youth Society meeting, writing it up in a 'catchy' style in the hope of attracting interest and attendance.

In the **Point Pass parish** the organised pattern of youth society activity was very similar to that in the Nuriootpa parish: monthly meetings, Bible study style devotionals and at times study topics, miscellaneous topics, socials. The difference was that more of my time was taken up in each month, as there were 4 societies (generally with good leaders): Point Pass, Robertstown (attended also by some Geranium Plain youth), Peep Hill, Julia. They were smaller than in the Nuriootpa parish, with a total membership that varies in the 60s and 50s during my ministry. Youth Camps were held in conjunction with the youth of the Eudunda parish (also with good leaders), in August 1960 at 'Adare', Victor Harbor, under the theme 'You are God's People', and in February 1965 at Lake Bonney, Barmera, under the theme 'Living in Christ'.

Women's and Men's Societies

Sisterhoods / Ladies' Guilds / Women's Guilds. In the Nuriootpa parish there was the *Nuriootpa Sisterhood* and the *Neukirch-Ebenezer Ladies' Guild*; in the Point Pass parish there were under our care – for Dorothy most of the time was President of all 5 guilds – the *Point Pass Women's Guild*, the *Robertstown Sisterhood*, the *Geranium Plain, Julia* and *Peep Hill Ladies' Guilds*. The term *Ladies Guild* apparently came into use, in preference to *Women's Guild*, as the English equivalent of *Frauenverein*; but that term arouses in me the perhaps absurd question: Should not a men's counterpart then be termed *Gentlemen's Society*? The term *Sisterhood* has had ongoing difficulty in becoming a standard term in the Church as the most fitting counterpart to *Brotherhood* (which also had its difficulties, despite the Scriptural word *brother*). Amazing however, at the time when I write this (2013) the gaudily pink-painted Priceline Pharmacy in Tanunda has instituted a *'Sisterhood'*, the members of which are encouraged to gain valuable points as they purchase non-prescription medical lines and especially plenty of cosmetics!

Whatever the name, the seven women's groups with which Dorothy and I were associated were a joy to work with; they were eager groups, who sought to study the Scriptures as their inspiration, and to serve the congregations and parish and Church in general with their gifts. They put the men to shame.

Celebrating 40th birthday with dear friends

The Nuriootpa Sisterhood was a large group, numbering 100 to 107 members, with Dorothy (President) and Hazel Mader (Secretary) a close working Executive nucleus. It sponsored some furnishings in the manse and improvements in the Church Hall, and strongly supported projects of the Lutheran Women's Association, especially Christmas Cheer for the New Guinea Mission. A substantial number formed the Sanctuary Helpers, who cared for the sanctuary and provided paraments. – The celebration of my 40th birthday (November 2, 1958) had particularly aspects that embraced sorrow and rejoicing. I was called in the afternoon to comfort the wife of J.F. Roocke, who had suddenly died that day. I returned home to find that a surprise evening, attended by 250 people, had been arranged by the Sisterhood. The cake had been iced by Mrs. J.F. Roocke and was still standing in a next-door room while I was ministering to the sorrowing widow. The Sisterhood announced that evening that as a birthday gift a new *Talar* (black robes) should be made for me, which was done by Miss Laura Pfitzner of Eudunda. Those robes served me till the end of my ministry.

Chapter 4

Once a year a few women from other guilds, and some men (including as a regular visitor Albert Doecke of the Immanuel College staff) gathered with some of the local women inside and outside the Nuriootpa Church Hall to prepare jam for Immanuel College and Seminary. Apricots in particular, and also plums, came from various Barossa quarters (diligently collected by Oswald Zilm of Nain). Inside, in the supper room, the fruit was cut; outside stood up to 10 well-cleaned coppers, in which the fruit was boiled and stirred with long stirrers. At least 100 gallons of jam – in a peak year 205 gallons – in 4-gallon kerosene tins were transported to Adelaide as a result of this happy day of activity. – Another individual project of guilds was to pickle eggs in 4-gallon tins for the College and Seminary.

Upon reflection I must say that the participation of women in the Point Pass parish was percentage-wise a little better than in Nuriootpa; there were over 100 members (111 in 1960, 102 in 1965) in the 5 guilds. Three of these (Geranium Plain, Peep Hill, Julia) had only 13 or 14 members each, but they were not weak or ineffective guilds – there was strong cohesion. For example, there was generally a 100 per cent attendance at a Geranium Plain meeting; if not, it could be assumed that the absent person was sick, away, or unexpectedly prevented from attending. I have often heard criticism of small congregations that have decided to continue despite pressures to close down; and I have defended them because they have almost consistently been more cohesive, and have been 'bright spots' in my three-parish ministry.

Brotherhood. The formation of men's societies as Brotherhoods was a mid-20th century development in the UELCA, and had only limited success; but they served their purpose well with those who were minded to join. Membership in existing community service groups like Rotary, Apex, Lions, Kiwanis, probably affected the response. This is demonstrated in the Parish Brotherhood in my two parishes. The Nuriootpa Parish Brotherhood was formed in mid-1955, and at the end of my ministry had 20 Nuriootpa and 5 Neukirch members. In the Point Pass the reorganised Parish Brotherhood had as membership: Point Pass 6 (1964: 2), Robertstown 6 (4), Julia 2 (-), Peep Hill 2 (2), Geranium Plain 1 (1), a total of 17, a proportionately good number, which however shrank to 9 at the end of my ministry. As I write this in mid-2013 the Langmeil Brotherhood of 5 members in a large congregation has quietly died. A 'Men's Shed' concept, not necessarily Lutheran in concept, has taken over within the LCA.

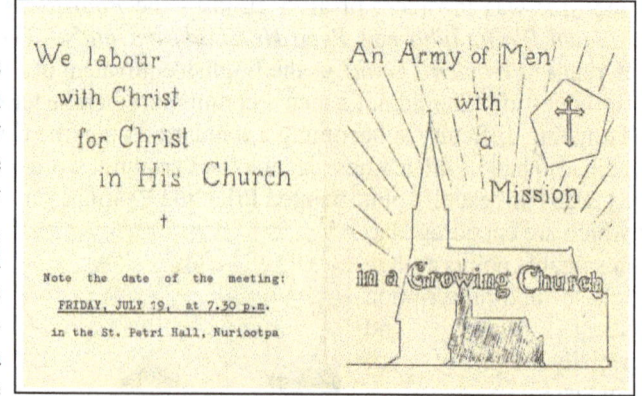

Miscellaneous Memories

Encouraging Giving. I was advised by the District authorities after I had accepted the call to Nuriootpa, that one of my early tasks would be to lift the financial awareness of the Nuriootpa congregation. It belonged to those congregations that (as one District Synod resolution expressed it) 'have not responded to the extent expected of them'. The other two congregations in the one-time St. John's, Tanunda parish had long complained that Nuriootpa was 'not pulling its weight'. I found that the practice in Nuriootpa, in addition to paying a fixed annual stipend contribution, was to have 24 special offerings (when there was a morning preaching service) for the funds of the UELCA. After one year I found that the average Neukirch contribution per communicant member to local congregation and UELCA needs was 3 times greater than the Nuriootpa average.

I repeatedly wrote encouragingly in the parish paper, stressing that it was 'much more than a matter of simple arithmetic in money matters. It is a matter of love toward God and His Church on earth, and it is a matter of Christian co-operation with fellow congregations that our Church may be able to carry out its necessary programme in the preaching of the Gospel'. However, in another issue, after stressing that each member should determine the 'proportion' of his income that he intended to set aside for Church purposes, I provided a mathematical guide how this could be divided between congregational needs and current and special requirements of the general UELCA. – In mid-1953 a review of the system of giving led to a meeting of the congregation allowing the introduction of a duplex-envelope system from October onwards for a trial of one year. The Treasurer of the congregation, not keen on the idea but not actively opposed to it, stated that he could not manage this system. A group of younger members under the experienced leadership of Theo Proeve, who had masterminded the scheme in North Adelaide, undertook to handle it, and it became an ongoing arrangement that gradually produced results. The weekly envelope had two pockets, the left one 'For the Congregation', the other 'For the Church'.

Chapter 4

Parish Papers. In Chapter III I wrote about the *Immanuel Lutheran* that I established. In the two other parishes that I served I immediately established parish papers to record and disseminate parish news. The *Nuriootpa Lutheran Messenger* began in April 1950 as a printed paper. After a brief period of printing by *The Leader* in Angaston I used Auricht's Printing Office as my regular printer. In January 1958, however, I began to duplicate it as a monthly folded-quarto publication. In Point Pass I duplicated monthly a new folded foolscap publication, the *Point Pass Lutheran*. It replaced the quarterly parish papers of the two preceding Point Pass parishes, the *Lutheran Messenger* of Immanuel and the *Lutheran Tidings* of St. Peter's. I did many a drawing on stencils – a rather labour-intensive process because of the danger of tearing the stencil – in an attempt to give these duplicated publications an attractive appearance. I also the changed the colour of the duplicating paper for each issue.

Nuriootpa Cemetery Saga. Congregational histories occasionally have stories about the problems that have arisen in reference to their trustees. I inherited a problem because Nuriootpa originally had trustees. It related to the local cemetery.

William Coulthard, the founder of Nuriootpa, gave a parcel of land on the western side of the township to the Nuriootpa congregation to serve as a cemetery. Early in the 20th century the trustees of the congregation divested themselves of the control of the cemetery by handing over the details of management to a Cemetery Improvement Committee, which they appointed. Its original members apparently were members of the congregation. Nothing of this was ever recorded in the minutes of the congregation, so that the congregation was unaware of the precise situation; the only record was encased in the inaugural minutes of the Improvement Committee. As the years flowed by the Committee took its own steps to fill vacancies with persons, whether Lutheran or not – there was no reporting to the congregation regarding its activities and decisions, which had treated it as a public cemetery. In 1951, when the Committee resolved to purchase the northern adjoining parcel of land and to add it to the cemetery that it 'owned', it discovered that it did not own the cemetery it was managing; and that in fact the Committee had no legal standing, and first had to become an incorporated body. Some hotheads on the Committee wanted to foist the cemetery back on the congregation. The congregation had no desire to take over what had become a 'public cemetery'; but it came to light that any decision by the congregation to transfer the cemetery to the Nuriootpa Cemetery Trust struck complications associated with caveats attached to Coulthard's original gift. For about two years Bert Teusner had discussions that wrestled with the mammoth task of finding a solution. For a long time it seemed that the only solution was an Act of the S.A. Parliament releasing the congregation from the caveats. Ultimately consultation between Mr. Teusner and the Attorney-General of S.A. devised a procedure that hopefully would withstand any legal challenge.

The requirements were that the congregation had to hold a special meeting of its voting members to adopt the carefully worded motions supplied by the legal experts. Notice of the meeting with the proposed motions appended had to be posted to every voting member. The ordinary quorum stipulated in the constitution of the congregation (which was often attained with difficulty) was not sufficient; a special quorum was required. It was an extraordinarily high percentage of all voting members, involving (as much as I can recall) well over 100 persons. I realised that the only way to be sure of having such an extraordinary quorum was to have the meeting immediately after a morning service. And so on August 30, 1953, when a service with three baptisms and Holy Communion had closed, the voting members were 'kept in', and the long-standing problem of the Nuriootpa cemetery was brought to a successful end.

Henry delivers the Christmas message at Nuriootpa

Joys and Sorrows in Pastoral Activity. The fact that my 10-year ministry in Nuriootpa was almost as long as the combined years (11¾) in North Adelaide and Point Pass possibly is the reason why the above is especially associated with Nuriootpa. In North Adelaide the sorrows were of a personal family nature, sharing with Dorothy the griefs in her family: her mother's death in April 1944 after suffering, then the joy of her father's second marriage, which was however plunged into grief only two months later through his death in December 1947 following a tragic car accident. As mentioned in Chapter II, when Gertrud Muetzelfeldt died I felt that in my youthful inexperience I could only inadequately be a *Seelsorger* to my respected teacher in a funeral sermon.

Chapter 4

Sorrow, but in Christian hope, came early in the Nuriootpa ministry: Carl Juncken, the Nuriootpa member who had contact with me before I came to Nuriootpa, was stricken with cancer. In addition to my personal ministration, there were weekly prayer gatherings at the request of his workmen. Arthur Reusch, the Nuriootpa chemist, took me to task that I always committed the answer to the Lord in His wisdom. He was inclined to be influenced by every religious figure that he encountered. One year, while he was in England, he sent to Oswald Krieg a tape recording by his latest 'discovery'; it contained the punchline *'Receive the Holy Spirit'*, followed by the sound of breathing strongly several times into the microphone. Oswald was by no means impressed.

Soon afterwards 20 year-old Verna Schiller was stricken with Hodgkin's Disease. I was called upon to tell her and her parents and siblings that her days were numbered. With believing heart Verna received the assurance of Romans 8, of which I reminded her as I gave her the news. It was a privilege to minister to her, and she comforted her family members as much as they comforted her. Romans 8,35,37-39 naturally was the basis for my funeral address. Her love for the Church of our Lord was demonstrated even after death with a bequest of £20 from her young estate.

Two suicides in Nuriootpa were the source of heart-searching, especially the first one. He was a sincere believer, but became depressed over the building of his house. He confided his temptations to me, and one night I sought to strengthen his faith with Scripture and prayer. Next morning I was woken with the news that he had hanged himself from the rafters of his house. A shocked pastor, mindful of all the evidence of trusting faith that he had witnessed, could only cry out in anguish, *Lord, have mercy*. At the funeral service I took refuge in the words of Jesus, John 16,33: "These things I have spoken unto you, that in me ye might have peace. In the world ye shall have tribulation: but be of good cheer; I have overcome the world." By the grace of God the spiritual life of his widow and family was not shattered. I had a third case of suicide in Point Pass.

One summer day I conducted a funeral in the Nuriootpa cemetery. The grave, we found out, had been dug a little too narrow at the 'shoulder' portion of the coffin. As a result the pallbearers at that end had to twist the coffin a little in order to lower it; the screws holding the lid popped, and the strong smell of death arose. With this smell still in my nostrils I left the cemetery without disrobing in order to enter the church and commence a marriage ceremony! – Last of all, I think of Christmas and its joy. One funeral in Nuriootpa was conducted on Christmas Day, and on this occasion I stressed that Christmas was not spoilt (as many people might say), because the true joy of Christmas was not centred on the usual Christmas celebrations but on the blessings for life associated with the birth of a Saviour. Many years later, on Kangaroo Island, I had to stress the same thought at a children's Christmas service (held before Christmas). I arrived at the service in time to give the address to the children. Why? Because I had been outside Kingscote comforting parents who had lost two children in an accident. I flew back to Adelaide with Christmas presents that were now earmarked for distribution to needy children. And years later, on December 26, 1993, I had to meditate on this same message about Christmas and its joy as I looked on a beloved wife who was 'asleep in Jesus' in the Royal Adelaide Hospital.

Joy fills my heart whenever I think of old *Mutter* Bartsch, a pious soul who went blind at about 18 years of age. She sat in the second row of pews close to the pastor's sedilia. Again and again I was amazed as she with quite a strong voice sang hymns in the German services. They were part of a treasury committed to memory, especially in the days of her confirmation instruction in Gruenberg. – On the other hand there was sorrowful concern in ministering to an older lady in Neukirch. She had developed religious mania, fed by programmes from sectarian sources (especially Jehovah's Witnesses) that she listened to on the radio. On one of my visits she became particularly negative. As I prayed before leaving she broke into the prayer with a loud *'Nein, nein, das ist nicht wahr!'* ('No, no, that is not true'), slumped on to her knees in front of the radio, and with arms upraised demanded of it to send her a proper pastor who did not talk nonsense *('der nicht plappert')*. Ministering to her was an ongoing burden.

Under this heading I must include joy that were not associated with pastoral activity, but the joys of a family head, enjoying two or three Sundays off each year on holidays with wife and children. A number of times these were interstate trips (to Queensland or Victoria), or breaks at the beach, sometimes in F.W. Albrecht's shack at Sellicks Beach, and especially after we purchased a simple asbestos cottage at Aldinga Beach. Parking and exploring on the wide expanse of beach, playing with my young family in the sand dunes, is one of the memories I treasure. I hope my children do too, because the manifold duties that I had to carry out week by week robbed me of such time that loving fathers would usually spend with their children.

Chapter 4

Church Anniversaries

As long-standing congregations both Nuriootpa and Neukirch celebrated milestones in their history.

Neukirch/Ebenezer Centenary. Further research into Neukirch history and for the first time research into Ebenezer history corrected initial impressions regarding the date of arrival (early 1852, not 1851) and the site of the first services (Schneider's property next to the Ebenezer church, not 'Mickan's triangle' at Neukirch – which applied only to Neukirch). The congregations therefore postponed their combined centennial celebrations till March 10, 1952, when a marble stone was erected in the Ebenezer grounds near the church. A morning service with guest preachers W. Riedel and R. Held was held in St. John's Church. In the afternoon we two local pastors conducted outdoor services close to the Ebenezer cemetery and then in the Neukirch grounds close to the original cemetery. The very simple folded-quarto history with a red cover (selling for 6 pence) that I duplicated is, as far as I know, the first time that a history of Ebenezer appeared in print.

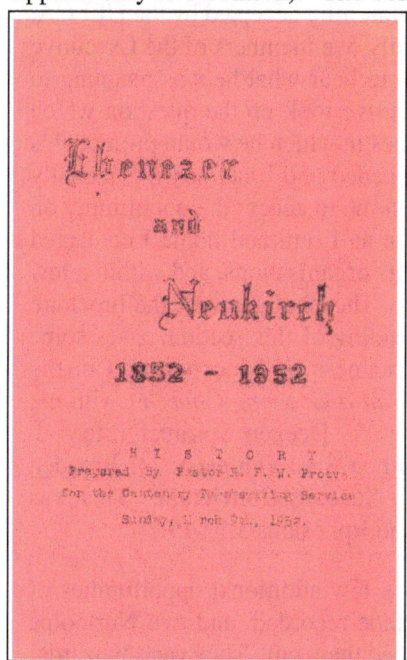

The Neukirch members were keen to keep their church and grounds in good condition. When electricity came to the district they renovated the interior of the church. The original cemetery near the church was lovingly cared for: pathways in the form of a cross were formed; a memorial stone was erected on the transept of these paths, bearing the names of all persons buried in it – I found out the full name connected with an incomplete church record; shrubs were planted to beautify it. This original cemetery had to be closed in the early years of the congregation: the water-table was so high that coffins had to be weighted to take them through the water to their last resting place. – The extensive strip of unused land along the entire northern boundary was gradually covered by several hundred pine trees of three species as beautification.

In <u>Nuriootpa</u>, as the 90th anniversary approached, the question became more urgent in mid-1956 what should be done about St. Petri church. My brochure, *'What Plans for the Future?'*, set out the situation regarding anticipated growth (possibly 870 baptised and 650 confirmed members in 1967), present size (usual seating 295, squeezed in 373), and condition of the church. Meetings in September and November (1956) resolved: 1. That the future planning regarding the church be based on the desire to build a new church or to rebuild the present one; 2. That for the 90th anniversary steps be taken to bring the church into reasonable repair by plastering of affected walls and the repainting of the interior, with expenditure to be kept at a minimum; 3. That a Centenary Church Building Fund be opened, and be added to each year at the time of the anniversary (November).

Photo on right: *Ebenezer history that Henry wrote in 2001-2*

So the first steps were taken for a major future development that took place under the next pastor, E.G. Stolz. Often when I look at the present St. Petri church I have a mental picture of one day when Erik von Schramek visited me while on a visit to the Barossa to monitor the progress on the Strait Gate Church in Light Pass that was being built. Expressing my concern that it appeared to me to be impractical to do anything to the St. Petri church, I asked what his thoughts were. With a stick Erik began to draw in the dirt of the allotment: a square *('The present bell-tower must be retained')*; a little to the north of the square a large rectangle running from the east (where the congregation now owned the adjoining allotment through the generosity of O.J. Krieg) to the west at Second Street *('The new church must have this orientation')*; two lines linking the square with the rectangle *('The tower must be connected to the church')*. That day I had a preview of what he designed in detail many years later.

Chapter 4

Two Noteworthy Events in the Parish

I close my memories of the Nuriootpa decade with two events in the latter and closing years of my ministry. I regard them as significant in the members' outlook on the Church and their Christian life in the Church.

1. Visit of Pastor M. David Fetter, 1957

Pastor David Fetter had a distinguished record of service in the American Lutheran Church, in which he built up large congregations in several cities. The Lutheran World Federation offered to make his services available to the UELCA for two years. This was gratefully accepted by the UELCA. After Pastor Fetter's arrival with his family, we members of the Executive of the General Church Council met him to hear what he was planning to do. When this had been done the Executive took up the question which parish should be the first of the six parishes in which he would promote his emphases. Because an early start was needed and I had heard personally his thinking, the other members called on me to accept the opportunity on behalf of the Nuriootpa parish. As soon as I returned home I contacted surprised parish officials and leaders of its organisations, and within a few days drew up a three-week programme. The photocopy of the brochure that I duplicated, reprinted under the heading of this section, gives some insight into the spiritual fullness and richness of 23 or so days in the Barossa. The theme was *'Spiritual Life in a Growing Church'*, with the sub-title *'Growth in Five Dimensions'*: 1. <u>Deepen</u> Spiritual Life; 2. <u>Heighten</u> Attendance Interest; 3. <u>Lengthen</u> Soul Outreach; 4. <u>Broaden</u> Organisation Participation; 5. <u>Intensify</u> Steward Conviction. This was completed with the encouragement to read Ephesians 3,17-19.

For three weeks Pastor Fetter used our home as his base; there he added a few additional opportunities of spreading his message. Every sermon, every talk, every presentation was tape-recorded, and two Nuriootpa sisters, Marie Schultz (later Heinrich) and Christine Schultz (later Dolling), typed them out. They were 'wizards' on the typewriter whose speed enabled them to turn the spoken words into written words, which were disseminated in duplicated form.

David Fetter worked under great nervous energy and pressure. For the first time he was facing the challenge of doing what he had done in American congregations in a parish where there was Australian thinking. Every evening he sat up with me (or us) and analysed, mostly into the wee hours of the next day, the reactions of the day among Australian Christians, and in what respect he might need to adjust his approach. Dorothy and I were not always able to fulfil his usual goodnight greeting, *'Sleep fast'* (rhyming with *hast*) before the morning called us up to necessary preliminary chores. When his visit was over we were fast asleep for an entire day!

In his farewell message David Fetter wrote: 'God be with you and strengthen you. … Your interest and enthusiasm exceeded my fondest expectation. … May your firm resolve be to put to work your time, talents and treasures, that neither your stewardship nor mine will have been in vain'.

Chapter 4

2. General Synod in Nuriootpa, September 23-28, 1959

An extra duty fell on me when the General Synod of the UELCA was held in September 1959: I was the pastor of the host parish. The wholehearted response in the parish, particularly by laymen who took on the responsibility for various aspects, preserved me from many a worry. Alma Linke very ably on behalf of her husband Edgar, the Quartermaster, found billets for 150 delegates in the district. Dr. Karl Basedow arranged displays of various works of the Church that attracted wide attention. Alf Cartwright made one half of his next-door store available for a temporary branch of the Lutheran Book Depot. Teams of men worked at the convention venue at the Soldiers' Memorial Hall and our church properties, including the daily parking of cars.

Over 100 voices from the choirs in the Barossa combined in practice from July onwards for a sacred concert; I planned the contents of this concert, based on the church year, with Norman Auricht, who relieved me of the necessity to be the conductor of the combined choir. Each church choir rendered an anthem under the baton of the respective conductor. Of the combined anthems I believe *'Hear my prayer'* with its soprano obligato *'O for the wings of a dove'*, by Mendelssohn, was the highlight; Hazel Mader's voice was at its peak at that time. The anthem for the Advent season that I duplicated, *'Veni Immanuel'* ("O come, O come, Immanuel') made such an impression on the choir conductors that I was inundated with requests for the music, so that they could use it in the forthcoming Advent season. Hundreds unfortunately had to be turned away from the SM Hall after the capacity attendance of 1,000 had been reached, and circumstances prevented a repeat of the concert. Dr. Carl Lundquist, Secretary of the LWF, who left for Europe next morning, declared that the sounds of this magnificent concert would continue to ring in his ears.

UELCA Pastors crossing the main street to go to the Soldiers' Memorial Hall

When the sisters of Nuriootpa and Neukirch came together to make arrangements for meals during the six days of the convention they amazed me with a proposal that I believe has remained unique: they insisted that the pastor and delegates of the Synod should be their guests in the full sense of the word, and that other visitors be offered meals at a very moderate price.

One feature that was the forerunner of later important connections was the presence of Pastor T.C. Sihombing, Secretary of the Batak Church. He was an interesting guest in our home.

Chapter 4

Pastors at the UELCA General Synod, Nuriootpa, 1959

The parish richly deserved the thanks that President M. Lohe expressed in a letter: 'On behalf of the United Evangelical Lutheran Church in Australia I desire to thank you very sincerely for the outstanding hospitality which you extended to the recent Synod in Nuriootpa. I want to assure you that the leaders of the Church, the pastors, delegates and visitors were overwhelmed, not only with the outstanding organisation and arrangements which were made, so that the Synod was able to proceed without hindrance. … The tributes of those who came from far and near were an indication of the excellence of the arrangements. I am certain that all those who attended the Synod at Nuriootpa will never forget the gracious hospitality, the kindness and the service, extended by the Nuriootpa parish'. The members of the Nuriootpa parish received some vision of the wideness of the Church in Australia, and I know that many interstate friendships were initiated.

Coronation service, Nuriootpa Oval, 1953

Hazel Mader & Henry practising for one of their many concerts

128

CALL

to

Pastor _Henry Proeve, B.A._

In the Name of our Lord Jesus Christ!

The Evangelical Lutheran Parish consisting of the congregations _St Petri, Nuriootpa_ _and_ _Pilgerkirche, Neukirch,_ assembled on the _thirtieth_ day of _August_, 19_49_, to elect in accordance with ecclesiastical usage a Pastor and "Seelsorger" with the result that you, Reverend Sir, have been chosen, which fact is respectfully made known to you by the undersigned through the presentation of this call.

I

The Parish trusts

1. That you will at all times teach and preach the Revealed Word of God of the Old and the New Testament in its truth and purity according to the Confessions of the Evangelical Lutheran Church of the year of our Lord 1580, in the _English and German_ language, and that your pastoral practice be regulated thereby;

2. That you will faithfully and conscientiously care for the instruction of the young in school and in confirmation class, _and Young People's Society._

3. That your pastoral care be directed especially to the weak and the doubting, the straying and the troubled, the sick and the dying; that you will visit, instruct, and generally deal with them after the manner of a faithful servant of the Lord Jesus Christ;

4. That you will preside at all congregational meetings, unless valid reasons forbid, and that you see to it that all things are done "decently and in order," and that church discipline be observed;

5. That you and yours, in word and deed, be an example for the young and the old in the congregation, and that you avoid giving offence through violating the scriptural and confessional standard, thus becoming a stumbling-block as is written 1. Timothy 3: 3-7; 2. Timothy 1: 6-11; etc.

II

On the other hand do we, the officers of the congregations above mentioned and all members thereof, declare ourselves in bond to you as our Pastor and "Seelsorger" as follows:

1. We one and all shall receive and honour you, and willingly submit ourselves to you as our Pastor and "Seelsorger" (1. Timothy 5: 17; Hebrews 13: 16-17); and we shall "communicate unto you in all good things" as is written Galatians 6: 6; 1. Corinthians 9: 7, 9: 10-14;

2. In proof whereof you shall receive a stipend of £_300_ per annum, which shall be paid to you in instalments every _month at Nuriootpa / 3 months at Neukirch_ months, a free dwelling, _Telephone rental £5, and reasonable travelling expenses._

3. For special ministrations you shall be entitled to special allowances, _such as baptisms, confirmations, weddings, burials; communion and festive offerings._

4. We grant you an annual vacation covering the time of _3_ Sundays, which may be determined by you.

May the Lord our God whose direction and guidance we have earnestly sought, through His Holy Spirit help you to find the answer well pleasing to Him, and may He, if such be His will, incline your heart to accept this call.

Dated this _thirtieth_ day of _August_, in the year of our Lord 19_49_.

For the Evangelical Lutheran Parish consisting of the Congregations—

Congregation: _St Petri Nuriootpa_ _A.E. Lange_

Congregation:

Congregation: _Pilgerkirche Neukirch_ _A.B. Kleinig_

Part of the Call document to Nuriootpa Parish, Aug 1949

Chapter 5

V. POINT PASS HALF-DECADE: 1960 (March) – 1965 (August)

V. A. POINT PASS PARISH

A fortnight after the General Synod closed in Nuriootpa I received a call to Point Pass. There had been a far-reaching development there – two complete parishes with four congregations in each one had been amalgamated into one parish. Two congregations in each parish had been amalgamated into two congregations (Point Pass and Robertstown), two churches were being closed (St. Petri, Point Pass, and Zion, Robertstown), the historic manse of Immanuel, Point Pass, would no longer serve as manse. So there were mixed feelings of loss among members of both congregations in Point Pass and Robertstown, as age-long separations were now to be healed; but there were some members in both places whose feelings still were pitched at the level of being inwardly, even verbally, opposed to the developments that affected their particular congregation. Thus, for example, I received a letter while still in Nuriootpa urging that I should refuse to move into the St. Petri manse and to demand that the Immanuel manse should be used.

Part of Call Document to Point Pass Parish, October 1959

I pondered over this call for about four weeks, and some of my colleague pastors expressed surprise that I elected to go to a totally rural 'backwater' area, where the parish centre was a tiny village with scarcely any facilities, where the closing down of the small telephone service over the weekend and public holidays meant that the Secretary of the UELCA could not be contacted on Telephone 3 during such closures. I was aware of that, and I was also conscious of the fact that Dorothy and the children were more in isolation than heretofore, especially when I was away with the car on some series of meetings. (For this reason one of the first purchases after our shift was one of the new gadgets that we had only admired and marvelled over through a shop window while in Nuriootpa – a television set; the reception at Point Pass was excellent and clear.) I was indeed aware of the negatives that could be directed at the call. But as Secretary of the long-standing Commission on Calls and Transfers of the UELCA, I was very conscious of two important points that the Commission had stressed. One was that it was expected of District Church Councils that they would by careful contact assess the situation in parishes and the suitability of pastors' gifts for such vacant parishes, and that both parishes and pastors should be mindful of Church Council recommendations and guidance. I was the pastor who had been nominated to the parish by the S.A. Church Council. The second point in the Commission's findings was that when pastors had served for 10 years in a parish they should seriously consider whether it was not time that they made their talents available to another parish. I had been in the Nuriootpa parish for 10 years. What I had written on behalf of the Commission on Calls and Transfers, plus some realisation that a small degree of reaction against my emphasis on a thorough period of confirmation instruction was becoming evident among some parents and confirmation-age children in Nuriootpa, said to me that it was time to go to a new field.

Photo on left: *Point Pass Immanuel church*

The changeover took place without a break. I conducted my farewell service in Nuriootpa on March 6, and on the following Sunday was installed in Point Pass. President Carl Pfitzner deemed it advisable in view of his lengthy involvement in the amalgamation negotiations to delegate the installation to Pastor A.J. Lohe of Immanuel Lutheran Seminary. Pastor Lohe based his sermon on the words: '*I will give you pastors according to mine heart*' (Jer. 3,15), which he explained in turn to the pastor and parish as a word of encouragement, of warning, and of guidance. I had thought long about the message that I should give. In the first issue (April 1960) of the new parish paper '*Point Pass Lutheran*' I provided a 3-page summary of my installation sermon, introduced by the words: '*It is our solemn duty before God, my dear members, to work together with our eyes fixed forward and upward. It is therefore in the spirit of seeking encouragement and guidance from the Word of God in this great task of ours that I offer you the following summary of my installation sermon based on Ephesians 4,3, "Eager to maintain the unity of the Spirit in the bond of peace".*' I led into the theme of my message to the people who were being entrusted to my pastoral care by pointing out that there were two types of inheritance: good (e.g. a farm, a monetary legacy) and those not so pleasant to receive and best got rid of (e.g. debts, mortgages). In spiritual matters the members had inherited from well-meaning fathers an inheritance of disunity and separateness. The first step to dispose of it had been taken in 1921; now they had recognised that the reasons for continuing the inheritance of separateness no longer existed. Now is the time to think of God's good inheritance, which He wants us to value and keep, described in Eph. 4,4-6. In enlarging then on my theme from Eph. 4,5 there were 3 main lines of thought that I dwelt on: 1. There is unity through the Holy Spirit; 2. This unity is to be kept in the bond of peace; 3. You and I must be eager and diligent to keep this unity.

Point Pass, St Peter, manse

Chapter 5

For about one year I had to deal gently and understandingly with some members in both congregations whose attitude was chiefly affected by the loss of 'their' church. In Point Pass it was mainly expressed by diffidence towards worshipping in the Immanuel church; in Robertstown (where an influential member caused concern) the fact the ELCA congregation had been granted permission to use the Zion church cast a shadow over the unity of the amalgamated UELCA congregation. It was a blessing that in both congregations men of high spiritual calibre, both of whom had 'lost' their churches through the amalgamation were chairmen: 'big' George Pfitzner in Point Pass (who was also parish chairman) and 'little' George Pfitzner in Robertstown. Both gave positive guidance to the members of their congregations.

Arrangements regarding Parish Care

Worship Services. I found that the parish awaited guidance from me regarding divine worship in the congregations – the Parish Committee had no preliminary plans. In the first issue of the duplicated parish paper that I immediately established, the *Point Pass Lutheran*, I could spell out my thinking: *'My present idea is to serve the 3 southern congregations* [Point Pass, Peep Hill, Julia] *on one Sunday, the 3 northern congregations* [Robertstown, Geranium Plain, Apoinga] *on one Sunday. ... The time of service will be rotated, so that each congregation will have in turn an earlier morning service, morning service, afternoon service'.* Under this arrangement any time of service that was unsuitable for someone normally only fell due every 6 weeks. This first issue already illustrated how festival seasons placed extra activity on my shoulders:

Maundy Thursday, Robertstown, H.C. 7.30 p.m.;

Good Friday, Point Pass, H.C. 9.00 a.m.; Geranium Plain, H.C. 11.00 a.m.; Peep Hill, H.C. 3 p.m.; Julia, H.C. 7.30 p.m.;

Easter, Julia, 9.00 a.m.; Peep Hill, 11.00 a.m.; Robertstown, 2.30 p.m.; Point Pass, 7.30 p.m.

```
              CALENDAR OF SERVICES
    (The list of services conducted by readers may be incomplete)

       Wednesday, March 30          April 14 (Maundy Thursday)
   8 p.m. POINT PASS: Lenten       7.30 p.m. ROBERTSTOWN, H.C.
                                   7.30 p.m. Point Pass (Reader)
          Friday, April 1
   8 p.m. ROBERTSTOWN: Lenten         April 15 (Good Friday)
                                   9 a.m. POINT PASS, H.C.
     April 3 (5th Sunday in Lent)  11 a.m. GERANIUM PLAIN, H.C.
   9 a.m. ROBERTSTOWN              3 p.m. PEEP HILL, H.C.
   10 a.m. Point Pass (Reader)     7.30 p.m. JULIA, H.C.
   11 a.m. PEEP HILL
   2.30 p.m. JULIA                   April 17 (FESTIVAL OF EASTER)
                                   9 a.m. JULIA
          Tuesday, April 5         11 a.m. PEEP HILL
   8 p.m. PEEP HILL: Lenten        2.30 p.m. ROBERTSTOWN
                                   7.30 p.m. POINT PASS
         Wednesday, April 6
   8 p.m. JULIA: Lenten              April 24 (1st Sunday a. Easter)
                                   9.30 a.m. GERANIUM PLAIN
          Friday, April 8          11 a.m. ROBERTSTOWN
   8 p.m. GERANIUM PLAIN: Lenten   10 a.m. Point Pass (Reader)
                                   10 a.m. Peep Hill (Reader)
        April 10 (Palm Sunday)     10 a.m. Julia (Reader)
   9 a.m. GERANIUM PLAIN           2.30 p.m. APOINGA
   10 a.m. Peep Hill (Reader)
   10 a.m. Julia (Reader)            May 1 (2nd Sunday a. Easter)
   11 a.m. APOINGA, H.C.           9.30 a.m. PEEP HILL
   2.30 p.m. POINT PASS            11 a.m. JULIA
                                   2.30 p.m. POINT PASS
   ─────────────────────────────────────────────────────────────
                    APRIL  MEETINGS
           Brotherhood                    Ladies' Guilds
   Thursday, Mar. 31, 8 p.m., at   Point Pass: Thursday, Mar. 31,
      St. Peter's, Point Pass.       2 p.m., in the manse.
   April meeting to be announced.  April meeting to be arranged.
          Youth Societies          Robertstown: Friday, April 1,
   Robertstown: Monday, March 28;    2.15 p.m.
     Monday, April 25.   8 p.m.    Geranium Plain: Thursday, Apr.
   Point Pass: Monday, April 4,      14, 2 p.m.
     8 p.m., in the manse.
   Julia: Thursday, Apr. 7, 8 p.m. Peep Hill: Wednesday, Apr. 20,
   Peep Hill: Monday, April 11,      2.15 p.m.
     8 p.m.
   District Youth Rally: Monday,   Julia: Thursday, Apr. 21, 2 p.m.
     Apr. 18, 10 a.m., at Point Pass.
```

From the Point Pass Lutheran April 1960

Chapter 5

In the Lenten Season I conducted three week-night (Tuesday, Wednesday, Friday) and one Sunday night Lenten services. My original arrangements remained in force throughout my ministry. I have noticed, to my surprise, that in 1961 I preached at 233 services.

Serving the parish involved **much travelling**: Divine Services, regular religious instruction in schools, monthly meetings of five ladies' guilds and five (later four) youth societies. Rural parishes in the UELCA often covered a wide geographical area – that applied to the Point Pass parish, particularly in its northern section. For example, when the two morning services involved Geranium Plain and Black Springs I had to hurry at least 25 miles (40 km) over three lines of hills that ran from south to north in the entire western segment of the parish; when the services were at Black Springs and Robertstown I covered 19 miles (32 km) in between. When I came to Point Pass the only bitumen stretch was the first 4 miles from Eudunda to Point Pass. During my ministry the bitumen was extended to Robertstown; at the time of construction it became a 'crystal highway' of windscreen glass. One day when E.W. Wiebusch hurried out to Robertstown he smashed the windscreen of two cars that he passed: on his return journey his own windscreen was smashed. My travel was on gravel roads with loose stones. The best car I ever owned, a Zephyr 6 with outstanding MacPherson struts attached to the front wheels, made cornering at speed a helpful possibility. Another example of its excellent qualities was provided on an interstate trip with the family towing a caravan; in response to an anxious 'thump' on the accelerator at the bottom of the steepest section of the Blue Mountains highway (at Mount Victoria) the Zephyr picked up speed from a dangerous crawl to take us past a slow-moving commercial vehicle.

Geranium Plain church and altar with pulpit above

The scattered homes of members increased the geographic dispersion. One Point Pass family ('Tom' Heinrich of 'Dutton's Trough', Worlds End) lived north of the Burra Creek, west of the Robertstown – Burra main road. Peep Hill members lived as far east as Sutherlands. Julia members lived south as far as Hansborough, as far west as Tarnma. One Robertstown family lived several miles north of Emu Downs. Geranium Plain members (Jaenschs) lived in the Florieton district, near the Morgan-Burra main road – one night, after a visit, I switched off my headlights to give a big mob of kangaroos a chance to clear off the road. Black Springs membership extended to the vicinity of Hanson and even to Farrells Flat. When Cynthia Heinrich of 'Dutton's Trough' married widowed Ross White and settled in their home at Andrews (north of Clare), I travelled at least twice to Andrews to give Ross the desired instruction in the Lutheran faith. His deep interest made this a pleasure; and he was received into the Lutheran Church at Black Springs. I later observed with joy and gratitude the strong leading role that Ross played in the life of the Burra congregation, when that came into existence.

Portion of the parish, especially the Geranium Plain congregation, lay outside the Goyder Line of rainfall; the western hilly portion lay in a good rainfall area. The result was a difference in farming experience. At an early morning service at Geranium Plain, for example, the farmers could report good prospects (*'the rain from the east has been just right')*, followed by the report at the later morning service at Apoinga that *'We have had too much rain at one time*!' On one such occasion Reg. Heinrich at Apoinga got his truck stuck, the tractor with which he attempted to extricate his truck likewise got stuck. He had to use his caterpillar tractor to extricate with difficulty both 'stuck' farm implements.

Chapter 5

Amalgamations in Point Pass and Robertstown

The amalgamations of congregations that had been decided upon in Point Pass and Robertstown still needed to be carried in legal form. This fell to me as the incoming pastor. I armed myself with the brochure that detailed the various actions that were possible under the Act that governed the incorporations under S.A. law.

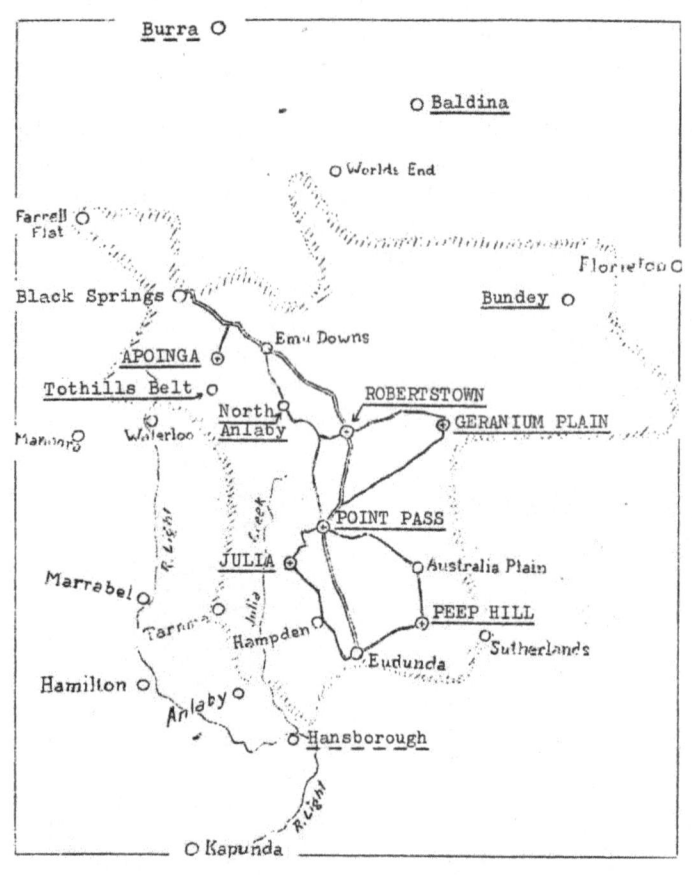

Both **Point Pass** congregations were incorporated. The section relating to the amalgamation of two incorporated bodies therefore applied. I prepared the draft of the rules of incorporation (i.e. constitution) that would apply in the future, on the basis of the model provided by the UELCA. As these rules would be the future constitution of both congregations, this work was done in consultation with the Church Committees of Point Pass and Robertstown. The one thing that the Point Pass Committee did not accept was my suggestion of the name 'Christ Church Lutheran' (reminiscent of Immanuel and of St. Peter, who confessed Christ), nor my alternative suggestion 'Prince of Peace'. The Church Committee preferred to leave the name as 'Point Pass Lutheran Church'. – The meeting in Point Pass that adopted the new constitution was an extraordinarily unusual one, seeing that the members were by resolution in reality already one body and had been acting as such. Emphasising that the step was necessary for legal purposes, I pointed out that the members first of all had 'mentally' to separate again into St. Peter's and Immanuel members. The two groups in turn had to vote that they were uniting with the other 'incorporated body', and had to adopt the new constitution. After this had been done by each of the two 'separate' bodies, they then together, voting as members of 'Point Pass Lutheran Church Inc.', had to adopt the new constitution. Imagine having to put the same constitution to the vote three times in a meeting that technically was three meetings! Because the Point Pass Committee, with membership from the former St. Petri and Immanuel congregations, had approved the draft I could dispense with the usual painful process of adopting the constitution clause by clause. – Little did I know that on that day I served my apprenticeship for similar action six years later at two separate conventions: the closing convention of the UELCA and the foundation convention of the LCA!

Black Springs church

Apoinga school building, used for church

Julia church

Peep Hill church

In **Robertstown** I faced a different situation. Zion congregation was an incorporated body, St .John's congregation still had trustees. But St. John's had not reacted to the death or removal elsewhere of its trustees, and instead of the obligatory seven it had only one left! At a meeting of the congregation I had to 'resurrect' St. John's: I had to announce that only the former St. John's members were allowed to vote to elect six new trustees, and to give the seven trustees the authority to transfer St. John's to the 'Salem Evangelical Lutheran Church, Robertstown Inc.' – I had prepared the draft of the new constitution in consultation with the congregational Church Committee, which accepted my suggestion of 'Salem', another name for 'Zion' (Ps. 76,2), the new 'JeruSALEM' seen by St. John (Rev. 21,2). As in Point Pass, this constitution was adopted without the necessity of clause by clause debate by the entire congregation as the 'Rules of Incorporation' of the renamed Salem congregation.

St John's church, Robertstown

Constitutional matters arose in other congregations during my ministry. In Julia, some clauses amended; in Geranium Plain 1964, election of trustees, bringing their number up from 3 to the required 7, followed by making the congregation an incorporated body instead of having trustees; in Black Springs, a new congregation established as an incorporated body, replacing the Apoinga congregation.

Organisations

In Chapter IV I included the activities of the organisations of the Point Pass parish in my presentation of these organisations in the Nuriootpa parish. My reference here is limited to the increased pressure on time that they involved.

Instead of two **Youth Societies** I initially had four: Point Pass, Julia, Peep Hill, Robertstown. After a couple of years Julia amalgamated with Point Pass. As a helpful guide to the societies a youth paper, *The Pointer*, was duplicated in the latter part of my ministry.

Dorothy in particular became heavily involved in the **women's societies** of the parish. There were five of them, Apoinga (later Black Springs) being the congregation that did not have one; in our first year she was elected as President by all guilds, and throughout my ministry she filled this position in most of them. The guilds in the smaller congregations enjoyed solid support; in Geranium Plain, for example with 12 members, if there weren't 12 present at a meeting it meant that someone was unwell or away from home.

The **Parish Brotherhood**, as in the Nuriootpa parish, had limited membership, but its members belonged to the spiritually alert and active members of the congregations.

Chapter 5

Miscellaneous Events and Observations

Manse Improvement. One feature of the manse in Point Pass was that the door to the kitchen on the south wing opened out on to a verandah, from which two doors led into the rest of the building, the first into the passage of the house, the second into the northern wing (large lobby and study) that had been added later. In mid-1961 the situation was made snug by enclosing this back verandah with bricks and louvres. – In 1965 the parish resolved that a new manse should be built, but this was held over when the possibility of a union between the UELCA and ELCA developed. Some years after my ministry Point Pass ceased to be the centre of the parish, and a manse was built in Robertstown.

Organised Sport. My Point Pass ministry was the one and only time that I took part in organised sport. The Point Pass Tennis Club was a little light on with players in the district competition. I was persuaded to join, and on Saturdays I played in various centres that reached as far as Allendale North near Kapunda.

'Pipes of Para'. The violinist Lyndall Henricksen (Mrs. G. Robson) of Kapunda contacted me in connection with her interest in the organs of Daniel Lemke, which were still extant in Ebenezer, Gruenberg, and Point Pass. Light Pass Immanuel had sold theirs to a Methodist congregation in Victoria. In the early afternoon of February 28, 1963, she arrived in Point Pass with an ABC photographer to take photographs of the Point Pass organ, and to record my comments on what I had done to the organ during my student days visits to Point Pass. This was in preparation for a documentary entitled *'Pipes of Para'*, which enjoyed widespread screening. I was scheduled to conduct a congregational meeting at Geranium Plain that afternoon. At the time Seminarist Kevin Zwar had been sent to me to assist me in my hymnbook task of typing out the texts of adopted hymns; he was not engaged in normal vicar activity. Knowing that a Geranium Plain meeting would be a peaceful one, I sent him out to open and chair the meeting until I could arrive, thus giving him the opportunity of gaining experience for the future. The meeting was nearing its close when I was able to attend. In the meantime I had been able to devote my attention to the Point Pass segment of the documentary with Lyndall.

Demolition of original Immanuel College. Part of the heritage of Point Pass was regretfully destroyed during my ministry. When the second and larger section of Immanuel College came up for sale the Point Pass Committee fell in with my idea that the three buildings associated with Point Pass – the Immanuel manse, the original building of the College (which was largely unused except for the rear portion that had served as a sleeping quarter for visitors to the manse), and the second larger and well-preserved College building – could be converted into a Retreat centre for S.A. District organisations; the Immanuel church could also be used for devotional purposes, and the original day-school on the church grounds for meetings. The large amount of unused land could be developed for some forms of sport. The District Church Council was not interested, so the idea was dropped. The deteriorating condition of the original College building made it a liability to the congregation. A series of wires slung from side to side over the roof and affixed to droppers cemented into the ground had for years prevented the roof from being blown off by the fiercely strong wind bursts that could sweep down from the open western range.

Immanuel College, Point Pass – left, second building; right, original building

So the historic building was demolished. The unused underground tank that had served the College was filled in with the rubble. The rubble included the German books that had been housed in the building. My one regret is that after extracting a few volumes that I regarded as worthwhile I did not make a list of these books of the *'Point Pass Bibliothek'* that shared this destructive fate. Such a list, together with similar remnants from other centres (e.g. Freeling, Tanunda) would have negated a widespread idea (not unknown even among metropolitan 'educated' Germans) that the Germans in rural areas were 'hayseeds' who had no literary interests.

The effect of war on lives. The parish did not have in its midst refugees from the Second World War in Europe. But such a family from Germany came for short time to work at the large 'Princess Royal Station' (I think that was its name), many miles north of Robertstown on the direct road to Burra. I went there on a visit, which did not result in membership; but it opened up a brief glimpse into the sufferings of persons who were caught up in the war. I was conversing with the mother of the family about their experiences. Suddenly a beautiful, fine-featured blonde maiden passed through the room, followed soon afterwards by a maiden with very dark hair and plain swarthy features. The mother looked at me and with a note of resignation in her voice said: *'Die Russen, wissen Sie'* (*'The Russians – you know'*, which in this context could also be rendered *'The Russians – you can tell'*).

Two Significant Events

On two occasions the action of a congregation regarding gifts warmed my heart and filled it with joy. These actions demonstrated that in spite of human frailties their hearts were filled with Christian love *(agape)*, and I was proud of them.

1. The first gift came from the Point Pass congregation.

Early in 1961 a delegation from Kadina, led by a former resident of the local district, Pat Fiedler, came to Point Pass. The small Kadina congregation was building a church, and the members were interested whether the furnishings of the St. Peter's church would be suitable. They expressed interest in all the furnishings (except the baptismal font, because they had one): viz. altar and its platform, pulpit, lectern missal stand, large candlesticks, pews, and aisle runner. When they asked about the price they were dumbfounded by the reply from the Point Pass Committee; *'Nothing. It is a gift!'*

Excerpts from the letters that I received reflect the deep impression that this gift made on the Kadina members. The Secretary (who had instigated the enquiry in the first place after a personal visit) wrote about this *'overwhelming offer'*: *'I hardly know how to word this letter to convey to you and the Point Pass committee and congregation our sincere appreciation and deep gratitude for your wonderful gift of the church furnishings; ... our congregation is absolutely delighted. It is our hope and prayer that God will richly bless you all for your generosity. Let me once more say a sincere thank you ...'* Pastor J. Sabel, the founder of the congregation, wrote: *'I feel that I would like you to convey to your people also my personal gratitude. I know what this wonderful gesture means to my congregation, and as this church building has been and still is my baby, you can imagine what this also means to me. Please convey therefore my personal gratitude and appreciation to the members of the congregation. Words cannot describe what this means to Kadina. ...'*

Kadina increased the length of its church, and the aisle runner from St. Peter's remained uncut! – The St. Peter's marble baptismal font was presented to the **Myponga** congregation, which had ties with Point Pass through various members. The newly established congregation at **Naracoorte** enquired whether a number of church vessels, including communion vessels and candlesticks, might be available; as far as I can recall these articles went there.

2. The second gift came from the Robertstown congregation.

When the ELCA was not interested in an offer to sell the Zion church and ceased using it at the end of 1963, development of the building as a church hall was effected. As the Zion congregation in **Frances** (many of whose members had links with this district in former years) was planning to build a church designed by Erik von Schramek, the Robertstown congregation presented to it the sanctuary furnishings (altar, including panelling and platform, pulpit, lectern), baptismal font and vessels, one hymn board, the altar furnishings (crucifix, single and triple candelabra, altar Bible, fair linen, altar and pulpit paraments, communion vessels), 15 pews of equal length, and the larger of two Sunday School organs. In August 1964 Frances brethren gratefully collected these items. Robertstown retained a few other items for its own use.

Anniversaries of Churches

With a history of up to 90 years behind them there were anniversaries of congregations, with which church renovations and other improvements were generally associated. In keeping with the custom of the time, the morning services generally were followed in the afternoon by a mission festival with two speakers. My contribution was that any recorded history was updated, and sometimes the history had to be more fully researched. Anniversaries began already in 1960. Peep Hill (70th anniversary, September 25) and Geranium Plain (60th anniversary, October 30) were the first two. In both cases the interior of the church was repainted.

Chapter 5

In 1961 there were three anniversaries: Robertstown (90th, February 5), Apoinga (25th, July 9), Julia (50th, August 13).

Robertstown marked the occasion by renovating the church, replacing the pulpit behind the altar with a new free-standing pulpit, renovating wall interiors, and repainting the exterior walls. I had commented that when I stepped into the pulpit I felt as if I was being tilted towards the congregation. The replacement of the pulpit revealed that this was indeed the case; the pulpit was barely fixed into the wall behind it, and therefore tilted forward to rest on the reredos of the altar when I entered it. One thing that could not be altered was the height of the door connecting the vestry with the church; it was not quite my height, and unconsciously I bowed my head a little every time I went through it. But on one occasion I hurried back into the vestry to pick up something before entering the pulpit, and I did not bow as I hurried through to mount the pulpit; the blow on my brow caused the first few minutes of my sermon to be a mechanical rendition.

Apoinga was on the point of relocating; at the time of its anniversary of 25 years in the disused Apoinga School it had already made a bid for the Anglican church at Black Springs.

Julia made great changes for its anniversary. The three sanctuary windows were replaced. I drew the designs for the new ones, with the ascending Christ as the figure for the central window; these designs were sandblasted into plate glass in Adelaide. The walls were painted externally and internally by voluntary labour; I was able to persuade the painters not to highlight the hat pegs affixed to the left wall (the traditional 'men's side'), but to help them to 'disappear' by painting them the colour of the wall. The guild replaced all carpets. I rewrote and brought up to date its history. In duplicated form it comprised 36 pages. An attaché case, which still renders good services, was the congregation's fine expression of thanks.

Julia church *Julia congregation at 50th anniversary*

Peep Hill again prepared to celebrate an anniversary, its 75th. Plans for this were made before our departure from Point Pass. I therefore completed my research into its interesting history, which had origins in Pastor C. Heinze's St. Trinitatis congregation in Eudunda – its church is now the Anglican church. The history was completed and duplicated in Adelaide, and I returned to my last parish to serve as liturgist at the Anniversary and Mission Services on September 26, 1965.

A Collapse and a Call

I cannot recall the precise weekday just after Sunday, May 2, 1965, when one morning I could not face whatever duties lay before me. It probably had been surreptitiously developing for a year or more. I was not as alert as I afterwards wished I had been to the preliminary signs in the case of a third suicide case (a Point Pass member) that distressed me in April 1964. In 1965 extra General Church activity had increased, and I had just had a heavy round of parish services, especially at the Easter weekend: Communion services in all congregations: on Maundy Thursday evening, and five on Good Friday at 9.00 a.m., 11.00 a.m., 1.30 p.m., 3.00 p.m., 7.00 p.m. Then four services on Easter Sunday at 9.00 a.m., 10.30 a.m., 2.30 p.m., 7.30 p.m. On Easter Monday I was involved in a Zone Youth Rally at Neales Flat.

A visit to Dr. D. Bowering in Eudunda put me on a course of valium tablets. I think it was the Parish Chairman who contacted the church authorities in Adelaide, and conducted a meeting of the Parish Committee on May 5 which granted me a month's leave of absence, commencing on May 9, and in consultation with my wife Dorothy made arrangements for care of the parish. L.W. Auricht and P.H. Proeve, Dr. M. Lohe, A.J. Lohe, H.W.R. Proeve conducted services in my absence, and Doug. Tscharke of Eudunda faithfully attended to emergency activities. Dr. Lohe arranged for his secretary, Pauline Fromm, to come to Point Pass and type out the manuscript for the May parish paper that I had prepared. Carol was a boarder at Immanuel College at that time, and Mr. and Mrs. Oscar Jenke, Peep Hill members living in Eudunda, in Christian love invited David and Philip into their home for four weeks.

For the first portion of my leave Dorothy and I went by invitation to Dorothy's sister Grace and husband John (Poolman) in Nhill, Victoria. As their house was next door to the express railway line, one disturbing element was the passing of the Adelaide express and the Melbourne express in the very early hours of the morning. The latter especially, on a downhill run into Nhill, seemed to come in through the back door and go through via the front door! There was understanding warmth during our stay. We did some sightseeing, especially in the Jeparit / Lake Hindmarsh / Rainbow area. While we were in Nhill I received a phone call from the Hymn Book Committee which was meeting in Adelaide; it sought some information from me that only I could give. – Laurie and Hazel Mader offered their comfortable beach house on the Esplanade at Christies Beach for the last fortnight of my recuperation. The open window behind our bed let in the refreshing breezes from the next-door Gulf; this was a wonderful relief for me, because for some reason I at times found easy breathing a difficulty. This was a time of undisturbed relaxation.

We returned to Point Pass on June 9, much recovered from the breakdown in nerves. The Lord's sustaining grace had been with me. District President Carl Pfitzner and local Seminarist Vernon Schutz gave assistance in services when I resumed duty. In the next parish paper I could record my general feeling of relief: *'Listening to the minutes of the previous meetings* [of the ladies' and youth organisations] *it was reassuring to notice that lay leadership rose to the occasion during my leave of absence. The meetings continued as programmed'*. One pleasing development that followed was that a beginning was made in all organisations that a member prepared and led the opening devotional section of a meeting.

A Call out of the parish ministry. I was very soon faced with a decision that was to affect my future ministry in the Church. In 1964 Dr. Lohe had returned from a visit to India that afflicted him with the debilitating ailment popularly called 'Bombay belly'. It troubled him greatly that it had affected his intended attention to duties, in which the Vice-President (Carl Pfitzner) and I helped out. So in March 1965, unknown to me, he had initiated discussion among the members of the General Church Council about the advisability of making the office of General Secretary full-time. When my breakdown meant that two of the Church's chief officers had been stricken, this discussion culminated in the General Church Council, without authorisation from a General Synod, resolving to extend a call to me. This call was handed to me at the end of June in Adelaide, before the commencement of a combined meeting with the fully represented ELCA Executive Committee. The call document defined my future obligations as follows:

(a) Fulfil your duties as Secretary of the Church;
(b) Assist the President of the Church in specially assigned tasks;
(c) Attend to such other duties as the Church or the Church Council shall from time to time direct.

I was not aware that after completion of the business of the combined meeting there was a combined meeting of the fully represented ELCA Council with representatives of our Church Council. It resolved, on the motion of two ELCA officials, that, should I accept the call, it be recommended that portion of my service be used in coordinating the activities between the two Churches towards amalgamation. When I was told of this it was not mentioned that the ELCA men had pledged a contribution to my salary!

The word 'tsunami' did not exist in 1965, but 'spiritual tsunami' is an appropriate term, I feel, to describe what hit the Point Pass parish at the end of June and the beginning of July. June 27 was the earliest date to announce that I had a call; on the next Sunday, July 4, the announcement was that I had accepted and that a call meeting would be held on July 18.

Chapter 5

What I wrote in the July issue of the *Point Pass Lutheran* best expresses the thoughts that went through my mind in this turning point of my life:

'After 22 years in the parish ministry and 20 years as Secretary of the Church, this call naturally placed before me the necessity of choosing between the two phases of my previous duties. Such a choice was by no means lightly made; for a parish ministry, with its personal pastoral functions, has many joys that act as a counterweight to its worrying and trying times.

'The following excerpt from my letter to Dr. M. Lohe expresses my thoughts on the decision I had to make: "In my answer I have sought guidance to the question: Where does my Church need me? The thought which has been so strongly emphasised in our long deliberations regarding calls and transfers, that the Lord gives guidance also through our Church Councils, received a peculiar emphasis in this case when the Church Council of the Church itself issued the call. Added to this was the reaction of the Executive Council of the E.L.C.A. last Thursday, which I could not lightly discard. I therefore accept it that at least until the time of the amalgamation of the two Churches (if my own Church should re-elect me to the position of Secretary) it is my duty to serve the Church in this official capacity".'

And last of all the plea to the parish: *'Let your prayers also rise that this decision, which also affects you through a change of pastorate, may prove to be a blessing to our Lutheran Church in Australia.'*

The Parish Committee resolved that the requirement of 3 months' notice should not be applied. I wound up the legal requirements re Rules of Incorporation in Point Pass and Robertstown, conducted four confirmation services, preached my farewell sermon at a parish service in Robertstown on August 29, 1965, and we departed from Point Pass to take up residence in Royston Park, Adelaide.

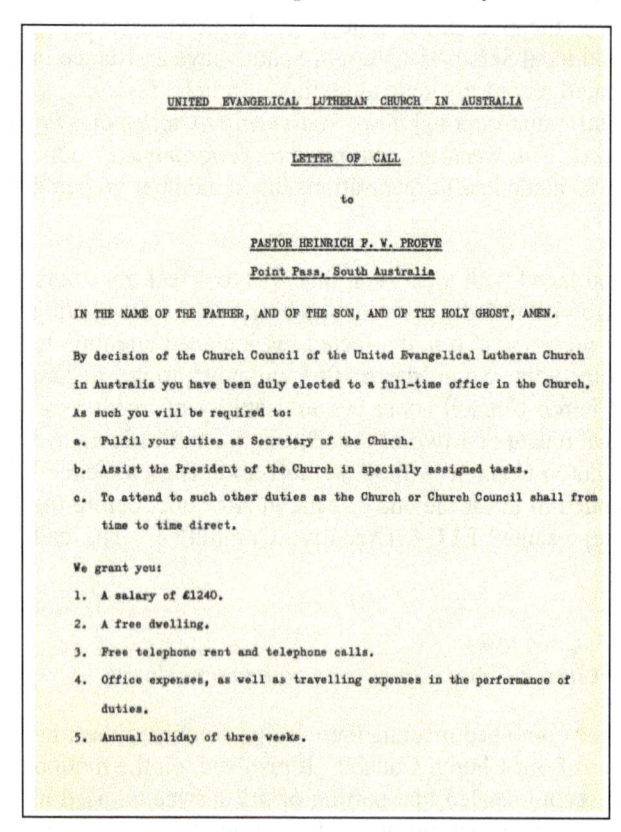

There were no regrets about the Point Pass parish to spoil our departure. Despite the suddenness of all developments that led to this departure, Point Pass was cared for without a break. The pastor who was called on July 18, Leo Graetz, accepted the call, with the proviso that he remained in his present parish till February 1966, to complete his confirmation course. Pastor Hartley Hage, who had been serving in New Guinea Mission, had to leave the Mission at that time on account of health problems in his family, and was almost immediately available as locum tenens until Pastor Graetz came.

For the last time a parish pastor drove his car the oft travelled route of 75 miles (120 km) to Adelaide, accompanied by those of his family who were in Point Pass, and arrived in Adelaide as a full-time church official.

Chapter 5

V. B. 'PART-TIME' CHURCH SECRETARY
DOUBLE DECADE: 1945 (August) – 1965 (August)

My adult 'working life' has been divided into two streams: the first, the normal career of a pastor, a 'Seelsorger' serving in a number of parishes of the Church; the other, the ordained pastor serving in some special field of activity in the Church. Or, to express the situation in a different metaphor, I was a pastor wearing two hats. In my case the second stream of activity ran completely parallel with my first and prime stream of activity almost from the very beginning. Up to this point in my Memoirs I have sought to concentrate on my memories of just over two decades of activity as a parish pastor. As my recording of such memories now closes it seems opportune to gather together in a summary the collateral areas of church activity during these two decades in which I was engaged. There have been some references to these in my previous chapters (e.g. 'Non-Parish Activities' in Chapter III). As I gather them together in this summary presentation I seek to avoid repetition.

Serving on Committees and Boards, beginning 1943 to 1945

1. Board of Archives. The general Church unwittingly drew me into an activity, from the very beginning of my ministry, that was going to involve me for most of my life, viz. the Archives of the Church. I was aware of the Archives, but not familiar with them, as a Seminary student: when the pastor who was associated with them, J.E. Materne, was removed from the scene by internment, I as the unofficial 'librarian' of the Seminary Library under Pastor W. Riedel occasionally checked on the Archives in the next-door room before the RAAF took over Immanuel College and Seminary. – In 1943 I inherited the care of those Archives as they were stored in a mountain of cartons on the platform of the Tynte Street hall; as the temporary 'custodian' I guarded them with an aura of liberally applied anti-vermin naphthalene flakes. – A change only came when the RAAF vacated the Immanuel College buildings. A small room attached to the northern side of the Lohe Library was set aside for the Archives, and a Board of Archives consisting of three persons, Pastors T. Hebart (Chairman), J.E. Materne (Chronist), and me (Secretary) was set up. Being custodian now as the Archivist began to have some practical meaning and purpose for me. Our meetings were especially occasions of sorting out material, and of interesting historical reminiscences by the two senior men.

This is a point where I can fittingly reflect on the two older men who were my first contacts and co-workers in the interests of the Lutheran Archives.

Pastor Theodor Hebart, after 36 years of ministry in Australia, and after two years of persuasion and three years of writing, had completed *'Die Vereinigte Ev. Luth. Kirche in Australien (Velka). Ihr Werden, Wirken und Wesen'* in 1938. He had the advantage of having a valuable basis in the Langmeil archives gathered by his predecessor J.C. Auricht, consisting among other things of minute books, German church papers, brochures on the history of several previous church bodies, and the manuscripts of three versions of the history of Kavel's church written by Auricht. In his mother tongue, German, Hebart was best able to express himself in a flowing, easily understood style. More importantly, he recognised the streams, trends, developments that marked the intricate history of Lutheranism in Australia; and at a time when there was still a sharp division between the two branches of the Lutheran Church he sought, as an historian, to present in his 480 pages these attitudes as objectively as possible (and I agree with Pastor J.J. Stolz, editor of the English version, that on the whole he succeeded). The concept of seeing the history of the Church as a stream was given visual expression in a long coloured attachment to his history that identified the various 'streams'.

Hebart's history differs markedly from that prepared by his counterpart in the ELCA, Dr. A.E.R. Brauer. Brauer's indefatigable detailed research led to the completion in 1947 of an interesting mammoth manuscript that the ELCA felt was too large for printing. When I was in full-time office in North Adelaide I arranged that my secretary, when not answering the phone and preparing morning and afternoon teas as the 'Girl Friday' of Lutheran Church House and doing such typing as I required of her, should type out the Brauer manuscript in multiple copies for a little wider dispersion. The difficulty that I had when the task was completed was to determine the order of chapters. Dr. Brauer's own notes indicated changes of mind. I believe that is the background to the assessment of Derek van Abbe, the German professor at the University of Adelaide, that *'Under the Southern Cross'* (the abbreviated version that appeared in 1956) was 'episodic' – the original, as interesting as it is, was not a 'flowing stream'.

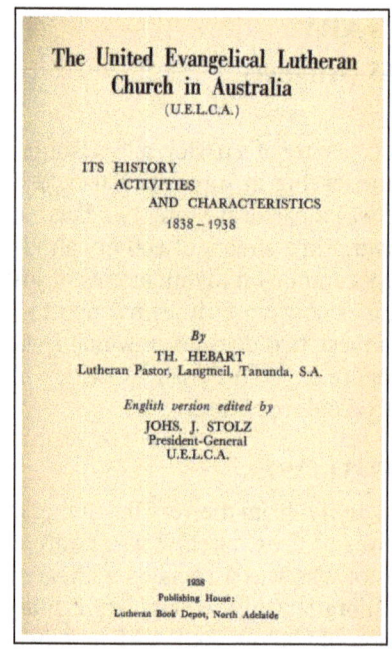

Chapter 5

Hebart's history also appeared in 1938 in English under the title *'The United Evangelical Lutheran Church in Australia (U.E.L.C.A.). Its History, Activities, and Characteristics'*. With President-General Johs. J. Stolz as the supervising Editor, this English version appeared, not as a translation but as a condensation and an abridgement (247 pages), prepared by no less than 18 revisers. As a result much documentary material is not available to English readers. Anyone with some knowledge of German should read the original version by Hebart to have this material and to enjoy his style of presentation.

Two Appendices in the English version, totalling 81 pages and providing brief outlines of the congregations of the UELCA and of the pastors who served the Church and its predecessors, have been a handy aid to researchers. The huge task of researching and preparing these outlines was carried out by one man, Ernst Materne. My personal copy of the 'Hebart-Stolz History', as it is generally called, contains a few corrections and additions in the margin. But it would be churlish to belittle the work done in those appendices. Materne summarised the history of 247 congregations and the curriculum vitae of 190 pastors, including pastors who returned to their homeland or died abroad.

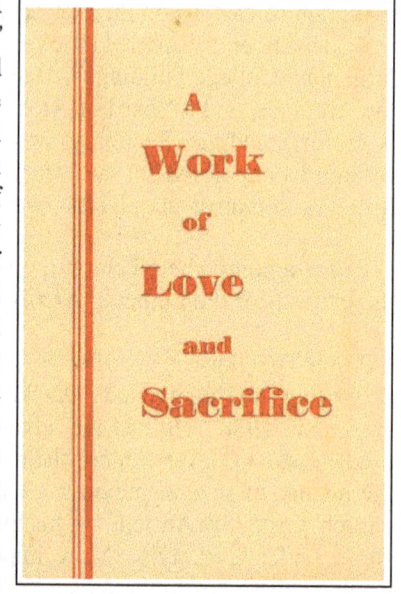

I was a frequent visitor at the State Archives as I researched non-UELCA sources in preparation for the appearance of *'A Work of Love and Sacrifice'* [Ed: about the start of the mission at Killalpaninna, which he co-authored with Uncle Ernst Proeve]. I got to know Mr. John McLellan very well; he was the State Archivist, and also in charge of the archives of his Church (Presbyterian). He gave me helpful tips; one of these was to index books in the Archives with ordinary numbers, and to prefix the numbering of brochures, letters, and loose sheets with a 'B'. There probably are many articles in the Archives which still give evidence of this early style of indexing. What especially impressed me was that the comparatively small building in which the State Archives were housed could hold so much material through use of a comparatively new style of shelving, compactus shelving. It was more expensive than ordinary shelving because it required a concrete floor with two tracks on which to run, and a winding apparatus to move each shelf. I proposed to the General Church Council that the Church should make maximum use of the small room for the Archives by installing a small compactus unit. Dr. Max Lohe was opposed to the idea; but Bruno Muetzelfeldt (the only other person in the Council who knew the system) supported me, and the General Church Council gave its approval. After he had seen it in action in our Archives, Dr. Max added to his strong support of Archives in general a strong promotion of compactus shelving for storage purposes in general.

While I was in Adelaide I was the Custodian of the Archives, but to fulfil such duties from the Barossa, was not logical – and other tasks were handed to me soon after I settled in Nuriootpa; Clem Schmidt took over the custodial duties of Archivist. During the period till the amalgamation of the Churches, however, I continued to be the Secretary of the Board, and handled many research enquiries. For example, Clem Zanker approached me for help in establishing the history of the Nain congregation; I was able to provide a good deal of new material relating to its beginnings. A request for help in providing material for the history of the Condowie congregation and its second (as they believed) church led to a rewrite of its early history: my comment, as I provided translations of early reports, that there appeared to be a reference to an earlier church led to senior members of the congregation recalling that there had been a building at nearby Zoar that served as the first church and then became the residence of Pastor A. Doehler's family.

There was co-operative contact between Dr. Fred Blaess, indefatigable Archivist of the ELCA, and me that lasted until his sudden death when he was then the Archivist of the LCA. My involvement in Archives in my years as fulltime Secretary was such that I reserve further reference to it for the next Chapter.

The S.A. District added four committee duties to my non-parish activities in the first two years.

2. Committee on Broadcasting (1944-1950).

Because I was its Secretary and the contact person with Station 5KA, handling all the material that had to be passed on for 'Fifteen Minutes with the Lutheran Church', I had to visit the station every week. The choice of hymns was difficult. 5KA had no list of recorded hymns; so I soon spent quite a lot of time viewing their vinyl records and setting up a list of useable hymns. In order to add some Lutheran hymns to our repertoire fellow committee-member W.W. Fritsch used a group of St. Stephen's members to make a record. I served until I moved to Nuriootpa; Kon Hartmann took my place, and served most efficiently for many years. – J.J. Stolz related to me an example of what could happen if a radio station chose 'suitable' hymns. Many years before when a devotional (I think by E. Rohde) was presented on the ABC, the station chose a 'hymn' that was obviously suitable because *'Gott'* was in the title. The devotional concluded with **'***Der Gott, der Eisen wachsen ließ' ['The God who caused iron to grow']* – a military national song, not a religious hymn.

3. Liturgical Committee of the S.A. District (1944-1947).

This was for me a period of apprenticeship that was the forerunner of a later lengthy association with liturgy.

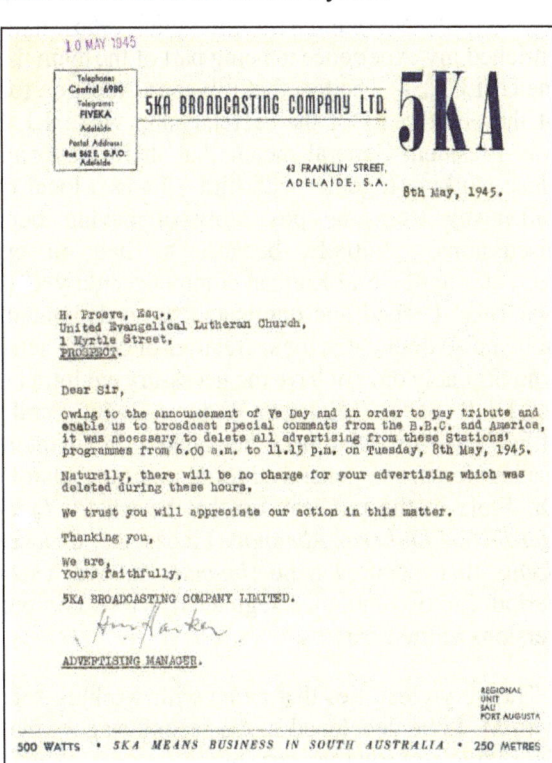

4. Lutheran City Mission Committee (1945-1949).

It was inevitable that I was appointed to the Committee that was set up to supervise the activity of my successor in the City Mission, Pastor A.F. Zinnbauer, serving first as its Secretary, then as its Chairman. The meetings of this committee were often quite difficult – but not between its members.

5. South Australian Council for Social Services (1944-1951).

This was an inter-denominational body, particularly promoted (I think) by the Methodist Church. The S.A. Church Council appointed W.W. Fritsch and me as the Lutheran representatives. As far as I can recall there were very few meetings, and I cannot recall any important decisions being made.

Secretary of the UELCA, 1945 – 1965

At the end of Chapter III, almost as an afterthought, in the paragraph headed *'A Pointer to the Future'*, I reflected on the unusual development that I became General Secretary of the UELCA in September 1945. I did not set my sights on being a Secretary of the Church. The Lord used the fellow-pastors and fellow-members of the Church to steer me into that avenue of service. I did not resist their decision; for somewhere during my life the principle was imprinted in my mind that if I was called upon by a responsible group to serve, and I felt I could serve, I should accept. But, whenever I look back over my career, the sense of amazement has never left me, that those pastors and members began this development in my second year, when I was scarcely 'dry behind the ears' (as a German phrase colourfully expresses lack of maturity)! I can't imagine that any other Church body has acted in a similar manner.

It was a blessing that I could grow into the requirements and responsibilities of the position. The provision in the new Rules of Incorporation of the Church that the General Secretary was a member of the General Church Council did not come into effect until 1947, so I was not a member of the Council to which I was still subject as a recent graduate. I could listen to and learn from the experience of five Presidents before being called upon to help make decisions. I think it may have been this 'listening' for two years to other people's opinions that helped to develop what Max Otto once described as a gift that he had admired in me because it speeded up the progress of meetings: *'You could listen to a debate, and after a while offer the meeting a resolution in draft form'*. It is indeed the case that very many resolutions recorded under the names of various movers and seconders were the wording that I offered.

Chapter 5

Serving under two different Presidents-General, J.J. Stolz (1945-1953) and M. Lohe (1953-1966), naturally enriched my experience in being part of the team that led the UELCA. – The fact that I lived in Adelaide for five of the eight years of the secretaryship while J.J. Stolz was President-General meant that there was ongoing close working together with him – I was a local phone call away from the possibility of having personal discussions. Initially, because he had no private secretary until Coral Koithan commenced duty a year or two later, I typed and duplicated some documents for him. I also duplicated for secretaries of church activities who probably did not have the necessary equipment, e.g. for J.T.P. Sabel (Ministers Widows Relief Fund), for H.F.W. Roehrs (Martin Luther Fund). In Chapter III I made reference to general editorial assistance that I gave Dr. Stolz in the publications that he edited, *Lutheran Herald* and *Lutheran Almanac*. I recast the *'Calendar of Saints'* that appeared in the *Almanac*, and over a six-year period (in two-monthly segments) wrote compressed versions of their careers.

The very close ties that came with working together with M. Lohe developed in the second stage – the full-time stage – of my secretaryship.

Page from Lutheran Almanac 1948

But I must mention that the concept of having 'necessary equipment' developed a little slowly in the UELCA. When I was elected in 1945 John Doehler with rather a wry smile handed over to me a 'Church' duplicator that had never been fit for use. I had in Dimboola been shown a Gestetner duplicator in the business of W. Bache, where Dorothy worked, and found that it was in perfect order, except that the feeding fingers were miss-set and dug into the paper instead of feeding it into the machine. At my request father Schultz, on returning to Dimboola from the General Synod, found out that it was still available – so I bought it. And I had my own trusty Corona portable typewriter to continue to write many a letter and cut many a stencil for many a year.

Still More Boards and Committees

6. Committee on Constitutions, UELCA (1947-1966). I heard myself dubbed 'the constitutional expert of the Church' so often that it almost hurt – it sounded as if I was not a pastor with theological background and interests, but a legalist. Of course I appreciated the role that constitutions, and rules and regulations, play in guaranteeing and maintaining good order – a bulwark against those who want to be dictators; but I did not set my sights on this sphere of activity. The gentle beginning was the action in North Adelaide to incorporate the congregation so that it could hold property. John Doehler was responsible for the next step: he asked me to join him in drafting a constitution for the recently formed Lutheran Women's Association in South Australia. I became a fixture in the constitutional field in 1947, when the General Synod elected me as a member of its Committee on Constitutions, and that committee then elected me as its Secretary.

It was a busy time for the Committee. Following the adoption by the UELCA of Rules of Incorporation in 1947, the Committee was charged with the task of preparing the By-laws of the Church and the rules of boards. As a newcomer into the field I had the advantage of working together with experienced men: Bert Teusner LL.B., the Speaker of the Legislative Assembly in S.A.; J. Edwin Theile, a farmer of Pinnaroo, and Chairman of the General Finance Council, a very clear thinker who loved his Church and served it with distinction; Pastor John Riedel, likewise a clear and sharp thinker. (Edwin Theile was a prolific contributor to synodical debates. On one occasion a group of younger pastors let out a cheer and announced to a bemused synodical assembly that it was the speaker's 100th speech at that convention. Much speaking indeed! But the rare occasions when it was not to the point was when his hearing had let him down.)

Chapter 5

I've never forgotten the General Synod of 1950 in Brisbane, at which these By-laws were adopted. Under the care of Mrs. Eisenmenger, wife of the St. Peter's College Bursar, I was laid up for a day or two with a severe cold in the head that affected my breathing. On the day that the By-laws were scheduled for debate Dr. J.J. Stolz committed the chairing of the convention to Vice-President John Doehler, who said something to the effect of: *'Henry, I am not familiar with this material; you will have to see it through'*. Heavy the head, but the By-laws got through.

General Secretary HFW Proeve with the Presidents at the 1950 General Synod:
from left, M Lohe (Qld), JTP Stolz (NSW), J Doehler (SA), JJ Stolz (General President), HFW Proeve, WF Stahl (V)

7. Finke River Mission Board (1950-1953). At the 1950 General Synod the long-standing member and Chairman of the Finke River Mission Board, John Riedel, did not seek re-election. His hopes that I would be elected to the Board were fulfilled. The former Secretary, Pastor R.B. Reuther, became the Chairman, and I was elected as Secretary by the Board. On September 17, 1951, the Board appointed us two to be a delegation to the mission field – there had been complaints from the field about a lack of visits. Our plans were speedily drawn up, so that we were on the field before Superintendent F.W. Albrecht went away on furlough leave. We left Adelaide on the Ghan on September 27, and the leisurely train journey gave us the opportunity to discuss what we would be looking for. In Marree I was given a surprise: the Aboriginals at the railway station expressed the surprised thought, *'Pastor Proeve, you have come back to visit us once again!'* This recognition came two years after my visit with Uncle Ernst. R.B. Reuther, of course, was also well known to them from earlier visits.

The day after we arrived in Alice Springs and Hermannsburg, October 1, was **Koporilja Day**. For the local community as far afield as Alice Springs and Haasts Bluff this was an annual 'national festival', marking the completion of the pipeline from the Koporilja Springs to Hermannsburg (a little less than 8 km) on October 1, 1935. A devotional opening, and a close in which blind evangelist Moses participated, and a picnic atmosphere of races and donkey rides for the Aboriginals marked the thanksgiving occasion.

Photo on right: *Hermannsburg old church*

Reuther and I visited and had discussion with the missionaries at all out-stations: Hermann Pech at Haasts Bluff, Werner Petering at Papunya, Alfred Koschade at Areyonga. I think that it was at the beginning of these visits that the truck that Superintendent Albrecht was using broke down west of Hermannsburg, and we spent a night on our swags on the sand of the Gilbert River while an Aboriginal made his way back to Hermannsburg to fetch another truck. We realised why there were kangaroo rugs on the truck for us when the bitter cold of early morning struck us. At Haasts Bluff there had been tribal fighting, and Pech had confiscated all boomerangs that landed in the area around his house; he gave me one as a souvenir that had been used for the purpose for which it was originally made. On the way to Areyonga we experienced an example of the problems the missionaries faced when travelling; the track at one point was so sandy that Albrecht laid down two long poles that he carried on the truck, which gave the twin back wheels traction through the sandy stretch.

Chapter 5

FRM Board 1951: Back row: LA Borgelt, BA Doering, HFW Proeve, CE Heinrich, Pastor AG Simpfendorfer.
Front row: AC Weckert, Pastor RB Reuther, Pastor FW Albrecht, HA Graetz.

We found that water was again becoming a problem, because the settlement was beginning to outgrow its supply. Somewhere a little west of Hermannsburg we stopped to greet Willie Wurst at his boring plant. This staunch member of the Appila congregation was so anxious to overcome the problem of water that he 'divined' at various locations and then bored for months in the severe weather conditions. He did not let any failures deter him from trying elsewhere.

Our visit to the field concluded with a lengthy Field Conference, attended by all missionaries, at which all concerns were carefully noted. Naturally it was the Secretary of the Board who did this.

On October 10 we flew back to Adelaide (Parafield) on one of the larger planes of that era. In those days these aircraft landed at Oodnadatta and Leigh Creek en route. – This was one instance where I served on a board for only one synodical term. I did not seek re-election because the duties that I was carrying out on the *'Lutheran Herald'* editorial staff were possibly going to be extended to chief editorship. But there was still some service to Finke River Mission possible when I was Secretary of the LCA.

Photo on right:
Henry and Pastor RB Reuther leaving Alice Springs

8. *'Lutheran Herald'* Editorial Staff. As soon as I transferred to Nuriootpa I replaced T.G. Obst, and joined S.H. Held and L.H. Leske as Associate Editors assisting J.J.Stolz in the production of the *'Lutheran Herald'*. I was involved with this church paper throughout my Nuriootpa ministry. The second issue in October 1950 unveiled the new style that was agreed upon by the combined staff: the newsprint paper was replaced by a better class (calendered) paper; presentation was upgraded: the material was arranged under headings with their own style of presentation – Devotional; Editorials; President's Letter (written in rotation by the five Presidents, partly in the hope of stimulating subscriptions throughout the Church); From our Exchanges; Mission News (i.e. Aboriginal and New Guinea); Church in Action (news on particular aspects of Church activity); News, with sub-headings Obituaries, Persons, Church at Home (grouped under Districts), Church Abroad; Announcements. Lawrence Leske was responsible for the entire News section, and covered it very well.

In March 1951 Dr. Stolz handed over the reins of editing to Pastor John Doehler after more than 30 years of editing church papers. When one takes into account that for some 10 years between two world wars this included the editing of the bi-weekly German *'Lutherisches Kirchenblatt'*, i.e. editing a 16-page issue of a church paper every week, plus annual English and German Almanacs, Dr. Stolz's services to the UELCA are all the more remarkable.

John Doehler's statement that he 'does not lay any claim to experience in this field' was unfortunately demonstrated by badly underestimating the amount of space that his contributed editorials and other material would occupy in one issue. Almost invariably it fell to me as the editor seeing the issues through the press (finally called 'Publishing Editor') to fill the issue. This happened in various ways: I provided the front page more and more, finally in the form of presentation of photos of church and potted history of congregations in the various Districts; series of historical articles under the title *'The Days Of Old, The Years Of Ancient Times'*. I arranged with L. Leske, who received the News Releases of the LWF, that he would keep an eye on interesting articles, or make LWF copies available to me, from which I wrote a collage of news items from other Lutheran Churches in the world. The easiest time for me was when J. Doehler was abroad for several months at an LWF Assembly, and I as Acting Editor-in-Chief could plan ahead. I even had a holiday in Queensland, knowing that the reliable compositor of Auricht's Printing Office, Alf Pfeiffer, could complete the issue, using material I had left with him.

Originally I 'worked on the stone' with the printers, i.e. arranging the typed items in the metal forme that held them in the printing machine; this involved reading the type upside down and in reverse. In the latter years this was changed to preparing a paste-up copy. J.F.W. Schulz used to bring the complete set of proof sheets to Nuriootpa on Friday afternoon, at the end of setting up on the linotype. This saved me from frequent attendance at the printery; but it put me under the continual week-end pressure, amid the confirmation instruction on Saturdays and services on Sundays, of proof reading and pasting up 16 pages before Schulz turned up very early on Monday morning (before the printery began operating for the day) to collect the proof-read and pasted-up copy. I had to do this many a time into the wee hours of the Monday morning (sometimes till 2.00 a.m. or later).

The experienced printer at Auricht's, Christian Obst, died suddenly in early 1951. In the 6 years that I knew him I often spent time with him in the cellar where he printed on the big Wharfedale machine, and thus got to know his skills and his love of the Church. I was able to draw attention to an immediate replacement for him, Dorothy's brother Clarence. Clarrie, a one-time pre-war printer at the *"Dimboola Banner"*, had been able to find work after his release from the RAAF only at Frearson's, who printed cartons. His knowledge of colour printing provided a valued addition to the range of printing that Auricht's could offer.

9. Hymn Book Committee. In previous chapters I have recalled my early interest and activity in the hymns of the Church. This has been a strong feature throughout my life that has given me much pleasure; unfortunately, as I write these lines at a time when hymnbooks have been replaced by screens and Lutheran hymnody is dying in the LCA, it is a matter of sorrow for me. — I was surprised, indeed disappointed, when a joint Hymn Book Committee was set up to prepare a new hymnbook for use in the two Lutheran Churches that I was not included as a UELCA member – in fact the UELCA representation was originally light-on (5 of 13 members). Together with two other UELCA and one more ELCA member I was appointed to the Committee in 1953, due (I believe) to the promptings of good friend Leslie Grope. As one of three surviving members (L. Grope and P. Renner the other two) it may be of interest to record miscellaneous recollections of that hard-working committee, especially now that the fruit of its long labours is being consigned to the dust-bin.

When I came on the Committee the research into hymns used in Lutheran circles and in English circles that G. Dohler had undertaken for many years had been duplicated in a list dubbed *'Codex Ipswichiensis'*. A preliminary choice of hymns had been made from this list of 1450 hymns as the opening basis for the new Australian book. These hymns in their various rubrics had been allocated to four Working Sub-Committees (S.A.I, with metropolitan members; S.A.II, with country members; Vic.-N.S.W.; Queensland) for study and recommendations according to the principles or guidelines that had been adopted.

Chapter 5

Throughout the activity of the Committee decisions were under review. There was little change to the decision 'Accepted', and was usually associated with an original conditional 'if required' or 'subject to translation'. The decision 'Deleted' likewise was rarely altered after it was made. The assessment 'Queried' kept many hymns under constant review until the reason(s) for the query (often 'better translation') no longer were regarded as applicable. I am sure that the average Church member has no idea of the vast amount of research that the Committee and its Sub-Committees undertook.

The Queensland Sub-Committee concentrated on providing further lists of hymns, and did so for very many years. S.A Sub-Committee II scoured the translations of two Danish translators to make about 34 suggestions. At the request of the Committee it studied the 500 German hymns that the combined Lutheran Churches in Germany had agreed upon in issuing the *Evangelisches Kirchengesangbuch' (EKG)*. This book was regarded by the Committee as containing the 'stock' hymns of the German Reformation; it also played a significant role in the development of the new liturgy for the LCA. – It has been estimated that at least 7,000 hymns were surveyed.

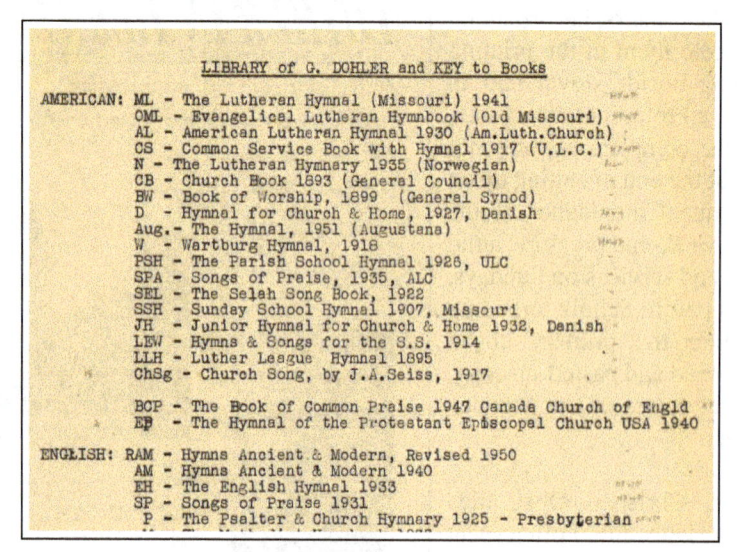

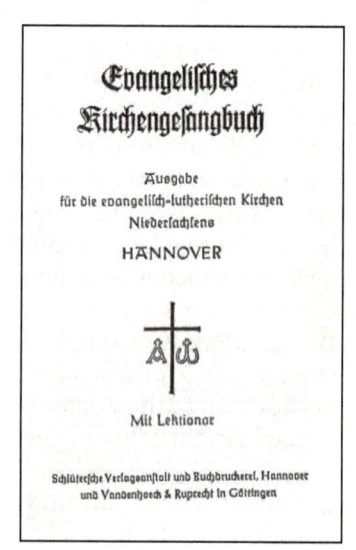

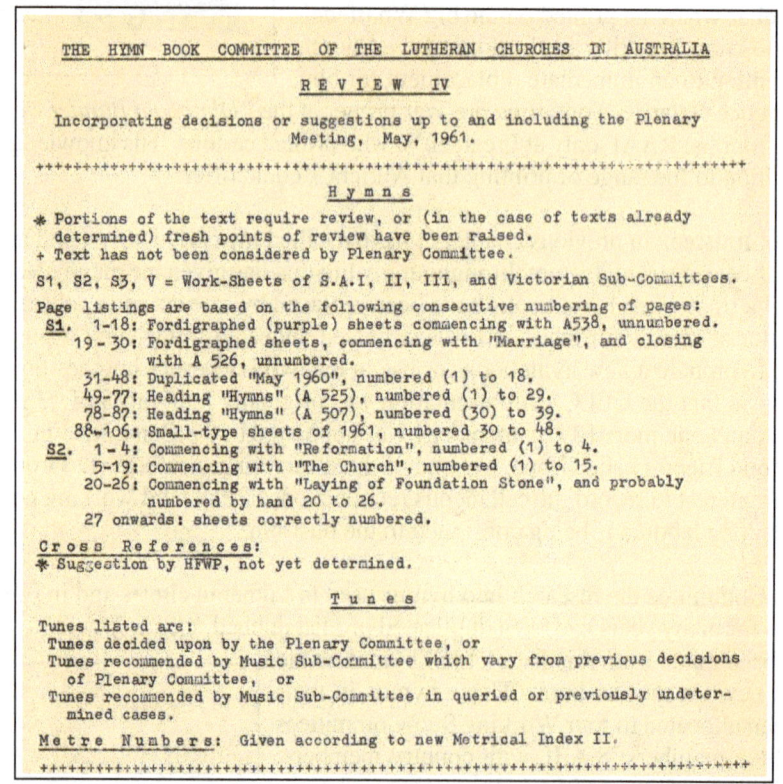

Example of the work involved in choosing the hymns from the list of 1450 hymns in Dohler's Codex Ipswichiensis

My activity in the committee developed very gradually; it was an unplanned development, and it was not fixed by any official resolutions. I was a member of S.A. Sub-Committee II, which in the initial stages was allocated the rubrics 'Reformation' and those associated with 'The Church', including 'Redeemer', 'The Ministry', and the 'Means of Grace', as its specific study. Fellow-members were O.E. Thiele (Carlsruhe) and, while they were in local parishes, W.F. Roehrs (Point Pass) and E.W. Wiebusch (Eudunda); finally for many years it consisted only of O.E. Thiele and me. The southern Sub-Committees recommended acceptance, tentative acceptance, queries, or non-acceptance of hymns, and provided proposed texts. If a discussion of texts by the Plenary Committee failed to reach a decision, the relevant problem was referred back to the Sub-Committee. Gradually the practice developed of referring deferred items to S.A. Sub-Committee II, partly (I think) because it appeared to meet more frequently than the others. I think that it was my habit of accurate note-taking and that I had equipment that led to my cutting the stencils when we reported on our work. This again led to my preparing new Reviews, which I gradually changed to indicate the origin of the hymns and the tunes accepted for them.

Hymn-Book Committee. Back: Pastor AT Miller, Dr LB Grope, Pastor HFW Proeve, Mr JB Thiele, Pastor HPV Renner. Front: Pastor G Dohler, Pastor EW Wiebusch, Dr M Lohe, Pastor OE Thiele, Pastor SH Held

The urge not to overlook good hymns or good tunes led to some interesting results. To help meet the expressed desire to have more *'Inner Mission'* hymns (a rubric which became *'Work and Society'* in the later Supplement of the hymnbook), Otto Thiele and I created the Hymn 238 (*'O God of mercy, hear us now'*), in which we recast the disjointed thoughts and phrases of an American author that had been accepted in 1956 from an additional listing by the Queensland S/C as a 'Queried' hymn. — The request from the Music S/C if possible to provide a text for a tune that was regarded as worth including led to several hymns being included. (1) J.P. Lohe's tune *Immanuel*, composed for *'Lord of the Church, we humbly pray'* (No. 245), was not adopted for that hymn, but it was regarded a good tune. My work-sheets show that I consulted 22 hymnbooks and listed 56 hymns. The hymn that O.E. Thiele and I submitted, No. 132, *'Spirit of wisdom, turn our eyes'*, was a complete recast of an anonymous hymn of c.1850 that emerged from further search, in which we highlighted the sevenfold gifts of the Holy Spirit. John Strelan wrote a hymn for travellers (No. 581) that provided a second acceptable hymn for the tune. (2) The second example of a recommended tune is *Houghton*. In a lesser known hymnbook of evangelical spirit, *Christian Hymns for the Christian Year*, I found a hymn (No. 367, *'O bring to the Lord your tribute of praise'*) that has met with immediate acceptance.

The principle that the original words of an author (except in translations) should be adhered to as much as possible caused a good deal of research to be undertaken by us in S.A. Sub-Committee II. The ascriptions in our hymnbook to many well-known English hymns taken over from *Hymns Ancient and Modern (HA&M:* caustically dubbed by some when it appeared as *Hymns Adulterated & Mutilated)* show that many hymns are popular in their altered form. To give an obvious example: No one dreams of singing *'Hark how all the welkin rings'* as the opening line of *'Hark, the herald angels sing'*.

Chapter 5

It was surprising how much alteration editors of hymnbooks were prepared to make. The English hymn, much favoured in our Australian Lutheran circles on account of its emphasis on 'justification by faith' (No. 331. Edward Mote, '*My hope is built on nothing less*') provided an example. I compared the version in 16 hymnbooks with Mote's original. No book carried Mote's version unaltered. Using the relevant mathematical formula, which I have now forgotten, I calculated that the alterations when spread out over all combinations would create 38,880 versions of the hymn! Even in preparing the text of the simple loved '*Away in a manger*' we among other variations had to decide the reading for <u>one</u> line between the lines that were offered by 25 books: *And stay by my cradle till morning is nigh,* or *by my side until morning,* or *my side till the morning,* or *my bedside till morning,* or *my cradle to watch lullaby.*

The <u>translation of hymns</u>, especially of the rich Lutheran heritage, figured very largely in the discussions of the Committee. It was not easily satisfied, and the notation 'improve translation' often continued to recur in the same hymn. Most of the attention to translations was devoted to the revision of translated hymns that had appeared in the *Australian Lutheran Hymnbook*. The most common purpose was to express the thoughts of the original more closely, but also to avoid crudities of expression, or to fit words better to the music. — The repentance hymn that commenced '*Alas my God, My sins are great, My conscience doth upbraid me; And now I find, That in my strait No man hath power to aid me*' remained under a cloud for many years because there was a feeling there was a weakness in this Winkworth translation by not having the internal rhyme in lines 1 and 3. I finally prepared a reworked translation, taking into account another Winkworth translation, and the hymn appeared as No. 309, '*Ah, Lord and God, How sore my load! My conscience doth upbraid me; My sins are great, And in my strait No man hath power to aid me*'. – In a hymn by Luther (No. 196), Thiele and I wrestled with a correct understanding of what Luther was saying when he wrote (in a literal translation): '*The silver, seven times proved by fire, is found to be pure; with the Word of God one shall expect the same at all times. It must be proved through the cross, then its power is recognised, and its light, and shines strongly into the lands.*' We appealed to Dr. Sasse for help. He replied that in the German '*there is a certain lack of logic. The silver is not only tried, but also purified. Thus the parallel is not absolutely valid. For the Word of God is only tried out, not purified*'. He explained the reference to the cross (which puzzled us) as '*when we bear our crosses*'. We still wrestled with the wording for years, with at least nine versions. The words that were printed were: '*Like silver, seven times purified And proved through much refining, The Word will ever pure abide, In all perfection shining. Neath burdened cross it proves its might, Till far and near men see its light And own its power to save them.*' — The change in another hymn also provides an example of our querying minds. The opening of the Hymn No. 218 in all translations was addressed to the Holy Spirit. The more we looked at all references to the Spirit in the hymn, the more Otto and I queried whether the initial reference was to the 'Spirit of the first witnesses who stand on the walls of Zion as faithful watchmen', and regarded it as a reference to their 'spirit' or 'zeal'. Again we appealed to Dr. Sasse regarding the correctness of our thinking; again he agreed with us. Thus the version of this hymn in our hymnbook differs from anything else previously offered: '*Arouse, O Lord, that zeal inspiring The faithful saints who witnessed day and night*'.

Dr Hermann Sasse

The large number of <u>hymns in the so-called 'Sapphic Metre'</u> received much attention. In its true Latin form the 11-syllable line fell into two parts, marked by two minims, in which the second minim opened the second part of the phrase. In the singing of English (and also German) words the cadence sounded more natural as a feminine ending. To illustrate the true Sapphic Metre and the English 'cadence' (underlining indicating the two minims):

'Of what great <u>crime   hast</u> Thou to make confession'   'Of what <u>offences</u>   must Thou make confession.'
'They give Thee <u>gall   to</u> drink, they still decry Thee'   'Gall do they <u>give Thee</u>,   harshly they decry Thee'.

When the proposal to make such alterations to this hymn (No. 55) was placed before the Plenary Committee the 'challenge' was issued to demonstrate how this would work out in the whole hymn. Immediately after that session I had to set out for Point Pass for the weekend duties. Because I knew very many of the stanzas by heart I mentally began the alterations during my 75-mile drive. On Monday morning I was able to return to Adelaide with a duplicated new version. In the years that followed the same 'cadence' alterations were arranged for all the hymns in the relevant metre.

We (Otto and I) mostly worked conjointly in a meeting, suggesting lines or phrases to each other. In one instance of this, each stanza finished with a recurring *'Meinen Jesum laß ich nicht'*, i.e. *My Jesus I will not leave*, or *My Jesus I will not forsake*. We suggested to each other as many words as we could think of to rhyme with *'leave'* and to rhyme with *'forsake'*. *'Leave'* won the day. In the Plenary Committee meetings the cry was sometimes humorously raised, *'O for a rhyming dictionary!'* One day Walter Roehrs put down a book on the table. It was *'The Improved Rhyming Dictionary'* by Jane Shaw Whitfield; and this became our useful official guide in Sub-Committee SA. II. — Sometimes Otto and I worked separately for a time until we were ready to offer a completed section, or we did this at home, to offer our work at the next meeting. The ascription *'Hymnal Compilers'* mostly covers the outcome of work that Otto and I did in this fashion.

The second aspect of work on translations was providing <u>new translations</u>. The thought of adding additional valuable hymns from the great heritage of German hymnody very much depended on good translations being prepared. In practice this was left to O.E. Thiele and me. Many of our versions ended up on the cutting room floor, because the Hymnbook Committee, in its critical assessment of texts, was not more merciful towards the work of its own members. The translation of No. 66, *'Seele, geh auf Golgotha'*, provides an illustration of what could happen. We worked separately, and submitted both versions. Otto's translation, *'Go, my soul, to Calvary'*, was adopted by the Hymnbook Committee; Philipp Scherer, editing the Aranda Hymnbook and receiving our work, however did not support the Hymnbook Committee decision and adopted my translation, *'Go to Golgotha, my soul'*, with the first line altered to *'Go to Calvary's mount, my soul'*. — The result of this translation activity was that (according to my count) 14 translations of new hymns were added: 5 by us 'Hymnal compilers', 4 by Otto Thiele (including *'Sun of righteousness divine'*, No. 185), 4 by me (including the difficult *'In Thee is gladness'*, No. 386), and 1 by P.G. Strelan (*'Beside Thy manger here I stand'*, No. 27).

One day in Carlsruhe Otto sombrely handed me a piece of paper. On it stood words he had composed while on vigil at the deathbed of his son James's wife. It was moving to read it, and I encouraged submitting it to the Hymnbook Committee; it appears in the Hymnbook as No. 417, *'Submissive to Thy will'*. — Another original hymn by Otto is No. 256, *'Not to us, O Lord, the glory'*, the only offering that could be accepted, from among about 12 other offerings responding to a Church-wide appeal, as a hymn that commemorated the coming together of the two Lutheran church bodies. — We even looked at some non-German hymns in the old hymnbook. John Larsen provided literal translations as a help in evaluating the translations of the Scandinavian hymns. We did make a few changes; but we certainly did not alter the opening line of a rather popular hymn, *'Built on a rock the Church doth stand'*. That line probably engenders a positive 'feel' towards the hymn; I doubt if there would be the same 'feel' if we in the pursuit of accuracy had reverted to the meaning of the original Danish, *'The Church, which is an old house'*!

In preparing *'Ljelintjamea—Pepa Lutherarinja'*, the **Aranda Lutheran Hymnal**, Scherer maintained liaison with me so that our hymnbook versions were used. In addition he included 6 other of my translations: *Thou Help of sinners, O refresh me* (No. 337, 10 stanzas); *Jehovah, Jehovah, Jehovah* (339); *Tiny Child, yet mighty God* (357); *This is the Lord's triumphal day* (365); *The best of friends is found in heaven* (385). In addition he listed, as a combined translation, *Two disciples, filled with longing* (368), a translation of *Zween der Jünger gehn mit Sehnen* (which T.G.H. Strehlow translated into Aranda); in this case I can only recall that I was not inspired by the German words to translate, but I must have provided sufficient phrases or lines that Philipp included my name.

Photo on left: *Pastor Philipp Scherer*

[Ed: The section in which Henry discusses the final layout is missing from his handwritten notes. It continues as follows:]

...set up in the later Indexes was followed as much as possible; exact chronological progression, however, was impossible because it was mainly hymns from English sources that could be used to complete the second page of a long Lutheran hymn. Where the space after a long Lutheran hymn was too little to accommodate a second hymn, we editors, borrowing an attractive idea from the *Evangelisches Kirchengesangbuch*, inserted longer or shorter Scripture passages related to the hymn section. The frontispiece three pages were based on drafts that I prepared.

Chapter 5

A number of features that were lacking in the work of the Hymn Book Committee showed up. 'Jim' Wiebusch and I attended to these, in most cases (if I remember correctly) drawing the Chairman's attention to this. I drafted 5 pages of 'Terms used in Worship'. Joint work supplied a variety of additions, 'Liturgical Colours', the Athanasian Creed (reprinted from Tappert's Symbolical books), 'Lessons for Matins and Vespers' (2 pages with Epistles and Gospels based on the German Eisenach series and the OT lessons selected from the other Series), 'Order for Emergency Baptism'. When we pasted up the chosen Psalms we discovered that there were a few pages where a psalm of suitable length could be included. The choice was made in conversation with Erich Renner (selections and printing) and James Thiele (selection of chant). – When the Tune Edition had been completed we set up the Melody Edition in the type face that had been chosen by the Hymn Book Committee.

A final comment about the **role of the Hymnbook Committee.** I cannot imagine that any committee could be more dedicated in preparing the best possible hymnbook for its Church than this one. But there is another valuable feature in its work. During my career I have often been asked by interested people, including non-Lutherans, what contributed to Lutheran union. In my reply I have made reference to the activity of the Hymnbook Committee. Its members by and large belonged to the influential section of their respective Church. They got to know one another through continual contact; they freely discussed the theological standpoint of the hymns, and they found that there was unity in their theological thinking on the vital doctrines of the Church. Critical attitudes were replaced by respect for one another, which extended beyond the committee. There was one occasion (I think it involved acceptance of a hymn) when someone in a jocular voice commented that the close vote was 'UELCA versus ELCA' – and everyone laughed, because it quite obviously was not an 'alignment' of church representatives. — For me personally this togetherness was particularly exemplified – and strengthened through joint labours in other areas – in my ever deepening friendship with Otto Thiele. Otto did not live to see the fruit of his labours appear in print in 1973. When he died in 1971 I was astounded (and the remembrance of it still deeply moves me) that his family did not approach any of the dozens of fellow-ELCA pastors, but chose me to give the funeral sermon.

Pastor Otto Thiele. His funeral was held at Bethlehem Lutheran Church on 29 Dec 1971.

Hymn Book Committee hard at work at Church House, Archer St
From left: James Thiele, Les Grope, Henry Proeve, Alf Miller, Otto Thiele

THE LUTHERAN, JULY 30, 1973. 3

President L.B. Grope accepts the new "Lutheran Hymnal" on behalf of the Church.

A BOOK OF WORSHIP

Although primarily prepared as a book containing hymns, the *Lutheran Hymnal* is more than that. It is a book of worship, designed to serve as a devotional aid in the congregation and in the home.

The singing of hymns, particularly in the Lutheran Church, takes place within the framework of liturgical orders of service which this Church has retained as a heritage linking it devotionally with the Christians of pre-Reformation centuries. In addition to the two chief Orders of Service and the Confessional Service already in use, the hymnal offers Matins and Vespers as orders for morning and evening (or afternoon) use respectively. The Order of Matins is available for the first time in our circles, and will undoubtedly be an enrichment to our worship, especially as this order and the Order of Vespers encourage a greater use of the Canticles and Psalms.

The first 128 pages in which these orders of worship appear also supply other material which is intended to give edifying variation within the optional portions of the orders or to make worship more meaningful.

In the section headed "The Propers", which contains the Introit, Collect, Old Testament Lesson, Epistle and Gospel for each festival or day of the Christian Year, the texts of the collects (the brief prayers which introduce the lessons) have been provided for the first time, in addition to the texts of the Introits. A table of Lessons for Matins and Vespers, listing alternative Old Testament lessons, Epistles and Gospels, and suitable Psalms, has been specially prepared for this book, based on a number of selections of pericopes (i.e. readings) in order to avoid duplication of passages, and chosen to harmonize with the general thoughts of the day. These may well be used also in home devotions.

It has been the Committee's aim to provide the text of various elements of worship, so that the congregation, if desired, may participate in recitation. The third Ecumenical Creed which our Church acknowledges, the Athanasian Creed, is made available in a modern translation. At Matins and Vespers, optional provision is made for a Responsory — "a longer grouping of Scripture verses, connecting the Lessons at Matins and Vespers with the Christian Year, and emphasizing their central thought" — to follow the Lesson, and for an Antiphon (literally "responsive strain") to introduce the Canticle. The text of Antiphons and Responsories suitable for the Seasons of the Christian Year has been provided.

Alternate General Prayers in responsive form appear in the form of the Litany, which Luther called "the best prayer on earth after the Lord's Prayer", and the Suffrages (General, Morning, and Evening). Suffrages "from the Latin *suffragium* 'assent', are short, concise petitions, to which the people assent by their response". The Morning and Evening Suffrages are particularly suitable for home use.

Members of the Editorial Committee, H.F.W. Proeve, left, and E.W. Wiebusch, examine the "Lutheran Hymnal".

Mr. James Thiele, music editor.

General Rubrics (i.e. "directions prescribed for the conduct of religious worship") give an indication of permissible uses of the available material which can add to helpful variation in the services. The liturgical colours have been explained in another section and their use in the Lutheran Church of Australia tabulated in a style which should facilitate easy reference.

It is natural and universally accepted that every aspect of life develops its own terms and vocabulary. This is also true in the religious aspect. As the technicalities of printing made the pages available, we have been able to include five pages which explain the terms used in worship. We believe that this will be appreciated by all who desire to worship with understanding. Several examples have been quoted in this article.

As any Christian has the right to administer Baptism in an emergency, the liturgical section of the hymnal closes with an Order for Emergency Baptism, which has been prepared for this book.

H.F.W. Proeve.

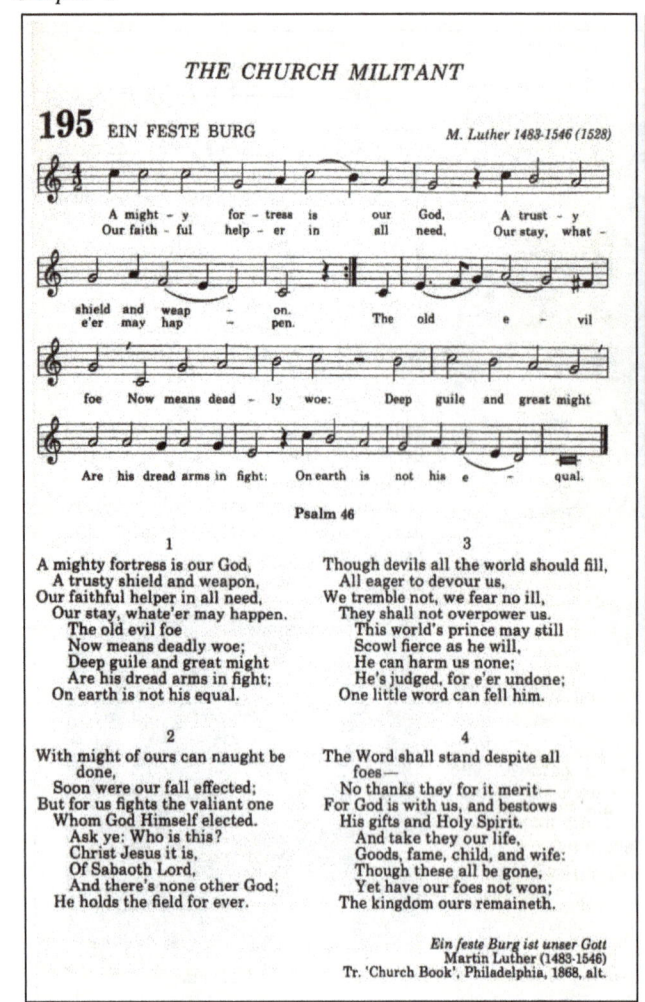

Photo above: *LPH Manager Martin Hoopmann presents Dr Grope with the Tune Edition in June 1973*

Photo at left: *A page from the Word Edition*

10. School Hymnal Committee. The above-mentioned activity in the realm of hymnody was supplemented in the years just before my removal to Point Pass and at Point Pass by other work connected with hymns / carols.

My memory has become unsure about the book of Christmas carols, entitled **'Beside Thy Manger'**, that we worked on and appeared in print. It contained a careful, wider choice of carols than what is generally available in books and records that appear from English sources. My basic memory is that it unfortunately did not meet with the success that had been hoped for. That was largely due to the fact the matter of publishing a tune edition struck problems at Lutheran Publishing House. A list of the tunes and the books in which they appeared was issued; but that was of little help, because it was highly unlikely that people would have the books that we had consulted. Otto Thiele, 'Jim' Wiebusch and I spent a good deal of our hymnbook time selecting and preparing the manuscript. After the amalgamation, when Everard Leske, who had a deep appreciation of German and other-language carols, was the Director of Publications, he edited a good collection of carols.

The other activity that belongs under this heading is the production of the 'Children's Hymnal', **'Rejoice and Sing'**, which was intended to be the School Hymnal of the two Churches. The word 'intended' already hints at the amount of success. — In June 1961 I was appointed by the Presidents of the two Churches to be the convenor of a School Hymnal Committee, and was subsequently elected as its Chairman. It consisted of an equal number of representatives of the ELCA and UELCA, elected by the relevant committees: Paul Gersch and Elizabeth (Mrs.S.K.) Bartsch (Sunday School interests), Bruno Matuschka and Gertrude Jacob (Day-school interests), Otto Thiele and I (Hymn Book Committee). Due to Otto's ill-health at the time, the formulations of basic principles and preparation of a list of hymns to initiate discussion at the first Committee meeting in September 1961 was undertaken by 'Jim' Wiebusch and me.

The Committee operated on lines very similar to those of the Hymnbook Committee: study of hymnals for children of varying ages (more than a dozen); four Sub-Committees: 1.Point Pass, 2.Barossa, 3.Victoria, 4.Adelaide, to give detailed attention to hymns in their allotted sections, making recommendations regarding inclusion or non-inclusion, and to provide the text of recommended hymns. Pastor Lionel Janetzki assisted Bruno in Sub-Committee 3, and Norman Auricht assisted Gertrude in Sub-Committee 2. Paul Gersch, well-known as a musician in the public and Church schools systems, and I served as the Music Sub-Committee, acting in collaboration with James Thiele of the Hymnbook Committee. Three types of hymns and tunes were kept in mind: Kindergarten (as a separate section; 36 largely one-stanza hymns), Junior and Senior sections, with the latter in particular leading into the hymnbook of the Church. In my estimation a striking feature of the book as a School Hymnal is presenting the hymns in one section under the various Parts of Luther's Small Catechism.

All the material of the Sub-Committees passed through my hands – and my stencil-cutting typewriter – 104 foolscap pages of it, plus 67 foolscap pages of three Reviews of hymns and their tunes, two Metrical Indexes, and Orders of Worship. Lesser personal contributions were being the person who added a stanza to a Kindergarten hymn of one stanza (No.5, Easter hymn), and three stanzas to a stanza by Isaac Watts to form a hymn on the Law of God (No.170). In addition I revised No. 212 (*O praise ye the Lord*) a little. — By the end of 1964 the Committee had completed its work, and the text of each hymn was available in manuscript, largely through the typing activity of Seminarist Kevin Zwar, to which I have referred in an earlier chapter.

The problems that lay ahead lay in the realm of publication, and started to show up officially in November 1962, when I met with the heads of the publishing houses of the two Churches. The ELCA Director of Publications had almost before we started work asked me: '*To whom is the School Hymnal Committee responsible?*' and '*Who is responsible (finance, production, and distribution)?*, and this was his cry at the meeting. He didn't need to worry about the expenses of the Committee – these had been taken over without fuss by the Lutheran Book Depot. It was left to the two publishing houses to make joint arrangements. Lutheran Publishing House had the printery that could take over the word edition. The stumbling block was the Tune Edition. What had been suggested as a possibility in November 1962 became the adopted solution: a brochure was published, **'Rejoice and Sing – Tune Resources'**, which merely indicated the tunes chosen for each hymn and the books in which they could be found. This solution was as unsatisfactory as the model on which it was based, '*Beside Thy Manger*', had been.

It seems to me that most Sunday Schools and Day Schools continued to use whatever books they had been using. Its use in the secondary schools possibly would have belittled the status that they were seeking to achieve in the general community. And there may also have been the beginning of an attitude that has grown in the years that have passed by, viz. to turn against the 'heavy' hymns of the Lutheran Church. This 'temporary' expedient lasted for almost 10 years. It was only after the amalgamation, when the '*Lutheran Hymnal*' of the LCA appeared in 1974, that E.W. Wiebusch, as the Director of Publications, in the second half of the year steered a Tune Edition of '*Rejoice and Sing*' through the press.

The fact that the Lutheran Church of Papua-New Guinea decided to make use of it helped towards – possibly ensured – its publication. The ability to make use of the art work of the many tunes that had appeared in the '*Lutheran Hymnal*' simplified the financial problem.

Tune edition – Papua New Guinea

Chapter 5

11. UELCA Committee for Intersynodical Negotiations. This was the last of the committees in this list of extra-parish activity. Appointed in 1956, I had been spared many years of taking part in the theological negotiations of the two Churches. All I had to do was to attend further negotiations and listen to the debate. The remnants of the 'sinful unionism' concept, at this stage involving the UELCA and the other Lutheran Churches that were members of the Lutheran World Federation, also affecting the joint mission work of the UELCA in Papua-New Guinea, were the final 'sticking point'.

In December 1964 I set out from Point Pass, fully anticipating another round on the same topic. On that day the amazing thing happened that a proposal from the Faculties of the two Seminaries became a suggested **'Document of Union'**. I drove home, pondering in amazement how 'God moves in a mysterious way His wonders to perform'. And then there followed a combined meeting of Executives in January 1965, and the divinely guided developments of that year.

Members of the Intersynodical Committee (15 members missing)

The memories of the first section of my career –

- in the parish ministry of the UELCA for 22 years;
- as its Secretary for 20 years; and
- as a participant in many aspects of its activity (the extent of which has surprised me now that I have been recording it) –

thus end with the dawn of a new era for the Lutheran Church in Australia on the horizon.

Chapter 6

VI. FULL-TIME CHURCH SECRETARY DOUBLE DECADE:
1965 (August) — 1984 (November)

VI. A. The Joint Union Committee (JUC) Years (1965 – 1966)

The memories that I am recollecting in my Memoirs now run across a time when the nature of my duties was changing. The new duties were added when my prime duty was to serve the Point Pass Parish, and my secondary duty was to fulfil the duties of a Secretary of the UELCA. Then the parish duties fell away, and my first duty was to serve as Secretary of the UELCA, my other duty was to continue to carry out those new duties. The answer to this riddle-like introduction is the follow-on from the December 1964 meeting of the two Intersynodical Committees – the establishment of a Joint Union Committee, and my task of being its Secretary. Those two years form the preamble to this Chapter and my new career in the Lutheran Church.

A feeling of forward movement was in the air at this time. The number of round trips of 150 miles (241 km) that I made from Point Pass to Adelaide increased. On January 11, 1965, the final draft of the *Document of Union* was adopted by the Joint Intersynodical Committees. Three days later I was for the second time in Adelaide: this time for a meeting of the Executives of the Executive Council of the ELCA and of the General Church Council of the UELCA. They recommended to their respective Councils that a Provisional Joint Union Committee should be appointed, consisting of the Presidents (ex officio) and four pastors and three laymen from each Church. There was no idea of waiting to see what the ELCA and UELCA would resolve at their conventions in March and October respectively. There was work that could be commenced in hopeful anticipation of a positive vote at Toowoomba in March (but with some uneasiness attached to that hope) and at Horsham in October. The uneasiness was proved warranted by the immediate resignation of one pastor and some laymen from the ELCA after its decision in March. — A little over 20 months of intense deliberation and decision lay before the 17 men who met 19 times in that period. They warrant identification in my memoirs, because the LCA owes them a great 'Thank you' for their faithful work:

- ELCA – The Pastors Dr. Clem Hoopmann (President until March 1965), Harold Koehne (President), Clem Koch, Otto Thiele (who from March replaced T.W. Koch), Everard Leske; the brethren H. Pfeiffer, L. Schuster, Peter Pearce (who in March replaced the deceased J.E. Dolling);

- UELCA – The Pastors Dr. Max Lohe (President), Carl Pfitzner (Vice-President), Siegfried Held, Dr. Victor Roennfeldt, H.F.W. Proeve; the brethren Mostyn Keller, Ken Leske, Max Otto.

At its first meeting, February 26, 1965, the JUC elected Dr. H. Koehne as its Chairman and me as its Secretary. Dr. M. Lohe, who was ill and absent from the meeting, was the Vice-Chairman. I am convinced that this was a good arrangement. The quiet nature of Dr. Koehne made his a mediating influence, which was particularly necessary in the Queensland District of the ELCA.

Photo on right: *Henry Proeve and Dr Harold Koehne*

There are memories that are very much alive about the months that followed, and there are many memories about aspects of them that have faded. Random sets of various minutes have aroused some recollections that had disappeared from memory. It was during the early stage of activity in the JUC that the volume of work in the Point Pass Parish, as the Secretary of the UELCA, as a member of the hardest working sub-committee of the Hymn Book Committee, and last of all as Secretary of the JUC, took its toll on my health, so that my temporary breakdown in health was followed by taking office in September 1965 in Adelaide as the Secretary of the UELCA full-time. This is recounted in Chapter V.A.

157

Chapter 6

Terms of Reference of the Committee. After the October Convention of the UELCA the Committee ceased to be 'Provisional'. The two Church Councils in the previous August finalised the Terms of Reference of the JUC. This resolution said:

The purpose of the Committee shall be to promote the cause of union in harmony with the Document of Union and the resolutions of the respective Church Councils prior to the amalgamation of the Churches.
To achieve this aim the [Provisional] JUC is empowered to deal with the following matters:

1. *To draw up a Constitution and By-Laws for the new Church, which is to be submitted to the Church Councils of the respective Churches;*
2. *To work in collaboration with the Church Councils of the Districts in order to prepare a uniform basic constitution for the Districts of the Church, for inclusion in the Constitution or By-Laws of the Church;*
3. *To consider the feasibility of drawing up a basic interim Constitution;*
4. *To prepare any necessary submissions dealing with legal matters, such as the transfer of properties, incorporation, and other associated matters;*
5. *To appoint sub-committees to work in specific areas affecting the amalgamation, and to receive reports from the same;*
6. *To receive Progress Reports from the Church Councils of the Districts of the Churches;*
7. *To authorise representation at District Conventions or conferences of the Churches or other meetings connected with amalgamation;*
8. *To draw up a timetable for various steps necessary for union;*
9. *To initiate discussions under the provisions of Clauses 12, 13 and 14 of the Document of Union.*

The JUC began to function shortly before the March Convention of the ELCA. After the ELCA removed doubt concerning its possible reaction by its positive answer, the JUC met more frequently and discussed matters in more detail, so that 5 of its 19 meetings were held before the UELCA met in Convention in October. Authorised on October 1 by the JUC to do so, but without any opportunity of submitting my progress report to the JUC for consideration and endorsement, I wrote and submitted a report to that Convention on the progress of discussions in eight areas of those terms of reference. — This is not a complete coverage of the activities of the JUC. That is excellently done in Chapter Thirteen of *'For Faith and Freedom'* by Everard Leske, written from personal experience on the JUC.

Matters affecting me as the Secretary of the UELCA

Before I begin an unbroken presentation of my recollections of the activities of the JUC until its task was completed, this is the point where I will best draw passing attention to my situation as Secretary of the UELCA at this time. There are three matters of UELCA import that ran parallel to JUC activity in the first ten months of 1965.

1. Removal to Royston Park. Dorothy played an important role in securing our residence in this suburb. The period available to secure a house was comparatively limited, and time passed by without any house coming into sight. While I was attending a meeting in Adelaide, Dorothy scoured the retail pages of houses for sale, visited some agents, and then drew the attention of relieved authorities in the UELCA to a corner house that she had inspected and considered suitable. It was an L-shaped house close to Carl Pfitzner's house, with a large tree in the yard. It was the home where our children developed into adulthood. — Carol completed her training as a primary school teacher, and when she was appointed to her first position at Brahma Lodge she learnt to drive the Austin A40 car that was secured for her from this home; the quiet streets of Royston Park provided the safe venue for the first steps of teaching her to drive. It was there that she introduced us to a friend John, and from which she left the parental home as a married woman. — David, more intent on practical things than on academic subjects, attended Norwood Technical College, and commenced work at Woolworths in Elizabeth. We helped him put many a rubber band around copies of the suburban free papers that he delivered on his bicycle to earn pocket money. — Philip attended Immanuel College; his interest in mechanics commenced when he took up casual bowser attendance at a motor service station in St. Peters, and led to his training as a well-qualified motor mechanic at the appropriate school in Croydon.

Chapter 6

2. Convention of General Synod UELCA, October 1965. Close attention to JUC matters had to take second place as the time approached for the UELCA to hold its Convention, at which the important matter of adoption of the *Document of Union* had to be considered. Long before that Convention was held I had to carry out all preliminary and then ongoing duties associated with the office: notices in the Church paper, preparation of Agenda, collecting Reports, printing of the Book of Reports by Auricht's Printing Office. Then came attendance at the General Pastors Conference and assisting Dr. Lohe in an explanation at the Convention of all the developments in the intersynodical scene. Finally the publication of the Official Report, and the correspondence arising from the Convention resolutions.

Pastors at the UELCA General Convention, Horsham, Oct 1965. (Henry seated in front row, 6th from left)

3. Declaration of Altar and Pulpit Fellowship. A memory associated with these gripping months that will never fade is the service on November 26, 1965, when altar and pulpit fellowship between the two Churches was declared. I have difficulty in finding the words to describe how I felt when, as the liturgist, I led the Presidents M. Lohe and H.D. Koehne and the Seminary Principals S.P. Hebart and H.P. Hamann into the sanctuary of the commodious Bethlehem Church. Awe, wonder, joy at what God had achieved in leading everything to this moment — a trembling, almost overwhelming sense of privilege as I turned at the altar to face the large combined congregation from two Churches and intoned the Invocation to worship and give thanks. The mighty 'Amen' that echoed through the Church in response affirmed that everyone was deeply conscious of the significance of the moment: two Churches were one in spirit in an 'official' service that was symbolical of the many similar services that would follow throughout Australia.

Standing at front: Drs M Lohe, C Hoopmann, H Koehne. Standing at altar: Henry Proeve

It was a similar experience for me when a year later it was my privilege to be the opening liturgist at the service with which **union of the two Churches** was initiated at Tanunda at the Constituting Convention.

Chapter 6

Recollections about the JUC

The JUC carried out its *'mammoth task'* (Ev. Leske's phrase) by arranging for five Sub-Committees to do the detailed preparation and to report to the JUC. These were: Sub-Committee on Structure (Chairman, Dr. Vic. Roennfeldt); S/C on Constitution; S/C on Salaries (Chairman, Mostyn Keller); S/C on Fellowships and Affiliations (Chairman, Dr. Max Lohe).; and S/C on Publications (Chairman, M. Lohe). Probably on account of the huge volume of various discussions that occupied my mind at the time, I have retained no recollection of some of these Sub-Committees, although I was the Secretary of all of them, who published each set of Sub-Committee minutes on its own colour of duplicator paper, so that the members of the JUC could easily identify which set of Sub-Committee minutes they were looking at. — A few of my particular recollections follow.

The S/C on Structure secured the freely given and valued advice of Oswald Heinrich as a consultant. Formerly a highly successful farmer in the Maitland district of Yorke Peninsula, Mr. Heinrich won great acknowledgement in the business world through his rescue of the important Horwood Bagshaw company from bankruptcy. His exposition of good business principles was accompanied by his attitude as a sincere committed churchman, who emphasised that not everything that applied to business applied to a Church – their purposes differed very greatly.

In the S/C on Constitutions we very quickly struck a serious difference of opinion that related to the position of the Ministry within the Church. We members of the UELCA anticipated that the statements regarding the Ministry in the adopted Theses of Agreement would facilitate adoption of a statement (like that in the UELCA Constitution) that the LCA consisted of *'congregations and pastors'*. An additional favourable factor was that the Lutheran Church – Missouri Synod Constitution added *'pastors and teachers'* to *'congregations'* as members. But Clem Koch of the ELCA was so adamantly persistent in his opposition to the inclusion of *'pastors'* that there was danger of a theological impasse. To make progress the word *'pastors'* was <u>not</u> written into Clause IV.1 of the Constitution; but at the insistence of us UELCA men the entire Article on The Ministry was brought forward from its original later position in the draft to become the Article that immediately followed Article IV, as an immediate statement of the importance and necessity of the Ministry of the Church (Article V, Clause 1).

Photo on right: *Leaving Bethlehem Lutheran Church after the Declaration of Altar & Pulpit Fellowship, 26 Nov 1965*

The S/C on Salaries, one of the earliest to commence work, initially requested the combined Seminary Faculties to provide a theological opinion. My main recollection here is that this opinion, which gave *'double honour'* (1.Tim. 5,17) an interpretation that raised eyebrows in the S/C, caused me to go to the Seminary Library for many days to study the modern commentaries that I did not have in my library. One of the lecturers noticed this frequent visiting, and rather suspiciously (I think) asked me what I was doing there. I finally wrote a study that took <u>all</u> Scripture passages into account, and applied them as I thought fitting to the entire matter of salaries (purpose, method of determining, etc.), and read it to the Sub-Committee. The outcome was that my study formed the basis of the report on salaries that was placed before the Constituting Convention on behalf of the JUC.

The S/C on Fellowships and Affiliations is a surprising blank in my memory, even though I was appointed to convene a meeting of one of its sub-committees, which was asked to consider the matter of overseas Churches. As the task of the S/C on Fellowships was to give further attention to the matter that had for years prevented the amalgamation – the matter of fellowship and working together with other Lutheran groups – its 16 members were selected from the membership of the Joint Intersynodical Committee. The Report of the Constituting Convention shows that most of the matter was left to the new Commission on Theology and Inter-Church Relations for careful attention as a united Church.

The JUC was especially concerned that its discussions and resolutions should be widely known in the two Churches. Its minutes were widely dispersed – not only to the members of the JUC and of the Church Council of both Churches, but also to the members of the District Church Councils of both Churches. The first official Minute Book unfortunately does not exist any more. An ELCA pastor well-known to me, Alf. Miller, sought a loan of it. The Lord soon after called him suddenly out of this life, and the family could not locate it when I made enquiries. The wide spread of these minutes, however, has ensured, I believe, that there are copies in the Lutheran Archives from the estates of deceased pastors.

```
PROVISIONAL JOINT UNION COMMITTEE, E.L.C.A. and U.E.L.C.A.

Minutes of Meeting held Friday, February 26, 1965, at 10 a.m.
             at Lutheran Church House, North Adelaide.

1. MEMBERSHIP OF COMMITTEE.
     The membership of the Provisional Joint Union Committee consisted of the
following persons, elected by the respective Executive Council and Church Council:
E.L.C.A.:  Dr. C. E. Hoopmann (President, E.L.C.A.); the Pastors H. D. Koehne, T. W.
           Koch, C. I. Koch, Everard Leske; the brethren J. E. Dolling, H. Pfeiffer,
           L. Schuster.
U.E.L.C.A.: Dr. M. Lohe (President, U.E.L.C.A.); the Pastors C. J. Pfitzner, S. H.
           Held, Dr. V. G. Roennfeldt, H. F. W. Proeve; the brethren M. G. Keller,
           K. B. Leske, M. A. Otto.
     All members of the Committee were present, with the exception of Dr. M. Lohe,
who forwarded an apology for absence due to ill-health.
2. OPENING.
     By general consent Pastor C. J. Pfitzner (Vice-President, U.E.L.C.A.) opened
the meeting. Pastor Pfitzner led in prayer, beseeching the guidance and blessing
of God in all further discussions and decisions connected with the union of the two
Lutheran Churches.
3. OFFICE-BEARERS.
(a) Chairman:  RESOLVED That Pastor H. D. Koehne be elected as Chairman.
(b) Secretary: RESOLVED That Pastor H. F. W. Proeve be elected as Secretary.
4. EXPRESSION OF SYMPATHY.
     Dr. C. E. Hoopmann expressed the sympathy of all present at the news of the
illness of Dr. M. Lohe and of Mrs. C. J. Pfitzner, and moved the resolution which
follows.
RESOLVED That we record our sympathy with Dr. M. Lohe in his illness and with Pastor
and Mrs. C. J. Pfitzner in the illness of Mrs. Pfitzner, and transmit to them our
message of goodwill.
5. MINUTES OF MEETING OF EXECUTIVES OF EXECUTIVE COUNCIL, E.L.C.A., AND CHURCH
     COUNCIL, U.E.L.C.A., held January 14, 1965.
     The minutes were read for the information of the members of the Committee.
RESOLVED (by motion and vote of the members of the Executives present) That we
regard the minutes as a correct record of the proceedings, and recommend their
adoption to the Executive Council of the E.L.C.A. and Church Council of the U.E.L.C.A.
```

The Sub-Committee that had the longest-lasting task was the **S/C on Constitutions.** It is possible to recognise this even through a casual perusal of the Official Report of the Constituting Convention:
- <u>Section II</u> — Constitution of the LCA, By-Laws of the LCA; Constitution of the Districts, By-Laws Part A of the Districts.
- <u>Section IX</u> — Model Constitution for Congregations, and Suggested By-Laws.
- <u>Rules of thirteen Boards</u> — including entire rules for Luther Seminary and for Lutheran Teachers' College.

In covering this wide range of subjects the Sub-Committee was often dependent on the speed with which other bodies, e.g. Church boards and corresponding District committees, provided a report on their suggestions how their area of activity should be carried out in the amalgamated Church. In preparing the Constitution of the LCA the Sub-Committee had access to the Constitutions of other Lutheran Church bodies in the USA (especially because those that were members of the LWF had exchanged their Reports of Church Conventions with the UELCA), but of course most of all it always considered the provisions in the existing ELCA and UELCA Constitutions. But the Sub-Committee also had to launch into uncharted waters. A new Article, <u>*X. Discipline, Adjudication, and Appeals*</u>, was drafted. The Germans have a saying, *'Wer A sagt, muß auch B sagen'*, i.e. *'He who says A, must also say B'* – the equivalent English saying is quite different, *'In for a penny, in for a pound'*. Our non-Lutheran legal consultant pointed out that what we started in an Article in the Constitution had to have a follow-on in the By-Laws, laying down how it was to be implemented. So Otto Thiele and I had to become lawyers, drafting rules for the 'judiciary system', taking into account that this was a Church that was spread over six States and two Territories of the Commonwealth.

We had before us the disciplinary regulations of the United Lutheran Church of America (which had the legal advantage of having high-ranking lawyers, even judges, in its membership), and the provisions in the Act of Parliament governing the Anglican Church in S.A. We consulted Bert Teusner when we sought some guidance; his concern was that the principles of 'natural justice' were not compromised. The concerns of us two drafting theologians who also thought scripturally (Matt. 18 and 1. Cor. 6,1) are reflected in a clause that I am sure does not appear in any law-book: *5. ... Such discipline shall be carried out in an evangelical manner in accordance with the procedure laid down in Matthew 18:15-17. Any charge shall be made where possible in the first instance within the congregation, parish and district within which it arose to the intent that the matter shall be confined to as small an area as possible. At all stages of the procedure the purpose of all ecclesiastical discipline – "to gain thy brother" – is to be observed'.* — Writing these by-laws was the least enjoyable of my tasks. I often sighed and said: *'For a Church that wants to preach the Gospel, we are writing an awful amount of Law!'*

Chapter 6

Working Documents. Comparatively early in 1966 the Sub-Committee on Constitutions had completed and presented to the JUC enough work that the JUC had a **Working Document A** printed. This contained the draft Constitution of the LCA and the beginnings of the By-Laws of the LCA. Copies of this Document were distributed much more widely than the minutes of the JUC, so that the widest amount of reaction could be obtained: the Church Councils of the two Churches, all pastors of both Churches, and the personnel of all District Synods of both Churches. — At the same time a **Working Document B** was also printed and distributed like Working Document A, with particular emphasis on District involvement, for this Document set out the proposed Constitution of the Districts, and, in part, the By-Laws Part A of the Districts, which were regarded as basic to the uniform functioning of the Church. The hopefully positive attitude of the Districts was important before the final presentation at the Constituting Convention.

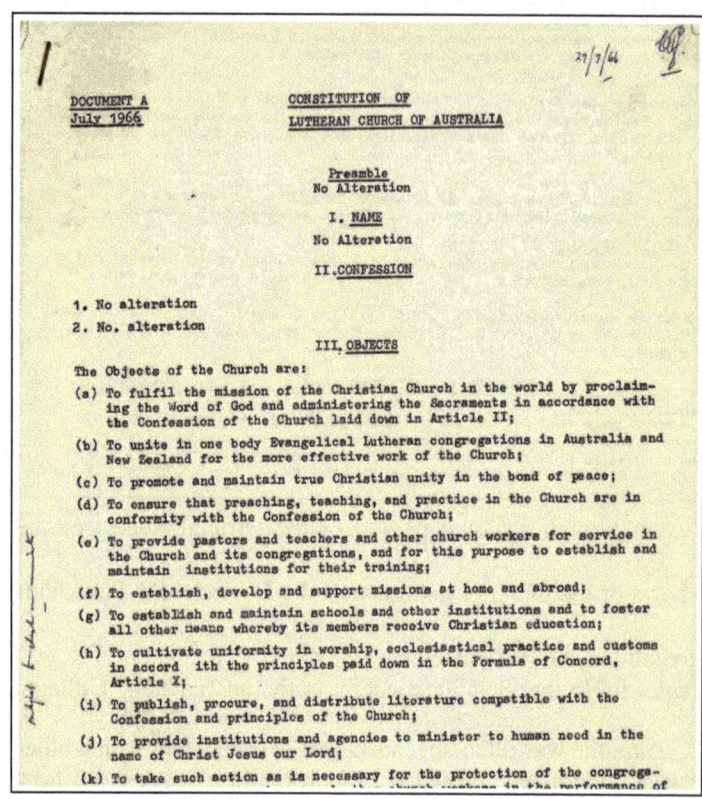

Correspondence between Lance Steicke, President of the Lutheran Church of New Zealand, and me led to the presentation in the first Working Document B of an amended form of the Constitution of Districts, headed 'NEW ZEALAND', which retained most of that Constitution, but took into account that this Church was the 'New Zealand District' of the LCA, but that it was at the same time a Church, the LUTHERAN CHURCH OF NEW ZEALAND, legally organised under the laws of another Dominion in the British Commonwealth of Nations. — When the JUC was considering what the LCA should be called, there was a suggestion that we possibly should avoid the word 'Australia' on account of New Zealand sensitivities, and include New Zealand by using the term 'Lutheran Church of Australasia'. The reply from New Zealand was a very firm 'NO'.

The Pressure of Final Months

As March 1966 approached the opinion was widespread that the latter part of October would be the time for the amalgamation. October 11-15 was suggested by Queensland as the most suitable for harvesting reasons; but, before the Queensland suggestion came to hand, in view of heavy bookings of facilities in the favoured Barossa, as safeguards the Tanunda Institute had been booked for a Pastors' Conference on October 27-28 (replaced by one of the Concluding Conventions), and the Tanunda Show Hall for a joint Convention on October 29-November 2. Behind us, on March 3, lay 53 weeks of work as JUC; ahead of us lay 34 weeks in which to finish a task that still had uncompleted matters in all sections of church activity. The necessarily careful way in which the preparation for the Constituting Convention was being made took precious time:

- Where necessary, suggestions from any existing general Church boards and eight District boards regarding a similar board in the LCA, made to the JUC and, for constitutions, to the S/C on Constitutions;
- All JUC decisions placed before the General Councils of both Churches for acceptance or review;
- Final presentation by JUC and the Joint Councils to the Constituting Convention.

At that March 3 meeting I placed before the JUC a draft *'Timetable of Preparation'* (attached below, except for points 11-13: District Church Councils; District Amalgamations; Formal Commencement of LCA and Districts). In it I in effect 'cracked a whip'. It gives some insight into the intricate amount of work that had to be completed. The fact that some Sections were late in being determined made the writing of the Report, which on the motion of Dr. C.E. Hoopmann was left in my hands at the second last (mid-September) meeting, an absolute nightmare for me. It was soon obvious to me that to provide a printed Report was completely impossible – it could not even be set up in stages and have consecutive page numbering. The only solution was to duplicate it. This was a task beyond the capability of my young "Girl-Friday" secretary. Carl Pfitzner generously made his experienced secretary, Rosemary Modra, available.

TIMETABLE OF PREPARATION

If the Constituting Convention of the LCA is to be held at the end of October 1966, the preliminary preparations will have to be controlled by a series of deadlines. These must take into account that it is proposed that the District Constituting Conventions be planned for the remaining two months of the year, and that the Districts depend on progress made in the general discussions for the completion of their own preparations.

The following is a suggested timetable:

Task	Deadline	Approx. wks. from Mar. 4	Meeting (week beginning)
1. **General**: Submission by District Conventions (completed by Qld. ELCA) and others of any points for review in Constitution of LCA and Districts. (Follow-on action in 3.)	May 14	9	
2. **Boards and Sub-Committees** (whose work involves Board structure). Submit their final suggestions regarding general set-up:			
x(a) those whose activities must be related with similar District Committees	May 21	10	
x(b) those whose activities are not closely related to District Committees	June 11	13	
x classification to be made			
3. **Sub-Committee on Constitution.**			S/C.March
(a) Complete preparation of By-Laws Part A for Districts and suggested uniform By-Laws Part B (immediate task) Forward to Districts, subject to any amendments at Stages 4(a) and 7.	May 21	10	April May 16
(b) Complete preparation of By-Laws of LCA (immediate task)	May 21	10	S/C.ditto
4. **Joint Union Committee.**			
(a) Review all constitutional matters submitted under 3. above	June 30 or earlier	16	May 23 or 30
(b) Complete proposals re Boards structure and Executive Officers			
1. In the case of 2(a) above and follow this by:	June 30	16	May 23 or 30
a. referring to Boards any detailed follow-up discussions.			
b. referring to District Church C'ls for implementation the establishment of related Dist. Committees (prior liaison to arrive at amicable understanding)			
2. In the case of 2(b) above	June 30	16	May 23 or later
5. **Sub-Committee on Constitution.** Complete rules governing Boards (follow-on of 4(b))	July 9	18	S/C July 4
6. **Joint Union Committee.**			
(a) Review all constitutional matters under 5. (Boards)	July 16	19	July 11
(b) Complete recommendations re procedures at Convention, particularly elections	July 16	19	July 11 or earlier
7. **Combined Church Councils**, etc.			
(a) Receive all progress reports (submitted from Stages 4 and 6); make decisions.	July 26 to 28 (meeting)	21	
(b) Selection of personnel (Boards and Executive Officers) ?			
(c) Prepare first Budget of LCA			
8. **Joint Union Committee.** Final review of total work in light of decisions at Stage 7.	Aug. 13	23	Aug. 1 or 8
9. **Body responsible for Constituting Convention**			
(a) Copy for reports ready for printing	Aug. 27	25	
(b) Printing of documents and reports completed	Sept. 24 (posted)	29	

Chapter 6

```
10. AMALGAMATION.
    (a) Preliminary combined session of
        Churches ? (to reach consensus
        on Constitution)                        Oct. 26        33½
    (b) Synods of both Churches (separate
        and concurrent)                         Oct. 27-28
    (c) Constituting Convention                 Oct. 29 to     34
                                                Nov. 1

11. District Church Councils.
    (a) Preparation of any special provisions
        in District Constitution required by
        State law. (cf. Working Document A,
                        Article IX.2)
    (b) Preparation of By-Laws Part B of Dis-
        trict (considering suggested uniform
        clauses provided by JUC after May 21;
        cf. Stage 3(a) above)
    (c) Establishment of District Committees
        related to a general Board (on basis
        of Stage 4(b)1.b.; after June 30)
    (d) Establishment of other District Com-
        mittees
    (e) Other preparations for District Con-
        stituting Convention.
    (f) Printing of documents and reports       4 wks. before resp. Convention
        completed                               October 8 onwards ?

12. DISTRICT AMALGAMATIONS.
    (a) South Australian conventions            Nov. 10-14 ?
    (b) Victorian conventions                   Nov. 17-21 ?
    (c) New South Wales conventions             Nov. 24-28 ?
    (d) Queensland conventions                  Dec. 1-5 ?
    (e) New Zealand: what action necessary?

13. FORMAL COMMENCEMENT OF LCA AND DISTRICTS
    (a) Official closing of all books           Dec. 31
    (b) Financial etc. operation of LCA and
        Districts begin                         Jan. 1, 1967.

                                                                HFWP
```

Dr Henry Proeve and the rainbow cake

In 1966 the task of pulling together all the threads of church union fell to Pastor Proeve, who had been appointed secretary of the Joint Union Committee. His assignment was to prepare the report on church union to the constituting convention of the new Lutheran Church of Australia.

Forty years after the constituting convention of the LCA, Dr Henry Proeve still clearly remembers the feeling of 'awe and wonder'

'I had each of the twelve sections of the report printed on different coloured paper', recalled Dr Proeve. 'It was like a rainbow cake.'

The last section could only be drawn up after 11 October, the date of a critical meeting about the place Luther Seminary would have in the unified church. The constituting convention of the new Lutheran Church of Australia was to begin just two weeks later.

'Nobody, not even the members of the general church council of either synod, saw the final report before it was mailed to delegates', said Dr Proeve. 'That was the level of trust they had placed in me. It was an enormous responsibility.'

Along with this was a deep sense of 'awe and wonder'. There was joy within both synods that the 120-year division had finally been overcome, Dr Proeve recalled. 'As far as the general public was concerned, too, the union removed the offence and puzzlement that these two churches could not get along. It was a very joyful time.'

After union there continued to be 'frank discussions', said Dr Proeve, 'but everybody was filled with the realisation that they were setting the course for this unified church. We were determined to make it work.'

Regarding the future of the LCA, Dr Proeve said that he could think of no better encouragement than the words he wrote at the close of his report to the constituting convention in 1966: 'We pray ... that the LCA ... under the blessing of our Lord will carry out its object "to fulfil the mission of the Christian church in the world by proclaiming the word of God and administering the sacraments in accordance with the confession of the church".

'It will be a church in the land under the Southern Cross, which will remain under the cross of our Lord Jesus Christ, rejoicing that there is, as its motto proclaims, *sub cruce unitas* [unity under the cross].' ∎

The original logo of the LCA (1996–1987)

Article in The Lutheran, *16 Oct 2006*

Piecemeal Preparation and Printing of the Official Report to Convention.
I devised a method of providing a manuscript. I divided the report into Sections. Each of these covered a specific aspect, and the manuscript was handed in when all decisions relating to the Section were complete; or, if only an identifiable portion was still awaited, the rest of the Section was handed in. Each Section was duplicated on a different coloured paper, and had its own page numbering. I particularly remember that for about a week I stayed in my study at Royston Park, with the request that telephone calls for me at Lutheran Church House should only be redirected to me at home if they related to what I was doing, or were really urgent. In the quietness of my home I could complete the collation of material that completed Sections.

Section IV. The Seminary of the Church' was the Section that caused the worrying delay in closing the Report. This was to be the first great project of the new Church, and as much detail as possible had to be provided. I don't recollect exactly when I completed the last manuscript. I think it must have been immediately after October 11, when the tenders of 17 firms were opened in the late afternoon. A Supplementary Report on the plans for the Seminary, and a Supplementary Report on the Church Paper had to be provided at the Convention. Apart from these and direct quoting from reports submitted to the JUC, every word of the Report was entirely my own summary of what the official bodies had decided. It concluded with the words *'Respectfully submitted on behalf of the Joint Union Committee, Executive Council of The ELCA, Church Council of The UELCA'* — but no one of any of those three bodies saw its wording until they received a duplicated copy! My report certainly had to be, and was, accepted in trust.

Queensland Problems. Throughout the period while the JUC was preparing the groundwork for the amalgamated Church, we were looking over our shoulder at the Queensland District. The ELCA District had been heavily indoctrinated by its long-standing President F.W. Noack, and that was where the problems might arise. In the early stages of the JUC work Dr. H.D. Koehne and I attended a Joint Pastors' Conference at Coolum to give an indication how the discussions were proceeding. Dr. Koehne in particular had to create, if possible, in some of the ELCA pastors an understanding of what was being accepted in both Churches. In April 1966, before the 1966 Convention of the ELCA District, he was again in Queensland. At a combined Pastors' Conference he faced a large number of points that raised basic issues about points that had already been accepted. They could be recognised as emanating especially, sometimes solely, from the ELCA pastors. (Their spokesman was Kurt Marquart, a pastor who had studied overseas. Two pastors, who were twin brothers, always supported him. One fellow-ELCA pastor once made the exasperated comment: *'They are twins, and have only one brain between them'.*). Dr. Koehne got in touch with me to provide an urgent answer from the JUC to the Queensland points while he was still in Queensland. It was impossible to convene a meeting of the whole JUC at such short notice; so I put the questions to the Sub-Committee on Constitution as a good cross-section. It met for three days, studying the points and their repercussions; and I sent a 7-quarto-page reply to Dr. Koehne.

It probably is instructive to a later generation to be given a brief summary of some of the 8 main Points that were thrown into the ring at this stage of the JUC deliberations. The basic point was expressed by Marquart: the Church should be *'a federation of Districts'*, and therefore the phrase *'as a part of the LCA'* should be dropped wherever it occurred in the Constitution of Districts. Closely associated with the above, and probably the hidden reason for this 'federation' idea, was the matter of *'withdrawal'* (by a congregation, but also possible by a District). The Queensland 'suggestion' to the JUC was *'to insert words somewhere to this effect: "The District shall belong to the LCA as long as in the judgment of the District the Church adheres to the confessional paragraph."'*. The idea did not enter the mind of those perfect members of this District who could sit *'in judgment'* on the Church that it was possible that the Church could judge that a District no longer *'adhered to the confessional paragraph'*! The influence of the mindset of some of the ELCA pastors (Marquart et al.) on the other pastors is revealed when the Queensland Conference 'passed the buck' to the JUC (my emphasis): *That in view of the wishes of some of the brethren of this conference, the JUC be asked to consider adding (in brackets) after "inerrant Word of God" in Article IV.1 the words "factually, historically, geographically, as well as theologically".*

We could not endorse the Queensland proposals; but we did recast the wording of some Articles a little. One change that did arise from our Sub-Committee was to make the General Synod a continuing body till the Convention of the next General Synod. I made the suggestion, borrowed from the Anglican Church and also the Old Prussian Church, that 'delegates' (who only acted as long the Convention was in progress) should become 'General Synodsmen', holding office until the next Convention, who could be called upon to vote on an important matter in the interim between Conventions. My suggestion was adopted. This term was used until the time came when *'man'*, whether used singly or in compounds, engendered a gender picture and therefore a mental storm in females with fixed ideas.

Chapter 6

This Queensland group had a soul-mate in S.A., the pastor of the Swan Reach parish. This parish obediently followed the constant insistence of its pastor (until he retired) and placed the same items on the agenda of several General Conventions (and on the agenda of annual District Conventions). It was even suggested by some in the LCA that we General Synod officials should refuse to accept these 'bobbing cork' agenda points. The Queensland group finally troubled us no more: Marquart went to the USA; the others under Clarence Priebbenow as a new theological leader and trainer of pastors formed a new truly Lutheran Church. In the meantime the persistence of these people had caused the LCA in its early Conventions to adopt Statements on several controversial issues.

Printing the Report. It was due to the devoted skill and organising ability of Rosemary Modra that the Report for the Constituting Convention still reached the 600 delegates within the barest of margins before the concluding Convention meetings began on October 27. With the permission of the relevant officials, she sought the assistance of other private secretaries in Lutheran Church House, especially when larger quantities of manuscript arrived from me. As a dedicated team, these ladies cut stencils and, using their office duplicators, duplicated on the coloured paper designated for the Section that they had typed. They collated as much of each Section as could be collated, for quite often there were only opening and/or closing portions. They carefully stored the collated material in the work-room, waiting for a middle section. As soon as consecutive Sections could be collated together, this was done in order to reduce the number of heaps. When the final middle portion of Section IV (Seminary) arrived – (this was the holdup in the completion of the Report) – the final burst of collating this portion into Section IV, and collating Section IV into its correct place between Section III and Section V, this completing more than 600 copies, then the 'rainbow' coloured foolscap-size Report could be stapled and posted to the delegates. These ladies did a magnificent job under great pressure.

Another Convention: Preparations. While all this activity was in progress there was another Convention for which preparation had to be made: the Closing Convention of The UELCA. I had secretarial responsibilities regarding that Convention. But Dr. Max realised that I was in an impossible situation. He kindly took over the detailed activity that I should be doing. Thus the Report to Convention was prepared, printed at Auricht's Printing Office, and posted in good time.

The Constituting Convention

The dominant memory of the Conventions that brought about the amalgamation of the two Churches is that of responsibility. I don't remember whose hospitality Dorothy and I enjoyed for six days in Tanunda. I don't recall the sounds of the anthems that the massed choirs of the Barossa joyfully rendered. I have already referred to my feelings as I led the opening service of the joint Convention in the Tanunda Show Hall. And a trivial, yet in these circumstances important, function that both Eric Mackenzie (as ELCA Secretary) and I had to keep an eagle on, stayed in memory, viz. to respond to every message that a delegate could/would not be present for a certain time by appointing a substitute delegate, so that the required equality of voting strength was preserved at all times – this has stayed in my mind. And I still feel the sense of responsibility that four of us felt as we sat on the temporary altar platform in front of the pavilion on the Tanunda Oval, and gazed on the estimated 10,000 joyful fellow-believers in front of us, who would see us installed as the chosen first office-bearers of a united Church.

First office-bearers of the Lutheran Church of Australia: Secretary Henry Proeve, Vice-President Harold Koehne, President Max Lohe, Treasurer Bert Doering

Procession of pastors at the Convention service

166

Chapter 6

Pastors at the LCA Constituting Convention, Tanunda Show Hall, October 1966
(Henry near the back, to the right of centre)

Convention service, Tanunda Oval, 30 Oct 1966 – view from altar of pastors and congregation

Chapter 6

VI. B. The Secretary of the LCA

Two years after the amalgamation of the two Lutheran Churches the General Church Council arranged a review of all full-time offices in the LCA. Max Otto interviewed me regarding **the function of the Secretary of the Church**. In my reply I picked up the symbolism of the Church being a ship: the President was the captain, whose position on the bridge made him the most visible. My place as Secretary was in the engine-room, with the task of ensuring that the ship could, and did, sail its course. On occasions, when Conventions of the General Synod were held, I appeared on the bridge with the captain to be his right-hand man, helping to pilot the ship through the convention waters. I know, and I'm convinced, that it is the Holy Spirit who makes things happen in the Church, as Luther's explanation of the Third Article in the Small Catechism says; but the Holy Spirit uses human instruments, and to have been instrumental with what I have is a privilege, I think, that has been given me.

The 19 years that I served as the LCA Secretary have naturally created many wide-ranging memories. In my Memoirs I attempt to correct my original rambling presentation by sorting them into two main groups:

- 1. My involvement in the large number of branches of Church activity, some together with the President; some as his representative, having oversight over selected boards / commissions of the Church; some as a member of such boards.
- 2. My service as a representative of the LCA in various areas.

The President and I at District Constituting Conventions

My first two visits to District Conventions (other than the South Australia District, where I was a member of its clergy) were connected with the establishment of Districts of the Church and therefore were visits of the President and Secretary of the Church. The first was the Constituting Convention of the Victorian District at Horsham in November 1966; the second was the Constituting Convention of the new Western Australia District in September 1967.

I naturally was present as a voting member of the District at the **Constituting Convention** of the **South Australia District**, which was held only 10 days after the close of the Convention of the LCA. Early in this convention there came a surprise – "shock" is possibly not too strong a term. Among the men of both Churches who were closely involved in the details of establishment there had been some neutral-minded 'counting of heads' concerning the possible composition of the General Church Council of the LCA in relation to the desire that it have 50/50 representation. It was considered that the likely set-up of pastors would be:

- UELCA, President and Secretary of the LCA; 2 District Presidents (S.A. and Queensland) = 4;
- ELCA, Vice-President of the LCA; 3 District Presidents (Victoria, New Zealand, probably NSW) = 4.
  (= 5, should an envisaged Western Australia District be established.)

The vote that chose the recently elected former ELCA President, Oscar Minge, in preference to the seasoned former UELCA District President and Vice-President of the UELCA, Carl Pfitzner, as President of the SA District, came as a complete surprise, also to Minge. His shocked reaction was visible to all as he clasped his face between his hands, and held them there for some time. Some of us believed that there was a reaction of sympathy among some of the UELCA delegates, following the recent LCA Convention, where they saw three UELCA men and one ELCA man installed into office, so that they wanted to give the ELCA a little more voice in the LCA. Oscar Minge gave quite good leadership to the District, where he enjoyed the co-operative support of the UELCA men; the personal relationship between him and me was very cordial.

1. Victorian District Constituting Convention. The composition of this Convention reflected the very great difference in the membership of the two amalgamating Districts. To the concern of Max Lohe and me, this voting advantage was allowed – one can even say 'encouraged' – by the ELCA District President to steam roller some decisions that contradicted the recommendations by the Joint Union Committee and the two Church Councils to <u>all</u> Districts. The names of the previous Districts of the two Churches had been a mixture of adjectives derived from the State names and (where such adjectives had a crude sound, e.g. New South Welsh, Queenslander) the name of the State. The unanimous recommendation, with a good model in the names in American Churches, was that the names of the State should be used. This was adopted by our Australian Districts – <u>but not in Victoria</u>! As it happened, the UELCA form had been *'Victoria District'*, the ELCA form *'Victorian District'*. Although Dr. Vic. Roennfeldt (UELCA) valiantly fought for the agreed form, he could make no impression on the ELCA heavies. A big listing of the form of the name adopted by public bodies was dragged into the debate, and a leading ELCA layman expressed the 'clinching' argument on the following lines: *'The only body that uses "Victoria" in its name is the 'Victoria Police Force", and we don't want to be associated with them, do we!'* A trivial matter, it is true, but symptomatic of an attitude.

This was demonstrated a second time. In the LCA amalgamation a General Finance Council was established to oversee the finances of the Church and make recommendations to the General Church Council, and the Districts mirrored this development, as recommended, by establishing a Finance Council. <u>But not Victoria</u>. The ELCA and its Districts had never had such an organised body – and the Victoria Convention stuck to the ELCA pattern. Max Lohe and I had reason to ponder after the Convention how co-operative former ELCA members would be. By the grace of God, Dr. H.D. Koehne and the influential pastors of the former ELCA and the great majority of its lay members were intent on making the union a blessed reality in the spirit of the Convention at Tanunda.

Victorian District Constituting Convention, Box Hill, Nov 1966 – (Henry Proeve 3rd from front right)

Here I would make a passing reference to <u>Queensland</u>. There the President of the amalgamated Queensland District, Herb. Schmidt (UELCA) faced the reverse situation. He successfully steered a District where the former ELCA was in a minority, but had a small and very vocal group of pastors that threw out theological bombs. He had to continue, as much as possible, the mediating influence that Dr. H.D. Koehne had to exercise prior to the amalgamation. In this case, when neither the Queensland District nor the LCA yielded to their demands, this group preserved its superior Lutheran status as a separate body, the Lutheran Church of the Reformation.

2. **Western Australia Constituting Convention.** Under the ELCA the Lutheran cause in WA (which was completely ELCA), with two parishes, Perth and Katanning, was regarded as part of the SA District. Its pastors, however, were empowered to make some decisions as a combined unit; I don't know or remember whether the seven congregations of the two parishes also met together. The now aged Pastor C.F. Graebner of Perth was the contact man for the WA unit, and this had given him an overwhelming degree of authority and respect. He, however, was not present at the LCA Constituting Convention. In fact, my memory did not recall what I now notice, as I have the 1966 Report before me, that WA was scarcely represented at that Convention: Pastors Max Mueller (Katanning) and Norman Bergen (Albany), and one layman, W.A. Heinrich (Morawa). Early in 1967 attention was turned to the possible establishment of a Western Australia District. This was done by Max Lohe and me, and G.O. Minge as President of the SA District. Two senior pastors were not in favour of the proposal: retired Dr. Graebner (who did not co-operate, neither did he act in opposition) and Max Mueller (who thought the District did not have the strength to be independent of SA). The positive reaction of the other pastors was accompanied by a fear that, few in number, they would be saddled with much board/committee work. We assured them that they did not have to establish as many boards as, for example, the SA District; it would suffice to establish a few important boards/committees. For the rest of the areas of church activity I would suffice to appoint a 'contact person', who would liaise with the relevant Church board, receiving and disseminating within the District any relevant information. — What did become clear, however, was that there was a lack of organisational experience among the young team of pastors in WA. It became my task to meet the need. The WA men submitted their opinions; I sorted them out and drafted the required wording. Thus the entire printed basis for the Constituting Convention took shape at my hands in North Adelaide, and was printed at Auricht's Printing Office at Tanunda, and then delivered in Western Australia.

It was deemed wise to visit as many parishes as possible before the Convention to explain to the members what was happening. Max Lohe and Oscar Minge flew to Perth; and visited in Perth and Katanning. Dorothy and I travelled by car, which provided more mobility in outlying areas – we visited four parishes before returning home. For both of us it was a very interesting trip, because we had never been to Western Australia. At that time the Eyre Highway was not yet bituminised in the long central portion (roughly Ceduna to Norseman). There were sections full of potholes. From Nullarbor the highway at that time ran due west through an area where there were large 'blowholes' hard against the road, through which air came up from far down in the earth.

Chapter 6

On the return journey we had to negotiate some sections with care, as the road had just been reopened to traffic and was still under water. We paid several visits on the way. We stayed the first night at Yaninee with cousin Elfriede and Ron Wilksch. Next day we called in at the Ceduna manse. We did not know Martin and Sigrid Wilke, but we reckoned that they received few visitors; and they were very thankful for our call. The Yalata Mission was close to the highway; so we called in, and promised Barry Lindner, the lay missionary, that we would stay longer on our return journey. On the second night, camped on open ground at the border settlement of Eucla, we had to rescue our tent from being blown away in the middle of the night.

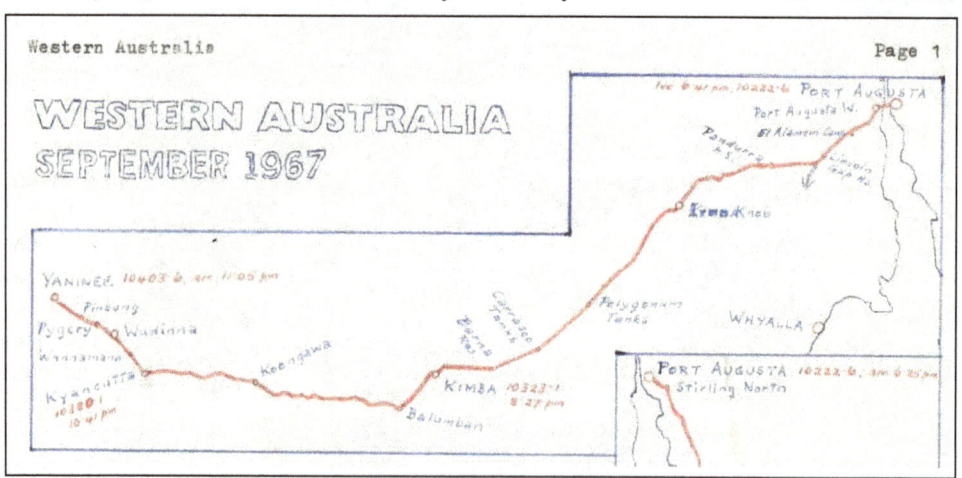

Part of the map Henry prepared for the trip to WA

Our official visit to the State began on September 3 at Norseman. Pastor Norman Bergen, of Albany, the pastor of the local congregation which used the Norseman Anglican Church for worship, had arranged that I should conduct a service, and had arranged accommodation in the very hospitable home of the Ed. Welke family. The rector of the local Anglican Church, whose name now escapes me (who later became Bishop of Kalgoorlie), was so well-disposed to the Lutherans, that he placed the baptismal font at the entrance to the sanctuary, because he thought that this Lutheran practice was preferable to the Anglican practice of placing the font at the entrance to the nave. Here, for the first time, I fulfilled the purpose of us LCA men coming to W.A. several weeks before the Convention: we explained to the congregations the purpose of forming a District, and sought to correct any misapprehensions regarding its effect on their congregational life. By taking over the whole service I spared Norman a round trip of 760 miles (1200 km). — The next day we were in Albany, at the manse with its unusual garden that (typical of Albany) still has original granite boulders in their original location. Bergen had arranged a special church service. One member who had attended the Sunday service on the previous day again travelled from his home, about 140 miles (220 km) away, to attend this Monday service! Long-distance travelling by members was typical of many W.A. country congregations. Quite a number of Latvian ladies belonged to the congregation; from their ethnic church background they had some difficulty in understanding the 'new' development in W.A. While we were in Albany Norman took us to the local whaling station to witness a rarity for Australia – the dismemberment of a whale.

The days of the Pastors' Conference and the Constituting Convention of the Western Australia District in Perth were busy days. We three LCA representatives from S.A., Dr. Lohe (as chairman), I (as secretary), and G.O. Minge, of course had to guide these meetings, providing much explanation. At the opening service on Saturday, Sept. 9, I served as liturgist and M. Lohe as preacher; the next day G.O. Minge and I were the preachers. We completed our service to the W.A. members when I prepared the official Report of this Constituting Convention in Adelaide, and had it printed at Auricht's Printing Office. Pastor Peter Kemeny, the Hungarian pastor living in Perth, whom we often saw when he came to the eastern States to conduct Hungarian services, and his wife had invited Dorothy and me to be their guests in Perth. Unfortunately, a car accident made this impossible. We were accommodated in the very fine home of Ross Garrett, a church-minded South Australian now active in the financial field of W.A., who was the obvious choice as Treasurer of this new District.

Albany Lutheran Church

170

Lohe and Minge returned to S.A. after the Convention; but our private mobility in travel was used to have Dorothy and me stay a week after the Convention for one more Sunday and visit two more parishes. We travelled, pausing at the interesting Spanish influenced New Norcia, to the northernmost parish at Morawa (235 miles, 380 km from Perth) under the care of senior pastor Alf. Lienert, with whom we felt very much at home. The first of three weekday evening services, at which I preached and afterwards as usual explained the new situation as a District, took place on the Tuesday of that week at Lienert's adjacent congregation Canna. Wednesday was spent in travelling south-east to Owen Klein's manse at Northam (200 miles, 320 km), where an evening service was held. We then spared Owen a 665 mile (1070 km) round trip to his other congregations. On Thursday night I conducted a service at Merredin (100 miles, 160 km) away; here I became aware of another instance of spiritual interest – a member drove in from a long distance to the north to worship at a weekday service. A Mrs. Reichelt, whom we had met earlier, had told us where to find the key and make ourselves comfortable in her home for the night. Next day we continued to Coolgardie (where we spent some sightseeing time) and Kalgoorlie (230 miles, 370 km from Merredin); on the way the highly visible pipeline carrying vital water to the goldfields impressed itself on our minds. I conducted a morning service at Kalgoorlie on the Sunday, and then we began the return journey, camping in our tent on the way. A remembrance of a new Church District, small in numbers but widespread in extent, with keen members, remained in our mind.

Lutheran Church, Perth

Photo on left: *Max Lohe and Henry Proeve at WA Constituting Convention*

Yalata Mission. We kept our promise to pay a longer visit at Yalata Mission on our return journey, enjoying the hospitality of Barry Lindner and wife, and the insight he gave us into the workings of the Mission. One of the main impressions that we gained at the time and which was strengthened on later visits was that many of the Aboriginals preferred to live 'bush' in wurlies than in the houses that were available to them. In later years I was associated with Yalata matters to an unexpected extent. Philip and his wife Jacqui accepted positions at the mission, Philip as its supervising mechanic, and Jacqui as a staff member in its store on the Eyre Highway; Neil Hampel was the missionary at the time. So Dorothy and I, visiting our family, gained further insights into the work.

The Board of Aboriginal Missions (SA) placed before the relevant Licensing Court a scheme, which the Court approved as 'an interesting social experiment', viz. to set up a canteen, open at specified times, where Aboriginals with an identifying card as their permit were permitted to buy one drink. The supervising mission official handed back their card when the 'open time' was finished. It was hoped by this means to counteract the problem that taxis from Nundroo dropped off liquor on the highway, and to control their drinking. The LCA had to be licensee in this experiment, so my name as Secretary and Public Officer appeared on the document, and I had to give the required evidence of what was proposed. At Lutheran Church House the scheme was facetiously dubbed 'Henry's Pub'! — Some time later (November 1971), when I dedicated the Lutheran Church at Ceduna, the energetic and capable head of the relevant Board, Ern Hansen, suggested that I should accompany him to Yalata to observe the canteen in operation; and so I handed over drinks to Aboriginals in my 'Pub'!

Chapter 6

Representing the President

In reference to representing the President the By-laws VIII.C.1 of the Church laid down, among other requirements, that the President *'as the spiritual leader of the Church'*: *(c) shall be an advisory member of all the Boards, Councils, Standing Committees, and Commissions of the Church and shall receive due notice of all meetings'*. Since there were 28 such bodies listed in the By-laws it was obvious that personal supervision and attendance at all these was a physical impossibility. There was, therefore, a provision that was common to the by-laws relating to the duties of President, Vice-President, and Secretary (VIII.8,3.(e) in my case), that these *'shall exercise particular supervision over those areas of responsibility which have been expressly assigned to them'*; and in addition the general provision that the President *'shall, at his discretion, appoint the Vice-President or another person to act as his deputy'*.

In June 1966 the JUC endorsed in principle a suggested division of duties between the three officials. With some minor adjustments, this provided a pattern for particular areas of Church activity [omitting general matters]:

(a) *President:* 1. Commission on Theology [however, transferred to Vice-President]; 2. Seminary: Council, Board, Faculty; 3. Bd. of Secondary Education; 4. Bd. of Primary Education; 5. Bd. of Tertiary Education; 6. Church Workers' Institute.

(b) *Vice-President:* 1. [Chairmanship Commission on Theology added]; 2. Bd. of Church Development; 3. Bd. of Aboriginal Missions (Finke, Koonibba/Yalata, Hope Valley); 4. Bd. of Overseas Missions; 5 Bd. of Pensions; 6. Bd. of Publications [generally to Secretary]; 7. Commission on Armed Services.

(c) *Secretary:* 1. Bd. of Social Welfare and World Relief; 2. Bd. of Archives; 3. Bd. of Radio and Television; 4. Commission on Public Relations; 5. Commission on Worship; 6. S/C. on Constitution [instead of Vice-President]; 7. S/C on Student Fund; 8. S/C on Salaries.

In addition to what was listed under (c) I was a member of the Commission on Theology and Inter-Church Relations, and at times had close association with the Board of Publications and the Lutheran Publishing House. — Such a range meant that as Secretary I had to keep in mind the needs of all its branches of activity, and not be focussed on one or two of them. I venture to believe that the majority of General Church Council members that I got to know approached their duties with the same attitude.

Representing the President at District Conventions

1. New Zealand. In 1970 (end of April – early May) I had the pleasure of visiting New Zealand and almost all parishes of the Lutheran Church of New Zealand over a period of 24 days. It began as a flight from Adelaide to Christchurch via Sydney. There was something heart-warming about the unusual greeting with which Gina (nee Ginters), Trevor Reu's wife, welcomed me at the Christchurch manse: *'I did not expect that, as pastor's wife, I would one day welcome you into our home'*. It aroused the thankful remembrance that Gina was one of the six girls that I had confirmed who married pastors. As my stay in Christchurch was going to be very brief, Trevor showed me the city and part of its surroundings in the afternoon after my arrival. Next day, Sunday, the normal pattern of my visit began: Preaching was limited to the Sundays, with a general talk on LCA matters following the service; weekday gatherings were only such talks. I preached at a harvest thanksgiving festival at Christchurch, and at the luncheon that followed addressed the congregation. Immediately after that I was winging my way in a local Air New Zealand plane over the northern ranges to the airport at Nelson. I felt some concern when I could feel the landing wheels being lowered while we were flying in heavy cloud. I learnt later that the high mountains to the west of Nelson require that planes often fly through a break in those mountains to the north-west of Nelson, near Upper Moutere. This is an area of long historical significance to the Lutheran Church, as its settlement dates back to the 1840s. Neil Hampel took me to Hope, his church in the historical Ranzau area, to address a congregational gathering that evening; then we continued on to the manse at Upper Moutere. My stay was for two nights. I addressed a gathering at Upper Moutere, and during the day had some interesting discussions with descendants of the original settlers.

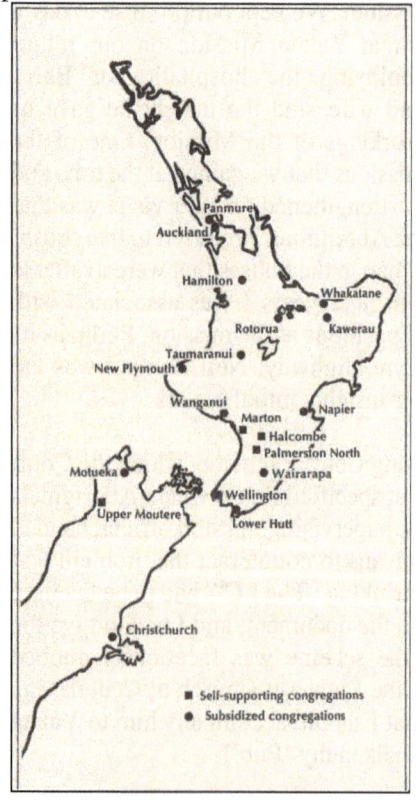

New Zealand map showing Lutheran churches Henry visited

Chapter 6

After three nights in the two parishes on the South Island it was time to make our way to the North Island for the official meetings of the New Zealand Church. I flew into Wellington to stay with Robert Wiebusch, and addressed an evening gathering at Lower Hutt. Next day we travelled together by car via Palmerston North to Marton, where Robert Strelan was my fourth host; in nearby Halcombe, part of the field under the care of President Lance Steicke, I addressed a gathering on LCA matters on that evening. There were 10 pastors in the North Island with whom I had contact in their home fields. Marton was the centre for the Pastors' Conference, and the Convention, at which I gave the synodical sermon. On a dairy farm at Marton I saw what seemed to be a widespread practice: the herds were fed in rich pasture land which was divided into successive strips by moveable fences. I could draw the attention of New Zealand brethren to an historical link with Australia: the layman Heinrich Goile who donated the block of land on which the Marton church stood came to New Zealand from Schoenborn in the Barossa Valley.

Robert Hamann took me with him to the manse at Rotorua. I spent four nights in this interesting volcanic country. The most enduring recollection is the sulphuric vapour that emanated out of the ground, even in streets. Visits to the geysers, and to a Maori dancing exhibition (which, apart from normal street contact, is the only 'contact' with Maoris that I can recall), were naturally of interest. My last two evenings there were devoted to addressing congregations – the first in Rotorua; the next day, after a trip to visit Robert's neighbour, Tony Lock, in Tony's congregation in Whakatane. Tony was one of two New Zealand-born pastors, the other being John Fraser at Panmure. Tony was married to an Australian girl, Olga, and I believe that the reason for the close of his ministry was centred in Australia.

Whakatane church

The next morning a small Geyserland plane carried me from Rotorua to Auckland. Ed. Koch and Gladys were my hosts for the two nights that I spent in Auckland. Through his kindness I had a good opportunity of getting an impression of this city. The hilly nature of its surroundings has made it a city with its main arteries on many ridges, like Brisbane and, with its ocean views, like Sydney. When he heard that in 1928 my family had travelled across the narrow neck of land to Onehunga on the Tasman Sea, he repeated the trip for me; the difference was that in the intervening years the area between the two places had been built up. There were two parishes in the Auckland area: the central city and Panmure in the south-east. Ed. took me to a congregational meeting at Panmure, because I would not have opportunity to address the congregation after the early service next morning. John Fraser, the pastor at Panmure, was the son of V. Fraser of Palmerston North, whom I had got to know in North Adelaide when Palmerston North (as remnant of the Danish Church in New Zealand) was still in altar and pulpit fellowship with the UELCA.

My final week in New Zealand had variety in it, and probably for that reason is one that provides the most memories. The Sunday provided a full programme. Immediately after my sermon at the early service in Panmure Ed.Koch hurried me to his Auckland church for its morning service (and subsequent address). During the afternoon he took me down to Hamilton, where Byron Klein was the pastor; there I preached at an evening service and addressed the congregation. — Byron's wife, who was a trained sister, immediately noticed and commented on my right hand; it still showed signs of the severe scalding it had received about five weeks earlier. On a visit to Meningie to see our first grandchild Simon, at Wellington East I screwed open a boiling radiator; although given some treatment at the Meningie Hospital, I had had extreme difficulty to use that hand for even the slightest control of steering – 'third degree burns', said Byron's wife. It was a great pleasure to have longer contact again with Jean (nee Warnest) and John King, because I had officiated at their marriage in Nuriootpa, and they now were highly valuable members of the Hamilton congregation and indeed active in the New Zealand Church.

Pastors Tony Lock, Lance Steicke, Henry Proeve

Chapter 6

Next day Byron decided to take me to the Waitomo Caves. Visiting hours had just ceased when we arrived; but a guide was willing to show us around. He was very relaxed and chatty as he rowed us around in the underground lake of the caves. He even took us to a portion of the caves where visitors usually were not taken. The sight of myriads of glow-worms lighting up on the walls and ceiling was of course absolutely fascinating. The guide related how an American tourist had asked him how many glow-worms there were! In reply he had said the American should count them while he named them! His stock reply to the frequent question about the difference between stalactites and stalagmites was: *'As the "mites" go up, the "tites" come down!'*

On that evening I addressed Byron's congregation at Taumaranui. One of the members, a Mr. Meyer, had spoken to me at the New Zealand Convention about a problem that worried him: the Lions, the service club to which he belonged, was due to host a luncheon to which all other service clubs in the district had been invited, but the guest speaker they had invited was now unable to come. Could I help? Politics and religion, however, weren't topics that could be used. After some consideration what I as a minister of religion could talk about, I agreed. This talk now took place next day before a goodly gathering of important persons in the area. Its topic was on the lines of *'About the Australian Aboriginals'*. Without referring to my background material as Lutheran Missions, I summarised Aboriginal life and customs as I had observed them at the Lutheran Mission I had visited, and elsewhere (Finke River settlements, Yalata, Hope Valley and Bloomfield; and also Cherbourg in Queensland, and Ebenezer in Victoria, and the activities, especially language, of the Dresden and Gossner missionaries). The audience contributed by commenting on the New Zealand situation regarding the Maoris. I still have a small Lions pennant as their expression of thanks. — The following day my host drove down to Wanganui on a road that followed every bend in the gorge of the Paraparap River, about 50 miles (80 km). I had to admit that we did not have such a long winding gorge road in S.A., but told him that we had a similarly long winding road to Lobethal and a shorter winding Torrens gorge road.

Arthur and Ruth Rathjen were my kind hosts in Wanganui, where I spent three nights and addressed congregational gatherings at Wanganui and New Plymouth. In taking me to New Plymouth Arthur made a 'round' around Mount Egmont, the striking mountain in the western bulge of the North Island. He showed me the area in the lower slopes of the mount where Missionary Blaess ministered to the Maoris in the now defunct Taranaki Mission. — On the Friday of that final week we travelled to Palmerston North for a Church Council meeting, but returned to Wanganui for a meeting of Zone elders. On the next evening I was with Robert Strelan in Marton for the last weekday address to congregational gatherings. – Next morning was my last Sunday in the Dominion, spent in Peter Wiebusch's Palmerston North congregation with two morning services. A noteworthy feature, probably indicative of Danish Lutheran influence, was that elders offered prayers in the vestry prior to the beginning and after the close of each service. By evening I was in the hilly city of Wellington, once more with Robert and Lynette Wiebusch, ready to fly to Adelaide via Sydney on the next morning. I think the main impression with which I left New Zealand was that I had seen a scattered Church of mainly small congregations (amounting roughly to the size of the LCA in the Barossa) in a mountainous Dominion, where the term 'Lutheran' probably did not mean anything to the majority of New Zealanders, who were strongly insistent that they were not part of Australia. I had a greater understanding of the problems that the Lutheran Church of New Zealand faced.

Marton church

2. Later District Conventions. I was the deputy for the President (by this time Les. Grope) at six later District Conventions. They did not have the same District 'visitation' nature as the preceding visits, except for a little of this in the WA visit in 1975; they were basically limited to attending the Pastors' Conference and the Convention, at which I delivered the synodical message. The significance for me of these visits to larger sections of the LCA — and also of pastoral activity in various congregations, to which I will make reference later on — may seem strange to some readers, but it was associated with the sense of loss when I was no longer a parish pastor. Theoretically I could accept the thought that I was one of a group of pastors for whom *'the LCA was the parish'*. These visits to Districts and congregations gave the theory a touch of reality. This summary listing of District visits (with little commentary) is a late-career reliving of those isolated feelings of the reality that one was indeed a minister of the Lord Jesus Christ and not just a recording instrument of the Church.

Chapter 6

In March 1973 I attended the Convention of the **Victorian District** at Tabor in Western Victoria. I had been in Tabor by invitation on a previous occasion, to preach the dedicatory sermon and to dedicate its newly restored organ. That day, December 17, 1967, was memorable for quite another reason. Malcolm Fraser, the local federal MP and Minister for the Army (to the best of my knowledge a sincere church-man) was present, and after luncheon mingled freely with his constituents; but suddenly we realised that he was no longer present. Harold Holt had disappeared in mysterious circumstances while swimming, and Fraser had been rushed to Melbourne in connection with the search for the Prime Minister.

Two years later (March 1975) I was in the **Western Australia District** for the second time. This was a trip by plane to Perth, but the next day I preached at Jack Shepherd's two morning services, at Bunbury and Collie. This was my only involvement outside the Synod. For two days the Pastors' Conference met at Morley, followed by the three-day convention in the Latvian congregation's complex in Perth. Its pastor Laimons Musinskis and wife Jean were my charming hosts. I preached the synodical sermon at the Sunday service. In my estimation Laimons was the most LCA-minded of the Latvian pastors in Australia. They were much inclined to use the strong nationalistic spirit of the Latvian people to hold a Latvian Church of Australia together as a national entity. Laimons integrated his congregation into the Australian Lutheran scene, and rendered valuable service as a District President of Western Australia. One of his interests was a close study of the occult. His collection of books on this subject would have done credit to the library of a theological Seminary. On Sunday night I was speeding homewards in the sleeping comfort and the scenic experience of a journey on the Indian Pacific.

Next year (March 1976) I flew to Sydney to be present and serve the **NSW District** in the usual manner at the Latvian church in Homebush. All that I can recall is that Mervyn Stolz jocularly made reference to the black 'Talar' that I was still wearing as pastoral robe. My equally jocular reply leapt from my mouth: *'I am not a parakeet of the Paraclete!'*

I was in the **Queensland District** in April 1978, a visit which was limited to its District Convention at Murgon, and to the preceding Pastors' Conference at Kingaroy (if I remember correctly).

In mid-October 1968 Dorothy and I made an eight-day trip to the Riverina in **New South Wales** to be present at the three-day District Pastors' Conference at Jindera and the three-day Convention at Albury. If my memory does not fail me, this was one of the occasions when we stayed with Mervyn and Dorothy (nee Rohde) Schoff in their lovely home in the rising land at the western end of Albury. The house had to be cut into the rising land to such an extent that one literally nosedived into the roomy garage under the house. The two Dorothys were close friends from Dimboola days, which made the Schoff hospitality especially warm.

Photo on right: *Henry Proeve, Max Lohe & Harold Koehne at Albury 1968*

One last time Dorothy and I again travelled by road to the **Western Australia District**. The travel conditions were good, because the sealing of the Eyre Highway had been completed, and motel accommodation was available at the Border Village on the border near Eucla. We were accompanied by Vic and Dorothy Hoffmann of Adelaide, who wished to go to Esperance. I appreciated the assistance that Vic gave in driving, especially from Eucla, when I inexplicably had a lightheaded day. We enjoyed a brief stay at Ed. Welke's at Esperance, but then continued westwards for that feature that made this visit memorable. Since the J.G. Schultz family reunion in 1981 we now had new close family contacts in W.A. We had a lovely stay at Witchcliffe, near Margaret River, with Ivy and Cliff Summerfield (of the Krueger branch). Based on their home, we explored the southwest portion of W.A., down to the tip of the continent at Cape Leeuwin, to Augusta, the south-western beaches, and the caves of the area. In Perth we resumed acquaintance with their daughter Gaye and Paul van Leeuwen. After that we made our way back to Adelaide.

I enjoyed my last visit to a District, which took place two years before I retired. I flew to Perth to attend the WA Pastors' Conference at Narrogin and the Convention at Katanning (February 1982). As return travel to Adelaide I enjoyed the experience of a sleeper journey on the Indian Pacific.

Chapter 6

Memories Associated with General Synod Conventions

- The Convention of the LCA that arouses the most memories in me is, of course, the First (Constituting) Convention. The stress of producing the official Report barely in time for the Convention, and the fact that that Convention depended almost 100 per cent on the Report that I wrote, has always remained a memory of those 'heady' days that cannot be erased.

- **'Get quotes'.** Another memory is connected with the printing of the Reports of the first few Conventions; and the passing of forty years or so has not totally eradicated its 'sour' taste. The two amalgamating Churches had had their long-standing arrangements regarding the printing of their publications and other general material. The ELCA had established its own press, Lutheran Publishing House (LPH), instead of using the printing firm of Hunkin, Ellis & King; the UELCA, already in the days when Pastor J.C. Auricht and his son printed for the Immanuel Synod, and throughout its own existence from 1921 to 1966 – and most its SA congregations – had used Auricht's Printing Office (APO) as the printery for the Church. When the amalgamation took place LPH 'automatically' took over the printing of the new Church paper and all other magazines and printed materials of bodies within the LCA – and it was very annoying that the Lutheran Laymen's League (LLL) continued to print materials that it was interested in distributing. LPH had much more than 'the cream' of church printing. To me it was natural, when I had to make arrangements for printing the Report of the Constituting Convention, to think of the faithful and efficient APO. And the same thought was in my mind for the 1968 Convention. Thus APO still received 'crumbs'; but they were 'crumbs' that would only fall from the LCA table every two years. It therefore came as a shock to me when action was taken at a General Church Council meeting to indicate than LPH was not happy (to put it mildly) that APO was given what I regarded as 'crumbs'. I was challenged by a member of ELCA background who had interests in LPH whether I had advertised for quotes. I of course had not done so; the UELCA had never asked for a quote, and I strongly believe that the ELCA too had never done so. So for the 1970 Convention I dutifully did what I had previously so 'neglectfully' failed to do: I sought quotes, even though I wondered how a printery could submit a quote when no manuscript could be submitted to show the size that the report would be. APO won the contract with ease.

In 1970 I again asked for quotes. This time LPH submitted a quote that was far below anything that it had previously quoted. The cost of the previous Reports that APO had printed was no secret. The detailed printed financial statements of the LCA made public what the 1968 Report, printed by APO, had cost. So LPH won the 1970 tussle. Realising the purpose that lay behind the whole procedure, in 1972 I handed the manuscript for the Report to Synod to LPH – without asking for quotes! And, lo and behold, I was never again quizzed whether I had sought quotes, and I was not criticised for 'neglect' to do so!! The trust I had had that in the LCA Christian ethics would always prevail received a severe jolt. I felt that in this new Church I could not be absolutely certain that the spirit of co-operation and understanding among Christians, and therefore helping one another, would always prevail over the spirit of coveting that can seep in and lead to unscrupulous actions similar to those that take place in secular business circles.

- **Valé! FRM Incorporated.** The 1981 General Convention in Indooroopilly has particular memories for me for an unusual reason. I have made previous reference to the problems that had developed regarding Finke River Mission Incorporated, with which the UELCA was unsuccessfully wrestling. The Immanuel Synod had incorporated the Mission, probably as a forerunner to becoming an incorporated Church itself. Laurie Leske, the Executive Officer of the Mission, repeatedly complained, echoing the longstanding worry, 'Can't you do something about the FRM Incorporated'? One day, probably with his words echoing in my mind, it struck me that I had on two occasions done all the paper work by which two incorporations disappeared into one body under a comparatively recent Associations Act, viz. two congregations in Point Pass in the 1950s, and in 1966 two Lutheran Churches. As a follow-on, the thought arose in my mind that in the case of FRM Incorporated the same might be achieved. A General Church Council meeting instructed me to seek legal advice. The lawyer I approached, Frank Condon (a member of St. Stephen's, Adelaide) affirmed that the provisions of the Associations Act certainly permitted this procedure.

Henry Proeve (Secretary), Lance Steicke (2nd Vice-President), Les Grope (President), and Clem Koch (1st Vice-President) at the 1981 General Convention, Indooroopilly.

The 1981 Convention thus took the unusual nature of first of all being another amalgamating convention, in which the proceedings had to be so arranged that the same set of resolutions had to be adopted twice: first by 'FRM Incorporated', the body that was to go out of existence by amalgamation with the LCA; then by LCA Incorporated. For the purposes of this incorporation we were adopting the existing constitutional provisions under which the LCA was operating and under which it would operate as the ostensibly 'new' LCA; and that saved a lot of detailed resolving. The tricky point was to determine who constituted the voting members of the 'Finke River Mission Incorporated'! Frank and I based our answer on the history of how the FRM became an incorporated body: *'The voting members are all former members of The UELCA who are synodsmen at this LCA Convention'*. These 'voting members' of FRM Inc. adopted the existing Constitution and By-Laws of the LCA; and so at long last the FRM Incorporated no longer existed. But there was one omission at the beginning of the Constitution. The excellent thoughtful and dignified Preamble to the Constitution of 1966 had to be left out because it no longer fitted the circumstances of this adoption. I regretted this loss, but it was unavoidable. I include it in these Memoirs, so that it is not just buried in the 1966 Report:

'We, the pastors and the members of the congregations which comprise The Evangelical Lutheran Church of Australia, and the pastors and the members of the congregations which comprise The United Evangelical Lutheran Church in Australia, severally and jointly declare:

• That by the grace of God and the guidance of the Holy Spirit we have been led together in the confession and unity of the one faith in our Lord Jesus Christ and of the one doctrine of His holy Gospel;

• That the Theses of Agreement 1966 which we have severally adopted are the expression of the common consent of our two Churches on matters which were held to be in dispute between us;

• That in confident reliance upon the Holy Spirit, who leads men to endeavour to keep the unity of the Spirit in the bond of peace, we adopt this Constitution to govern our activity as we in the name of our Lord Jesus Christ unitedly undertake to proclaim His Gospel and to administer His Sacraments in accordance with His will'.

• **Board of Public Relations.** This was a small board of four members. I was the sole pastor on it, probably because in theory I was one of the most likely persons who would know what newsworthy developments were taking place in Australia that were grist for the media mill. We had a newspaper editor and one-time newspaper reporter on the board; but with half the members located in Victoria it is no surprise that the board did not flourish and bear fruit in its brief existence. It has disappeared from my memory lane.

Some Noteworthy Events in the 1970s

• **Canberra Consultation, 1970.** Dr. Lohe, Clem Koch, and I did a four-day 'flying' trip to Canberra. It was literally 'flying', not in the air but on the ground, especially when Clem was driving. We reached Canberra in one day. The purpose was to investigate the situation in Canberra, together with NSW authorities, and to make recommendations about the development of the local congregations. I had enjoyable quarters with Des Pfeiffer (a member of the Canberra newspaper staff) and his wife in the western portion of Woden Valley. On the first day of our meeting in the church at Reid it was arranged that I followed Des (who was riding his motor bike) in his Volkswagen into the city, a route on which some road works were in progress. When the day's sessions were over, which was after lighting-up time, my troubles began. I had not been shown where the Volkswagen light switches were, and it took some searching to find them. Then the layout of Canberra like a French horn posed a problem for me, because the road works diverted the route that I had taken in the morning, and I could not see that route in the dark. I started to follow the huge roundabout that lay on the south-side of the city. At last I was able to hail a policeman who was on night patrol. He after much thought gave me directions which I later was able to plot on a map as a long roundabout route. I continued on the roundabout street on which I was travelling to a road that led me south-east to a suburb called Forest Hill; there I had to turn right and drive westward over hill and dale, and so I arrived in the Woden Valley centre from the east (instead of the north). In the dark I had to recognise the one street that led into the western network of streets that included Des Pfeiffer's street. After several vain attempts I always returned to the slightly better-lit junction near Woden Valley centre that I knew was correct. I decided that if necessary I would remain at that spot until Des arrived at about 3.00 a.m. on his way home from work. Fortunately, when I made one last attempt I recognised the correct entrance street, and rejoiced to see the welcoming light of Des's home. It was almost 1.00 a.m.

Chapter 6

- The story of the **Siebenschläfer** (Seven Sleepers), who were listed in our Lutheran almanacs for June 27, aroused such a measure of interest that I made myself familiar with it at the time when Dr. J.J. Stolz and I were revising the calendar of saints in our UELCA almanac. Many local people held to the European folklore that if it rained on June 27 some rain would fall during the seven weeks that followed. At the beginning of 1971 two correspondents used the popular letter pages of the *'Women's Page'* that appeared in *'The Chronicle'* (a weekly paper with news roundups for country readers), to offer different explanations of the origin of the story. I wrote a letter of correction to the editress of the *'Women's Page'*, Mary Broughton. In reply she appeared at my office in Lutheran Church House, interested in obtaining further information. I brought out W. Löhe's *Märtyrologium,* and provided a running on-the-spot translation of his story of seven Christian brothers who were walled into a cave near Ephesus on account of their faith, and awoke from their sleep 196 years later, thinking it was the next day. From that time on they were honoured as seven saints. Mary Broughton wrote up the story as I told it, and printed it.

In 1977 *The Chronicle* ceased publication, and Mary Broughton came to my office once again. From all the articles that had appeared in the *Women's Page* she had chosen 30 to form a farewell volume called *Chronicle Cameos* – one of these was the article on the Siebenschläfer that had fascinated her, and she wanted to reproduce it with the colourful front page of one of the German almanacs that I had. On this occasion she dropped her anonymity, and on a number of official occasions I had further contact with her as 'Alison Dolling', the descendant of a prominent German family.

Photo on left: *The German almanac referred to*

- **Visit to Coober Pedy, 1972.** Ern Hansen, the Executive Officer of the SA Aboriginal Mission Board, who had persuaded me to accompany him to Yalata after the dedication of the church at Ceduna [*see photo of foundation stone laying in 1971 on page 217*], approached me to go to Coober Pedy to conduct a Communion service. At that time the Board had a lay missionary, Audley Grieger, in Coober Pedy to minister to the Aboriginals (in particular) and European Lutherans in the area. I travelled up by bus, and while there had opportunity to watch mining operations. The bedroom that I used lay in the rear portion of Audley's house, which was underground – the front portion stood in the open air. The gross darkness of the bedroom was a bit eerie. I cannot recall what the congregation was like, and it appears to me (without checking in any official report) that the Coober Pedy project folded up soon afterwards. The return trip was by plane, which landed at Andamooka (which I recall as a rough and ready looking collection of iron buildings), and Leigh Creek.

- **November 1973: Deaths -- Recreational Leave.**
This series of recollections begins with November 2, 1973. It's my 55th birthday. Dorothy and I go to Tanunda to visit Mother and Father. Mother has been in the Tanunda Lutheran Home for about two years because she has suffered a stroke. Father, who has been visiting her every day, is now in the Tanunda Hospital because his ill-health has become worse. Dorothy and I return to Adelaide in the afternoon; and then a telephone call comes from Paul that Father has died. We return to Tanunda in sad shock. Three days later (November 5) Father is laid to rest in the Tabor Cemetery.

Two days later (November 7), and Paul and Gwen are stricken with the loss of their first-born, Robert, a victim of cancer in the chest; Dorothy and I seek to console them in Angaston. We are in a heart-rending quandary: Robert is our beloved god-child; but we have completed arrangements for my Recreational Leave (we do not call it Long Service Leave), and are booked to leave Melbourne on November 9 with our car on board the *'Princess of Tasmania'* bound for Devonport, Tasmania, and the following three Sundays are booked for three services (Burnie, Hobart, Launceston) in the two Tasmanian parishes. Paul and Gwen understand that we have to travel to Melbourne on the day of Robert's funeral (November 9). That was not a day of happy anticipation of visiting Tasmania. We carried with us the copies of the recently published *'Lutheran Hymnal'* that had been ordered by the three congregations we were visiting.

The 16 days we spent in Tasmania were highly interesting to both of us. The places we visited were of our own choosing, based on what we had read in brochures. The pastor at Launceston arranged that we stayed with a Mr. and Mrs. Cuthbertson in Burnie, who were very hospitable hosts for several days while we visited areas like Sheffield and Cradle Mountain, Stanley (and its distinctive Nob) and Smithton. On the trip down the western side of the island we viewed Zeehan before reaching Strahan via Queenstown. We took a cruise up the Gordon River and in Macquarie Harbour. The one-day trip from Strahan over the high country to Hobart was somewhat strenuous because the weather was rainy and the side-tracks in the extensive road-building area were slippery. In Hobart Dennis Obst and wife were our congenial hosts in the manse, while we visited the apple country of the Huon Valley and the convict settlement of Port Arthur. We travelled up the inland highway to Ross before heading for the east coast at Bicheno, and ultimately to Launceston. Pastor Schultz and wife were away, but he arranged that we had the use of his manse, which was our base for a little inland touring around the Great Lake. The day after the service in Launceston we boarded the ship for our overnight return to the Australian continent.

St Peter's Lutheran Church and manse, Hobart, purchased from Methodist Church in 1973

- **Jury duty:** It is a surprise to see such duty listed against the name of a minister of religion, but that has happened to me on two occasions. When the notice came, Les Grope as President of the LCA attempted in vain to have it set aside. It appears that because I was in full-time service in an office the normal exemption did not apply to me. So for an entire month my daily duties were subject to my frequent morning attendance at the court to find if I had to serve. Sometimes I could return early to Lutheran Church House if enough potential jurors had been selected without me; sometimes this happened only after enough jurors had been empanelled without me. On one occasion, when a Supreme Court case was involved, I was challenged by the lawyer for the defence before I reached the jury seats; reasons were never given, but I suspect that it was my occupation that may have been the cause. I sat on two cases; the second has faded almost completely from memory – I think it involved a young man, but I cannot recall the charge. We found him guilty.

The first case, which the Crown had hoped would be heard at the end of October 1974 by a 'seasoned' jury, came on at the beginning of the next month. A grandmother was charged with ill-treating her very young granddaughter. We were shown very graphic photos of severe chain marks around her neck and other injuries. The grandmother had obviously been 'used' by her selfish daughter as a baby-sitter to such an extent that she finally had snapped. We had to find her guilty, but we added a 'strong recommendation to mercy'; and so she escaped being jailed. Some jurors bluntly said in the jury room that it should have been the daughter who was charged. There are three comments that I would make arising from my stint of jury duty.

- The first is that I took note of the actions of the fellow-jurors while we were waiting in the jury room before we were called up. On the first occasion one man was quite talkative, expressing all sorts of opinions. When we had been empanelled I immediately moved (successfully) that he be the foreman, and thus I escaped the possibility of being elected to that position.

- The second comment is that after hearing the explanation by two magistrates of what constitutes 'reasonable doubt', I was quite bamboozled whether one could ever be sure that there was no reasonable doubt; so I relied on my own sense.

- The third, believe it or not, concerns listening to sermons. In this modern age the human cry is that sermons are 'too long' if they exceed 15 or 20 minutes. I know there is a difference between a sermon and a long piece of evidence or a long summary by lawyers or a judge, but long, intense listening is common to both. Is the Crown naïve in continuing to expect that the members of a jury can listen intently and absorb what is said, even for days?

Chapter 6

- **Social Welfare**: Sydney Bartsch, the head of Australian Lutheran World Service in Albury (Bonegilla), gave good guidance to the activities of this Board. He was also the valued NSW representative in the General Church Council. He gave candid insight of the activities of the many organisations in Australia engaged in welfare work, especially in reference to the percentage of donated money spent on advertising and administration. — One meeting of the Board stands out in my memory. In 1976, accompanied by the SA representative, Eric Blaess, I travelled in my car. One day, when visits to various welfare centres were arranged we plotted our course through Sydney suburban streets to one of these, but those NSW men we followed lost their way and finally arrived late. When the tour was over we found that I had locked my keys in the car. I had to wait in pouring rain for an hour on the main road with little to guide the NRMA down the long approach to the establishment. The heavy rain had sparked a host of emergency calls.

- **An unforgettable Funeral (Jan 1977)**: When John Biar was absent from his North Adelaide parish the emergency calls for his services were directed to me. In his Seelsorge he had befriended a Geoffrey Medlon Smi…(?), a huge man of about 38 years, who roamed the streets of North Adelaide. From my office window I noticed him at times in O'Connell St, always alone. Geoff died while John Biar was away. At the Centennial Park Crematorium the funeral director led me downstairs for a necessary 'viewing of the coffin'. At the door to the furnace careful measurements were being taken to check that the specially-made timber coffin would go through the door with millimetres to spare. Then we proceeded upstairs to the chapel where coffins are normally lowered. The funeral director stood on one side of the empty spot and I on the other – and there was not one soul in the chapel who was there for Geoff's sake. In a type of shock I had instantaneously reduced the order of burial cremation to those sentences that seemed appropriate to the complete absence of family and mourners. — There was an aftermath 25 years later. I received a phone call in Tanunda from the funeral director; a brother David was seeking information! All that we had is in this reference.

- **Publications**: My activity in Publications was mostly with individuals, not with the Board. As I prepared the write-up of this section the recollection suddenly struck me that I had received and declined a call to serve as Director of Publications. Everard Leske accepted the call, and filled the position admirably. – He was not overwhelmed by the radical demands that started to be expressed in some quarters and which influenced the attitude of some later Directors, notably John Pfitzner.

- **'God's People at Prayer'**: In 1977 Everard approached me to work with him on a book of prayers for public worship, prayers for general use, seasonal opening paragraphs and prayers for seasonal use, being prayers for all sorts and conditions of men (now in modern times cleaned from all hidden masculinity by being 'human beings'). We then drew in the prayers that had been prepared by Harry Wendt for every Sunday, and published our collection under the above title.

Everard Leske

The identification 'Chi-Rho' on the title page was my suggestion to LPH. One day [April-May 1973] as I was leaving Lutheran Publishing House a group of men was gathered near the exit discussing the matter of having a distinctive title. As I sat down in my car near the entrance I, as usual, saw the large lamp that was emblazoned in one of the windows: at the left end was a large X, at the right end a large P in its design. I went inside to the group, and said: 'How about 'CHI-RHO', which is on your lamp.' For a number of years (I don't know how many) this logo was used. It included a Chi-Rho series of explanation of books of the Bible.

- **All Asia Lutheran Seminar on Mission, Hong Kong (Kowloon), January 9-14, 1978**: The only time I left Australasian shores on behalf of the LCA was an interesting, if stressful, time for me. The occasion was the first All Asia Lutheran Seminar on Mission. The retiring Director of the LWF Department of Church Co-operation, Dr. Carl-J. Hellberg, wrote: *'I have noticed a very encouraging growing together of your churches as well as your neighbouring church in Australia. It has indeed been a very stimulating experience for which I give thanks to God'*. The Chairman of the LWF Commission on Church Co-operation (James A. Scherer) described it as a *'momentous venture. The Lutheran churches of Asia are giving a shining example to the other churches of the Federation for missionary zeal and commitment to the ongoing task of sharing the Gospel with all people.'*

Chapter 6

I still have the printed Report of 189 A4 pages plus 6 pages of photographs, entitled *'Asian Quest for Mission'* to aid my memory. There were 70 participants, 57 of whom were delegates from about 29 groups, chiefly Lutheran Churches. I have not analysed the listing thoroughly enough to give an exact figure. This amazing array of people came from Hong Kong (about 6 Churches and other groups), Taiwan (2 Churches), Korea (2), Japan (4), India and Bangladesh (5), Malaysia and Singapore (2), Indonesia (4), Philippines (1), Papua New Guinea (2), and Australia (LCA). There were only about 10 European Caucasian faces visible at this Seminar. Dr. S.P. Hebart and I, the two LCA delegates, were two of these European faces. Unbeknown to me, I was not a delegate who could sit quietly in a corner, absorbing as much as possible what was being said at the Seminar.

For the first time in my life I experienced how one could be whisked away in a day over thousands of kilometres into a totally different world. In the morning of January 9 I stepped into a Qantas plane at the Adelaide airport. During the morning the Australian continent disappeared below me and was replaced by sea. Through a window on the right side of the plane the distinctive neck of western New Guinea was seen in clear outline; then the islands of the Philippines appeared below me.

Landing at Manila we were very much made aware that there was military control in the Philippines as we, flanked by armed soldiers, made our way to the Transit Lounge. Night-time had begun when we headed into the blaze of lights that flanked the Kowloon airport. A girl called Shirley (which always sounded to me like 'Sherry' or 'Cherry' when it was said), a member of the staff of the Chairman of the Seminar, quickly sought me out, got me through Customs with amazing ease, and bundled me into a taxi. At that stage I did not notice the tall buildings that lined the streets of Kowloon; my heart was in my mouth as my eye measured how many centimetres separated us from the vehicles alongside as we squeezed between the heavy traffic. At a tall building, typical of Kowloon buildings, a lift took the two of us up many storeys to the church that (according to my memory) was Truth Lutheran Church. And so, approximately 12 hours after leaving Adelaide, I stepped into the opening service that had just begun, at which the Kowloon-based Seminary professor and Vice-President of the LWF, Dr. Andrew Hsaio, preached on the theme 'Why the Asian Church must talk about Mission'.

Delegates in a session at Truth Lutheran Church

The Chairman of the Seminar, Dr. Andrew Chiu, of the staff of Concordia Lutheran Seminary in Hong Kong, greeted and welcomed me after the service, and added: *'You know that we have a job for you – to be the Recording Secretary of the Seminar!'* I certainly hadn't received any such message in Australia. I don't know who made this suggestion, but I believe that it could have been the Asia Secretary of LWF, Dr. Kunchala Rajaratnam, who had visited the LCA in the previous year and with whom I had had some contact. My task was, after the reading of the lectures that formed a large part of the programme, to record comments made by participants, and to record any resolutions carried during plenary sessions. That meant I had to seek to understand every speaker, ranging from the accent of many Indians and the higher-pitched accent of many Chinese to white speakers with European accents; and I had to ensure that I identified every speaker correctly.

Chapter 6

Even on the last day I struggled. I understood the Chinese Chairman to say: *'That the motion be adopted as a mandate'*, and proceeded to write that down, even though I thought it was a remarkably binding statement; the Chairman however repeated his words, and I wrote down: *'That the motion be adopted as amended (as a-mand-et)!'* For five days (Tuesday to Saturday), when the sessions were over and the delegates were free to move at will in Kowloon, I worked on my report, sorting out my scribbled notes and writing up the record of each day in legible form. When the Seminar closed at 12.45 p.m. on Saturday I had my final flurry, because Rajaratnam was catching an early flight to Geneva, and wanted to take my Report with him. When it appeared in print in the official Report of the Seminar it occupied 13 pages.

I was asked to lead in the opening prayer when business sessions began on Tuesday, and was then formally elected as the Recording Secretary. The first four days began with a Bible Study on passages from the 'Patriarchal Period' in Genesis, conducted by Dr. Richard Deutsch of Basel Mission Switzerland, who was serving in a College in the Chinese University of Hong Kong. Three papers were read on that first day, and the other two on the next. Generally two Reactors had been chosen to provide an 'official' reaction to these papers. The absent third writer, Dr. M. Abel, had to be replaced 'through changed circumstances'; and so the two Reactors, Mrs. M. Mamora of Indonesia and I (I had not received information about being a Reactor) likewise were excused. Dr.Rajaratnam provided an essay, probably written for another occasion, in place of the above.

For the discussion periods, which especially occupied Thursday and Friday, the Seminar was divided into groups, chiefly on geographic and ethnic lines: Hong Kong/Taiwan/Malaysia; India; Indonesia; Japan/Korea; Papua New Guinea; Australia/Philippines/English-speaking delegates (including representatives of European Mission Societies). Hebart served as the chairman of the Australian group and was much involved in its report. Hebart also provided an evening devotion, and served as the reporter of the three-man Evaluation Committee that was appointed on Friday to assess the Seminar. We were accommodated nearby in the multi-storey YMCA International House at 25 Waterloo Road. My room-mate was Dr. Jose Fuliga, President of the Philippines Church and head of its Seminary, who was one of the essayists at the Seminar. He was a very pleasant companion.

Some of the participants at the Assembly. Henry in back row, 6th from left.

Kowloon depended on China for its supply of water; this was turned off every day for a length of time that I have forgotten. Our hotel, however, stored up a reserve supply, so that we were not aware of any lack, apart from the request to be careful in the use of water. Our meals there were very good. On the Wednesday we were given a Chinese meal in a restaurant; in typical Chinese style there were very many smaller courses. That meant there were chop-sticks; but the Indians with whom I sat were as helpless as I. When I saw them put aside their chop-sticks and pick up forks I thankfully did the same.

Chapter 6

On Thursday we were taken by bus on a 60-mile trip through the New Territories, the additional land that was leased from China as part of the Kowloon area of Hong Kong. The days of Hong Kong as British territory were numbered (I believe it was still two years at that time), and the imminent return to China was a subject of much anxious discussion. We were taken to some higher ground close to the border, from which we viewed the People's Republic of China that lay a mile away below us. On the return part of the trip we passed through the suburb of Shatin, where one of the Lutheran Seminaries was located – and also the active horse-racing fraternity.

When the Seminar was ended and I had handed in my report on Saturday afternoon I wandered through the central part of Kowloon. In gratitude for my time-consuming work as Recording Secretary I was allowed to stay an extra night so that I could see more of Hong Kong. Next morning I looked across the water towards the island of Hong Kong in the hope of being able to enjoy the highly-commended view from its peak; but everything was so murky that this was impossible. So I visited the streets and shops of Kowloon, and shopped for the last of the mementos for my family before joining the early evening Qantas flight for Australia. I did not sleep very well during the disturbed night, for we once again moved past the armed military line-up to the Transit Lounge in Manila. To my disappointment I found that the Chinese-English newspaper that I had been reading and wanted to keep as a memento was no longer on my seat when I returned to the plane. And on this flight there was a second visit to a Transit Lounge – around dawn on Monday we found that we had to move into the lounge at the Brisbane Airport.

My eyes needed match-sticks when we arrived in Sydney; but I was unexpectedly greeted by Robert Paech, President of the NSW District. He desired to take me that morning to Parramatta to show me for my approval the arrangements that had been made with the King's College for the General Convention of the LCA to be held there later in the year. I believe that I nodded my head quite often – always to indicate approval?

- **Second Australasian Congress on Genealogy and Heraldry, Adelaide, April 1980**. [Henry was guest speaker at this Congress. His topic was "Lutheran Records in Australasia".]

- **Last Day at the Office.** [from *The Lutheran*, 24 Dec 1984:
In the late afternoon of November 30, 1984, the staff at Church House, North Adelaide, spoke their final farewells to Pastor H.F.W. Proeve. The convention at Croydon, Victoria, back in August had already taken note of the fact that Pastor Proeve was relinquishing office after 39 years as secretary of the Church, first of the United Evangelical Lutheran Church, and then as the secretary of the Lutheran Church of Australia. In this long period of service Henry, as he was affectionately known, was faithfully supported by his wife, Dorothy. Officials and office staff paid warm tribute to the outstanding contribution which Pastor Henry Proeve made to the work of the Lutheran Church in Australia. We wish the Proeves well in retirement.]

Henry, Dorothy and President Les Grope

Chapter 7

VII. THE RETIRED COUPLE DECADE:
1984 (December) — 1993 (December)

Editor's note: Henry was unable to complete the final sections of his memoirs. We have included some additional information which fits this chapter of his life. This is indicated inside square brackets.

- **Friends of Lutheran Archives.**

The great success of this organisation is a matter of deep satisfaction to me. It was I who conceived the project. Any researcher of its history needs to study the minutes of the Board of Archives to discover the full story.

In May 1984, as Secretary of the Board of Archives, I successfully moved that the formation of a Friends group be investigated, and I was entrusted with the task. I studied such documents as I could think of, like the Friends of the Public Library, and finally submitted – in April 1986 – the structure for an organisation, to be known as **'Friends of Lutheran Archives'**, as a body that gathered together people who would support the Archives in as many ways as possible, especially financially. The Board of Archives adopted my draft.

Lutheran Archives at 101 Archer St, North Adelaide

The actual foundation of the Friends of Lutheran Archives had to be organised in Adelaide. The keen interest of Joyce Graetz put into effect in October 1990 what I had conceived several years earlier.

Putting the plan into action unfortunately suffered delays. As far as I personally was concerned this was due to my shifting from Prospect to Tanunda about that time, aggravated by problems associated with this move. In addition to the normal involvements of settling in I was faced with a lengthy struggle with the local District Council. I needed to have a building erected to house my library, with a modified garage plan as its basis. The height of the building necessary to accommodate my library shelves (2.74 m) was disallowed by the Council as exceeding the permissible limit of 2.4m. I lodged a challenge to the Council ruling on the grounds that there were other buildings of a similar nature in the vicinity that exceeded the limit. My son David helped by providing photographs of these buildings. I prepared and presented my own case before the Planning Appeal Tribunal in Adelaide. This absorbed my time for months, and even resulted in my non-attendance and non-participation as a Consultant at the 1987 General Synod, because the Tribunal sat at the same time.

Study at 37 Homburg St, Tanunda

Chapter 7

- **Shifting to Tanunda, 1987**: After continuing to live in Airlie Avenue, Prospect, for about two years after my retirement, Dorothy began to canvas the idea of shifting to Tanunda, in order to help David and Kaylene in caring for their handicapped son Andrew. The first requirement was to find a home in Tanunda within the price range that we could expect to receive for our Prospect house. There was not much choice, especially when one room had to be set aside as a study. **37 Homburg Street** was inspected several times. The rooms were on the small side, the ceiling was much lower than anything we had ever lived in. None of the bedrooms were suitable to be a library. Dorothy was keener than I to purchase it because it was only half a kilometre from David's home.

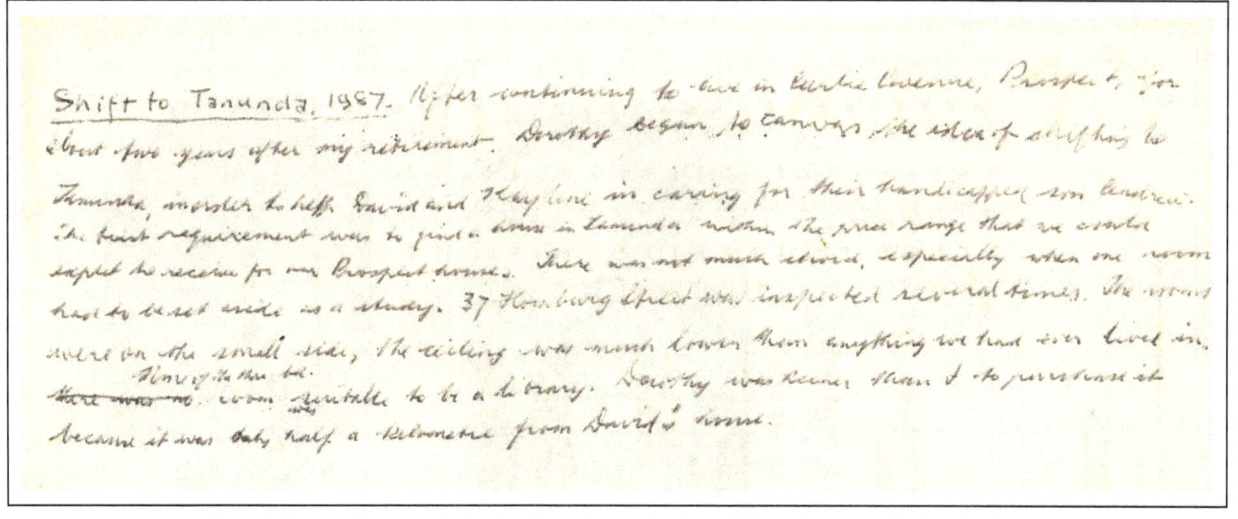

Henry's last written words for the Memoirs, early Sept 2014, a few weeks before he died.

[**Continued LCA involvement**: Despite being retired, Henry was still asked to continue on some of the LCA committees and share his wisdom. He continued on the Commission on Theology and Inter-Church Relations until 1987, on the Board of Archives and Research (as Secretary) until 1990, the Standing Committee on Constitutions until 1990, and the Commission on Worship - Department of Liturgy and Hymnody (as Consultant) until 1997.

Cemeteries Association of South Australia Inc.
Henry was an original member of the Cemeteries Association of South Australia, when it formed in Dec 1977. He represented the Lutheran Church. He served as a committee member (1977-1991), Chairman (1980-1981) and President (1981-1983, 1986-1991).]

Henry in mid-2014

185

Chapter 7

Dorothy: Dorothy suffered from various illnesses in the last years of her life. She died on December 26th, 1993.

Below: *Henry's first Christmas letter, December 1994*

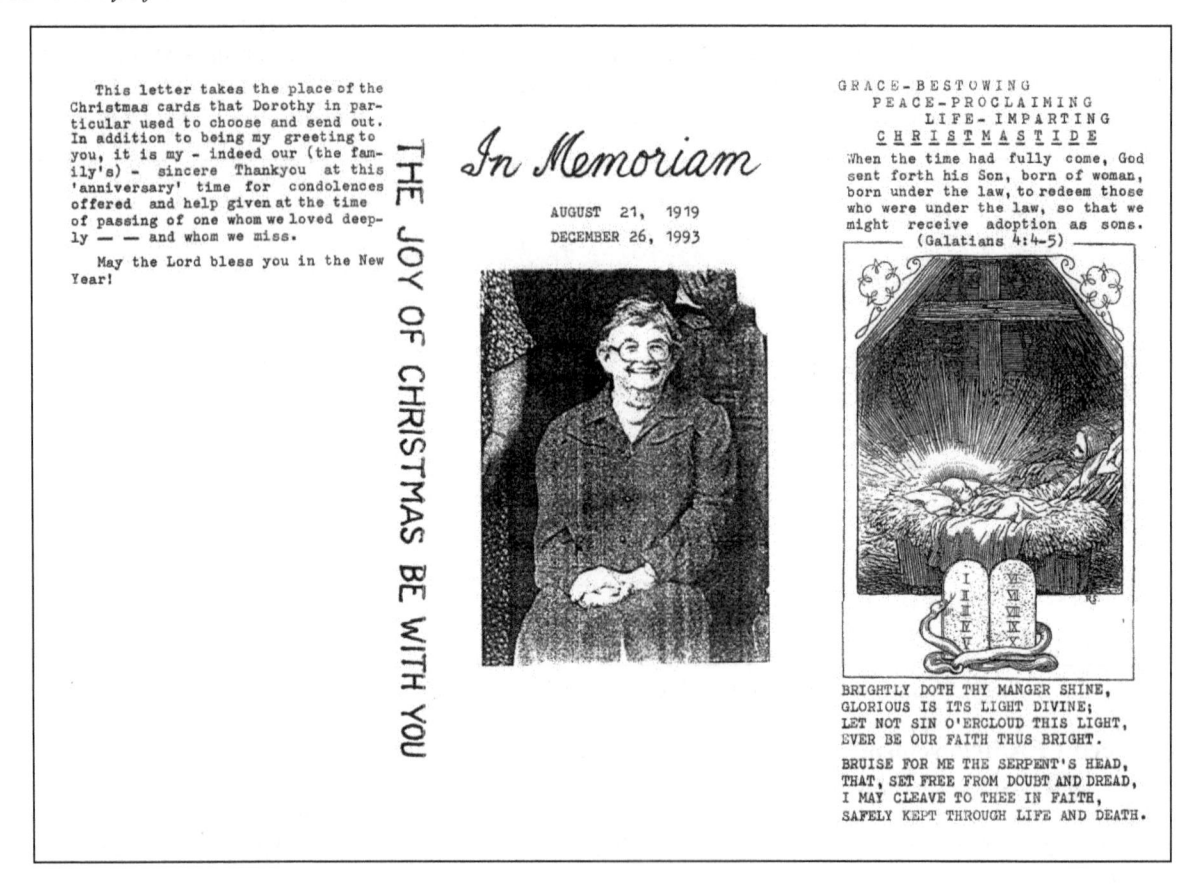

> This letter takes the place of the Christmas cards that Dorothy in particular used to choose and send out. In addition to being my greeting to you, it is my - indeed our (the family's) - sincere Thankyou at this 'anniversary' time for condolences offered and help given at the time of passing of one whom we loved deeply — — and whom we miss.
>
> May the Lord bless you in the New Year!

In Memoriam

AUGUST 21, 1919
DECEMBER 26, 1993

THE JOY OF CHRISTMAS BE WITH YOU

GRACE-BESTOWING
PEACE-PROCLAIMING
LIFE-IMPARTING
C H R I S T M A S T I D E

When the time had fully come, God sent forth his Son, born of woman, born under the law, to redeem those who were under the law, so that we might receive adoption as sons.
— (Galatians 4:4-5) —

BRIGHTLY DOTH THY MANGER SHINE,
GLORIOUS IS ITS LIGHT DIVINE;
LET NOT SIN O'ERCLOUD THIS LIGHT,
EVER BE OUR FAITH THUS BRIGHT.

BRUISE FOR ME THE SERPENT'S HEAD,
THAT, SET FREE FROM DOUBT AND DREAD,
I MAY CLEAVE TO THEE IN FAITH,
SAFELY KEPT THROUGH LIFE AND DEATH.

[*from Dorothy's obituary:*

Dorothy was born in America into a pastor's family. Her father was Australian and her mother was American. They came to Australia in 1921. She was confirmed at Dimboola in 1932; she attended Immanuel College, North Adelaide, in 1934, and later began training as a nurse at the Horsham Hospital. Her mother died in April 1944. On August 29, 1944, she married Henry Proeve.

This was the beginning of life as a parish pastor's wife. Having served as an organist in her father's parish from the age of 13 years, and as a Sunday School teacher, she was happy to continue these activities, particularly in the North Adelaide field. Women's activities in the congregations were of special interest to her, and she served as the President of the Guild that her husband organised in North Adelaide, of the Nuriootpa Guild, and finally as President of four of the five guilds in the Point Pass parish. She was also, as Doctor J.J. Stolz once expressed it, the 'spark' that began the women's organisation in the SA District of the former UELCA. When it was formed under the name 'Lutheran Women's Association' Dorothy was elected as its first secretary, and as the business manager of its official publication 'Lutheran Women'.

When Henry became General Secretary of the LCA and they moved to Adelaide, Dorothy found opportunities of service in the guild activities in the North Adelaide congrgegation, and the activities of its catering section, and also for a time as Treasurer of the congregation and member of its Church Council. To this she added many hours of voluntary assistance in Henry's office, and took particular joy in being involved in the often pressured activities associated with general conventions of the Church.

Several operations in later life, a severe attack of facial shingles some ten years ago, also slight strokes, gradually decreased her bodily stamina and mobility; nevertheless her decline and death at 6.35 p.m. on December 26th 1993, very soon after an operation at the Royal Adelaide Hospital, came with startling suddenness. Dorothy was buried in Langmeil cemetery.]

Chapter 8

VIII. THE GERMAN-LANGUAGE MINISTRY IN ADELAIDE

- **My 'Macedonian Ministry'.** In the Lutheran Church particular emphasis is laid on being properly called to carry out a ministry in the Church. For about three decades I officiated in a ministry for which I did not have a Letter of Call. I dubbed my call the 'Macedonian Call', which had the unwritten wording 'Come over and help us'. It emanated from three areas where German services were held: Warradale, North Adelaide, Bethlehem Adelaide.

My ministry to the **Warradale** German Lutheran Congregation began on Good Friday, March 24, 1978. German services had been begun in the ELCA Warradale Church by Pastor A.B.C. Hoff. After the amalgamation of the two Lutheran Churches the bilingual Pastor F. Schafranek continued them in the Faith Lutheran Church, and when he accepted another call Pastor Peter Strelan served the German group as a visiting pastor. He died suddenly before the Good Friday; John Biar telephoned me whether I could take the service at short notice. I did so, and when the time came for the next monthly service on the second Sunday in April I went again, and without question that became the normal routine. The time when the service began had to be fitted in with the increasing requirements of the host congregation; 8.00 a.m. became 7.45 a.m. for many years, until in May 2000, when the German-speaking group had shrunk to below 10, it ceased to use the church and gathered at the more comfortable time of 10.00 a.m. in a series of private homes. On Good Friday, April 14, 2006, two persons (including the stalwart of the congregation, Otto Bienert) plus Elvira gathered for the last service, and the German-speaking group that I had served for 28 years had closed.

Photo on left: *Warradale church*

Conducting German services in **Albert Park** preceded my ministry at Warradale. The early pastors at Albert Park were capable of ministering to the German sections of their congregation. My first two services were widely separated in June 1969 and January 1972, when I served the parish as guest minister, followed by an ongoing stint of five services in 1977. At the request of the bilingual local pastor W. Stolz, I officiated 7 times between 1979 and 1981. That ensured that he could at times remain with his Woodville West members instead of immediately rushing off to Albert Park for the German service.

Albert Park was the scene of one of the most embarrassing happenings that I had in a service. The communion vessels stood on the altar, the chalice of course covered by a veil. What no one had noticed was that the chalice stood <u>on one end</u> of the veil. When I pulled the veil away from the chalice it pulled the chalice over, and its contents saturated my gown as well as the altar linens. I had two more communion services that day, North Adelaide (late morning), Bethlehem (afternoon), and finally a baptism after that in a Hungarian service – and everywhere I reeked of wine!

I conducted many German services at **North Adelaide**. The first took place during my North Adelaide ministry, when immigrants started to arrive from Europe. When Dorothy and I returned to Adelaide in 1965 and joined the North Adelaide congregation this congregation included a German-speaking congregation that had been absorbed during Kon Hartmann's ministry, and was provided with services on the 1st and 3rd Sundays of each month. For many years the pastors of the congregation (K. Hartmann, C.J. Pfitzner, J.H. Biar) were bilingual. My assistance consisted in officiating when they could not, or when there was a vacancy. One such vacancy lasted for a year, during which time the fellow North Adelaide Pastor A.J. Lohe and I served the whole congregation. When bilingual pastors were no longer called by the congregation my ministry in German became ongoing, especially when Pastor Biar shifted to Queensland in 1995.

Henry giving the Benediction at North Adelaide on July 4, 2010

Chapter 8

The ministry was then taken over by the long-standing trio of pastors who conducted German services in the Adelaide area during the twentieth century, which consisted of Erich Renner, Maurice Schild, and me, with help for a number of years from Gunther Bayha. This trio was broken when ill-health put a very sudden end to my ministry in 2011. There is a twinge of sadness and disappointment in my mind that I was not able to close my public ministry where my called ministry began, viz.in North Adelaide – the idea to officiate for the last time in North Adelaide on Sunday, November 2, could not be carried out.

Photo on right: *After the service at North Adelaide on July 4, 2010 – with Erich Renner and Robert Pfitzner*

The '**Macedonian Call**' finally came also from the **Bethlehem Adelaide** German Lutheran congregation, established by the burly, somewhat blusterous Berliner, Pastor M. Pachur, that worshipped in the Bethlehem Church. After Pastor Pachur's retirement in 1973, various German-speaking pastors served Bethlehem until 1977, and the North Adelaide congregation agreed to an approach that its Pastor John Biar, who was the pastor at North Adelaide, would look after the Bethlehem German congregation as well. John Biar took over its care and did so with passionate zeal. He built up financial security by collecting and selling newspapers (which filled his garage), and the sale of used clothing and household goods. He and his wife Elsie encouraged the women in the congregation to provide the goods, especially eatables, that were sold at trading tables in an annual Fair in St. Helen's Park, Prospect. – Two services in 1973 and two in mid-1979 were very early forerunners to the occasional services that I conducted usually one or two times per annum during the 1980's and early 1990 until John Biar's removal to Queensland.

Leaving Bethlehem church, 2011    *In Bethlehem church*

Bethlehem was then looked after by North Adelaide by the long-standing trio of pastors during the 20th century: E. Renner, M. Schild and me, and also for a number of years, G. Bayha. Bethlehem, however, had services every Sunday at that time. At the annual meeting at the end of 2003, however, the surprising decision was made by the congregation to reduce the number of services to one per month, on the 4th Sunday of the month. On the 24th July 2011 I preached sermon number 4592 (according to the ongoing numbering in my 36 record books) in Bethlehem with 10 persons present and 7 communing. What I did not know was that this was the final service in my ministry [*see photo above right*].

Chapter 8

At the 60th anniversary of the Bethlehem German congregation May 22, 2011
Photo on right: Dr Maurice Schild, SA President David Altus, Henry Proeve, Dr Erich Renner

For a short time I still served the German-speaking groups by continuing to edit the *Bethlehems Bote*, which I had been doing since September 2006. I ceased to do this with the December 2012 issue and left it to Renner, Schild and Peter Fleig (Bethlehem chairperson) to produce it.

Der Bethlehems-Bote

Gemeindeblatt der deutschen evang.-luth. Bethlehemsgemeinde, 170 Flinders St. Adelaide

60. Jahrgang, Nr. 2   Jahresbeitrag $5.00   März — Mai 2012

Seite 8

GOTTESDIENSTPLAN:	MÄRZ — APRIL — MAI 2012		
März 2: Passion 2, Reminiscere			
11.00 Uhr North Adelaide		Hl. Abendmahl	Dr. M. E. Schild
März 18: Passion 4, Lätare			
11.00 Uhr North Adelaide			Dr. J. T. E. Renner
März 25: Passion, Judika			
14.00 Uhr Bethlehem		Hl. Abendmahl	Dr. M. E. Schild
April 1: Passion, Palmsonntag			
Kein Gottesdienst in North Adelaide: Verlegt auf **OSTERN**			
April 6: Karfreitag			
14.00 Uhr Bethlehem		Hl. Abendmahl	Dr. J. T. E. Renner
		Prediger: Dr. Friedemann Hebart	
April 8: OSTERFEST			
11.00 Uhr North Adelaide		Hl. Abendmahl	Dr. J. T. E. Renner
April 15: Ostern 1, Quasimodogeniti			
11.00 Uhr North Adelaide			Dr. M. E. Schild
April 22: Ostern 2, Misericordias Domini			
14.00 Uhr Bethlehem			Dr. M. E. Schild
Mai 6: Ostern 4, Kantate			
11.00 Uhr North Adelaide		Hl. Abendmahl	Dr. J. T. E. Renner
Mai 20: Ostern 6, Exaudi			
11.00 Uhr North Adelaide			Dr. M. E. Schild
Mai 27: PFINGSTFEST			
14.00 Uhr Bethlehem		Hl. Abendmahl	Dr. J. T. E. Renner

Auskunft über Taufen, Konfirmationen, Hochzeiten, Beerdigungen
Geben die in Adelaide wohnenden Pastoren:
Dr. J. T. E. Renner (North Adelaide)   Telefon 8267 4329
Dr. M. E. Schild (Prospect)   Telefon 8344 1671
    E-mail: mschild@internode.on.net
Vorsitzender / Kassierer: Herr Peter Fleig Telefon 7329 1609
    Mobile Phone: 0420 859 438   E-mail: fleig@adam.com.au
Redakteur Bethlehems-Bote: Dr. H. F. W. Proeve Telefon 8563 2098
Organistin: Frau Sonia Bradtke   Telefon 8258 4929

Gottesdienste werden gehalten: *Adresse*   *Gewöhnliche Zeit*
Bethlehemkirche 170 Flinders Street, Adelaide   14.00 Uhr am 4. **Sonntag**
Immanuelkirche 139 Archer Street, North Adelaide   11.00 Uhr am 1. & 3. Sonntag

FÜR DIE HAUSANDACHT *(Fortsetzung von Seite 7)*
Mai 27: PFINGSTEN *4.Mose 11,11-12.13-17.24-25 / Apostelg. 2,1-18 / Joh. 14,23-27*
Es soll nicht durch Heer oder Kraft,
sondern durch meinen Geist geschehen, spricht der Herr Zebaoth.   *Sacharja 4,6*

Chapter 9

IX. THE LAST CHAPTER

> **Editor's note**: After Dorothy's death in 1993, Henry wrote a Christmas letter each year from 1994 to 2013 to his family and friends in which he reported on the activities of the year, and much of the following story is compiled from these letters. We have chosen appropriate photos to include.

1994:

I have been fending for myself this year. That, of course, has meant a greater amount of time than heretofore in the kitchen, the laundry, the house in general, and among the pot plants and garden plants: study activities, like bookbinding, have taken the time-cut. Treasured friends have had me regularly in their homes for meals; others have brought food around; and (if I want to) I can go over to Kaylene's and David's table, ½ km distant.

Monthly German services at Warradale for the faithful little group have continued; likewise assistance as required elsewhere for services, bible studies, and the like. Being President of the Trust administering the local Museum, some historical projects, working on documents written in the old handwritten German script, are among the items that have filled in time.

The trip to Gippsland which Dorothy and I could not do last year on account of floods, turned this year into a 3-week 5000km tour (October) by us two widowed 'cobbers', Les Grope and me, along the highways and byways of lush-green Gippsland, as well as Eden, Alpine Way and Omeo Highway, and the Mornington Peninsula. Very enjoyable – but also with thoughts of what might have been coming to mind at times.

1995:

Since the beginning of the year, due to the removal of class-mate John Biar to Queensland, there has been increased co-involvement in ministering (primarily conducting 28 services) to the German-speaking groups referred to earlier.

Planning (and in the first half-year conducting) the Tanunda Town Walk for tourists [has] provided another area of interest and activity.

General thinking about 1996 includes the hope that I may once again visit Queensland and the cousins there. And comparative recent information, which I followed up in Nhill, that gives the promise of locating the missing fourth branch (Johann Gottlieb Schultz jr.) of Dorothy's ancestral family (Joh. Gottlieb Schultz sr.) points to Gippsland as the area for further enquiry.

1996:

The highlight of this year no doubt was a 45-day motoring trip with brother Paul and his wife Gwen (Sept. 10 – Oct. 23) in his trusty Mazda. The Queensland-based Proeve/Prove family has now reached the stage that its 'advanced' line consists of 31 living first cousins: Queensland (20), NSW (1), SA (6), Victoria (4). In fact I am now the 'old man of the tribe'! For us three travellers – and we believe the same applies to the relatives with whom we spent some hours or some days – it was a heart-warming experience to be together in the realisation that we were linked in the bonds of kinship. In some instances this personal contact had only taken place once or twice in an adult lifetime. Covering some 13,000 kms, we met all Queensland and NSW cousins (except 1) and their spouses, and on occasion some of the next generation. And we could include the three interstate children of Paul and Gwen at Alice Springs, Darwin and Springwood. All told, 75 to 80 kinsfolk!

So our travelling took us to Alice Springs and Darwin in the Northern Territory; in Queensland to Townsville, Mackay (including Seaforth), Yeppoon, Gympie, Blackbutt (near Yarraman), Dalby, Chinchilla, Mundubbera, Pittsworth, Toowoomba (and nearby Wellcamp), Gatton, Indooroopilly and Chapel Hill (Brisbane), Southport; in NSW Maclean, Springwood (Blue Mountains), Deniliquin. Associated with this was an update of family information, in the hope to produce a printed record of the Proeve/Prove family, now 110 years in Australia.

We are thankful to the Lord for His protection on our journey, and grateful to the 'family' for all love and kindness.

Chapter 9

Other areas of interest and activity have included the reading, transcribing, and translating of documents on the old German handwriting, various kinds of research (some theological, some historical); presiding over the affairs of the Barossa Valley Museum in Tanunda; and being an interviewee for journalists, documentary-makers, and visitors to the Barossa. The outcome of one such occasion was that the co-worker of two Berlin visitors, a Proeve living in the ancestral area, made contact by sending out a printed version of the history of the Australian Proeves written by my father for the 'Pröven-Tag' (family day) in the early 1920's.

1997:

German as well as history has figured strongly in other week-by-week activity, sometimes created by sudden, unexpected approaches: one of a panel of 6 speakers in a seminar during the Barossa Music Festival to launch Dr Noris Ioannou's latest book on the Barossa; radio interviews, in English for BBC London Radio, in German for South German Radio; quite a number of requests relating to family research, where in 2 cases the printed story of the beginnings in Australia will have to be radically changed; translating German originals; transcribing, and if necessary translating, German handwritten documents, such as Prussian documents relating to the 1830's held in microfilm in the Lutheran Archives – and minute books from 3 congregations have been lodged with me. – My association with the Barossa Museum in Tanunda, as President of its Barossa Valley Archives and Historical Trust, brought me into contact with some interesting enquirers and visitors, such as the German Consul-General in Melbourne. I served as selector and annotator for an audio cassette of hymns and other musical renditions (organist Mark Whitfield) to mark the opening in the museum of a restored 1865 Krüger organ, built in western Victoria.

Photo above: *Ivan Venning, MP, Roger Jones, organ builder, & Henry at restored Krüger organ*

1998:

This year has passed by quite satisfactorily for me, for which praise and thanks are due to our Heavenly Father. It has been marked by several noteworthy events. As chief of these I daresay I should place the birthday milestone that God graciously granted me: the 80th birthday on November 2. The children arranged the celebration for November 8, a day when Carol and John and almost all the children could be present. At least 135 people were at The Langmeil Centre; a most heart-warming aspect of this was the presence of so many members of the parishes I served (even though this was 33 or more years ago).

As in earlier years, historical and research activities have continued, and they have not lost their interest factors. I addressed three touring groups – and in one case led two searching descendants to the grave of their ancestors ('somewhere in the Barossa'), because I unveiled a commemorative plaque on it many years ago. A filmed interview at 5 minutes notice with a team from German Studio Television Singapore; a taped interview with a Deutsche Welle reporter from Cologne. (I do not know the outcome. Some years ago it was very interesting to receive a copy of the article in an English newspaper in Djakarta which summarised large portions of my statement to an Indonesian interviewer.); guest speaker on Barossa history at a Retreat in Nuriootpa for Mt. Barker-based Caregivers; twice the after-dinner guest speaker: a regional conference of the Wisemen (SA, Vic., NSW; and organisation giving support to YMCA) in Tanunda; and on Dec. 28 at Glenelg at the Proclamation Day Dinner of the S.A. Pioneers' Association, attended by 74 people, on the subject, 'German Migration 1836-1845'.

Photo on left: *Henry relaxing at home (taken by German reporters)*

The Neldner family had a reunion at the end of October, commemorating the 140th anniversary of arrival. As Dorothy's grandmother on the paternal side was a Neldner, I served as the Schultz branch representative on the committee that produced the family history.

Chapter 9

1999:

As has no doubt been the case with everyone, there has been much normal routine in my life since last Christmas; but also particular markers both of joy and sadness within the family circle. – The prefix 'great' was added to 'grandfather' with the birth of Nicholas Adam Wilksch (to Matthew and Sandra) in May. Matthew's ordination to the Holy Ministry (with 11 others at Faith Secondary School, Tanunda) followed in November. His appointment to the Rosewood parish in Queensland has for me the interesting historical connection that my father conducted his first service in Rosewood in July 1928. The marriage in May of Carol and John Wilksch's eldest son, Simon, to Christine, took us South Australians to Melbourne for a weekend. – The death of younger brother Paul on September 13 (in sudden deterioration, yet not unexpected) was not an event in my original thinking about the future – but man proposes, God disposes (much better expressed in 'der Mensch denkt, Gott lenkt'). Prior to that we had celebrated sister-in-law Gwen's 70th birthday (February) and Paul's 50th anniversary of ordination (April 11); happy occasions, but not without the background feeling that restoration to strength and reasonably normal activity was scarcely to be expected. In November David accompanied me to Dimboola, Vic., for the funeral of Dorothy's brother Charles, the 2nd-last surviving member of the Schultz family.

A highlight of the year was the visit of American cousin Loretta (Becker) Emeott, of St. Paul, Minnesota; but it was associated with a veritable emotional roller-coaster. Repeatedly encouraged by Paul to do so, she carried out her desire to visit Australia by joining a touring party. On Sept. 15 (2 days after Paul's death) she arrived on the Ghan in Adelaide to spend the two nights' stopover in Murray Bridge. Paul and Gwen had seen her in St. Paul; for me it was the first time after almost 72 years. And the 72-year-old records of the time when we were together was a Christmastide 1928 snapshot of a 9-year-old Henry and an 8-year-old Loretta sitting in grandmother's home with Loretta holding a 15-weeks-old Paul [*see photo on page 24 of memoirs*]. The farewell to Loretta was in the morning of Sept. 17, when I took her back to Adelaide to rejoin her departing party; the earthly farewell to Paul was a few hours later at the funeral in Murray Bridge.

2000:

The highlight of this year was part of an historical project that has been on the simmer for a long time – writing the history of the Proeve family. This provided an impetus to undertake a car trip to Queensland, in order to visit 20 cousins (or deceased cousins' spouses). I enjoyed having the company of my good friend, Les Grope, for most of the days of this 7,000 km journey. (In Toowoomba and partly in Brisbane we followed our own courses for about a week.) We began on September 25 as passing sightseers via Hay to Griffith, Cowra (Japanese War Camp and Cemetery; Japanese Garden), and Gulgong (heritage mining town), admiring good wheat crops, and in the Riverina area the mixture of lush green and gleaming canola gold. The visiting of cousins began at Maclean (near Grafton), and then continued: Toowoomba/Wellcamp, Gatton, Pittsworth, Blackbutt (near Yarraman), Brisbane (Indooroopilly, Chapel Hill, Marsden), Southport, Gympie, and Yeppoon (near Rockhampton) – 16 cousins in all, plus spouses, and a few of the next generation. I owe a deep debt of gratitude to all of them. They received me with open arms. The time spent with them went all too quickly as we shared family news, and reminiscences, and also updated the information that I have been collecting regarding each family.

Dear friends, Les Grope and Henry Proeve

Les and I also took the opportunity of visiting our two Seminary classmates in Queensland, Colin Scheer (Kippa-Ring) and John Biar (Bundaberg); also two retired co-workers in ministry, David Siegle (Glasshouse Mountains) and Vic. Pokela (near Gympie). The saddening part of the trip was to see the longstanding very dry condition of the country, worsening as we travelled northwards from Grafton. This pleasant trip came to an abrupt halt at Yeppoon. As an all-night attack of intense pain, following a shorter similar attack three nights earlier, was diagnosed as kidney stones, I decided to return immediately to South Australia to await developments and any further treatment. So the visiting of cousins in Mackay unfortunately had to be cancelled; and we commenced a 3-day 2400 km dash home on October 15. An ultrasound down here and the lack of later problems would indicate that the critical stage must have been that night of October 13.

The planned family history has the title: '*PRÖVE – PROEVE – PROVE. (1380-) 1886-2000)*'. Its three parts would comprise: 1. The Roots (1380 onwards); 2. The Transplanted Stem (H.W. Proeve); 3. The Branches (10 children; 7 families). Now I have to make contact with the southern (SA and Victorian) cousins.

2001:
I have taken a bold step this year. I am now more seriously a 'Sorceror's Apprentice' on a computer. And this Christmas letter is a test whether it is true that (as the Apprentice said in Goethe's poem, but in my wording): *Words and acts I noted, And the usage too; With their power devoted I'll work wonders too!* The 'sorceror' whose words and actions I've noted (if he hasn't done them too quickly) is David, and he's the master to whom I run when my commands are stubbornly disobeyed.

It is natural, no doubt, for those in 'senior' years to develop a certain standard pattern of activity. At least, that is how mine have been developing. There are some fixed features of duty, and it's the Lord's mercies that the health and strength to carry them out is still with me. The strongest feature continues to be that I am still part of the four-man team that provides German services in Adelaide.

Outside these 'features' there's participation in the activities of the Executive of the Barossa Valley Archives and Historical Trust, the Langmeil Men's Fellowship, and meetings of the Friends of Lutheran Archives. Some events have had their interesting moments: speaking to groups of tourists has happened only twice, one of these being a German group at Seppeltsfield; launching a book at Lyndoch for the local Historical Society; preparing two CD programmes in German on the Barossa which will be used as teaching aids for German classes in Victorian secondary schools; participating in the 125th anniversary celebrations at Point Pass, with 'Memories of Point Pass' as an afternoon segment; guest speaker on the Moravians at a Barossa Valley Rotary Club dinner.

I have now accepted an invitation to be the Patron for 2002 of the recently established Barossa Valley Family History Group. Assistance in research, transcription of old German, and translation continues to be an interesting 'hobby'. Work on the Proeve family history falls into that category. I am at present also preparing the history of the Ebenezer congregation for its 150th anniversary in May 2002; hitherto unused (because unknown) information can be incorporated into its interesting story.

Another member of our originally 10-member class at Immanuel Seminary reached the 80-year mark this year, namely Hermann Pech. The four surviving South Australian members of that group, Les Grope, Erich Renner, and I (travelling in my station-waggon), and Vic Wenke had the pleasure of celebrating with Herman and wife Elizabeth (likewise 80) in Box Hill in May. Such ties of long-standing friendship are precious.

2002:
The pattern of activities associated with my interest in the two branches of my studies in Melbourne about 65 years ago, History and German, does not become boring, since each year brings fresh requests with interesting differences that open up new vistas. An interesting example of this relates to two arrivals on the ship 'Alfred' in 1849: one an emigrant from the Wendish area of Bautzen (Kaulvers); the other a Roman Catholic priest who established the well-known settlement, Sevenhills near Clare (Father Kranewitter). A Melbourne researcher, Tom Darragh, has translated their writings; this year Pastor Clem Schmidt and I carefully checked the Kaulvers story, and I will be doing the same with the Kranewitter. The totally different background and SA experiences of these two men makes such work interesting.

Photo on right: *Clem Schmidt and Henry*

Requests for help in family research often falls into this category of 'interesting'. One surprise has been that requests have come from New South Wales through word-of-mouth referral; one couple made a point of making personal contact with me in Tanunda when they visited SA. I was asked to conduct the thanksgiving service of a Graetz family in March. An invitation to attend the official launching of the latest volume of the 'Australian Dictionary of Biography', this time in SA by the SA Governor, provided me with an opportunity to meet some fellow-contributors whom I had not seen for quite some time, even years. At the Lutheran Archives my standing offer is to try to decipher the 'tough nuts' – and they can be tough; but they are a challenge!

Chapter 9

There have been commemorations and celebrations of a varied nature. Leo Kalleske celebrated the 50th anniversary of ordination (January, at Langmeil) – I was the survivor of the 3 ordaining pastors. Then there was quite a run of celebrations. Immanuel College Old Scholars commemorated (April 27) the '1942 Move' that we had experienced from North Adelaide to Walkerville – a nostalgic day of activities. Seminary classmate Erich Renner celebrated his 80th birthday, and 5 of his classmates could be present on May 1. On May 5 the Ebenezer congregation commemorated 150 years; completing its 67 A4-page history book took me till March, comprising (the printer told me) 42,000 words.

The Proeve history is gradually taking shape. I have been concentrating on writing-up the earliest section, commencing with 1380, so that the final step will be the presentation and final update of the Australian families.

2003:

As part of my family history project I opened up the 1982 issue of 'Heimat-kalender für die Lüneburger Heide' ('Home Almanac for the Lüneburg Heath'), which was sent to me at the time by Anagret Arbeiter, the daughter of family historian Dr. Heinrich Proeve of Celle. As one of its feature articles it reproduced portion of a 1925 document prepared by my father, entitled '*Die Proeven in Australien*' *(The Proeves in Australia')*.

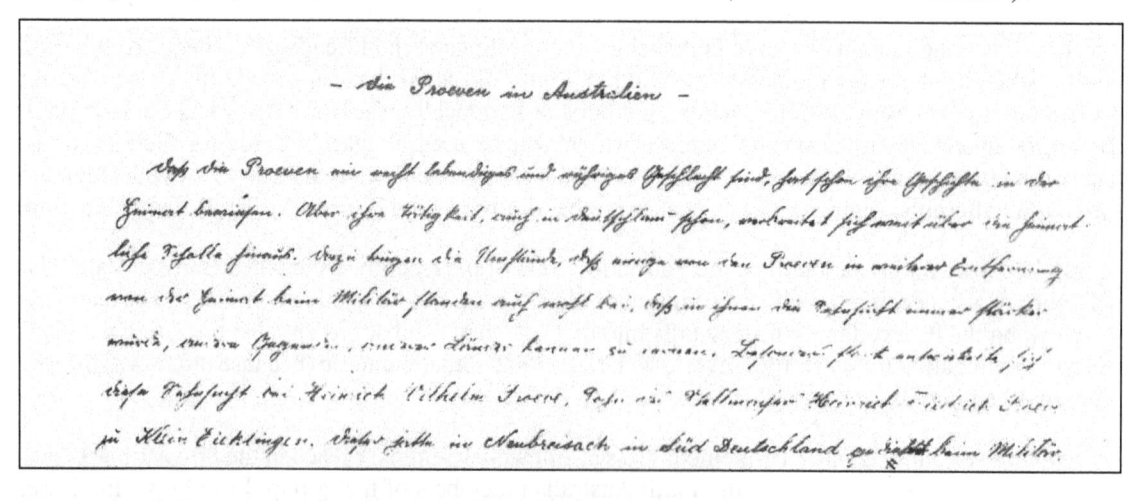

Celebrations are events that usually linger in the memory, and that has applied this year. The 60th anniversary of my ordination to the Ministry fell on the 28th March this year. The rite took place in St Paul's Church, Warramboo (on Eyre Peninsula, about 25 km south of Wudinna) – the congregation and building do not exist any more. Father, assisted by uncle Ernst Proeve, ordained me. My home congregation of Langmeil took note of the occasion at the first service on March 30.

Photo on left: *Pastor David Preuss with Henry at the 60th anniversary of his ordination at Langmeil church*

Two Sundays later (April 13) six of us classmates who graduated during 1943 came together in the Immanuel Church, North Adelaide, for a combined celebration. John Biar (down from Bundaberg, Queensland), Herman Pech (from Melbourne) and I, the three who were ordained early in 1943, served in the liturgical portion; the other three in the celebration were Leslie Grope (preacher), Erich Renner, and Colin Scheer (from Redcliffe, Queensland). It was a time of heart-warming fellowship; but our seventh class-mate, Victor Wenke, was not with us; he had died suddenly exactly one week earlier.

Chapter 9

Photo below: *Ian Lutze (North Adelaide pastor), Les Grope, Henry Proeve, Eric Renner, Colin Scheer, Mike Semmler (LCA President) celebrating their 60th anniversary, April 2003*

The second celebration centred around my 85th birthday on November 2. The home of Carol and John at Hope Valley was the venue that day for a wonderful extended family gathering of the children and SA grandchildren, cousins in SA and sister-in-law Gwen – some 17 in all. Eight days later our close-knit classmate group, Leslie, Erich, Herman and Elizabeth Pech (on a visit to Adelaide), Dulcie Held, and Nancy Wenke, honoured me with a dinner and afternoon of fellowship in North Adelaide. It was a time to bless the Lord for all His benefits.

My three long-standing interests have helped to keep this year interestingly occupied. My commitment to ministry in German has remained about the same (29 services on 19 days), supplemented by 4 services in English. The latter included a family reunion in Tanunda (Arnold), during which I also unveiled a memorial plaque on a paternal ancestor's grave 65 km away on a now-deserted church site at Angas Valley.

The involvement in historical matters in general and assisting family researchers (often involving translation of German originals) has continued. The delayed reworking of the Royal Geographical Society's publication, now entitled *Enjoy the Barossa,* was launched by the Governor, Margaret Jackson-Nelson, in April at a winery function to which I was invited as a contributor.

In June the small committee charged by the Barossa Council to be concerned about the treasures of the Barossa arranged an evening function to honour 'Live Treasures of the Barossa', viz. the 5 chief authors of the Barossa history, *The Barossa – A Vision Realised* (Reg. Munchenberg, Don Ross, Geoff. Saegenschnitter, Anne Hausler, and I) plus Angela Heuzenroeder (the author of a book on Barossa cookery). We had to tell how we came to be involved in such activity, and signed our names on a newly acquired table, till then only graced by the signature of the Cliff Richards!

Photo below: *Geoff Saegenschnitter, Don Ross, Anne Hausler, Henry Proeve, Reg Munchenberg.* Inset: *Angela Heuzenroeder*

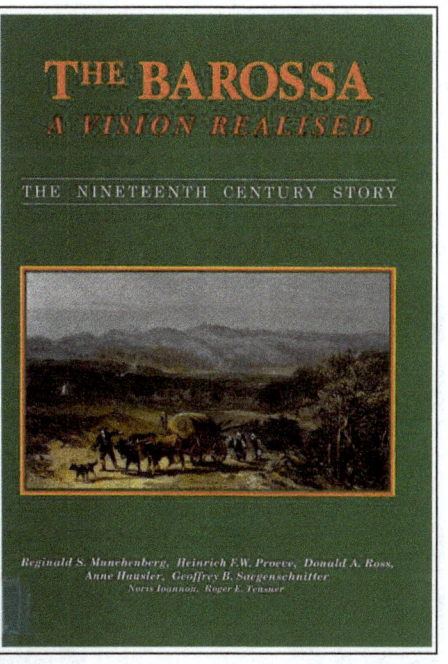

195

Chapter 9

2004:

2004 has been a pleasant year for me, graciously blessed by the Lord our God. It has had a rather unusual number of unexpected surprises. The first of these, a surprise to relatives and friends when the award of an OAM (Medal of the Order of Australia) was announced on Australia Day, was of course a presignalled, confidential, surprise to me: Sept 26, 2003 ('you are being considered') and Dec 19 ('has been approved'). The citation read: 'For service to the Lutheran Church of Australia, and to the community of the Barossa Valley as an historian'. It was a particular pleasure that I could invite my three children, Carol, David, and Philip, to be present at the investiture on April 6 at Government House. A dinner at the Hotel Archer (formerly our Lutheran Church headquarters), with the spouses John, Kaylene, and Jackie also present, concluded our celebrations, which had the additional feature of being a celebration of Carol's birthday that day. Since 'only two given names can be published in the Commonwealth of Australia Gazette and engraved on the medal insignia' I regretfully had to decide which part of my personality, as expressed in my name, I would amputate. (HFWP has long been my personal 'logo'.) I must already have been partly brain-washed by business computers who identify me as 'H.F. Proeve'. Later quiet reflection suggests that I should have fixed on 'H.W.' as retaining that portion of my grandfathers' three names (H.W.Proeve/F.W.Becker), which were their 'Rufnamen' ('calling names').

Henry, Philip, Her Excellency the Governor (Marjorie Jackson-Nelson), David, & Carol at Government House

The other two surprises did come quite literally out of the blue. At its annual meeting in August the Barossa Valley Archives and Historical Trust awarded me Honorary Life Membership. It's a body that I have been happy to serve in full membership since we came to Tanunda in 1987; prior to that I had been a guest speaker in its early years, and held associate membership as a non-Barossa resident. I have been on its Executive Committee since 1987, including a period (1990-1998) as its President. In its citation the Trust stated, among other things: 'The outstanding contribution to the Museum is your meticulous work in producing the map of the German origins of Barossa settlers'.

SA Governor awarding OAM to Henry Proeve

Then, at the beginning of November, at its annual general meeting, the Friends of Lutheran Archives conferred Honorary Life Membership on me, 'in appreciation of services in translating historic documents, and collecting, researching and recording the history of The Lutheran Church of Australia'. My own reaction to this is deep appreciation of such unexpected recognition of activity which has been a delight to me, helping to enrich the days of retirement.

Photo on left: *Henry receives Life Membership of Barossa Valley Archives and Historical Trust from President James Falkenberg*

Chapter 9

faces and places

Our Lutheran living treasure

When Pastor H F W (Henry) Proeve speaks at the Lutheran Archives, everyone stops and listens. For he has become the authority on the history of the Lutheran Church in Australia.

So it came as no surprise when he was awarded a Medal of the Order of Australia (OAM) in the Australia Day 2004 Honours list for his contribution to the Lutheran Church of Australia and to the community of the Barossa Valley as an historian.

For over 60 years Pastor Proeve has served the Lutheran Church as pastor. He also played a major role in the formation of the LCA.

> The shape of the new Lutheran Church of Australia at the time of church union in 1966 was very much the work of Pastor Proeve

Pastor Henry Proeve (photo: Colin Hentschke)

Adelaide (1943–1950), Nuriootpa (1950–1960) and Point Pass (1960–1965). When I asked him how he managed both positions, he replied: 'The Lord gave me the strength'.

It was unusual for so young a man to hold the General Secretary position, but God was preparing Pastor Proeve for a bigger task. The shape of the new Lutheran Church of Australia in 1966 was very much his work. The year that he spent as Secretary of the Joint Union Committee was a highlight of his life. The wording of the new constitution was Pastor Proeve's job. He became the obvious choice as the initial LCA General Secretary, a position he held until his retirement in 1984. For 22 years he also served as secretary of the Commission on Theology and Inter-Church Relations.

The production of the *Lutheran Hymnal* in 1973 was a great thrill for him. He served on the Hymn Book Committee, sharing in the translation and revision of over 100 hymns. Ten translations bear his name alone. Four of his modern translations also appear in the *Supplement to the Lutheran Hymnal*.

He believes that the *Lutheran Hymnal* was a great production, containing valuable hymns which are rich in meaning and thought. It saddens him that much of this Lutheran hymnody has disappeared from our congregations today.

With a deep love of history he enjoyed service as UELCA Archivist for

At the LCA General Convention of Synod in 1970, Dr M Lohe (president) and Pastor H F W Proeve (secretary)

Ordained in 1943, he began his parish ministry at North Adelaide. Within two years he was elected General Secretary of the UELCA, a position he held for the next 22 years. It was remarkable that at the same time he continued to serve as parish pastor: at North

20 years and LCA Archivist for three years, in addition to his other full-time work.

Over the years Pastor Proeve has written many congregational histories. As one of the authors of the book, *The Barossa, a Vision Realised* (1992), he made an important contribution to this definitive history with his chapters on early German settlement and the churches of the Barossa Valley.

His linguistic ability in reading the difficult old German handwriting and translating it into English has been invaluable for the study of our Lutheran history, and he willingly gives his time to many who seek his help.

As the authority on the history of the Lutheran Church in Australia, he has contributed to the *Australian Dictionary of Biography*, providing entries on the Lutheran figures J C Auricht, G A Heidenreich, G J Rechner and G F Leidig.

Twenty-six years ago Pastor Biar asked Pastor Proeve to take a German service for a migrant congregation in Adelaide. He was 'happy to use his gifts', and he still regularly conducts German services.

We thank God for his gifted and humble servant, Pastor Henry Proeve, who for over 60 years has enriched the church as parish pastor, synodical secretary, historian and hymnologist.

Lyall Kupke
LCA Archivist

Article in The Lutheran, *3 May 2004*

Chapter 9

2004 *cont.*

The Lord has given me the health and strength to continue in the areas that have taken up my attention for many years. I have continued to assist in conducting German services in three Adelaide centres; but these have been reduced through the somewhat radical decision of the Bethlehem German congregation at Flinders Street to hold its Sunday services only on the fourth Sunday of each month, not on every Sunday of the year. This year I have taken over the two German services for the entire Barossa (Good Friday, and Second Christmas Day) in St John's Church, Tanunda. — The Neukirch congregation in the Nuriootpa Parish (which I served 1950-1960) asked me to mark one of its five Sundays in August that celebrated its 150th anniversary with a service in which the sung responsive portions of the traditional liturgy followed the pattern: pastor in German, congregational response in English. The Lessons for the Day were read bilingually, and the Male Choir brushed up (for younger members, imparted the pronunciation of) German for its anthems. Period costume was worn that day. — In Langmeil I continue to help out by giving private communions, and by participation in the activities of its small Men's Fellowship, an endangered species of organisation in the Barossa and LCA.

My other local involvement continues to be that of being the Patron of the Barossa Family History Group. There continue to be local, and also outside, approaches for help in deciphering and/or translating German documents or inscriptions – in some instances a challenge, in most cases a delight because of the variety of subjects. Pastor Ted Prenzler recently asked me to indicate the possibility of translating/summarising his father's diary, which related particularly to his studies at Hermannsburg, Germany, before, during, and after World War I. Almost the first volume I opened gave a detailed account of his bicycle trip with my father and Uncle Ernst Proeve, – quite unknown to me – as my father made a farewell visit to his German relatives immediately before leaving Germany to continue his theological studies in the USA! How can I say 'no' to the request! The requests for assistance that come in from distant researchers have again led to some very pleasurable personal contacts.

The Archives continues to be an interest of mine, although I have not been functioning as a specific, ongoing, volunteer. My offer is to try to crack the 'hard nuts' that are around.

This year I was asked to write an article for the Journal of Friends of Lutheran Archives, outlining the history of The Evangelical Lutheran Synod of Australia 'auf alter Grundlage' ('On the Old Basis') – popularly known as the 'Heidenreich Synod' –, which was officially established in 1904 and amalgamated with The United Evangelical Lutheran Church in Australia in 1926.

And at the annual meeting of the Friends I gave a talk about this church body.

Top right: Start of Henry's article in FOLA Journal 2004

Bottom right: UELCA Synod at Bethany, 1926

THE EVANGELICAL LUTHERAN SYNOD IN AUSTRALIA a.a.G
Its Genesis and History

H F W Proeve, OAM

When the 20th century dawned, there were six Lutheran church bodies (termed 'Synods') in Australia. Their separate existence was due in part to theological differences, in part to geographical, colonial factors. One hundred years ago, in 1904, another one was formed: the Evangelical Lutheran Synod in Australia a.a.G (hereafter ELSAaaG). In due course it entered into intersynodical negotiations, and ended its separate organised existence after 22 years (in reality, 24 years).

The anagram 'a.a.G' may well be a mystery to many. It is the German abbreviation for *'auf alter Grundlage'* (in English: 'on the old basis') The equivalent anagram in English, 'o.o.B', is awkward and unpleasant, and was never used by that church even when it began to publish its reports in English. In adopting its title, it indicated that it had been part of the Evangelical Lutheran Synod in Australia (abbreviated as ELSA), which was also known as the 'Australian Synod'.

The reason for adopting the phrase *'auf alter Grundlage'* was already hinted at in a 1902 conference of the relevant parish (Bethanien, now Bethany), and then formally stated at the inaugural meeting of the ELSAaaG in 1904:

198

2005

2005, in its second half, has been a year of surprises for me.

A *Rundschreiben* (circular letter), via that remarkable means of communication, the e-mail, also came to Australia, saying the a *Prövetag 2005*('Pröve-Day') would take place this year in Eicklingen, near Celle, to mark 625 years' occupancy of property granted under the feudal system in 1380 to Hinrik Prove. The willingness of daughter Carol and her husband John to accompany me meant that an 86-year-old could contemplate and undertake a journey for the first time to Germany, and visit the village from which my grandfather emigrated. Sister-in-law Gwen Proeve made up the fourth member of our party; we were 4 of the 16 members of the Australian branch who attended. (It was an indication of the effect our great Australian distances has within families when we had to introduce Australians to Australians at the *Prövehof* in Eicklingen!)

Photo on right: *Welcoming Henry at the Pröve Day*

After the flight from Adelaide via Singapore (overnight, Aug. 20) to Frankfurt and Hannover, the first part of our visit was to relatives in my mother's family in Westphalia (2 nights in Rödinghausen). Then in Eicklingen (for 7 nights), where the family celebrations took place from August 26 to 28, at which about 140 were present (of whom some had come to our local family centenary celebration in Brisbane and Toowoomba 20 years ago). The thanksgiving service took place in the church at Wienhausen in which grandfather was baptised. The family atmosphere of these 10 days made them particularly memorable. This included some local family research, questions about another Proeve who went to Australia (partly researched by me) and about a female Proeve, said to have gone to Australia (completely unknown); it included plenty of translation, German into English and vice-versa. In Celle, a beautiful city with old half-timbered houses, it was a delight to view 3 Pröve houses, dated 1576, pre-1602, and 1699. We were right royally treated by our German relatives.

Pröve Hof at Eicklingen

We spent 5 more nights in Germany: in the two Luther cities, Eisleben (where John and I were allowed, as Lutheran pastors, to enter the pulpit from which Luther preached his last sermons before his death), and Wittenberg (2 nights); one night each in Leipzig and Nürnberg. This was the end of our travelling in a hired vehicle, in which John courageously tackled driving on the European side of the road, quite often on Autobahnen. A speedy ICE-train took us to Vienna for the second stage of our visit.

Photo on right: *Clawes Pröve house, Celle, 1576*

This stage was quite different from the first: no longer the company and normal daily contact in homes with family or warm-hearted fellow-Lutherans, but the daily regimen of an organised tour through Central Europe from hotel to hotel, to visit castles, cathedrals, and cobble-stoned market places (carefully studied in order to remember which narrow street led back to the bus). Leaving Vienna, 2 nights each were spent in Budapest, Krakow, Warsaw (via Auschwitz), Berlin, Prague (via Dresden), and Vienna. There were sights and special activities that made it an interesting tour: old-world grandeur everywhere; but also reminders of communist rule, e.g. in the vast series of dull apartment blocks, which (we were told) often had inferior materials that allowed damp to seep through and create mouldy apartments. The vast amount of rebuilding after the devastation of World War II (e.g. Warsaw, Berlin, Dresden; but not in unscathed Prague) was quite an eye-opener; but it has also caused me to reflect – 'untouristly'? – that extensive sections of what I saw were actually of more recent construction than in our Australian cities, but reproduced in the grand old traditional style, where possible with some old material.

Chapter 9

Upon the return from a memorable trip on Sept.21 it became obvious that, despite using much of the 'free time' during the tour to rest up, some quiet days were needed to replenish the bodily stamina and do some mental sorting out.

Below: Assorted photos from the trip.

At Wittenberg church door

Luther monument in Wittenberg

Photo on left: *Henry reading the Lesson at Wienhausen*

With a Proeve relative

The second surprise came only a few days after my return. It was a message that the Australian Lutheran College (one-time Luther Seminary) proposed to confer on me the title of Doctor of Divinity honoris causa (D.D.) on November 26. In the shorter citation on the document it is stated that this is 'in recognition of him as a teacher of the church in ecclesiastical history, liturgical theology and constitutional law'. It is still a complete surprise to me that I should receive (as the longer citation expresses it) 'the first honorary doctorate awarded by the LCA as it prepares to celebrate the fortieth anniversary of its foundation'. I had the pleasure of being able to invite my immediate family and all my Proeve cousins in South Australia to the ceremony and to the reception that the Church authorities organised.

Through the Proeve cousins of my generation and some of the next generation I sent out about 100 copies of a circular letter regarding the possibility of having a Proeve reunion next year to mark the 120th anniversary of the arrival of grandfather Heinrich Wilhelm and the young lady Emma Beuschel who was to become his wife. After a final consultation with cousins in Brisbane and Toowoomba a Proeve Reunion was planned for October 2006.

Photo on left: *Henry holding his doctorate award*

2006

For a time I had in mind to visit all interstate cousins this year, but that did not eventuate. The Lutheran Church officials, however, kindly organised a trip to Toowoomba, Queensland, to attend the national Convention of its General Synod as a guest at the beginning of October, during which the 40th anniversary of the amalgamation of the two Lutheran Churches was commemorated. It was a highly interesting experience; causing sober reflection on the fact that I was the sole survivor of the four officials elected 40 years ago. *(see The Lutheran article on page 164 of Memoirs)*. It was a deep pleasure to visit my 88-year-old 'twin' cousin, Karl Mutze, and to meet his nephew Michael in Toowoomba, and to spend time with cousins Freda and Max Kanowski and Gwyn Prove in Brisbane at that time.

A number of us southern cousins could join with George Mutze in celebrating his 80th birthday in Adelaide in September. A trip to Melbourne by car (thanks to son Philip) to attend the funeral of class-mate Herman Pech at Box Hill in March, gave opportunity to visit the Wimmera sisters-in-law in the Schultz family, Thora Schultz (Dimboola) and Verna Oldfield (Nhill).

The Lord has blessed me with regard to health, and so this past year has in many respects been able to follow the course of previous years. That, of course, includes the duties of daily living, but also allows other interests. There have been a few opportunities of helping out locally in conducting services, but there has been a decrease in reference to German services. Serving at Warradale, which I took over 28 years ago on a Good Friday, ceased on Good Friday this year – now replaced by Private Communion ministration to persons in retirement homes. I again was reminded how varied pastoral experiences can be.

In January I conducted a bilingual burial service in St John's Church, Tanunda: a young German genetics lecturer had recently arrived with his family of two young children to take up a position at Roseworthy Agricultural campus, and they had attended the German Christmas service that I conducted in St John's; so he turned to me when his wife was the innocent victim of a road accident about ten days later. A couple of months later, following doctrinal discussions (in German), I could participate in the reception of a lady, Elvira Boehler, into the Lutheran Church and our local Langmeil congregation. Her ongoing in-depth study of the theology of Dr Martin Luther continues to provide theological discussion. I will be conducting two German Christmas services this year: in North Adelaide on December 25, in Tanunda on December 26.

Chapter 9

Requests for transcriptions and translations from the German, for help in researching family history etc. continue to come in; the common interests that we have, however, has resulted in Elvira coming to my aid with transcription and translation. An undertaking that required of me that I completed my research was an address on the life and activity of an independent Lutheran pastor in South Australia, Andreas Kappler; this I gave in April at the Hope Valley Retirement Village in Adelaide to a well-attended meeting arranged by the Friends of the Lutheran Archives. I don't recommend to others, however, the manner in which it became an 'eye to eye' presentation: I inadvertently left my well-prepared manuscript at home in Tanunda!

I still enjoy involvement in the Barossa Museum as a member of the Executive of the Trust that runs it, and in the Barossa Family History Group as its Patron.

ANDREAS KAPPLER: An Independent Lutheran Pastor
(including his ministry at Hope Valley, c.1849-1860)
Dr Henry Proeve

Only a comparatively few people who read or closely study the history of the Lutheran Church in Australia are likely to be aware of the presence and activity of Andreas Kappler. His 26-year-long ministry belongs to the ministries of those pastors who are classified as 'independent', because they were not associated with any of the synodical church bodies that developed within the Lutheran Church in this continent. The upshot has been that the Australian church histories, generally written on behalf of a synodically organised branch, have by and large ignored the activities of the 'independents', unless a congregation that they established survived and was received into a synodical

Pastor Andreas Kappler

Henry's article in FoLA Journal 2007

My generation in the Proeve family has suffered two unexpected losses. Cousin Marie Hardy (nee Dunemann) of Maclean, NSW, died on February 22 of a sudden heart attack in the Lismore Hospital, one month short of her 80th birthday. Sister-in-law Gwen Proeve (widow of brother Paul) died suddenly at home at Murray Bridge on December 13 of a heart attack; she was 77 years old. Gwen took the place of a sister in my life, and our travels together in Europe last year remain a constant memory. The openness of her home for many a Christmas/New Year get-together of as many southern members of the Proeve family as could manage it will be fondly remembered by those who participated.

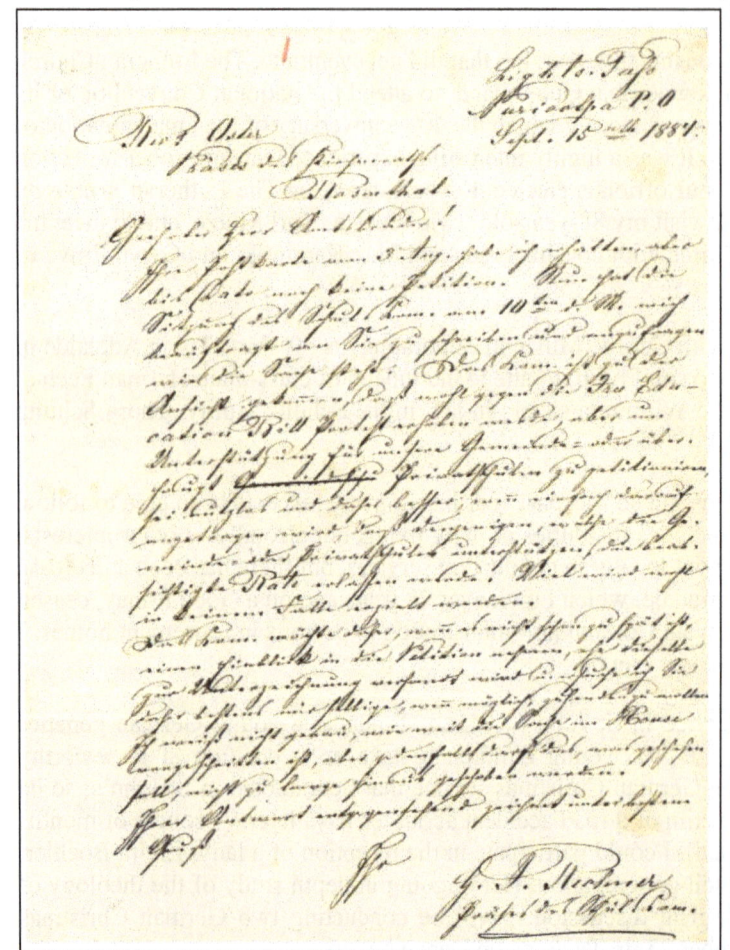

The completion of the Proeve history has been very much on my mind this year. My draft presentation of the history of the ten children and the details of their families has been passed on to family members for checking, correction, or addition. Several factors led to a postponement of our Proeve Family Reunion. It is scheduled for Saturday (in Brisbane) and Sunday (in Toowoomba), April 14 and 15, 2007. The Reunion, marking 120 years since Grandfather Proeve's arrival in Queensland, hopefully will bring far-flung family members together in a happy gathering. It is proposed to launch the family history on this occasion.

Example of German handwriting by Pastor Rechner that Henry frequently transcribed and translated

Chapter 9

2007

As I reflect on the past year I have to say in deep thankfulness: 'The Lord has been merciful and gracious'. I have to record as first in reference to time of year and definitely first in reference to importance the event that took place on Saturday, February 24, in the Langmeil Church – entering into marriage with Elvira Boehler. I made reference to her in my letter last year – Elvira reminds me, she helped in the closing stages of the mailing out of my letter. The very high regard in which I held her qualities as we continued to study theological matters and to work together in projects for the Barossa Museum developed into mutual love. The local pastor, David Preuss, conducted the ceremony; the witnesses were Margaret (Proeve) Auricht (chosen because she was the link with the day in August 1944 when I married Dorothy at Dimboola and she served as our organist), and a longtime friend of Elvira, Peter Griffin (of Alice Springs).

Elvira was born in Ulm in South Germany, but grew up in Singen, near Lake Constance. Orphaned at 6 years by the death of her mother, she was sent from the grandparents' home at the age of 17 to Australia, where she found it necessary to fend for herself. The process of melding two independent lives together began when just prior to the wedding, the premises in which her business, *Bohemian Concepts*, was located were sold, the business was closed and its stock had to be relocated at Elvira's home property in Tanunda. Homburg Street has had changes made to it to be our home – with a garden under the care of a green-fingered wife – and Elvira's Jane Place home is let.

Pastor David Preuss leads the celebrations

The newly-married couple

The second significant event was the Proeve Family Day in April. We took the opportunity of making it a journey by road in Elvira's diesel Land-Rover; for me, as a co-driver, it meant mentally repeating what I had not done for many years: 'Remember to use the clutch'. We left Tanunda on April 11, stayed overnight in Hay and Narrabri, and then enjoyed Gwynn Prove's hospitality. We met at two venues: St Peter's College at Indooroopilly, Brisbane, on Saturday, April 14, and next day in Trinity Church, Toowoomba, for the Thanksgiving Service, which I conducted, basing my sermon on Psalm 145,4.

The experience of meeting around 100 family members in one 'gulp' was not quite as overwhelming for Elvira (who has very few family contacts) as could be feared – she felt warmth from many of you who were there. For me it was again the happy experience of being together with relatives I have known for many years.

Chapter 9

Our return journey, commencing on April 17, turned out to be troublesome. Following a stay in Lismore with Elvira's daughter Shiralee and grandson Jack, a serious fuel pump problem caused us to limp into Tocumwal on the Murray. The weekend, and the complicated negotiations connected with the repairs, enforced a stay of 3 nights in Tocumwal, and 2 nights in Wodonga. As a result a visit to an aunt of Elvira in Airey's Inlet was abandoned; but we were able to visit sister-in-law Verna Oldfield in her care-unit at Nhill. Our journey of 5,000 km ended on April 24.

Photos from the Proeve Family Days, April 2007

The third event of significance is the completion of the Proeve family history. The text was complete at the time of the family reunion; the addition of photos proved to be an ongoing challenge on my computer. The Friends of Lutheran Archives have arranged that there should be a public 'launching', set down for the afternoon of February 10, 2008, at Hope Valley Retirement Village.

2008

2008 has had enough variation to make it an interesting year. It began with the last 'hurrah' over the family history that appeared at the end of last year. South Australian cousins gathered in Tanunda on January 12 to mark its appearance with a celebratory meal. In February the Friends of the Lutheran Archives insisted on a public launch of the book at one of its formal meetings with guest speaker, who in this instance was the author! The quality of these meetings of FoLA have enticed Elvira and me on a number of occasions to attend and then undertake late night returns of 70-75 km from Adelaide to Tanunda.

Henry launches the Proeve family history at Hope Valley, Feb 2008

The other main reason for visits to Adelaide is continued service, with three other pastors, in the Bethlehem, Adelaide, and North Adelaide churches for the German-speaking members, my contribution being 8 services. It has now devolved on me to produce, per my computer, the quarterly parish paper that serves them, the 'Bethlehems Bote'. The availability of an ever-increasing number of retired pastors has made it a rare event to be called on to conduct an English service. One of the three that I conducted was in Langmeil on January 1, and as this day (contrary to suggestions from within the local Committee of Worship) managed to escape being struck out as a day of worship I am scheduled to do it again at the coming turn of the year. The other pastoral activity in which I have been engaged for almost 20 years, administering Holy Communion to shut-ins, has ceased, mainly through the death of the people I was serving.

The year has been a significant one for me. The 65th anniversary of ordination passed by quietly in March; the 4 others who were ordained around that date were no longer alive for a possible joint celebration. There are plans that I will join on February 8 [2009] with my two treasured classmates, Les Grope and Erich Renner, when their 65th anniversary falls due.

Chapter 9

The other significant event was my 90th birthday, which the Lord graciously permitted me to celebrate. Elvira and family members arranged an afternoon function on the day, November 2, in the Langmeil Hall. About 100 persons attended; greetings came from many others. My sincere thanks to all readers to whom this applies. That day demonstrated how unexpectedly remarkable life can be. A stranger and his wife made themselves known to me. Quite a number of years ago by correspondence with them at their NSW address I helped them in family research. Now resident in SA, they somehow became aware of my birthday and carried out their desire to meet me personally.

Elvira & Henry at the 90th birthday   *Elvira, Henry, Les Grope & Les Auricht singing a German hymn*

Various activities have involved us away from home. The Barossa and Light Pastors' Fraternal meets almost monthly and we have also been attending meetings of the Adelaide Retired Pastors' (and wives) Fraternal. I continue to participate in the Men's Fellowship at Langmeil; and Elvira is a member of the church choir. Members of the Order of Australia in this area gather about twice in the year.

Our strongest involvement has been connected in various forms with the Barossa Museum in Tanunda; both Elvira and I are members of its executive committee. Elvira and fellow committee-member Reg Munchenberg have been spending many hours improving the displays and their presentation. The comments of visitors have been most appreciative. Elvira and I have been providing German documentation and display titles where this has been found helpful. We contributed to an interview by a researcher from Germany; and I am involved in joint discussions that are to lead to the erection of historical markers in Tanunda. Elvira and I have also helped a keen researcher friend in Melbourne and the Lutheran Archives with some translation work.

And here at home: Elvira's keenness and green fingers as a gardener have created in the front a complete bush garden of young native shrubs, creeping plants, lilies, and timber features, and a lesser version of this in the area behind the house.

Elvira and I travelled to Airey's Inlet on the Great Ocean Road in Victoria, and stayed in a cabin in the local caravan park from June 3 to 6, to visit an aunt Gisela, whom Elvira had not seen for years. A visit to the local lighthouse was a feature of the stay; the climb up 130 winding steps was a test of stamina and the prelude to a glorious view.

On the return journey we stayed in Horsham, worshipped there on the Sunday, and then spent a happy period with Verna at the excellent facility where she is now cared for in Nhill.

Photo on left: Back: *Henry, Eileen Schultz, Thora Schultz.*
Front: *Verna Oldfield (Dorothy's sister)*

Chapter 9

2009

The home and garden have been receiving attention. Elvira began a transformation into a native garden almost three years ago. More native shrubs and ground covers have been added. The pavers we have laid, plus old bricks, stones, and pieces of timber, help to make the effects of her non-ceasing care increasingly evident.

Photo on right: *Henry admiring our work in the front garden at the Tanunda home*

In the public scene our interest has continued to lie in the Barossa Museum located in Tanunda. As members of the Executive it has fallen to both of us to serve as once-a-week volunteer caretakers for half a year, through lack of tenancy in the 'shop' (original post office) area. Contact with visitors from abroad and interstate has provided interesting moments. Translation of German material has continued. Elvira has spent many hours in a two-person team that has been improving the displays in the Museum. A proposal to have historical markers in Tanunda was taken up by the local Town Committee, for which fellow-historian Don Ross and I have been providing the historical information. We've been at this since January. We struggle with the problem of correcting the presentation of a professionally employed person in reference to historical accuracy, unnecessary repetition, and even suitable English expression.

Photo on left: *Elvira, Don Ross and Henry at the Oral History presentation in the Barossa*

Another 'standard' feature has been that I have continued to assist in the ministry at North Adelaide and Adelaide Bethlehem churches to Lutherans of German background by providing ten services, in addition to drawing up the roster of officiating pastors. I continue to edit the quarterly *Bethlehems-Bote*. There has been an occasional request to serve as a guest pastor in the Barossa.

Our journeyings have not been as extensive or striking as those of some of our local friends or relatives. We again visited one of the very few relatives that Elvira has, her aunt Gisela at Aireys Inlet. This time we used Mt Gambier as a half-way house in travel along the Coorong in South Australia (each way) and on the Great South Road in Victoria (on the forward journey).

Day-trips in South Australia, as far afield as Clare (Sevenhill R.C. Church and winery) and Polish Hill River (Polish Museum) in the north and Goolwa in the south, have made Elvira familiar with areas unknown to her.

Henry, Elvira, Gisela & her granddaughter Tanya

In July I had a cataract removed from my right eye in an operation at Calvary Hospital, North Adelaide. The result was that I really only needed glasses to read fine print. The left eye, however, found it difficult to work in unison with the other. I have therefore been using new glasses. On January 4 [2010] I will be in Adelaide for arrangements to be made to remove the cataract in the left eye.

My 10-year driver's licence expired in November. With nothing more than the usual questions that a doctor has to ask annually, the Department of Transport offered me a further 10-year licence to 2.11.2019. I took it.

2010

We marked our birthdays with a stay on a holiday house for church workers at Port Hughes, near Moonta. Locally we have continued to make day-trips, whereby Elvira gets to know this part of South Australia more and more. A different type of interest has been the cemeteries of two now defunct Lutheran congregations: Magdala (on the road to Hamley Bridge), originally a church centre of Dr Carl Muecke; and Schönfeld (a forerunner of nearby Freeling) where the tombstones can scarcely be seen amid the tangle of tall cactus plants.

Our outside interests remain as in previous years, with an addition or two. In our local congregation I participate in the small Men's Fellowship (with Elvira a welcome attender). Elvira is a member of the Langmeil Choir, which celebrated its 150th anniversary this year, but suffers from scant interest in being involved. (My own voice is ceasing to be a reliable singing voice.) We attend the meetings of two Fraternals: Barossa and Light Fraternal (monthly with a few exceptions), and the Adelaide Retired Pastors and Widows Fraternal (roughly quarterly). The meetings of Friends of Lutheran Archives (FoLA) are interesting, and we have had the definite benefit of being able to travel to the night meetings with an interested local member, Geoff Saegenschnitter. Elvira and I continue to do some translating for the Lutheran Archives, and others.

As far as German services are concerned, I reduced a little my help in conducting these in Adelaide (to 7); but I am still editing the quarterly *Bethlehems-Bote*. Last Christmas I decided not to conduct a German service in Tanunda, nor did I arrange any German services this year. So Good Friday 2009 evidently became the day when a strong component of 157 years of history in the Barossa expired weakly. It is left to "snitzels", German cake, and Bavarian hats and hotpants to present the German culture that tourists are urged to seek and enjoy.

Both of us continue to be members of the Board of the Barossa Valley Archives and Historical Trust, controlling the Barossa Museum. Elvira and fellow-member Reg Munchenberg have spent very many hours preparing displays. Elvira and I are now members of the Barossa Bushgardens group and of the Friends of the Kaiserstuhl Conservation Park. Elvira is the active hands-on member in our twosome, especially in the activities of the latter group, which is seeking to rid the Park of its non-indigenous growth.

2011

The entire year has been punctuated by very many visits to the local GP and (in Adelaide or Gawler) to specialists. What has to carry my faithfully and lovingly caring Elvira and me into the new year is hope – the hope for an improvement.

We did manage to have three brief breaks away from home: to mark our 4th wedding anniversary, 2 nights in February at Loxton as the base to visit Renmark and the one-time internment complex at Loveday; 1 night in September at Mannum, celebrating Elvira's birthday; and in November, 2 nights on Hindmarsh Island for my birthday. We joined brief cruises on the Murray, at Renmark and Mannum – quite enjoyable experiences. A third cruise, at Goolwa, had to be held over to a later date. The River at Morgan or Blanchetown has also been the venue for some of our Sunday afternoon outings.

Photo on right: *Enjoying a cruise at Goolwa*

Our joint historical interests continue to have their outlet on the Executive of the Barossa Valley Archives and Historical Trust. Our volunteer work in the Lutheran Archives is concentrated on translations for a German researcher of Nehrlich family material transcribed in Germany. Pastor GD Fritzsche married into this family. A 20-page letter written by Lisinka Nehrlich about her voyage on the *Hermann von Beckerath* in 1847 (which breaks off at Rio de Janeiro), when she was on her way to bring her mother back to Germany, and a 12-page letter written by Pastor Fritzsche to Lisinka Nehrlich (his sister-in-law) about the death of Dorchen, nee Nehrlich, his wife, challenged our ability to express curious phraseology, and our durability in wanting to continue to exhume their thought processes.

Chapter 9

The daily insecurity of personal well-being affected my public activity for many months. I have not considered myself able to assist my friends Drs. E Renner and M Schild in conducting German services in Adelaide; I have not done so since July 24 at the Bethlehem Church. Prior to that, on May 22, we three led a service commemorating the 60th anniversary of the establishment of the German-speaking Bethlehem Congregation. The dwindling attendances (even at an anniversary service) indicate that the time will come when such services will cease. I am still editing the quarterly *Bethlehems-Bote*.

Photo on right: *Henry at the 60th anniversary of the Bethlehem German congregation.*

2012

God's thoughts and ways are not always what we picture for ourselves and wish. That has been my experience. Doctors were puzzled throughout 2010 and 2011 by my problems. Answers slowly began to come through in 2012. So we have to take each day as it comes, hoping that there will be appetite at each mealtime, with no adverse feelings developing in the stomach. We are thankful to God for every day that has passed by well.

Some of my activity is curtailed. I functioned in worship only once: in the Good Friday German Service at Flinders Street, reading a Lesson. I have still been editing the *Bethlehems-Bote*, but have been contemplating giving it up.

Elvira and I are still translating German documents for the Lutheran Archives; and we are still Executive Members of the Barossa Valley Archives and Historical Trust. We are involved in the development of the original Auricht's Printing building on Langmeil land as the Langmeil Heritage Centre. As a private venture my Memoirs still occupy my time, but the spirit needs stimulating at times. Elvira enjoys the careful, loving tending of our garden, both shrub and vegetable.

Friedemann Hebart, Henry & Erich Renner at the Good Friday service at Bethlehem Church

We've celebrated our birthdays or special days by trips of several days' duration. One interesting trip was a 40-km voyage in an historic wood-fired paddle steamer, the "Oscar W". We went upstream on the Murray from Blanchetown to Morgan. We made our own memento of the voyage by sitting on deck, where one could look down into the engine room, watching the fire burn, and also watching the river scenes passing by. The sparks that flew up provided the memento on my jacket.

Photo on right: *Aboard the "Oscar W"*

Chapter 9

2013

The year 2013 has had some concerns for us. The concerns of earlier years have not gone away, but our close observation of daily occurrences, and constant consultation between Elvira and me, guided by the medical advice that has been given, have achieved a reasonable measure of control.

In March I was permitted to celebrate a special and rather rare anniversary – the 70th of my ordination on March 28, 1943, in the little wood and iron church at Warramboo. I am the sole survivor of the five candidates of theology who were ordained at that time. (God willing, three of the five members of our class, who graduated at the end of 1943, will celebrate their 70th anniversary on Feb 6 next year, viz. Erich Renner, Leslie Grope, and Colin Scheer. – *see photos on next page*).

My anniversary was celebrated on the Sunday (March 24) before the actual date in the Langmeil Church, with Julian Bayha as the liturgist. The retiring President-General, Dr Michael Semmler, preached the sermon for the occasion and led the thanksgiving rite. I spoke the opening Invocation, read a Lesson, and pronounced the final Benediction. A community luncheon in the church hall followed.

Photo on right:
Pastors Julian Bayha, Henry Proeve & Mike Semmler at his 70th anniversary service at Langmeil church

Henry with Proeve family members who came from far and wide for his 70th anniversary

Chapter 9

Photos below: *At the 70th anniversary service at St Stephen's church, Feb 2014*:

Photo on left*: Drs Renner, Proeve & Grope*

Photo on right: *Pastors standing: Rob Kempe, Peter Lockwood, Kevin Schmidt, Ted Prenzler, James Winderlich, Vic Pfitzner, Maurice Schild*

On the following Sunday, Easter Day, as a kind of after-celebration Elvira and I attended the German service in Immanuel Church, North Adelaide, conducted by Erich Renner. We were mindful that I had long connections with North Adelaide: the first congregation that I served, 28 years of membership and locums tenens ministry, and many years serving the German section of the congregation in my retirement. To mark this occasion I read the Epistle lesson.

Elvira lovingly refused to let the personal health problems of the time cause my 95th birthday to pass unnoticed. She invited about 30 family members and relatives and friends to an outdoor afternoon tea at Homburg Street. With the willing assistance of helpers a pleasant time was enjoyed by all.

Another surprising indication that the years have been accumulating came at a function that the Royal Automobile Association (RAA) of SA, organised in Tanunda to greet its Gold Members (members for 50 years or more). It transpired that I was the longest standing member there, a member of 69 years standing since 1944.

Apart from the above celebrations and very many visits of a medical/health nature in the Barossa and Adelaide by me, life in general changes very little for us two. We did less translation for the Lutheran Archives than in previous years. We have also continued our involvement in the affairs of the Barossa Museum in Tanunda. A favoured spot for a little relaxation has been the River Murray, especially at Morgan.

Relaxing at Morgan

And at Mannum

HEINRICH FRIEDRICH WILHELM PROEVE

2nd November 1918 - 27th September 2014

FUNERAL SERVICE

LANGMEIL THANKSGIVING LUTHERAN CHURCH
TANUNDA

3rd October 2014

Elvira wrote this at Christmas 2014:

Many of you know that Henry has gone to his heavenly home and for those who do not know, he was taken by his Lord on September 27, 2014, after two weeks in the Tanunda Hospital. Henry's physical strength had been weakening very much this year, but he was blessed with mental alertness to the very end.

I was with my beloved Heinrich when he took his last breath – God called his faithful servant home.

Henry had written his memoirs up to 1987 and the last sentences were written one week prior to being admitted to hospital. To honour Henry I have decided with the help of friends to continue the memoirs as a biography from 1987 on until 2014.

It was always important and a joy for Henry to "compose" his Christmas letter with meaningful messages, rare hymns loved by him, and family news. I will not attempt to do anything like it. This year would have been Henry's 20th Christmas letter and I am writing this to honour Henry. Family and friends were important and dear to him and therefore to me as well.

Chapter 9

The hymn, *Go forth, my thoughts, in faith and wonder,* was a special hymn for Henry [*see Memoirs, page 7*]. It was sung at his funeral service. Here, on the next pages, is his translation of the complete hymn, including his change to the title. It differs from the version in the *Supplement to the Lutheran Hymnal* (No. 871), which only included 6 verses.

Henry preaching the Gospel at Neukirch, one of the many churches in which he preached in his lifetime. He kept the details of over 4000 services he conducted.

GEHT HIN, IHR GLÄUBIGEN GEDANKEN	**GO FORTH, MY THOUGHTS, IN FAITH, IN WONDER**
Epheser 1,3-8	*Ephesians 1,3-8*
1 Geht hin, ihr gläubigen Gedanken, 　ins weite Feld der Ewigkeit, erhebt euch über alle Schranken 　der alten und der neuen Zeit; erwägt, daß Gott die Liebe sei, die ewig alt und ewig neu.	1 Go forth, my thoughts, in faith, in wonder, 　To range afar o'er fields sublime As on eternity you ponder, 　Unhindered by the bounds of time; Recall that God is love so true, For ever old, for ever new.
2 Der Grund der Welt war nicht geleget, 　der Himmel war noch nicht gemacht, So hat Gott schon den Trieb geheget, 　der mir das Beste zugedacht; da ich noch nicht geschaffen war, da reicht er mir schon Gnade dar.	2 Before God laid this world's foundation, 　Before the world in splendour stood, His heart was filled with inclination 　To bless me with the greatest good; Before life had its earthly place He poured on me abundant grace.
3 Sein Ratschluß war, ich sollte leben 　durch seinen eingebornen Sohn; den wollt er mir zum Mittler geben, 　den macht er mir zum Gnadenthron, in dessen Blute sollt ich rein, geheiliget und selig sein.	3 This was the will of my Creator; 　That I through His own Son should live, Whom He would make my mediator, 　And as my mercy-seat would give; Cleansed in His blood, from sin set free, Holy and blessed I should be.

Chapter 9

Reading the Gospel at Bethlehem Church, 2011

4 O Wunderliebe, die mich wählte 　vor allem Anbeginn der Welt und mich zu ihren Kindern zählte, 　für welche sie das Reich bestellt! O Vaterland, O Gnadentrieb, der mich ins Buch des Lebens schrieb!	4 O wondrous love, that deigned to choose me 　Before this world in time was reared, That children's right did not refuse me, 　For whom the kingdom is prepared! O grace which moved the Father's hand, That in His book my name should stand!
5 Wie wohl ist mir, wenn mein Gemüte 　hinauf zu dieser Quelle steigt, von welcher sich ein Strom der Güte 　zu mir durch alle Zeiten neigt, daß jeder Tag sein Zeugnis gibt: Gott hat mich je und je geliebt.	5 How blest am I, when now my spirit 　Up to this heavenly fount can rise, Whose bounteous stream, without my merit, 　At all times grace to me supplies, Whereby each passing day will prove: God loves me with unending love.
6 Wer bin ich unter Millionen 　der Kreaturen seiner Macht, die in der Höh und Tiefe wohnen, 　Daß er mich bis hierher gebracht? Ich bin ja nur ein dürres Blatt, ein Staub, der keine Stätte hat.	6 His creatures fill the earth and ocean, 　Fashioned in millions by His power; O what am I in this creation, 　That He has helped me to this hour? Naught but a faded leaf am I; I am as dust that soon may fly.

Chapter 9

Henry preaching at Trinity church, Toowoomba, at the Proeve Reunion, April 2007

> 7
> Ja, freilich bin ich zu geringe
>   der herzlichen Barmherzigkeit,
> womit, O Schöpfer aller Dinge,
>   mich deine Liebe stets erfreut;
> ich bin, O Vater, selbst nicht mein,
> dein bin ich, Herr, und bleibe dein.
>
> 8
> Im sichern Schatten deiner Flügel
>   find ich die ungestörte Ruh.
> Der fests Grund hat dieses Siegel:
>   "Wer dein ist, Herr, den kennest du."
> Laß Erd und Himmel untergehn,
> dies Wort der Wahrheit bleibet stehn.
>
> 9
> Wenn in dem Kampfe schwerer Leiden
>   der Seele Mut und Kraft gebricht,
> so salbest du mein Haupt mit Freuden,
>   so tröstet mich dein Angesicht;
> da spür ich deines Geistes Kraft,
> die in der Schwachheit alles schafft.
>
> 7
> Maker of all, I bow before you,
>   Whose love sets joy before my face,
> For I indeed am never worthy
>   Of all your mercy, love, and grace.
> I am, O Father, not my own:
> Yours am I ever, yours alone.
>
> 8
> Beneath your wings no danger fearing,
>   I rest, O Lord, in calm repose;
> My steadfast trust this seal is bearing:
>   'Those who are His, the Lord God knows'.
> Let heaven and earth now pass away,
> I know this word of truth will stay.
>
> 9
> Yea, when my soul grows faint in sadness
>   Amid the strife of woe and pain,
> You then anoint my head with gladness,
>   Your face then comforts me again;
> And then I feel your Spirit's might
> Which works all things, when weak my plight

Chapter 9

Henry's grave at Langmeil Cemetery

10	10
Die Hoffnung schauet in der Ferne	My hope in confidence now gazes
durch alle Schatten dieser Zeit;	Beyond the shades of earthly years;
der Glaube schwingt sich durch die Sterne	My faith mounts up to heavenly places
und sieht ins Reich der Ewigkeit;	And looks upon eternal spheres;
da zeigt mir deine milde Hand	I see there, guided by your hand,
mein Erbteil und gelobtes Land.	My heritage and promised land.

11
Ach könnt ich dich nur besser ehren,
 welch edles Loblied stimmt ich an;
es sollten Erd und Himmel hören,
 was du, mein Gott, an mir getan;
nichts ist so köstlich, nichts so schön
als, höchster Vater, dich erhöhn.

11
Ah, could I better honour render,
 What noble praise would I intone!
Then earth and heaven would hear the splendour
 Of all that you, my God, have done.
Precious indeed, exalted Name,
'Tis to exalt my Father's fame.

12
Doch nur Geduld, es kommt die Stunde,
 da mein durch dich erlöster Geist
im höhern Chor mit frohem Munde
 dich, schönste Liebe, schöner preist;
drum eilt mein Herz aus dieser Zeit
und sehnt sich nach der Ewigkeit.

12
Have patience, wait the hour victorious;
 My spirit then, set free by you,
Most glorious Love, with strains more glorious
 Shall sing in nobler choir of you.
So hastes my heart from earth away,
And longs to see the eternal day.

Johann Gottfried Herrmann (1707-1791)

H. F. W. Proeve, August 2001
(original version 1960)

Chapter 9

A long, well-lived life in pictures

Top left: *Relaxing on holiday, 2008*
Top right: *Laying the foundation stone at North Adelaide, Aug 1955*

Middle left*: Henry's map of Germany at the Barossa Museum showing villages of early settlers*
Middle right: *Graduation photo, 1943*

Bottom left: *Elvira and Henry, Sept 2012*
Bottom right: *Ordination at Warramboo, 1943*

Chapter 9

Top left: *In 2009, visiting the lane behind the Grovedale manse, where the Proeve brothers played cricket as children*
Top centre: *Henry in the snow in front of his grandparent's house, St Paul, USA, in 1927*
Top right: *Unveiling the foundation stone at Ceduna, 1971*

Middle left: *Playing his piano at home in the late 1940s*
Middle right: *Success at balancing the nails puzzle, Mintaro 2009*

Bottom left: *Henry and Dorothy at the Constituting Convention, Tanunda 1966*
Bottom right: *Erich Renner, Les Grope & Henry Proeve near the 65th anniversary of their ordination, 2009*

217

Chapter 9

Top left: *One year old Henry & parents*
Top right: *Paul and Henry, 1932*

Checking a map for a trip

Henry, Father & Paul, 1949

Henry & Elvira at the Proeve Family Day, Brisbane 2007

Relaxing at the Blue Lake, Mt Gambier, 2009

Chapter 9

Henry, 2004

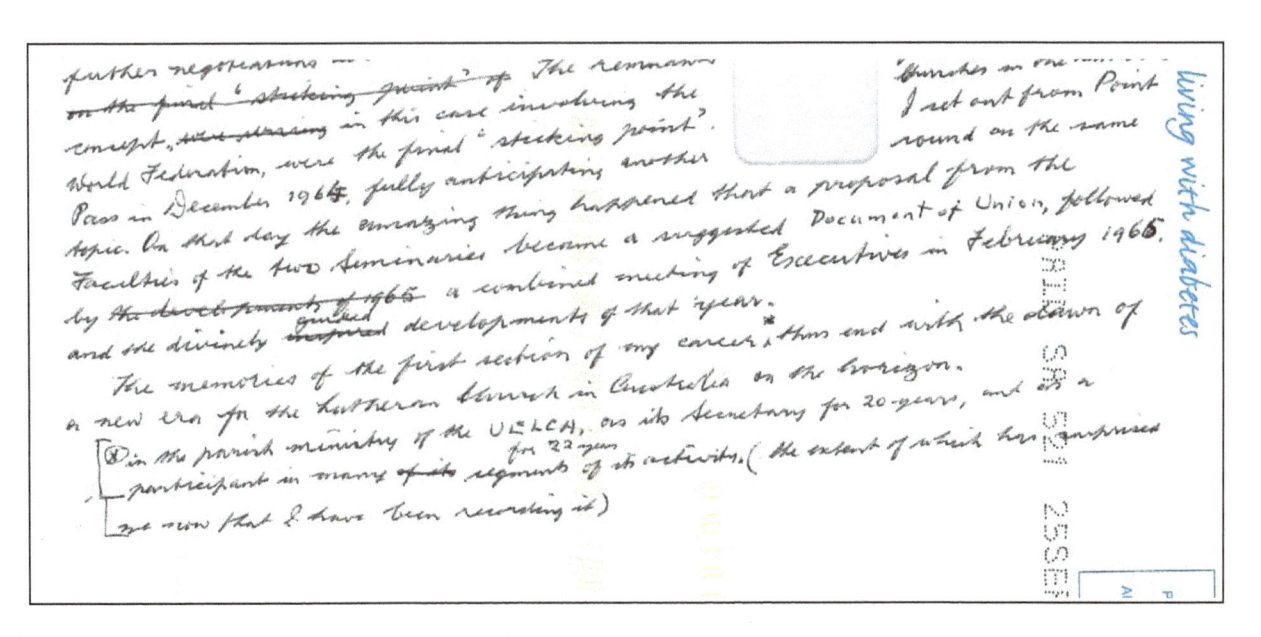

Part of his manuscript, written on an envelope.

Milton Keynes UK
Ingram Content Group UK Ltd.
UKHW050014191124
451263UK00004B/17